A SLOW RECKONING

A VOLUME IN THE NIU SERIES IN

Slavic, East European, and Eurasian Studies
Edited by Christine D. Worobec

For a list of books in the series, visit our website at cornellpress.cornell.edu.

A SLOW RECKONING

THE USSR, THE AFGHAN COMMUNISTS, AND ISLAM

VASSILY KLIMENTOV

NORTHERN ILLINOIS UNIVERSITY PRESS
AN IMPRINT OF
CORNELL UNIVERSITY PRESS
Ithaca and London

First published 2024 by Cornell University Press

Library of Congress Cataloging-in-Publication Data

Names: Klimentov, Vassily, 1986– author.
Title: A slow reckoning : the USSR, the Afghan communists, and Islam / Vassily Klimentov.
Description: Ithaca [New York] : Northern Illinois University Press, an imprint of Cornell University Press, 2024. | Series: NIU series in Slavic, East European, and Eurasian studies | Includes bibliographical references and index.
Identifiers: LCCN 2023023253 (print) | LCCN 2023023254 (ebook) | ISBN 9781501773808 (hardcover) | ISBN 9781501773815 (ebook) | ISBN 9781501773822 (pdf)
Subjects: LCSH: Islam and politics—Afghanistan. | Islam and politics—Soviet Union. | Communism and Islam—Afghanistan. | Afghanistan—History—Soviet occupation, 1979–1989—Religious aspects—Islam.
Classification: LCC BP63.A54 K55 2024 (print) | LCC BP63.A54 (ebook) | DDC 297.2/7209581—dc23/eng/20230712
LC record available at https://lccn.loc.gov/2023023253
LC ebook record available at https://lccn.loc.gov/2023023254

To Arianna, Sasha, and Nastya

Contents

List of Illustrations   ix

Acknowledgments   xi

List of Abbreviations   xiii

Note on Transliteration   xv

Introduction   1

1. The Basmachi and Soviet Islam   18

2. Khalq's Islam and the Decision to
    Intervene   28

3. Ideology in the Karmal Era   53

4. Najibullah's Islamization   103

5. The USSR, Afghanistan, and the
    Muslim World   141

6. Moscow's Islamist Threat   180

    Conclusion   227

Notes   235

Bibliography   277

Index   289

Illustrations

Figures

0.1. Monument to the Afgantsy built in Moscow in 2004   8

2.1. The Front Page of *The Kabul New Times*, 1 April 1979   30

2.2. Leonid Brezhnev and Andrei Gromyko   37

2.3. The mujahideen in central Afghanistan, 1982   44

3.1. A downed Soviet aircraft in the Panjshir Province, 1981   64

3.2. Young mujahideen in a destroyed mosque in Herat Province, 1987   68

3.3. A mujahideen propaganda poster about Karmal   82

3.4. Last meeting between Babrak Karmal, Mikhail Gorbachev, and Andrei Gromyko (to Gorbachev's right) in Moscow, 1985   100

4.1. A meeting between Mohammad Najibullah, Mikhail Gorbachev, Eduard Shevardnadze (to Gorbachev's right), and Anatoly Chernyaev (to Najibullah's left) in Tashkent, 1988   106

4.2. A PDPA propaganda poster of a man with his land ownership document received from the government   108

4.3. A meeting between Mohammad Najibullah, Mikhail Gorbachev and Raisa Gorbacheva, Eduard Shevardnadze, and Rafiq Nishanov, the first secretary of the Uzbek CPSU in Tashkent, 1988   120

4.4. Ronald Reagan receiving mujahideen leaders at the White House, 1983   131

4.5. Ahmad Shah Massoud talking with a mullah in the Panjshir, 1981   136

5.1. Ronald Reagan signing Proclamation 5621 that designated 21 March 1987 as "Afghanistan Day," amid US and Afghan policymakers   147

5.2. Front page of a mujahideen journal   169

6.1. A mural poster in Afghanistan in the late Najibullah era, 1989   184

6.2. Ronald Reagan, Mikhail Gorbachev, and other policymakers
in the Oval Office, 1987   204
6.3. Front page of the Hezb-e-Islami journal following the
Shahnawaz Tanai coup in Kabul   211

Maps

0.1. Historical map of Afghanistan   xvi
1.1. Historical ethnic map of Afghanistan produced by the CIA,
1979   22
4.1. Historical map of areas controlled by insurgent groups in
Afghanistan produced by the CIA, 1985   132
6.1. Areas of control in Afghanistan between Soviet and Afghan
communist forces and the mujahideen, 1988   181

ACKNOWLEDGMENTS

This book has been a long-haul project that I am proud to have undertaken. It is based on the research I conducted at the International History Department at the Graduate Institute of International and Development Studies in Geneva. I would like to thank the many people who have helped me along the way, providing counsel and guidance, sharing insight and recommending literature and sources, and commenting on my work. They have made the completion of this book possible.

I sincerely thank Mohammad-Mahmoud Ould Mohamedou from the International History Department for the exciting discussions we have had about my work, for the always sound advice he gave me, and for writing all these reference letters and introductions to archives. I also thank Keith Krause from the Department of International Relations and Political Science for the tremendous help he provided me by reviewing my articles and drafts of chapters. Although my research ended up being more International History than International Relations, I believe it is fundamental to understanding present-day Russia and Afghanistan.

The Graduate Institute's International History Department is the place where I spent the most time between 2016 and 2020. I thank Jussi Hanhimäki, who has instructed me about the Cold War and read my papers and articles, and Cyrus Schayegh and André Liebich, who have also read my work and provided great advice. My special thanks go to Davide Rodogno, who has been of great help at the time of my application to the Graduate Institute.

At the Graduate Institute, I also thank Alessandro Monsutti from the Department of Anthropology and Sociology, our in-house Afghanistan expert, for reviewing one of my articles on Afghanistan. My heartfelt thanks go to Claire Somerville, whom I have assisted as a teaching assistant for four years. This list would be incomplete without mentioning the Master's students, PhD candidates, postdocs, and other colleagues whom I have befriended at the Graduate Institute. Some of the ideas in this book came from our discussions. I especially thank Severyan Dyakonov, Joel Veldkamp, Aditya Kiran Kakati, Oksana Myshlovska, and Cholpon Orozbekova for their support.

This research has also benefitted from the support of scholars from other universities, including the European University Institute in Florence, where I finalized this book between 2020 and 2023. I am especially grateful to Artemy A. Kalinovsky from Temple University, who has provided contacts of interviewees, advice on archives and literature throughout the way, and helped me write the book proposal. Without his support, this book would not have been possible. I moreover heartily thank Olivier Roy from the European University Institute who has reviewed the many articles and papers I wrote during my time there.

I also want to acknowledge the institutions that have funded my research. The Graduate Institute has provided me with scholarships and employment as a teaching assistant, and the Swiss National Science Foundation has funded my research through two successive grants. The Pierre du Bois Foundation has funded part of my research and provided funds to finalize the manuscript that led to this book. I personally thank Irina du Bois, the Foundation's President, for her help and support.

I am also thankful for the many people at Cornell University Press and North Illinois University Press who have helped in revising this manuscript. I am especially grateful for the support and availability of my editor Amy Farranto. Likewise, this book has immensely benefitted from the feedback of Eren Tasar from the University of North Carolina and of an anonymous reviewer during the peer-review process.

I also want to thank the many people who have agreed to be interviewed for this research. Although I cannot list all of them here, I especially thank those who have become nods in a network, linking me to other interviewees and who have shared documents with me. My genuine thanks hence go to Ghaus Janbaz, Vladimir Snegirev, Davlat Khudonazarov, Andrei Grachev, Gennadiy Khobotov, and Vasili Kravtsov.

Finally, I thank my family and friends for supporting me through this long endeavor. My parents, Natalia and Alexei, have been of great help. My wife, Arianna, has perhaps more than anyone else seen the slow but steady progress of this book. I am sure she is as glad as me to see it come to fruition. Although they were certainly not fully aware of what was happening, I also have here a thought for our son Sasha and our daughter Nastya. These are all people who have made this achievement possible for me.

Abbreviations

AAPSO	Afro-Asian People's Solidarity Organisation (pro-USSR)
AIC	Afghanistan Information Centre (Pakistan)
CARC	Council for the Affairs of Religious Cults (USSR)
CC	Central Committee
CFM	Council of Foreign Ministers (OIC)
CIA	Central Intelligence Agency (US)
CIS	Community of Independent States
CRA	Council for Religious Affairs (USSR)
CPSU	Communist Party of the Soviet Union
DFLP	Democratic Front for the Liberation of Palestine
DOMA	Democratic Youth Organisation of Afghanistan (Afghan Komsomol)
DRA	Democratic Republic of Afghanistan
GRU	Glavnoe Razvedyvatel'noe Upravlenie (Main Intelligence Directorate) (USSR)
IEWSS	Institute of the Economy of the World Socialist System (USSR)
IRP(T)	Islamic Renaissance Party (of Tajikistan) (USSR/Tajikistan)
ISCHS	Islamic Summit Conference of Heads of States (OIC)
ISI	Inter-Services Intelligence (Pakistan)
Ittehadiya	Ittehadiya Islami-ye Wilayat-I Shamal (Islamic Union of the Northern Provinces) (mujahideen/ Pakistan)
KGB	Komitet Gosudarstvennoi Bezopasnosti (Committee for State Security) (USSR)
KhAD	Khadamat-e Aetela'at-e Dawlati (State Intelligence Agency) (DRA)
LCST	Limited Contingent of Soviet Troops (USSR)
MIA	Missing in Action
MID	Ministerstvo Inostrannykh Del (Ministry of Foreign Affairs) (USSR)
MWL	Muslim World League (pro-Saudi Arabia)
NAM	Non-Alignment Movement
NATO	North Atlantic Treaty Organization (pro-US)

NFF	National Fatherland Front (DRA)
OIC	Organisation of the Islamic Conference
PDPA	People's Democratic Party of Afghanistan (DRA)
PDRY	People's Democratic Republic of Yemen (South Yemen)
PFLP	Popular Front for the Liberation of Palestine
PLO	Palestine Liberation Organization
POW	Prisoner of War
SADUM	Spiritual Administration of the Muslims of Central Asia and Kazakhstan (USSR)
SAFS	Soviet-Afghan Friendship Society (USSR)
SALT	Strategic Arms Limitation Talks
TASS	Telegrafnoe Agentstvo Sovetskogo Soyuza (Telegraph Agency of the Soviet Union)
Tudeh	Hezb-e Tude-ye Iran (People's Party of Iran)
UN	United Nations
NSC	National Security Council (US)
WMC	World Muslim Congress (pro-Pakistan)

NOTE ON TRANSLITERATION

For words in Cyrillic, this book uses the simplified transliteration system adopted by most academic journals and books. It keeps, however, the common spelling for the most well-known proper nouns (for example, Yeltsin instead of El'tsin) and words. The transliteration table is available at: https://files.taylorandfrancis.com/CEAS-RPSA-transliteration-table.pdf. Since it relies primarily on Soviet and Russian sources, including for translations of Afghan and Central Asian sources, the book transliterates Dari, Pashto, and other foreign words based on their Russian translation using the same table. This may, at times, lead to unusual spellings.

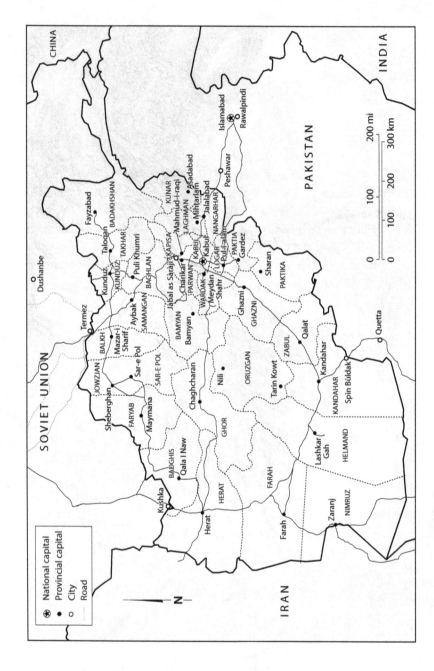

MAP 0.1. Historical map of Afghanistan.

A SLOW RECKONING

Introduction

The Soviet-Afghan War (1978–89) was the defining conflict of the late Cold War. It pitted the Soviet Union and its People's Democratic Party of Afghanistan (PDPA) client against the mujahideen—the combatants of jihad, the holy war against the infidels.[1] The mujahideen enjoyed the military support of Pakistan, Iran, the United States, Saudi Arabia, and many other countries. In nine years, the conflict killed over 15,000 Soviet soldiers and between 600,000 and 1.5 million Afghans.[2] Over 6 million more Afghans fled to neighboring Pakistan and Iran. Because of the formidable economic and military burden it created, the public criticism it attracted in the USSR during Mikhail Gorbachev's rule, and because of Soviet inability to make its modernization model attractive to Afghans, the Afghan War, as it is called in the post-Soviet space, had a profound effect on the Soviet Union. Although it was not the main cause of the Soviet collapse, it certainly contributed to Moscow's difficulties in the late 1980s. At the same time, the Soviet-Afghan War showed to many in the Third World that communism's appeal was running out of steam. Even in the Soviet Union, it led members of the Communist Party of the Soviet Union (CPSU) to question the dogma of an ineluctable transition to socialism for developing countries. This ideological aspect loomed large during the war. Marxism-Leninism represented an all-encompassing worldview for Soviet policymakers and the advisers and military personnel they sent to Afghanistan, but Islam served a similar purpose for many Afghans. These two systems vividly came into conflict during the war and came to define it then and thereafter.

Although even in the 1980s many saw the Soviet-Afghan War, much as the war in Ukraine in the 2020s, as the pivotal struggle of their time, its effects were still felt long after the Cold War and, in many ways, the world feels them still. In Afghanistan, the Soviet support to the PDPA, the Afghan communists, and the ensuing war ushered the country into a spiral of conflicts that saw the rise and fall of the mujahideen, the Taliban's arrival in the mid-1990s, and the US-led intervention after 9/11.[3] Meanwhile, Afghanistan became the world's main producer of opiates. Even at the time of writing in 2023, the country is not at peace, and many Afghans blame the rash Soviet decision to intervene for transforming a limited internal conflict into a Cold War proxy battlefield and for creating tens of thousands of professionals of violence. Over 2.5 million Afghans are still refugees because of these successive conflicts.

In Russia, the Soviet-Afghan War became a negative point of reference in the post-Soviet period, giving rise to the expression "the Afghan Syndrome" and launching a plethora of historical and political controversies over its legacy. The military sees it as the Soviet Union's glorious swan song. Red Army commanders make it a point of honor to emphasize that the Soviets left Afghanistan "undefeated."[4] General Boris Gromov, the last commander of the 40th Army, which constituted the bulk of the so-called Limited Contingent of Soviet Troops (LCST) sent to Afghanistan, noted that "unlike the Americans in Vietnam [the Soviets] had accomplished their mission." For him, the Red Army's job was to "help the government of Afghanistan stabilize the domestic situation [and] prevent an aggression from abroad," which it did, not to defeat the mujahideen.[5] Since the 2010s, there have been initiatives in the State Duma, the lower house of the Russian parliament, to celebrate the war, the veterans of Afghanistan (the Afgantsy), and even to rehabilitate the decision to dispatch the LCST.

Against the backdrop of the perceived success of the intervention in Syria, the Soviet-Afghan War is also being reevaluated positively in Russia. The grand celebration at the Crocus City Hall in Moscow of the thirtieth anniversary of the Soviet withdrawal in February 2019 saw General Mikhail Moiseev, former head of the General Staff of the Red Army and deputy minister of defense, praise the LCST for doing its "international duty" and "guaranteeing Russia's security." Moiseev traced a parallel between the Afgantsy and the troops that carried out their "sacred duty" in Syria. The ceremony was noteworthy for having an Orthodox priest make a speech before Moiseev and General Viktor Ermakov, one of the commanders of the 40th Army. The event showed the odd syncretism that sees praise for communist internationalism be intertwined with religion in Russia. It showed how the necessary support to and rehabilitation of the long socially marginalized Afgantsy, the majority of whom were conscripts, comes together with a problematic rewriting of history that presents Afghanistan as the first Russian war against Islamist terrorism.

This reevaluation of the Afghan experience has nonetheless allowed Russia to reengage politically and economically with Kabul in the 2000s, with the involvement of many Afgantsy. In the 2010s, Moscow has participated in the intra-Afghan peace dialogue, including by hosting Taliban delegations. In June 2022, a Taliban delegation joined at the St. Petersburg International Economic Forum. That visit testified as much to Russia's interest in stabilizing Afghanistan, as to coalescing with anti-American forces in connection with the war in Ukraine. The latter conflict is also changing the perception of the Afghan War in Russia. As talks of a new Cold War spread, Russian authorities present both wars as being about opposition to Western hegemony. Because the invasion of Ukraine is justified by the necessity to preemptively oppose NATO in Russia's perceived sphere of influence, so was the Afghan War, the Kremlin argues.

Beyond this neo-imperial parallel, the Soviet-Afghan War also traced a continuity between the Cold War and the post-1991 order regarding the rise of Islamism, a philosophy that "conceives of Islam as a political ideology," an aspect of the conflict that has received considerable attention in the West and in Russia and which has sparked endless scholarly and political debates.[6] Theorized in the late 1960s by Muslim philosophers, including Abul A'la Maudoodi from Pakistan, Sayyid Qutb of Egypt, and the Iranian Ayatollah Ruhollah Khomeini, Islamism redrew the boundary between the world of Islam and the rest of the world beginning after the 1973 Arab-Israeli conflict. Crystallizing with Saudi Arabia at its political center, Sunni Islamism reanimated ideas of pan-Islam and a Muslim world in opposition to or at least as different and isolated from Western ideas of modernity.

According to the historian Cemil Aydin, Islamist ideas of Muslim internationalism and of a mythicized Muslim world that remained politically and culturally diverse in the 1980s owed much to perceptions dating back to the nineteenth century. Yet the Cold War and the contestation of its dominant paradigms had since replaced anticolonialism and ideas of the Caliphate.[7] The Islamism of the 1970s was a product of its time. The idea of a violent and egalitarian revolution that its proponents advocated had similarities to Marxist-influenced projects.[8] The Iranian revolution saw an early convergence between Islamist and communist forces. In Afghanistan, Maoism had originally attracted Ahmad Shah Massoud, one of the foremost mujahideen commanders. Even more extraordinary, Gulbuddin Hekmatyar, the staunch Islamist leader, had early on gravitated toward the PDPA.

During the Soviet-Afghan War, a strand of Islamism led to the emergence of what scholars now call Salafi-Jihadism or radical Islamism.[9] A transnational militant form of fundamentalist Islam, radical Islamism was theorized by Abdullah Yusuf Azzam, a Palestinian Islamic scholar who came to Pakistan during the conflict. In a theological innovation, Azzam argued that it was an individual (*fard al-'ayn*) and not a collective duty for Muslims to participate in the Afghan jihad. He made fighting in Afghanistan one of the pillars of the faith.[10] His preaching motivated thousands of fighters from Saudi Arabia and other Arab countries to join the mujahideen after 1984. During the conflict, Pakistani, American, and Saudi support to the Islamist Afghan parties and foreign fighters rather than to the moderate traditional Islamic and royalist Afghan armed groups was crucial in stunting Soviet and PDPA attempts to control Afghanistan. Radicals, particularly the Afghan Hezb-e-Islami (Islamic Party) of Hekmatyar and the Arab foreign fighters—known as the Arab Afghans—became increasingly influential in the resistance due to that support. After the Soviet withdrawal, they tried to impose their fundamentalist views on postwar Afghanistan, and this was one of the reasons for the widespread and muddled fighting among the mujahideen in the 1990s.

Meanwhile, the foreigners who had joined the Afghan jihad found themselves without a cause when the Soviets left. The conflict increasingly became an intra-Afghan affair. The rapid transformation by Mohammad Najibullah, the last communist ruler installed by the Soviets, of the Soviet-looking institutions of the Democratic Republic of Afghanistan (DRA) into the Islamized institutions of the Republic of Afghanistan contributed to blurring the lines. At that point, radical Islamism took on a life of its own as thousands of Arab veterans from Afghanistan engaged in other conflicts involving Muslims around the world, including in Kashmir (1989), Algeria (1991), Bosnia (1992), Tajikistan (1992), and Chechnya (1995). They brought with them their militant fundamentalist views and set out to violently purge Islam of what they saw as the corrupt influences introduced since the time of the Prophet Muhammad and return to a literalist interpretation of the Koran and the Sunnah. This put them at odds with other forms of Islam that had developed in these regions, and with secular and nationalist forces within the Muslim parties they supported.

As the USSR collapsed and despite the outburst of violence and terrorism connected to that ideology, the debates over Islamism's vitality were replaced by postmortem analysis of a phenomenon that many saw as having peaked during the second part of the Soviet-Afghan War. It was only after 9/11 and the reinvigoration of Osama bin Laden's al-Qaeda during the American interventions in Afghanistan and then Iraq that debates over Islamism, and especially its transnational militant form, resurfaced. They took a new color as Western politicians increasingly cast Islamism as the main threat to Western modernity, giving it the place that communism had once held. Strikingly, in Afghanistan, the United States encountered the same challenges as the Soviets had in their military operations and state-building project, including as to what to do with Islam.[11] It took the United States years to begin learning from the Soviet experience.

History and Memory

The Soviet-Afghan War has long fascinated historians as the conflict that saw the mighty Red Army get bogged down in an international backwater and, ultimately, as the one that ended the Cold War. Since 1989, the number of publications on the conflict has fluctuated based on the availability of archival sources and recollections from participants and its perceived relevance to understanding the present. Considering the opening of new archives on the 1980s across the world, the long-running US war in Afghanistan, and Russia's return to a neo-imperial foreign policy, interest in the Soviet-Afghan War has again been on the rise in recent years. As in previous periods, today's concerns color the interpretation of the past. This book is part of this reassessment of the Soviet-Afghan War.

Although there was no critical literature on the Soviet-Afghan War in the USSR, Western scholars wrote about the conflict as it unfolded. Most of this output is now outdated, but some books and articles written by eyewitnesses remain relevant to this day.[12] The golden age for the study of the Soviet-Afghan War came after its end and stretched from the mid-1990s to the mid-2000s. The research was at the time informed by documents released from Russian archives, and by the memoirs and accounts by Soviet, Afghan, Pakistani, and American decision-makers, intelligence and military officers, and journalists. International conferences such as in Lysebu in Norway in 1995 brought together Russian and American cold warriors.[13] In this context, scholars reassessed the Soviet decision to intervene in Afghanistan, and examined the war's military aspects, the dragged-out process of the Soviet withdrawal, the negotiations for a never-to-be-possible Afghan coalition government, the Soviet and Afghan decision-making processes, and the Afghan social and political milieu that produced the communist revolution in 1978.[14] Few focused on the traumatic experience of Soviet soldiers.[15] Other books highlighted the war's violence and the abuses committed by both sides.[16] Subsequently, the historians and social scientists Thomas Barfield, Gilles Dorronsoro, Antonio Giustozzi, and Barnett R. Rubin studied the Soviet war in the broader context of Afghanistan's twentieth-century history, writing some of the best comprehensive accounts.[17]

Surprisingly, communist policies on religion and the Soviet view of Islam during the conflict received little attention. In terms of dedicated studies, only one article by the historian Chantal Lobato and, more recently, another by the historian Eren Tasar dealt with "communist Islam."[18] A chapter in the historian Yaacov Ro'i last book moreover dealt with the Soviet-Afghan War's impact on Central Asia and the experience of Central Asian soldiers in Afghanistan.[19] These contributions proved lacking. Lobato's research gave a brief overview of the policies on Islam of Babrak Karmal, the ruler installed by the Kremlin in 1979, but it said nothing of the Soviet perspective on the question, relied on a limited corpus of sources, and was tributary of the ideological Cold War context. It dismissed communist attempts at working with Islam and ended its analysis in 1985. Tasar's article, despite its quality, overstated Soviet interest in Islam in Afghanistan in the early years of the conflict. Finally, Ro'i's important book focused on all aspects of the Soviet experience in Afghanistan, leaving only a modest place to Islam. This fascinating gap in the historiography contrasts with the numerous studies on Islam's importance for the mujahideen that developed after 9/11.

By examining communist views and policies on Islam in Afghanistan, this book enhances our understanding of the multilayered oppositions structuring the Soviet-Afghan War. It shows how—beyond the military aspects—the conflict was also an ideological battle in which the communist side adapted its message and tactics as the conflict went on. It helps us understand the evolving Soviet perceptions of and goals in Afghanistan and the enduring tension between ideology and pragmatism in Soviet decision-making. The latter discussion feeds into the larger debate over the influence of ideology in Soviet foreign policy during the Cold War. Following the historian Jeremy Friedman's research on the Soviet Union's support of leftist regimes in the Third World, it begs for more comparative studies looking at Soviet and local leftist and nationalist parties' policies in pro-Soviet Muslim countries such as Iraq, the People's Democratic Republic of Yemen (PDRY or South Yemen), and Syria.[20]

This book also adds to the research on the Soviet-Afghan War that emerged in the 2000s. US researchers, markedly including the journalist Steve Coll, then questioned the policies of the Reagan Administration and its support to the mujahideen in the context of the al-Qaeda threat and the US engagement against the Taliban.[21] Eventually, scholars and the military also looked at the Soviet experience as a cautionary tale of fighting a war in the "graveyard of empires" and of failed nation-building. As the US war in Afghanistan continued, interest in the Soviet experience remained high. Artemy M. Kalinovsky examined the process of the Soviet withdrawal, Paul Robinson and Jay Dixon researched Soviet economic and development policies, Rodrick Braithwaite covered the overall Soviet involvement, Daniel B. Edwards analyzed the evolving perceptions of suicide bombing from the Soviet period to the present, Ro'i looked at the conflict's influence on the Soviet people, and Elizabeth Leake wrote an international history of the conflict.[22] There has furthermore been a growing interest in the study of Afghanistan's global integration with books by Timothy Nunan and Robert D. Crews dedicating chapters to the Soviet period.[23] This book connects to this rich historiography, demonstrating how, unlike the United States in the 1980s, the Soviets were aware of and concerned about Islamism's rise. Despite that, they eventually dismissed its importance.

The Soviet-Afghan War has also garnered significant interest in Afghanistan and Russia. Most of the contributions by Afghans remain difficult to procure outside Afghanistan and are heavily biased toward one or the other of the warring sides. This book uses some of the more influential Afghan accounts discussing the PDPA's policies. Russian historiography and political circles have, meanwhile, remained fixated on the question of why the politburo, the highest decision-making body in the USSR composed of just over a dozen members, sent troops to Afghanistan. This obsession has led it to disregard other aspects of the conflict, save perhaps for the question of the withdrawal that many military and political leaders and advisers saw as a betrayal of the Afghan communists. A sentiment one often hears from veterans and that can be found in their memoirs was that even though dispatching troops to Afghanistan may have been a mistake, leaving in the way it was done was a crime. Overall, memoirs have dominated Russian scholarship, introducing biases in assessments of the war. The authors who wrote the most scholarly and influential contributions, including Vasili Khristoforov, Nikolai Kozyrev, Vladimir Plastun, and Vladimir Snegirev, are themselves either veterans or former advisers.[24] In parallel, several Russian researchers and Afgantsy have reassessed the Soviet-Afghan War in the context of the troubles in Central Asia and the North Caucasus in the 1990s and 2000s and increasingly of the Syrian conflict.[25] These deterministic accounts are naturally problematic.

The Soviet-Afghan War has also entered Russian popular culture. Contrasting with how the United States produced Cold War-type action films in the 1980s, including *Rambo III* and the much better *The Beast of War*, the Soviet-Afghan War made it to cinema screens in Russia only in the 1990s. Critical of the war, the films of the 1990s, including *Noga* (*The Leg*), went along with its negative portrayal in memoirs. By contrast, the 2000s saw the action film *9 rota* (*The 9th Company*) that, like many accounts of that period, heroized the

Figure 0.1. Monument to the Afgantsy built in Moscow in 2004 (Author's Photo). The monument testifies to the heroization in Russia since the 2000s of the "Soviet internationalist soldiers" who fought in Afghanistan.

Soviet experience. Released in 2005, *9 rota* has been immensely influential in shaping the war's memory. The movie tells the tragic story of conscripts sent to Afghanistan as the conflict was winding down in 1988. It highlights the war's religious component while presenting Soviet soldiers in a favorable light. In 2010, another popular movie in a similar patriotic mode, *Kandahar*, also dealt with Afghanistan. Based on true events, the movie's plot revolved around the capture of a Russian plane of weapons by the Taliban in 1995. At many levels, *Kandahar* traced a surprising continuity between the Soviet-Afghan War and the post-1991 period when Russia supported the former mujahideen's anti-Taliban alliance. Today, the Soviet-Afghan War's memory remains contested in Russia, as shown by the hostile reception from veterans and politicians to the film *Bratstvo* (*Leaving Afghanistan*), released in 2019. Seen as critical of the war, *Bratstvo* came in contradiction with the heroic-patriotic mode promoted in official depictions of the conflict. This tension around the memory of the Soviet-Afghan War illustrates the broader difficulty for Russia in coming to terms with the memory of the Soviet period.

The Soviet Ideology and Playbook

Leaving Kabul in November 1988, Nikolay Egorychev, the Soviet ambassador who oversaw the withdrawal of Soviet troops at the end of the Soviet-Afghan War, bitterly reflected on the entire enterprise. Like US policymakers in 2022, the Soviets were painfully trying to figure out how things could have gone so wrong in Afghanistan after such an auspicious start. In his personal notes, Egorychev candidly listed the factors that he believed had worked for and against the Soviets.[26] In the left column, he noted how the Soviets had been able to establish control over Afghan provincial centers, how tens of thousands of people had joined the PDPA, and how the communists had held an advantage in weapons and equipment. In the right column, he noted as his first point— "Islam. Infidel people." He went on to list other factors that had helped the mujahideen such as the mountainous terrain and the support they received from abroad. Still, Islam had come first. This, Egorychev believed, had been the main impediment to the Soviets in Afghanistan.

By the end of the Afghan War, even a staunch communist like Egorychev, the former first secretary of the Moscow City Committee of the CPSU, had to acknowledge that the Soviets' inability to deal with Islam in Afghanistan had been their undoing. This assessment contradicted the core of Marxist-Leninist ideology, which predicted that Islam would have been a minor concern. Afghans' embrace of the Soviet modernization project should have marginalized religion. Yet the opposite had proved true: communism's appeal was nothing compared to Islam's in Afghanistan. After having dismissed Islam and Islamism at the start of the conflict, the Soviets had to adapt and embrace religion as a political force in Afghanistan in 1986, discarding Marxism-Leninism. Much as the United States decades later, they had, by then, lost the battle for Afghans' hearts and minds that they were sure they would win.

The explanation of the Soviet failure in Afghanistan connects to the ever-pregnant debate about the competition between ideology and realpolitik in driving decision-making during the Cold War. Amid the opening of new archives, that debate animates historians investigating Soviet-American relations, decolonization and the conflicts in the Third World, and the Sino-Soviet split. This book, along with the historians such as Vladislav Zubok and Melvyn Leffler, emphasizes the role of ideology in Soviet decision-making.[27] The Cold War's main characteristic was that it was a "clash of ideologies" in which Moscow and Washington articulated alternative views of modernity and of the future economic, social, and political development of humanity.[28] As the historian Odd Arne Westad wrote, "some of the extraordinary brutality of Cold War interventions [in the Third World]—such as those in Vietnam or Afghanistan—can only be explained by Soviet and American identification with the people they sought to defend."[29]

Ideology gave structure and meaning to how Soviet and American policy makers formed ideas about the world and their country's place in it. It provided a set of fundamental notions connected to their specific cultural and historical contexts, and to "relationships of power, and the creation, transmission, and interpretation of meaning."[30] Ideology held the two systems together domestically and internationally as part of military and economic alliances. This is not to make the reductionist argument that other factors were not important—Soviet, American, and other decision-makers, for example, observed the geostrategic situation and made realist calculations, and personalities also played a role—but to underline that ideas were central during the Cold War.

While stressing ideology, it is important to recognize its protean nature. Ideology did not need to be coherent, fully developed, or even entirely shared to be important. Scholars have shown how ideology first fostered the Sino-Soviet alliance and then drove the split. Between communist China and the Soviet Union, Marxism-Leninism was a shared ideology and a topic of divergence. The latter was characteristic of the communist world and of domestic fights for power in the Soviet Union. Decision-makers, while adhering to or claiming to adhere to similar ideas, could have diverging, including wrong, interpretations of the tenets of Marxism-Leninism, anchored in their varying knowledge of it. They could also use, in good faith or in a cynical way, Marxism-

Leninism's inherent ambiguities to advance their interests. Marxism-Leninism was both a belief system and a political tool.[31] Its ambiguities were not only a source of tension inside the Kremlin and in Soviet dealings with foreign communist leaders; they also produced conflicts at lower levels in the CPSU. As this book shows, they created endless disagreements in Afghanistan between the Soviet advisers and Afghan communists and among the Soviet advisers themselves.

Ultimately, Marxism-Leninism was for the Soviets and many of their communist allies not a set of stable beliefs or values; it was, as Friedman notes, "a systematically simplified way of understanding reality that facilitates judgment and action."[32] The historians Lorenz M. Lüthi and Michael M. Hunt similarly emphasize that it was a way to process and simplify the information by fitting it into an easily comprehensible model and a call to action, setting a number of methods to achieve a utopian goal.[33] Having come to Afghanistan expecting to see "class conflict," Soviets at all levels noted its presence against all evidence well into the mid-1980s. Whatever happened, they fit it into a preexisting and rigid model, and the way to address the issues was through methods they knew and that were based on the Soviet modernization experience; that is, they had only one playbook. The latter had, nevertheless, undergone momentous changes since the October Revolution.

The Road to "Real Socialism"

The early years of the Soviet Union under Joseph Stalin saw the defining of the tenets of Marxism-Leninism and the violent attempts at implementing them in real life.[34] Amid the mass repression against real and supposed dissent, the USSR went through the collectivization of agriculture and the resulting horrific famines in Ukraine, Russia, and Kazakhstan and rapid industrialization using the forced labor of the GULAG, the state agency dealing with camps for political prisoners and criminals.[35] By the Second World War, Stalin established a centralized political system in which the CPSU duplicated the state organs and ran the country. The period was marked by Stalin's public reinterpretation of Marxist-Leninism's cannons in the *Pravda* and elsewhere, leading to the revision of the Soviet Constitution and the definition of the "socialism in one country paradigm." While Stalin and his associates set the Soviet doctrine, they eliminated the earlier generations of Soviet communists and intellectuals, artists, and religious leaders who may have had alternative views. Soviet society was mobilized to achieve the rapid modernization of the country and forced to surrender political power to the CPSU. This system withstood the shock of the Second World War and the post-war period saw the return of repressions, although in a less radical form. The Stalin period was the time when communism gained ground worldwide, relying on the prestige gained by the USSR after its victory in the Second World War. European communist parties in France and Italy gained significant power in democratic elections, the USSR installed pro-Soviet regimes in Eastern Europe, anticolonial and anti-imperialist struggles in Asia, Africa, and Latin America developed under left-ist ideas, and, in 1949, China, the most populous country in the world, turned communist.

After Stalin's death, Nikita Khrushchev attempted to reform the Soviet system from 1953 to 1964, getting rid of Stalin's personality cult and stopping political repressions.[36] Having undermined the authority figure of Stalin, Khrushchev appealed to Vladimir Lenin's writings to legitimize his policies. His reformism aimed at recapturing the zeal of the October Revolution and, indeed, improving the lives of ordinary Soviets with economic reforms while preserving many aspects of the centralized Stalinist regime, including its constitution. In foreign policy, because European communist parties had failed at capturing power and the spreading of world communist revolution by the USSR became impossible in the nuclear age, Khrushchev focused on supporting liberation struggles by leftist movements in the Third World. The latter marked a major shift in the "Soviet model of the global revolutionary process," also fostered by the Sino-Soviet split.[37] The focus was no longer on the communist revolution in the "developed world" but on the communist revolution in its anti-imperialist component in the Third World. Although these two revolutions were connected, they were not the same. This was even more so as most leftist movements in the Third World had only a vague grasp of Marxism-Leninism and a practical impossibility to follow its basic postulates due to the absence of an industrial base. The Soviet ideology already then became less about a complex system of thoughts and more about, on the one hand, professing basic political ideas in foreign and domestic policy, and, on the other, endorsing the regime that had consolidated in the Soviet Union. There, the communist utopia as envisioned by Marx was left for the future while pacific competition prevailed with the West. Khrushchev's reformism and unpredictability in foreign policy appeared, however, too risky for some CPSU elites who removed the mercurial first secretary.

The ascendency of Brezhnev in 1964 was when what anthropologist Alexey Yurchak aptly named the "last Soviet generation" entered the stage.[38] These new Soviet elites made the argument that the Soviet system was already at maturity, meaning that this "real" or "developed socialism" was as good as it would get. The Brezhnev-era elites gave up on having Marxism-Leninism as a living ideology that could be debated or reformulated and used it mostly as a tool of identification within the CPSU in-group. The Marxist-Leninist ideology as such became circular, funded by the emulation and referencing of past achievements, myths about the October Revolution, and statements by Lenin. It was about the reproduction of approaches and techniques in party and state organizations at all levels, notwithstanding that these had already failed to improve living standards, bolster industrial and agricultural productivity, and ensure accountability within the CPSU. The Soviet system was marked by the fear of innovation that could expose its proponent to accusations of lacking Marxist-Leninist rectitude.

The consolidation at the head of the Soviet Union of aging elites amplified this trend. By 1979, politburo members such as seventy-three-year-old Brezhnev, sixty-five-year-old Yuri Andropov, the head of the Committee for State Security or KGB, seventy-year-old Andrei Gromyko, the minister of Foreign Affairs, seventy-one-year-old Dmitry Ustinov, the minister of defense, and sixty-eight-year-old Konstantin Chernenko, Brezhnev's longtime associate, were afraid to depart from decades-old protocols and communist incantations. They remained convinced communists who trusted that their system would prevail, that the "world would go their way."[39] They had expanded Khrushchev's policies of support to leftists around the world, raising Soviet commitments to Fidel Castro's Cuba, Hafez al-Assad Syria, Salvador Allende's Chile, Agostinho Neto's Angola, Mengistu Haile Mariam's Ethiopia, and other countries as part of the "Global Cold War" with the United States. This support though ironically asked less and less of these Third World leaders in terms of ideological commitment to Marxism-Leninism. By the 1970s, being pro-Soviet was enough for a country to be labeled as having entered the "non-capitalist path of development."[40] Soviet clients, meanwhile, enjoyed considerable freedom in dealing with Moscow, often charting their own domestic and foreign policies. As this book shows, this would also strikingly be the case of the Afghan communists.

"Real socialism" was a mixed blessing for ordinary Soviet citizens. It meant rising living standards for most people, including better access to state services in health and education and consumer goods. It also meant stagnation as this rise slowed down in the late 1970s, and the Soviet system increasingly dropped behind the West. In parallel, the regime's gigantic and largely unaccountable bureaucracy made the Soviet system ineffective and led to significant disconnects between central and local policies. As shown by historian Artemy A. Kalinovsky regarding Soviet development policies in Tajikistan, it is wrong to see central policies as well-integrated and rigidly applied locally. Strategies decided in Moscow were reworked at the point of contact, being often transformed as they were implemented.[41] The CPSU officials in Soviet republics had considerable freedom in both what they took from the Kremlin's instructions and in how they reported about the situation in their republics. Interestingly, the same would be true of Soviet policies in Afghanistan where Soviet advisers and military and the PDPA had considerable room for maneuver. It was even more so as Soviet military, intelligence, and civilian agencies would compete to dominate policy making during the war, often submitting distorted and contradictory reports to Moscow.

The "last Soviet generation" also benefited from the relaxation of state control and increasingly looked at the West as an alternate model of modernity, being influenced, notably through the radio, by Western culture, music, and social codes. This did not mean that most ordinary Soviets rejected socialism and opposed Soviet power. Many stayed attached to the communist ideal, and the core tenets of the system were inculcated to them through primary and secondary education, various cultural and sports clubs, and CPSU youth political organizations such as the Komsomol. Until the end, many Soviets inside and outside the CPSU believed that their system, despite its many flaws, was benevolent and egalitarian and could serve as a model to the Third World. This was a striking paradox given that most ordinary Soviets partook in communist rituals and traditions in a way that was mostly symbolic and did not ask from them a conscious engagement with ideology. Still, as dramatically clear from testimonies of advisers who went to Afghanistan, most of them traveled to Kabul firmly believing they would bring modernization and progress to Afghans.

Marxism-Leninism, Islam, and Afghanistan

The Soviet-Afghan War tested the Soviet system and the Marxist-Leninist ideology that had crystalized by the 1980s. The two were by then indissociable. Ideology in the USSR was less about interpreting what Marx and Lenin had written than about replicating forms of political organization, social and labor organization, and repeating worn-out party slogans that had become ingrained among the elites and in society and served a symbolic function. Ideology for the Soviets was as much about actual ideas as about discursive markers and ways of doing things. It was a modernization model for export that espoused the old Stalinist ideas of the collectivization of agriculture, the emphasis on heavy industry, the replication of a party-state structure on the Soviet model that included Soviet political organizations such as the Komsomol and atheism. The Soviets struggled with imposing their model in Afghanistan at all levels, but they encountered particular difficulties with religious policy.

As much as it catalyzed the emergence of radical Islamism among the mujahideen, the Soviet-Afghan War was also the time when Soviet elites rethought the "Islamic factor." Although the Soviets occasionally used the term narrowly to mean Islamism, they usually saw it as encompassing the entirety of Islam—everything related to the social and political role of Islam in Muslim areas. As they encountered the mujahideen, the Soviets reassessed Islam and had to decide if Islamism could be a threat to Soviet Central Asia. As they struggled with their modernization project in Afghanistan, they faced the challenge of reconciling their atheism and Marxist-Leninist ideology with the need to placate Islam to gain support among the local population. Soviets wondered to which extent special policies toward Islam may be needed in Afghanistan. As they worked together with the Afghan communists, the Soviets had to decide who should reach out to Afghan Islamic leaders. As Islamist parties became dominant among the mujahideen and Arab fighters arrived, the Soviets, too, had to adjust their approach toward Islam in Afghanistan. Ultimately, the Soviet relation to Islam offers a unique angle through which to assess their nation-building enterprise in Afghanistan.

When the Soviet Union invaded Afghanistan in 1980, the politburo assessed the country as being socially, politically, and economically backward. Still, it had to be transformable using scientific Marxism-Leninism. As this book shows, the Soviets had extensively criticized the PDPA for its radical policies in 1978 and 1979, including on Islam, but these disagreements had to do with tactics. Moscow took the same ideological approach to modernizing Afghanistan in the 1980s. Although its mistakes were less blatant, they were of the same nature as the ones made by the PDPA early on. Like the Afghan communists, the Soviets were prisoners of Marxist-Leninist ideology. Their policies were unable to solve the tension between the tangible reality of a feudal and Islamic Afghanistan and the idea, pushed by the International Department in the Central Committee (CC) of the CPSU, that Third World Soviet-aligned countries had to be moving toward socialism. This duality reflected in how the USSR perceived Islam in Afghanistan and explained the evolution of the Soviets' and the PDPA's relationship with Islam from 1978 to 1989. Only late in the conflict and as the LCST prepared to leave, the Soviets and the PDPA made serious efforts to co-opt Islam in support of the regime, realizing that no amount of sovietization would transform the DRA into a proto-Central Asian republic. The Soviets' attitude toward Islam served as a litmus test for their reformist project.

Soviet views of Islam in Afghanistan connected to their assessment of religion at home. The KGB had used the term Wahhabism disparagingly to denote non-state-controlled Islamic practice in Soviet Muslim regions since the 1950s. These negative perceptions, echoing tsarist preoccupations, focused on an "unorthodox Islam" that did not fit with the religious knowledge, "rooted in the privileging of a limited textual canon," of Soviet atheist Orientalists and Islamologists.[42] Beyond their suspicion of deviations in Islam, tsarist elites were preoccupied with pan-Islamic movements and the loyalty of the empire's Muslim elites on which the authorities relied and which had, over time, proved loyal during the wars with the Ottoman Empire.

As this book shows, this concern carried into how the Kremlin saw Islamism during the Soviet-Afghan War. However, it did not crystallize into firm beliefs as confusion dominated in assessing the threat that the Afghan Islamists represented for the USSR. The Kremlin did not conceptualize an independent and non-state-based Islamist threat and the Soviets did not use the term Islamism, speaking instead of the Islamic factor, Islamic fundamentalism, Islamic fanaticism, or Islamic extremism to denote the idea of a militant political Islam. At home, Soviet authorities remained reluctant for Islam to have any place in the social or political life of Muslim regions and suspected foreign forces from Afghanistan, Iran, or the United States every time Soviet Muslims played up. Gorbachev and his team branded Islam a retrograde factor despite the local tolerance for private Islamic practices that existed in Central Asia. Accordingly, they failed to take the Islamist ideology in Afghanistan seriously.

Structure of the Book

This book develops its arguments across six chapters. The first chapter briefly presents the Soviet relation to Islam at home since the October Revolution. The second chapter then discusses the policies of the PDPA's Khalq faction after it took power in 1978, stressing the extent to which its policies were anti-Islamic. In parallel, it examines how Islam featured in the Soviet politburo's debates about Afghanistan in 1978–79 and Soviet policy advice to the PDPA. The chapter also examines the events before the start of the Soviet-Afghan War in 1979 and argues that the threat of an Islamist contagion from Afghanistan to Central Asia, which preoccupied the KGB, played a role in triggering it. It was nevertheless a relatively minor concern.

The third chapter shows Karmal's, the Afghan leader installed by the Soviets, attempts to present his regime as respectful of Islam and to co-opt Islamic scholars into the regime's institutions. While this was in sharp contrast to Khalq's approach, the chapter stresses Moscow's inconsistent influence in pushing for these policies and the communists' collective belief that a makeshift Islamic facade would be enough to diffuse criticism of the PDPA on religious grounds. Despite having discussed it in the run-up to the intervention, the Soviets neglected Islam in Afghanistan and Marxist-Leninist ideology and military considerations dominated the decision-making.

The fourth chapter focuses on Najibullah's drive to integrate Islam into his regime as part of his policy of national reconciliation after he took power from Karmal in 1986. This thrust came together with a now-proactive Soviet interest in the religious aspects of the conflict on the eve of the withdrawal. Moscow pushed Najibullah toward scrapping Marxism-Leninism both rhetorically and practically—an interesting contrast with Gorbachev's attempt to salvage socialism at home—and toward Islamizing his rhetoric and the regime's institutions. While the Soviets and Afghans jointly initiated national reconciliation, the Afghans retained flexibility in piloting it. The chapter thus challenges the orthodox view of Soviet control over the PDPA.

The fifth chapter shows how the PDPA, with Soviet support, courted the Muslim world after most Muslim countries, including some Soviet allies, condemned the intervention. The USSR staged an international information campaign displaying the Islamic character of the Afghan communist regime to boost its political legitimacy in Afghanistan through recognition by the Muslim world. Afghanistan's diplomacy toward Muslim countries remained, in parallel, limited to Soviet clients and, unlike its domestic policies, entirely dependent on Moscow. In turn, Soviet influence among Arab countries long ensured that condemnations of the Afghan communists remained limited in the Organisation of the Islamic Conference (OIC).

The sixth chapter examines Moscow's assessments of Islamism at the end of the Soviet-Afghan War and in its aftermath. It points to the role of India and of Najibullah in raising Soviet concerns over the Islamist threat. The chapter shows how the risk of the consolidation of an Islamist regime in Afghanistan and the influence that Islamism might have on Soviet Muslims evidently worried the Kremlin. It also explains that the USSR was unable to conceptualize an independent Islamist threat and saw it as more like a tool for Pakistan, the United States, or Iran to use against it. In the end, this threat was of limited concern for the politburo while other domestic and international considerations dwarfed it during Gorbachev's reforms. This belief flowed from the Soviets' conviction that Islamism and nationalism were retrograde ideologies whose influence should not be overestimated.

CHAPTER 1

The Basmachi and Soviet Islam

The relationship with Islam in the USSR influenced Moscow's perceptions of the coup d'état that brought the PDPA to power in 1978, the PDPA's antireligious policies, and the Islamic Revolution in Iran. This attitude was tributary of the longue durée of Moscow's relationship with Muslims where layers of perceptions superposed over centuries.[1] Significant continuities exist between the imperial, Soviet, and post-Soviet periods.

Russia's relationship with Islam has always been ambivalent. Moscow fought Muslims as its empire expanded, especially the Ottoman Empire in a dozen wars between the sixteenth and the twentieth centuries. Russia also had a proximity relationship with Islam and an integrating trend toward Muslims.[2] The empire's administration co-opted Muslim elites while tolerating religious practices and institutions in Muslim regions. In Central Asia, *sharia* courts existed and many Muslims willingly submitted to the tsar's authority. The state used Islam as one of the pillars of its legitimacy in the same way it used Orthodoxy. By 1897, some 20 million Muslims lived in the Russian Empire.[3] They had accrued as the empire annexed the Khanate of Kazan to the east in the sixteenth century and the Caucasus and Central Asia to the south in the nineteenth. These regions were then integrated into the Soviet Union and experienced the harsh Stalinist policies in different ways.

The historiography of Islam in the USSR has evolved since the 2000s, but a substantial part of it dates to the 1980s and is problematic in various ways.

The Soviet historiography is ideologically biased and sees religion as an archaism that delayed Soviet modernity. However, the historiography pioneered in the West by Alexander Bennigsen, Chantal Lemercier-Quelquejay, and Marie Broxup is also outdated.[4] These authors contended that Soviet Muslims, especially the most religiously inclined who belonged to Sufi orders and evaded state control, would come to challenge the regime and that Soviet authorities were exceedingly concerned about that Islamic threat. Even in the 1980s, scholars questioned these claims, calling them "Cold War wishful thinking" that ascribed Soviet Muslims of the 1980s "ideas and sentiments of Islamic thinkers or activists of the 1920s."[5] The Bennigsen school misinterpreted anti-Islamic propaganda in the USSR as a response to political mobilization among Soviet Muslims. Although the sequence of events that led to the Soviet Union's breakup ultimately discredited its theories, their influence lingered.

The opening of the archives of the Soviet agencies tasked with regulating religion, including the Council for the Affairs of Religious Cults (CARC), which was replaced by the Council for Religious Affairs (CRA) in 1965, and the Spiritual Administration of the Muslims of Central Asia and Kazakhstan (SADUM) that oversaw Islam in Central Asia, and field research among (post-)Soviet Muslims led to the emergence of a new historiography. This replacement also had its issues, and some scholars were criticized for their inability to critically deal with Soviet archives, reproducing Soviet-era ideological stereotypes, recycling Soviet terms such as "unregistered clergy" to describe the diverse religious specialists and practitioners not part of state institutions and taking at face values assessments and policies made in Moscow.[6] Yet there was a gap between the Marxist-Leninist ideology, how the policies were formulated in the Kremlin and written in CARC and CRA documents, and how they were implemented in Muslim regions after 1945.[7] Overall, the Soviet attitude toward Islam alternated between tolerance and repression.

In the wake of Lenin's call in 1919 to "All the Toiling Muslims of Russia and the East" that promised Muslims that their beliefs, customs, and rights to worship would remain "free and untouchable," the Bolsheviks originally embraced Islam. The next year they called on Muslims to engage in a "red holy war" against "world imperialism" at the Communist International-sponsored First Congress of the Peoples of the East in Baku, even though their focus remained on worker parties in Western Europe.[8] In territories under their control, they allowed mosques and madrasas (Islamic schools) to function. The Bolsheviks' strategy was, however, a tactical ploy. As Grigory Zinoviev explained, "the alliance of Bolshevism and Islam could not happen at the expense of capitulation to religious ideas." The Bolsheviks already saw the potential spread of pan-Islamic ideas as a threat.[9] By the 1930s, Stalin unleashed an antireligious campaign that closed and often destroyed thousands of churches and mosques and led to wide-spread abuses against the Christian clergy, Islamic scholars, and the believers of both religions. The Soviets executed some 14,000 Islamic scholars and leaders during the Cultural Revolution and the Great Terror in Uzbekistan alone.[10] Yet, unlike Orthodox Christianity, Islam proved more resilient to repression. One reason was its ability to operate underground without mosques. Others were related to the nonhierarchical structure of the community of Islamic scholars and leaders, which made them more difficult for the authorities to control, and the absence of ordination in Islam.

In the postrevolutionary period, the young Soviet state witnessed its only challenge from a Muslim insurgency. The latter experience was formative for Soviet leaders and continued to influence their and their heirs' worldviews long after the insurgency's end. The Basmachi, a name formed from the Turkish verb *basmak* meaning "to oppress, to violate" and used by the Soviets for Central Asian insurgents, developed in the late 1910s and continued into the early 1930s when the Soviet authorities crushed them.[11] Outbursts of contestation occurred until 1942.

The Basmachi had originated to protest conscription into the tsarist army during the First World War, a conflict in which the caliph's Ottoman Empire was on the opposite side. They became more potent as the Bolsheviks tried to assert control over Central Asia following the breakdown of the Turkestan (Kokand) autonomy in 1918. Allied to the anticommunist White forces during the civil war, the Basmachi grew on the resistance of the traditional local authorities—feudal aristocracy, tribal leaders, Islamic scholars, and large and middle landowners—to Soviet social and economic reforms. They especially opposed the Bolsheviks' antireligious drive that closed *madrasas* and *sharia* courts and nationalized *waqfs* (mosques and other lands owned by Islamic institutions and scholars). The fact that many Basmachi had ties of kinship with local Bolsheviks who were former tribal leaders made fighting them more complicated for Moscow.[12]

After Turkestan's fall, fighting spread to Central Asia with many engagements occurring in the Fergana Valley, shared between present-day Uzbekistan, Tajikistan, and Kyrgyzstan. By the early 1920s, the Basmachi were some 20,000 fighters strong, divided into groups led by local leaders—the *qo'rboshi*. In the newly established Soviet Turkestan—which encompassed present-day Turkmenistan, Uzbekistan, Tajikistan, and Kyrgyzstan—save for the small Bukharan People's Soviet Republic, the countryside supported the insurgents while the Soviets controlled Tashkent. The early 1920s marked the height of the Basmachi, revitalized after the arrival of General İsmail Enver, the former

Turkish war minister, in 1921. As it increasingly fought under Islamic and pan-Turk slogans, the movement consolidated control over the Bukharan Republic and swathes of Soviet Turkestan.[13]

At this point, the Bolsheviks changed their strategy to make Soviet power more attractive to the local population. New measures included amnesties for Basmachi who joined the Soviets, land reform, food aid to the population and to Basmachi defectors at a time when famine loomed large, the introduction of Lenin's New Economic Policy that eased pressure on the peasantry, and the suspension of anti-Islamic legislation. In parallel, alliances emerged between the Soviets and Muslim Jadid intellectuals—modernist reformers who combined anticolonial and national ideas and Islam.[14] In 1921–22, the Soviets restored *sharia* courts, returned *waqf* lands, and reopened *madrasas*. Although they tried to convince Islamic scholars of their tolerance toward Islam, most measures only lasted until the Basmachi's strength decreased. By the late 1920s, the authorities had reintroduced restrictions on *sharia* courts and *madrasas* and bans on Islamic scholars' participation in local affairs.

As they battled the Basmachi, Soviet leaders used Afghanistan as a bridgehead to steer uprisings among British India's Muslims. Moscow promptly recognized Afghan independence under Amanullah Khan in 1919 and signed a Treaty of Friendship with Kabul in 1921. The Bolsheviks then toyed with the possibility of supporting a push by Afghanistan toward the sea. Moscow definitively abandoned its hopes to start a front against Great Britain in Afghanistan only after Amanullah refused to transfer weapons and propaganda material to Pashtuns on the other side of the Afghan-Indian border.[15] The USSR continued to consolidate its influence in Afghanistan until a popular rebellion overthrew Amanullah in 1929. The Bolsheviks remarkably then set up a covert operation to try to restore the king to his throne. This showed the strategic importance they placed on the region. After Amanullah fled abroad, the Soviet forces, which had already taken the northern cities of Mazar-i Sharif and Balkh, retreated.

Anti-Islamic campaigns and collectivization revitalized the Basmachi in Tajikistan in the 1930s. In addition, Amanullah's short-lived successor, the Tajik Habibullah Kalakani, allowed them to use Afghanistan as a base. In 1931, Ibrahim Bek, the last *qo'rboshi*, led an attack of 2,000 men into Central Asia. Accompanied by the executions of Soviet officials and abuses against peasants, it resulted in a loss of support for the movement. After the Soviet authorities captured Bek, the Basmachi declined, although raids from Afghanistan and sporadic uprisings across Central Asia continued until the Second World War. As late as 1937, Stalin ordered the People's Commissariat for Internal Affairs to

Ethnic Groups in Afghanistan

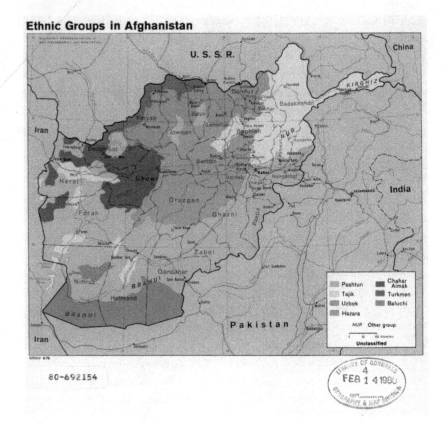

MAP 1.1.   Historical ethnic map of Afghanistan produced by the CIA, 1979 (Library of Congress https://www.loc.gov/item/80692154/).

deport mullahs who had returned from Afghanistan and all Afghan nationals.[16] Overall, thousands of Turkmens and Uzbeks ended up in Afghanistan following the Soviets suppression of the Basmachi and lost contact with their kin in the USSR.[17] Many of them and their descendants continued to identify by their place of origin and be staunch anticommunists.

Remarkably, Islam played a central role in ensuring the Basmachi's cohesion. The Basmachi pictured themselves as fighting a jihad. People who refused to fight were at risk of condemnation under *sharia*. Islam was also omnipresent in Basmachi's declarations. Fighters in the Fergana Valley called themselves "an army of Islam" and *qo'rboshi* declared fighting either for the "defense of *sharia*," "the solemnity of Islam," or "in the name of our founder and Prophet, Muhammad."[18] The Basmachi opposition to the Bolsheviks went beyond the rejection of collectivization; it was about keeping a holistic role for religion as structuring all the domains of life in Central Asia, something impossible under Soviet rule.

The Soviet historiography has naturally assessed the Basmachi negatively as a reactionary amalgam of feudal landlords and Islamic clergy who abused peasants and against whom Soviet soldiers fought valiantly, succeeding in imposing the progressive order of the October Revolution. In the post-Soviet period, these perceptions changed to the opposite in the Central Asian states where Basmachi became akin to Muslim freedom fighters or mujahideen.[19]

The Basmachi have, over the years, received considerable attention in Soviet popular culture. Their uprising notably served as the background for the film *Beloe solntse pustyni* (*White Sun of the Desert*), one of the most popular Soviet productions ever. An action-drama with elements of comedy, *Beloe solntse pustyni* gathered 50 million viewers in Soviet cinemas in 1970. Its plot follows Fyodor Sukhov, a Red Army soldier who is returning home after years of fighting in the civil war in Asia and is now passing through present-day Turkmenistan on the eastern shore of the Caspian Sea. Unfortunately for Sukhov, he becomes embroiled in local affairs and must fight Abdullah, a *qo'rboshi*. Sukhov subsequently undertakes the mission of protecting Abdullah's harem because Abdullah is set on killing his wives in revenge for them not committing suicide after being separated from him. After a multitude of twists and turns, Sukhov accomplishes his mission, protecting all but one of the women and defeats Abdullah. He then continues his way home as the film suggests that he may have to again defend the progressive Soviet order along the way.

Beloe solntse pustyni is notable for how it presents tropes of Russian and Soviet Orientalism.[20] Abdullah, the savage enemy, is romanticized as a fearless and noble warrior whom Red Army soldiers and local people respect. Yet he defends a perceivably archaic ideology of subversion of women to men. The film similarly evokes other common themes about the East, including the blood feud and honor debt for saving someone's life that are at the same time condemned and admired. Many of the same stereotypes will be then applied to the Afghans as the Soviets essentialized them as either "noble savages," or "cunning Easterners."

Over the years, *Beloe solntse pustyni* became a repository for popular quotes and wisdom—including the phrase *"Vostok delo tonkoe"* (The East is a delicate matter) said by Sukhov—and there is no doubt that most soldiers going to Afghanistan saw it. Even more fascinating, Soviet propaganda units showed the film in Afghan villages to elicit support for the USSR.[21] This exemplified the Basmachi's lasting impact on Soviet perceptions. For the Soviets who analyzed Afghanistan in the 1980s, the Basmachi were the archetype of what an Islam-inspired rebellion against Marxist-Leninist reforms looked like. They accordingly often called the Afghan opposition the Basmachi, alongside mainly *dushman* (enemies).[22] According to KGB and military officers, the Soviets transferred the methods and policies used against the Basmachi to Afghanistan.[23] As this book shows, that parallel was more misleading than helpful for the Soviets.

In Central Asia and in other Muslim regions, anti-Islamic policies continued until the Second World War. That conflict transformed Soviet society even though Stalin moved to reassert his domestic authority after the victory. It also allowed for an easing of the regulations on religion that led CARC and SADUM to normalize their relationship with Islam. After Stalin's death, Khrushchev restarted antireligious campaigns but these were nowhere near as potent as the purges of the 1930s. The role that Islam now occupied in Soviet diplomacy also mitigated them. Although it was a barely concealed enterprise in propaganda and intelligence collection, with KGB operatives accompanying religious leaders on Hajj, the Soviets' Islamic diplomacy through CARC/CRA and SADUM and state-to-state diplomacy in the Muslim world allowed them to develop relations with Muslim countries.[24] This brought rewards to Moscow which publicized the support it received from foreign Muslim figures. The Turkish minister of state for Religious Affairs and Waqfs, for example, visited the USSR in 1978 and found the situation with Islam to be quite satisfactory there.[25] By Leonid Brezhnev's time, a cohabitation between communism and Islam had crystallized in many Soviet Muslim regions. Depending on the region and the party officials in charge, hard and moderate lines toward Islam coexisted.

In Central Asia, a relatively tolerant attitude reminiscent of imperial policies toward Islam had evolved by late Stalinism. The authorities tried to control and channel Islam in support of the regime rather than eradicate it. As Tasar notes, "the Islamic sphere—the constellation of Islamic practices, sites, figures"—was an "organic and evolving part of being Muslim under Communist rule."[26] Even local CPSU leadership abode by Islamic rituals in the 1970s–80s—the first secretary of the Kazakh CPSU had his son circumcised—while the party downplayed the "Islamic factor" to get rid of Moscow's scrutiny.[27] Although most did not follow an Islamic way of life in the way Afghans understood it, Central Asians identified as Muslims and many partook in the rituals associated with the faith. This is a striking aspect that one finds when analyzing Central Asian soldiers' attitudes during the Soviet-Afghan War. Religiosity was especially high in Tajikistan and Uzbekistan in Central Asia, and in Chechnya-Ingushetia and Dagestan in the North Caucasus.

CARC/CRA and SADUM, meanwhile, became an interface between the state and Islam as ideological and political alliances emerged between national and local institutions. SADUM mediated between party authorities, Muslim leaders, scholars, and believers, adapting to inflections in the national policy on religion. It also promoted its agenda of asserting control over all Islamic scholars. In practice, this meant that the distinction, which Moscow saw as clear-cut, between the registered clergy that reported to SADUM and the unregistered clergy that operated independently was blurred, with both categories remaining ill-defined. SADUM could be flexible toward unregistered scholars if they recognized its spiritual authority. Many registered and some unregistered actors and believers understood in return that, although it was part of the Soviet state, SADUM had some of their interests in mind.

Still, the USSR remained a proudly atheist country. While touring India and Burma with Central Asian politicians and intellectuals in tow in 1955, Khrushchev noted that these people were of "a Moslem creed" and "worthy members of the great Soviet Union."[28] The Kremlin saw Tajiks and Uzbeks as cultural Muslims—atheist Muslims who would eventually come to abandon Islam. This view predominated after the Khrushchev era and its echoes are present in how advisers in Afghanistan saw Soviet Muslims. Throughout the Soviet period, the state hence conducted atheistic propaganda tailored to each Soviet region. Its goal was to "restrict religious practice, particularly in its more demonstrative forms and to prevent children and young people from being imbued with religious tenets or from being taught religious rites."[29] The fact that this propaganda's effectiveness was low did not mean that no opposition to religion existed. Atheistic propaganda and state pressure on practicing working age and urban Muslims led to widespread dissatisfaction. The lack of mosques in Central Asia and the Caucasus remained another major issue. Islamic leaders and believers accordingly criticized the state and the institutions dealing with religion, sometimes branding the latter as uneducated sell-outs, not real Muslims and under the KGB's control.[30]

At the same time, the Kremlin, some republic-level party authorities, and the KGB viewed the unregistered clergy with suspicion. They associated "itinerant mullahs" with foreign-influenced "deviant" practices contrary to what Soviet scholars saw as "proper Islam." The Islamologist Devin Deweese notes the irony that "the Communist Party and the Soviet academic establishment were essentially allied with the official Islamic clergy (not to mention fundamentalists abroad) in adopting a 'rigorist' interpretation of what constituted 'real' Islam."[31] This criticism appeared in the Central Asian media that denounced the "confusion between religious and national traditions" and the tenacity of foreign "religious archaisms" such as inscriptions in Arabic in local cemeteries.[32] In this context, the KGB and local communist authorities often branded unregistered mullahs "fanatics"—an undefined category—and saw them as potential spies for foreign countries.[33]

Anatoly Chernyaev, Gorbachev's foreign policy adviser, noted the confusion and concern about Islam at a politburo meeting in 1984. Amid a corruption scandal, Muhammetnazar Gapurow, the first secretary of the Turkmen CPSU, explained that in his republic "people lived publicly by Soviet norms but at home, in the village, according to *sharia*. [Mullahs] circumcised boys, conducted 100% of burials according to the rules of the Koran, etc. There were 40–50 immolations a year." Beyond this, mullahs celebrated weddings, there were thousands of "unregistered mullahs" and young people, including from the Komsomol, paid bride prices and conducted bride kidnappings. The KGB, in parallel, reported that groups of *murids*—disciples following a religious figure such as a *sheikh* in Sufism—were common and that amid this high religiosity "anti-Soviet and anti-Russian feelings" were widespread in Turkmenistan. This description astounded Gorbachev and the Russians at the politburo. The Soviet leader could not understand how "67 years after the October Revolution," Islam thrived in Central Asia. Gapurow's revelation also reminded those present about the ongoing Soviet-Afghan War. If such was the situation in Central Asia, how should the USSR go about sovietizing Afghanistan?[34]

Turkmenistan's story summarizes the points made above. Belief in Marxist-Leninism and the limited information coming from Muslim regions hid the actual situation with Islam from the Kremlin. Soviet leaders were oblivious to the accommodation between Islam and communism that had developed in Central Asia and believed that religion was dying out in the USSR. This perception then extended to much of the academic and political elite in Moscow that, although aware of the theoretical "Muslim danger," did not take it seriously.[35] Although the Kremlin was cognizant of the issue, it did not see the Islamist threat as a priority.

Doubts about Soviet Muslims' loyalty, fostered by the appearance of Islamists among Soviet Muslims, grew after the Iranian Revolution and the start of the Soviet-Afghan War. They led to anti-Islamic resolutions strengthening ideological and atheistic work. One such document noted "the increased activity of Shias in some regions bordering Iran" as a potential threat the KGB had to monitor.[36] Since 1980, other signs showed the rising concern. The local KGB head in Azerbaijan commented in the media that "given the situations in Iran and Afghanistan, US special services were trying to use the Islamic religion as one of the factors in influencing" the USSR.[37] The KGB thenceforth remained at the forefront of Soviet concerns about Islamism.

These concerns were two-fold. First, the KGB feared that "identification with the *ummah*, the worldwide Muslim community" or the Soviet Muslim community may challenge proletarian internationalism—the "friendship of the people" narrative in the Soviet Union.[38] Second, it suspected that the Islamists, called fanatics and Wahhabis, would come to oppose the Soviet order on a mixed religious and nationalist basis. The KGB saw that risk as connected to a foreign hand, showing a lack of understanding of the Islamists' local roots and often nonpolitical nature at that stage. Beyond this, the KGB remained as much concerned with the Islamists as with Sufi networks—the *murid* groups noted above. Such perceptions carried into how the Soviets saw Islam in Afghanistan.

Finally, the Soviets had to reconcile their concerns with Islamism and Marxism-Leninism, which argued that, in some countries, Islam had a progressive role. Yevgeny Primakov, then director of the Oriental Studies Institute, explained that the Islamic movement "comprised several trends. There was a radical trend which was strongly charged with anti-imperialism. And there was . . . a bourgeois-landowner trend which was loaded with a large charge of anti-communism." While the first trend was apparent in Iran, where leftist forces had supported the Islamists, Primakov claimed that the United States tried to use the second against the Soviets in Afghanistan.[39] Others later made similar arguments. One Soviet scholar opposed how the United States, China, and "Muslim reactionaries" tried to abuse Islam while, in reality, as Soviet ally President Chadli Bendjedid of Algeria had stated, Islam was "a progressive religion based on social justice," meaning that it could be a steppingstone toward Marxism-Leninism.[40] These perceptions also carried into how the Soviets saw Islam in Afghanistan, leading to considerable ambiguity.

CHAPTER 2

Khalq's Islam and the Decision to Intervene

> There are 15 thousand mosques by which there are
> many tens of thousands of religious figures (according
> to some sources these are up to 180 thousand people)
> in Afghanistan. The influence and the role of the
> Muslim clergy in the social and political life of the
> country are very important. Mullahs are not only
> religious figures but also judges . . . and teachers.
>
> —Soviet Afghanist, 1964

> [Amin] liked to repeat: "Comrade Stalin taught us how
> to build socialism in a backward country: First, it
> would hurt, and then it would be great!"
>
> —Soviet advisers in Afghanistan, 1979

The PDPA's Marxist Playbook and Islam

The communist coup in Afghanistan on 27–28 April 1978 came after a period of political turmoil that started with the ousting of King Zahir Shah, who had reigned for forty years and whose reign many Afghans associated in retrospect with prosperity and stability, by his former prime minister and cousin Moham-mad Daoud Khan in 1973. Leading to the creation of the DRA, the Saur (April) Revolution as it was called, was a home-grown affair whose striking success came as a surprise to the Kremlin, although informants had tipped off KGB operatives in Kabul shortly before it began.[1] The rise of the PDPA was unexpected given the party's membership of only a few thousand, mostly in Kabul and in the military, and given its bitter factionalism. For Moscow, the PDPA's accession to power posed a problem because it removed Daud who, despite having sidelined the PDPA and moved closer to Iran and the West, remained the USSR's man.[2] As put by Andrey Grachev, who then worked in the CC CPSU International Depart-ment, the PDPA "had managed to get rid of Daud with whom the USSR had no issue but, on the other side, if [Moscow] got such a gift what could it do?"[3]

Since its inception in the 1960s, the PDPA, which stood on a Marxist-Leninist line, was split between two groups—Khalq (People) and Parcham (Banner)—

that competed for influence among its constituency and favor in Moscow. That split had led to diverging loyalties. While Parcham was closer to the KGB and seen as most favored by the Soviets, Khalq was closer to the Main Intelligence Directorate, the military intelligence known as GRU. While Soviet agencies competed to shape information on and policy in Afghanistan, this division remained, however, fluid. One KGB general would recall years later that not being able to choose between PDPA factions had been the KGB's biggest mistake in Afghanistan because it was clear from the 1970s that no reconciliation between the parties would be possible.[4]

Aside from personal enmities, the two groups differed in their proposed approach. Parcham was ready to work through Afghan institutions and make alliances to rise to power. Many of its members, including its leader Karmal, had been part of the parliament and the government at the beginning of Daoud's presidency. It was also more flexible toward the Islamic clergy. That faction comprised intellectuals and many whose families, including Karmal's and Najibullah's, came from among the higher ranks of civil servants, often from urban areas, and had a higher representation among northern ethnic minorities. Conversely, Khalq was more radical and numerous. It relied on support in the army and the lower ranks of civil servants such as teachers, often in rural areas. Because of its influence in the military, it retained significant support within the LCST even after Karmal's arrival to power. Khalq was also Pashtun-dominated—Pashtun nationalist by some accounts—having more links in the south and southeast of the country.[5]

After the April Revolution, Khalq dominated Afghan politics with its leader Nur Muhammad Taraki becoming the general secretary of the CC PDPA. Ideology aside, this marked a monumental switch in tribal and political equilibrium. After the reign of the Durrani Pashtuns since the mid-eighteenth century, with Dari-speaking groups in a secondary position, the power had passed to the Ghilzai Pashtuns. This, too, played a role in reinforcing the break with the previous period. Unlike previous rulers, Taraki made his speeches in Pashto and not in Dari.[6] As important as the end of the previous dynasty was that Taraki was childless and came from "a poor and insignificant family," factors that would have normally made him illegitimate to rule in the traditional Afghan society that valued wealth and lineage.[7] This, more than anything else, incarnated the break represented by Khalq.

To consolidate power, Taraki, with the support of his number two Hafizullah Amin, sidelined Parcham, appointing Karmal as ambassador to Czechoslovakia. Then, Khalq decided to remodel Afghanistan using the Marxist-Leninist playbook. In a radio speech on 9 May 1978, Taraki announced a program of far-reaching domestic and international policies. The first measure the regime

FIGURE 2.1. Front page of a communist journal one year after the April Revolution (*The Kabul New Times*, 1 April 1979, https://digitalcommons.unomaha.edu/kabultimes/). The personality cult of Nur Muhammad Taraki, referred to as the "Great Leader," is in full swing. Parchamis have been purged from the leadership.

wanted to adopt was land reform; the second—the abolition of "old feudal and prefeudal relations," meaning landowners, traditional leaders, and mullahs. Khalq's program was full of Soviet-inspired jargon, talking of the "scientific planning" of the economy, the "democratic solution to the national question," and the "liquidation of the influence of imperialism" in the economy. In foreign affairs, it pledged to follow a nonaligned policy and, at the same time, "support national-liberation movement[s] in Asia, Africa, and Latin America."[8] In short, Taraki promised Afghans sweeping changes at all levels. As he told Soviet ambassador Alexander Puzanov, Afghanistan was to embark "on the road to building socialism." This though had to be done "with care," Taraki cautioned, because the PDPA could not directly tell Afghans its "real purpose."[9]

Interestingly, besides the traditional Islamic introduction and a nod to respect for Islam, Taraki's radio speech was devoid of Islamic references and none of his twenty-eight measures dealt with religion. The program's early lack of attention to Islam came as a surprise to observers. The US embassy in Kabul reported that the PDPA was putting itself at risk by discarding its "initial veil of 'Islamic nationalism'" and not doing more to assuage the people's feelings that Islam may be in danger with the new regime.[10] In reality, it was understandable in a party whose leaders were secularized and who, as recalled by Abdul Darmanger, one of the PDPA's founders, did not fast during Ramadan.[11]

Taraki's program proposed measures but no ways of implementing them. The PDPA was unprepared to assume power, having neither a plan nor a constituency. As noted by Soviet analysts, even by 1981, it would have only a few hundred members per province with Kabul being the only area with several thousand.[12] At the same time, it had no idea about how Afghans would respond to its program of action. The Afghan Marxists thought—against available evidence—of Afghanistan as a whole, refusing to make exceptions to accommodate disparate social and ethnic groups. They applied their measures and reforms, including military conscription, border customs, and seizure of lands for land reform, indistinctly to the entire country.

The issue with Khalq's program had to do with both the policies and their implementation. The reforms, although not necessarily antireligious, went against traditional economic and political elites, including Islamic authorities, and challenged centuries-old traditions associated with Islam.[13] The new regime initiated land reform to redistribute Afghanistan's land. Plagued by corruption, conducted with little planning and without having consolidated control in the countryside, the reform was a critical factor in mobilizing the population against the PDPA. It failed to integrate the crucial aspect of water provision in the countryside and did not have a plan to provide poor farmers who were ready to take the land with seeds and traction animals to cultivate it.[14] To Khalq, the land reform was a beacon to show their Marxism to the world. "Until the land reform is done, nothing is done," Taraki once declared to Puzanov.[15] Other measures, such as literacy programs for women, mixed girls' and boys' classes, and the abolition of the bride price by which girls were given into marriage, though laudable, also led to protests in the conservative countryside. The latter was at times associated with demands to abandon traditional clothes such as the *chadaree* (or *paranja* in Central Asia), a robe for women that covers the head and the body, which was common in rural areas.

The regime's drive to reform led to misbehavior by party cadres with witnesses reporting the beating and killing of landowners, mullahs, and ordinary peasants, looting, desecration of holy sites, and burning of religious books.[16] They noted other attacks on Islam, including when party cadres in one village forbade the *namaz* (morning prayer) and brought donkeys into the mosque or called on people to give up the Koran for Marx's and Lenin's books.[17] Although exacerbated by the revolution, these conflicts were also the result of preexisting tensions between Afghans in the city and the countryside. Rural Afghans perceived the often-young urban PDPA cadres as disrespectful of Islam and tradition, a view based as much on their behavior and looks—bare head or long hair instead of the cap or turban, failure to pray five times a day, and lack of deference to the mullah—as on the policies they came to implement.[18]

Khalq surprisingly failed to appreciate that Islam in Afghanistan was an "all-encompassing way of life."[19] Even in small details, the party was out of touch with Afghan reality. One telling example was the use of the term "communist" by some PDPA cadres in the countryside. To Afghans, the latter sounded like a combination of Dari and Pashto that meant basically "no God." Interestingly, this same problem was afterward present for the Soviets, and it took until the mid-1980s to adapt terminology and alert advisers to the issue.[20] Since the beginning, the new authorities had also proclaimed their opposition to Islamist currents, making the Muslim Brotherhood its number one enemy without explaining what exactly this organization was and why the PDPA was so bent on attacking its affiliates.

The principal problem was that Khalq did not pay enough attention to Islam. Speaking with the Soviets, the governor of Ghazni Province complained that the land reform and the mixed school classes did not consider religious issues.[21] Afghan scholars pointed out that, in addition to the problems mentioned above, some peasants refused to take the land because it seemed an "illegal" and "immoral" act in their "religious beliefs system."[22] According to Georgy Kornienko, the Soviet first deputy foreign minister, the reform of the Afghan judiciary system modeled on the Soviet system posed problems because it deprived countryside mullahs of their role as arbiters of disputes. This antagonized both the religious figures who lost a source of material benefit and the people who had to travel in search of a judge.[23] In both cases, the authorities, with Soviet advice, did not direct the reform against Islam, but people saw them as such all the same.

Other measures tried to impose Soviet-style symbols on the DRA and had a clearer anti-Islamic aspect. In October 1978, Khalq changed the country's flag to make it red and removed all Islamic symbols. Although the regime down-played the measure's importance, it had a lasting negative impact. The regime then decided to skip the preamble, "In the name of God, the Most Gracious, the Most Merciful" (Bismillahi Rahmani Rahim), at the beginning of official statements and to have justice officials in Kabul forgo all Islamic references. Another badly received decision forced Kabul residents to paint their doors red to celebrate the new regime while officials released red-painted pigeons to cel-ebrate the new flag.

In summary, conservative tribes, Islamic leaders, and the rural popula-tion's Islam-inspired opposition to Khalq's reforms resembled the opposition faced before by Amanullah and Daud. Afghanistan had some 300,000 reli-gious figures who were affiliated with one of its 45,000 mosques and *madra-sas*.[24] The mosque was the structuring building in villages and the mullah's role went far beyond that of a prayer leader. He resolved disputes and was a folk-healer. Religious specialists were, for example, engaged in variolation campaigns in Afghanistan before being co-opted as part of the World Health Organization's campaign for vaccination against smallpox.[25] As noted by the political scientist Olivier Roy, Islam in rural Afghanistan provided "a system of norms, a code regulating human relations, a social morality."[26] Such popular religion, akin to the role Christianism played in medieval Western Europe, was connected to all aspects of everyday life. Through the numerous reli-gious figures, the religious buildings, and the ever-present shrines of Muslim saints to which Afghans went on a pilgrimage (*ziyarat*), Islam was visible in the environment. By contrast to village mullahs whose role was central in communities and who, depending on the region, formed part of the elite, the influence of religious figures in cities had eroded by the late 1970s following attempts at modernization, the introduction of new civil institutions, and secular schools.

As summarized by the US embassy, the opposition's grievances that had crystallized "appeared sufficient to sustain long-term fighting" against the PDPA. Two aspects stood out: "the virtually universal perceptions that the DRA leadership was made of 'godless communists'" and the belief that it had "sold Afghanistan's soul and future to Moscow." For descendants of Central Asian refugees, it evoked unfortunate memories of the sovietization follow-ing the Basmachi revolt. Conversely and ironically, the US embassy believed that the regime's reform program, while it had "provoked some scattered op-position," was not the main problem that "sustained the hostility" against the PDPA.[27] Symbols played a bigger role in spurring opposition.

Puzanov, who tried to temper the pace of the land reform to no avail, ex-tensively criticized Khalq's leftist radicalism in 1978–79.[28] Soviet allies made similar points. The Bulgarian ambassador in Kabul noted that some PDPA cadres were "hurried in their actions" and volunteered advice based on Bulgaria's experience of dealing with the clergy's influence among the masses. The PDPA, he explained, had to adopt a more "cautious approach" when moving to "liquidate the lands owned by the high clergy."[29] The East German ambassador was even more disparaging, claiming that Khalq had rejected his advice and been utterly incompetent about land reform. Poor peasants were refusing to accept land because of "religious scruples" and fear of retaliation. Khalq's "accelerated program" had failed, and the country now had to deal with this "Khalqi mess."[30] This also exemplified how since the beginning the PDPA had refused to follow its big brothers' advice.

By 1979, the PDPA's already limited Islamic credentials had further eroded. It did not help that its leaders occasionally boasted of their disdain for Islam. To Vladimir Kryuchkov, the head of the First Chief Directorate of the KGB, Taraki once promised that Afghan mosques would be empty within a year.[31] The fact that an Afghan officer from a remote garrison repeated that claim to Vasili Zaplatin, a visiting Soviet general, suggests that this message circulated in the PDPA.[32] Interestingly, in return, Zaplatin engaged in a surreal attempt to explain that a class struggle was underway in Afghanistan. On the Soviet side, too, ideology drove many people. In that, Amin was thought to be the most radical of all. Bent on taking Stalin's ruthless policies as an example, he talked of establishing a "dictatorship of the working class" in Afghanistan.[33]

Facing opposition, Khalq repressed the groups it saw as threats, including religious and tribal leaders, students and teachers, military officers, and Parchamis. The regime executed some 50,000 people between April 1978 and September 1979, including 12,000 inside Kabul prisons, and jailed many more.[34] Even more Afghans fled to neighboring countries. Afghanistan's Shia Muslims—the Hazaras—were particularly affected. The violence included the indiscriminate bombing of civilians and executions of tribal elders who had come to Kabul to negotiate with the authorities. As repressions grew, Khalq more extensively targeted Islamic scholars from late 1978, executing the Islamists jailed under the previous regime.[35] In February 1979, it went a step further, killing several dozen male members of the Mujaddidi family of Naqshbandiyah Sufi scholars, Afghanistan's most influential Islamic authorities. These repressions underlined Khalq's anticlerical character and even led some PDPA cadres to complain to the Soviets that Taraki's war on "bearded men" was fueling the insurgency and preventing moderate insurgent commanders such as Sayyid Ahmed Gailani, the leader of the Qadiriyyah Sufi order, from negotiating with the regime.[36] In March 1979, shortly after the executions among his family, Sibghatullah Mujaddidi, now an insurgent commander in Pakistan, called for jihad against the Kabul regime, supporting earlier calls to jihad by Hezb-e-Islami.

By the spring of 1979, no more than 10 percent of Islamic figures among lower and middle ranks supported the regime. Khalq had, in effect, lost Islam to the opposition, while most Islamic scholars considered Taraki and Amin unfit to rule. Some 1,300 mullahs fought among the insurgents, including over 400 who commanded military units.[37] This religious aspect was central to structuring the insurgency. The "popular tradition of jihad" had mobilized the people in a largely spontaneous way and around traditional religious and tribal leaders.[38] Speeches by mullahs condemning PDPA reforms at the mosque often served as a prelude to local mobilization and attack on a symbol of state power, typically a guard post. Despite the communist authorities' frequently blaming adepts of the Muslim Brotherhood for the violence, only in a minority of cases, such as in Herat, did structured Islamist groups linked to Jamiat-e-Islami and Hezb-e-Islami, played a role. Islam was not, however, the only factor that led to mobilization. The PDPA's reforms, the importance of traditional tribal, clientele, and patronage networks, the reaction to Khalq's abuses, Pashtun nationalism, and the traditional opposition of some regions to centralizing attempts all played a role.[39]

Against this backdrop, in March 1979, the authorities faced a revolt in Herat, a city near the Iranian border with an important Hazara population. Opposition to the regime's policies advocating for girls' education, the draft, and land reform spurred initial and largely spontaneous discontent. As a result of the uprising, some 20,000 people died and insurgents lynched party cadres and several Soviet advisers.[40] Accounts received by the US embassy indicated that the executions of Soviets involved "great brutality, such as beheading, being flayed alive, or being cut into pieces."[41] The Herat events reflected the already negative attitude toward the Soviets—the Shuravi as the locals called them in Dari—in Afghanistan. The population saw them—wrongly, as we will see—as the puppeteers behind Khalq's disruptive policies.

The revolt also testified to the insurgency's strength and led to the first call from Kabul for a Soviet military intervention amid paranoia over the Afghan military's loyalty. Talking with Alexei Kosygin, the chairman of the Soviet Council of Ministers, Taraki claimed that the Herat population was "under the influence of Shia slogans." A Soviet intervention was necessary because the Afghans trained in Soviet military academies under the previous regime were unreliable. They were all "Muslim reactionaries."[42]

1979: The Road to Intervention

After a brief wavering, the Soviet politburo rebuffed the PDPA's calls for action. On 17 March 1979, it agreed that an intervention would require the USSR "to wage a war in significant part against the [Afghan] people." At the same time, the politburo, under perhaps the PDPA's influence, was mindful of the Islamic component of the insurgency. Andrei Kirilenko, one of Brezhnev's lieutenants, Gromyko, Andropov, and Ustinov all spoke of either "religious fundamentalists," "religious fanatics," or "Islamic fundamentalists." Kosygin summarized the collective thinking by stressing that Afghans were "all Mohammedans" whose faith was "sufficiently strong that they [could] close ranks on that basis." The real problem was with Taraki and Amin's wrong tactics, including regarding Islam. The Soviets had to instruct them that: "Executions, torture and so forth could not be applied on a massive scale. Religious questions, the relationship with religious communities, with religion generally and with religious leaders [had to] take on special meaning."[43]

Based on that conversation, Brezhnev instructed Taraki that "appropriate work must be done with the clergy to split their ranks." The PDPA should only target Islamic scholars "who spoke out against the revolutionary government."[44] These discussions are central to understanding the evolution of Soviet thinking on the April Revolution. According to Grachev, this was the moment when the Soviet leadership's vision, encouraged by Ponomarev, of Afghanistan as another Third World country moving toward socialism began to waver. This perception grew during 1979 and even officials in the International Department began to talk about how to reconcile Khalq with the population, including by integrating Islam.[45] In April, a Soviet team of CPSU advisers, without any religious leaders, arrived in Kabul to help Khalq conduct propaganda among the population. While it suggested practical steps to "break [the clergy] apart and attract most of it to cooperate with the regime," the CPSU advisers remained focused on showcasing the progressive reforms of the April Revolution.[46] Ironically though, Khalq was not interested in such attempts to impose moderation on its policies even if its plan to remake the old social and political systems to impose progress was not working.

The Soviets did not curtail their economic and military support to the PDPA even though some of them felt that their initial "supportive attitude had grown into an obligation that was more and more constraining."[47] For ideological reasons, Moscow could not refuse support to the Afghans. As in Ethiopia, Angola, and Mozambique, this was the impasse reached by the USSR as ideology drove foreign policy. There were no precise requirements for Moscow to label a Third World country as having entered the noncapitalist path of develop-

FIGURE 2.2. Leonid Brezhnev and Andrei Gromyko (United Archives GmbH | Alamy Stock Photo). The General Secretary of the CPSU and his minister of foreign affairs look grim. Gromyko is part of the triumvirate that leaned on Brezhnev to intervene in Afghanistan.

ment to become a country of socialist orientation. It was not about the development of industrial forces, the existence of a working class, not even the existence of a communist party, but about being pro-Soviet in foreign policy.

In the following months, politburo discussions continued to stress that Khalq was mismanaging the situation at multiple levels. It had problems working with religious authorities that were prominent in the "counterrevolution" and encouraged "Islamic fanaticism," it was unable to find relays in the countryside, lacked "political flexibility" despite Soviet recommendations and was inefficient in its domestic propaganda. Among other things, the Soviets advised the PDPA to tell Afghans about the accomplishments of Soviet Central Asia, notably emphasizing the religious freedom enjoyed by Soviet Muslims to defuse some of the criticism.[48] Moscow even afterward organized radio propaganda on that topic through the deputy head of SADUM whose speech Amin had republished in the Afghan media.[49]

Discussions at the politburo showed awareness of the religious factor in Afghanistan that Soviet policymakers connected to their memories of the Basmachi. A major issue was, however, that when Soviet policymakers spoke of the Basmachi, they thought of the Central Asia of the 1970s whose people were different from their ancestors.[50] In any case, Soviet leaders had little knowledge about Soviet Muslims' beliefs. Based on such flawed analogies, their advice to Kabul was vague and decontextualized. Karen Brutents, then Deputy Head of the International Department, notes that it was superficial. He recalls Brezhnev telling Taraki to just "close the border with Pakistan and Iran" (something the LCST would never be able to do during the war) and "organize committees of poor peasants," short-lived village-level institutions supporting the Bolsheviks in 1918–19.[51] Overall, the Soviets believed that one could deal with Islam in Afghanistan by simply tempering Khalq's most radical policies, better explaining the reforms, and reconciling Khalq and Parcham. Then, Afghanistan could, in principle, become a place to consolidate Soviet presence. This flawed assumption determined the Soviet policies even after the intervention.

Moscow was, nevertheless, reluctant to do itself what Khalq had been unable to do. In 1979, the Kremlin similarly declined another fifteen calls for military action by Taraki and Amin.[52] In June, it again pressured the PDPA into tolerance toward Islam. Taking stock of "false reports" that spoke of abuses against Muslims, of the "canons of Islam [being] trampled," and of anti-PDPA and anti-Soviet propaganda by the "reactionary clergy," the politburo instructed the Soviet ambassador to help the PDPA "counter this malicious propaganda [and] attract an ever-greater number of Muslim *ulemas* [scholars] to the Revolution's side." For the Soviets, the regime was not doing enough in "convincing the broad masses of Muslims that the socioeconomic reforms carried out by the PDPA and people's power, the need for which is advocated in Islam, [did] not affect and [would not] affect Muslims' religious beliefs."[53] The Soviets were also advising the PDPA to provide material benefits to loyal Islamic leaders and to promise to severely punish anyone in the PDPA who attacked religion. Following the cue from Moscow, Puzanov conducted seventeen meetings with Taraki and thirty with Amin in two months to enjoin them to better work with Islamic leaders and pay attention to Islam, finally managing to get, first, a recognition from Khalq that it had lost the middle and small clergy, and, second, a commitment to change its policy.[54]

The Kremlin then decided to send more military advisers and economic help, make new recommendations, and mobilize all means of Soviet propaganda to denounce the interference by Pakistan, Iran, China, and the United States in Afghanistan. In parallel, it instructed the KGB and the GRU to notify India about insurgents' plans to include Kashmir and Afghanistan in a "world Muslim republic." This, the Soviets hoped, would drive New Delhi to "take resolute steps to oppose the anti-Afghan activities of Pakistan."[55] From early on, the Kremlin had expected that India's fear of Islamism would lead it to support the USSR's position in Afghanistan, and it was right, as we will see in chapter 6. India's ambassador in Kabul told the Americans that a victory by the opposition might mean "fundamentalist Islam spilling over the borders" of Afghanistan.[56]

Following the revolt in Herat, KGB operatives also started paying more attention to the religious factor. The agency's office in Kabul outlined a five-point plan to Moscow to deal with Islam: (1) better take into account the "possible reaction of the Muslim clergy" to the authorities' policies; (2) use KGB contacts to push the authorities to stop repressions against the Muslim clergy; (3) work more actively with the official clergy; (4) organize visits to Afghanistan by Soviet Islamic authorities; and (5) increase contacts through KGB agents with the moderate insurgent leader Gailani to convince him to return to the DRA.[57] Among these measures, those that depended on the Soviets started to be realized immediately; others appeared long unacceptable to the PDPA.

Regarding the official clergy, the KGB highlighted two aspects. First, Soviet advisers had to understand that the authority and influence of Islamic leaders were not correlated to their position in the state apparatus. Second, the KGB's Afghan colleagues from the Department for Safeguarding the Interests of Afghanistan, which would become the State Information Services (KhAD) after the intervention, were already working with Islamic scholars and leaders, monitoring mosques to check for antiregime propaganda. Yet, the KGB complained, they failed to understand that mullahs conducted such propaganda in private while visiting believers' homes. These observations underlined how superficial were the Soviet and Afghan strategies at dealing with Islam and the lack of religious specialists to work alongside intelligence operatives and Soviet advisers. These problems would carry over into the next period.

One should also assess Soviet recommendations in the context of the confusion that accompanied reporting and decision-making on Afghanistan. The KGB was unquestionably the main source of information for the Kremlin. As bitterly recalled by Anatoly Adamishin, the soon-to-be deputy minister of foreign affairs under Eduard Shevardnadze, "there was the not very smart idea that the KGB knows best and more." Hence, the politburo thought, "surely the ambassador is alright but how much does he actually know by talking to people in Kabul and reading the newspapers?"[58] Besides the KGB and the embassy, the military and the GRU also sent information to Moscow. These entities were under orders from their superiors whom they tried to please, sometimes distorting reality in the process, but they had little choice in a system that put a premium on ideological rectitude. In one telling example, Ustinov instructed the military advisers and the GRU to "arm the working class," an absurd statement in the context of Afghanistan.[59] Amid corruption and personal enmities, these three entities—joined by CPSU advisers after the intervention's start—competed to shape the narrative and blurring the message received in Moscow. This did not give the politburo a proper understanding of the situation in Afghanistan and rendered decision-making difficult.

Despite this confusion, the tendency throughout 1979 was clear: the contrast of outlook between Afghans and Soviets grew more important in how to fight the insurgency, how to broaden the base of the regime, and how to implement reform. Khalq sought a maximalist interpretation of the socialist ideal while the Soviets saw it as unsuitable for Afghanistan. Islam was a case in point. The Soviets carried atheistic propaganda in their Muslim regions with limited resources and had long abandoned repression. Conversely, Khalq's execution of Islamic leaders and attacks on Islam in an environment considerably less secularized than Central Asia appeared surreal to Moscow. Even the Kremlin's limited understanding of Islam was enough to see that Khalq was jeopardizing the Marxist-Leninist revolution.

The PDPA's factionalism and unreliability, fostered by competition among Soviet agencies in Kabul, also appalled Moscow, especially as Afghan communists attempted to involve the Soviet embassy in their quarrels.[60] After purging Parcham, Khalq turned to infighting. In October 1979, the assassination of Taraki by Amin's supporters aggravated tensions.[61] Before that, muddied initiatives from different Soviet agencies, including a plot against Amin backed by the KGB and simultaneously an attempt by the embassy to engineer a Parcham-Khalq reconciliation had complicated things even more. Although the DRA remained aligned with the USSR, Amin's increasing unpredictability was crucial in altering the Soviet position on nonintervention. The main factor was his unsuccessful attempt to engage the United States. Clearly, Moscow "could not allow a second [Anwar] Sadat close by," Ponomarev noted.[62] Rumors that such a shift may happen already circulated in Kabul. At the same time, the KGB pushed the anti-Amin line—an aspect that historians often overlook. Since the summer of 1979, at the time of the failed attempts against his life and while Taraki was still alive, its operatives argued that Amin was no friend to the USSR. Interestingly, many in the Soviet military argued, on the contrary, that Amin was a strong leader and a reliable partner, testifying again to the differences in perspectives among agencies.[63] However, the KGB was the main source of information, not the military.

Complex Motivations

The motivations for the intervention have been extensively debated, but the officials of the various Soviet agencies have downplayed their and their chiefs' roles in the decision-making process. The MID pointed out that the embassy in Kabul had sent reports advising against going into Afghanistan and that Gromyko was the last to agree to it in the triumvirate he formed with Andropov and Ustinov.[64] The KGB downplayed Andropov's role.[65] The military noted that Ustinov forced them into agreeing to the deployment while the General Staff opposed it. Ponomarev's International Department seemed to have had a limited influence.[66] Overall, reconstructing decision-makers' motivations based on these competing accounts is difficult, even more so as these evidently varied from one agency to the next and many key discussions were either not recorded or have not yet been declassified. Still, we know some things with a high degree of certainty.

The Cold War's geostrategic framework was one of the two main factors that influenced Soviet thinking. Amin's attempts to balance between superpowers worried the Kremlin, especially because it believed that Washington was looking for new allies in the region following its loss of Iran to the Islamists. Amin's fateful meeting with US chargé d'affaires Archer Blood in October 1979 made the Soviets especially anxious. However, that exchange of opinions, where Blood found Amin to be exuding "an air of quiet self-confidence," never went beyond a deal not to further jeopardize bilateral relations.[67] To be fair, Soviet fears were also the product of Amin's attempts at putting pressure on Moscow. The Khalqi leader played with fire in telling Soviet diplomats that the United States was willing to provide more aid to Afghanistan if it accepted a decrease in Soviet military presence.[68] Amin also increasingly showed his displeasure with Puzanov, whom he had Moscow replace with Fikryat Tabeev, and was less welcoming of Soviet advice than Taraki. He resented Moscow's support to Parcham and seemed suspicious of its motives.[69]

To date, many former military and intelligence operatives believe that if the Soviets did not intervene in Afghanistan, the United States would have established military bases and put surveillance equipment there and used it to destabilize the USSR.[70] The need to counter the Americans was also the reason for intervention given to the LCST. Soldiers believed that "they had beaten the Americans by only a few hours" to Kabul.[71] Although the United States certainly planned no such intervention, Soviet claims, at the time widely dismissed, that it was aiding the counterrevolution in Afghanistan proved to be true. The United States had provided nonmilitary aid and propaganda support to the mujahideen since July 1979.[72] Although the initial US effort was small, it had huge symbolic importance. It signaled to Pakistan and countries in the Arab world that it was all right to back the mujahideen.

Evolutions in the global balance of power with the United States also affected the Kremlin's assessments of Afghanistan. By December 1979, the Soviets believed that there was less at stake internationally. If in March, Gromyko had noted that a conflict might lose the Soviet Union the benefits of détente and the already agreed upon Strategic Arms Limitation Talks (SALT) II Treaty, the thinking now was that the increasingly aggressive US policy had already jeopardized them.[73] The previous summer, the United States had failed to ratify SALT II. It then decided to deploy new medium-range nuclear "Pershing" missiles to Europe immediately before the intervention. In Asia, the Americans were increasingly using the China card against the Soviets. Meanwhile, Moscow continued to see détente as a bilateral USSR-US affair independent of support to Third World liberation movements.

Ideology, no doubt, was the second main factor that pushed the Soviets toward intervention. While the PDPA's flaws had been a cold shower on their revolutionary zeal, Soviet policymakers could not but see Afghanistan as their chance to stand in the same row as their glorious predecessors who had seen Eastern Europe, China, and Cuba join the socialist camp. Afghanistan was their time to shine. Anatoly Dobrynin, the long-time ambassador in Washington, argued that Marxist-Leninist ideology was "the key factor" that led to intervention.[74] People did not declare so during the decision-making process, but it unconsciously shaped thinking in the politburo, he noted. Ideology's importance was similarly emphasized by Grachev, who recalled how Gromyko could engage in lengthy monologues on how "Marxism-Leninism in one thousand years would be lightening up the world," while other Soviet leaders listened.[75] The Soviets truthfully believed that the world was going their way and that they could not but support an Afghan regime set on building socialism. Ideology ensnared the Soviets. Andropov summed up this idea in 1981: "The imperialists had grasped that the situation was developing to their disadvantage—e.g., in Angola, Ethiopia, Afghanistan, Central America. They had understood that maintaining the policy of détente would benefit us more and cause greater damage to them."[76]

There was no doubt in his mind that the USSR "and capitalism could not live on the same planet."[77] Although not all Soviets ascribed ideology the dominant role, all noted that it was the background against which decisions were taken. It colored seemingly pragmatic assessments.[78] This crystallized in the collective belief that Afghanistan may ideally become a second Mongolia or a new Central Asia.[79] There was also a connection between the geostrategic framework and ideology in the Cold War's logic. Brutents summed it up best by noting that "the loss of a [strategic] position (of a country) meant more than the [strategic] position itself. It was seen as a defeat, a retreat of a superpower, and the socialist camp, as the loss of initiative."[80]

In addition to these two main factors, some authors argued that military adventures like Afghanistan were unavoidable given the size of the military-industrial complex in the USSR. Foreign policy was determined not only by realism and ideology but also by the policy instruments available. Soviet leaders felt they had to somehow use the military-industrial complex.[81] Ustinov ended up being one of the main advocates for the war because it was a convenient way to test new weapons with limited risk.[82] According to Aleksandr Maiorov, the chief Soviet military adviser in Afghanistan in 1980, Ustinov once revealed that he saw Afghanistan as a "military-technical testing ground . . . of world proportions." Testifying as to the difference in perceptions in the politburo, Ponomarev then instantly corrected him by saying that Afghanistan was instead "a political and economic testing ground," but Ustinov did not budge.[83] This was a remarkable skirmish that demonstrated how military testing ground and ideological testing ground were two sides of the same coin for members of the politburo. Ideology permeated realist assessments and instrumentalist arguments.

Developments inside Afghanistan also factored into Soviet calculations. Amin's inability to either quell the insurgency or alter his policies by taking Soviet advice for restraint convinced some Soviets that, without intervention, Afghanistan may be heading for a prolonged civil war or worse—an anti-Soviet Islamic regime. Some Soviets argued that there were furthermore humanitarian motivations for the intervention. General Valentin Varennikov, the chief Soviet military adviser during the last phase of the war, noted that the Kremlin wanted to prevent Amin's genocide of his people.[84] However, this looks like an after-the-fact interpretation. Although the Kremlin saw Amin's methods as excessively harsh, it took issue with him for other reasons.

What is less clear is if the Soviets believed that Amin's regime could fall. For the US embassy, it was in no real danger of being toppled in December 1979.[85] By contrast, Tabeev thought, albeit commenting long after the events, that there was a "real threat of a counter-revolutionary coup under the banner of the Islamic fundamentalists."[86] In retrospect, it is difficult to assess what the regime's long-term prospects would have been without Soviet intervention. Until the end, Amin controlled the provincial capitals and retained Khalq's support including in the military, and parts of Afghanistan were still relatively calm, even the Pashtun areas around Kandahar. No insurgent army was approaching Kabul. Militarily, the situation would be significantly worse throughout the Soviet occupation. Nevertheless, the idea that the regime may fall played a role in reinforcing the Soviet conundrum: it meant that a "progressive revolution" would be overturned by "reactionary forces."[87]

In this context, several policymakers had concerns that a victory of Islamism in Afghanistan might stir trouble among Soviet Muslims. The influence of this last factor is difficult to assess because the politburo did not conceptualize it clearly, leading the historiography to underestimate it. There were two reasons

FIGURE 2.3. The Mujahideen in central Afghanistan, 1982 (Courtesy of Olivier Roy). The early mobilizations before and after the Soviet intervention of December 1979 happened along tribal lines. Most people had old and outdated firearms.

for that. First, most of the politburo had only the faintest idea about the situation in the Soviet Muslim regions and the syncretism that had developed there between Islam and communism. Second, even for those in the KGB who knew more, openly talking about an Islamic threat to Central Asia from Afghanistan would have been questioning Marxist-Leninist ideology. No one at the politburo was ready to do that in 1979. In any case, Islam was not an issue for domestic stability in the USSR. Although there was no telling how Afghanistan and the Iranian Revolution might affect Soviet Muslims, memories of a Muslim rebellion dated back to the Basmachi—ancient times even for the elderly Soviet policymakers.

Nevertheless, the Kremlin was aware that it had to monitor the Islamic factor. The Islamic Revolution had raised Soviet concerns as to the region's stability. The Kremlin wondered how this Islamic renaissance may affect Afghanistan and the millions of Soviet Muslims. At the same time, it worried about the United States, Pakistan, and other Muslim countries growing support for the mujahideen, some of whom claimed that "they would carry the struggle" to "Soviet Central Asian."[88] Although the threat was vague, it heightened fears over an Afghan spillover into the USSR that hostile foreign powers could engineer. Kryuchkov, then head of the KGB's First Chief Directorate dealing with foreign operations and intelligence activities, made this concern into no less than one of the main reasons for the intervention: "In Moscow they operated based on the assumption that . . . Islamic fundamentalism in Afghanistan would also quickly spread to the Central Asian region of the Soviet Union. The Muslim part of the population of the USSR is very heterogeneous. The overwhelming majority of believers behave relatively passively. But it is not this silent majority that defines the social-political climate in the republics, the mood is set by the minority—active in the religious domain and rather aggressive politically."[89]

Kryuchkov overplays the Soviets' awareness of the Islamist threat, even noting that they feared that Afghan Islamists would try to destabilize other Soviet Muslim regions. However, the KGB was clearly sensitive to Islamism because it dealt with anti-Soviet activities by religious groups.[90] This fear of Islamism was likely more specific to the KGB, including its local operatives as in Azerbaijan and Tajikistan, than widespread in the politburo. Following the Soviet-Afghan War, Red Army generals, including Gromov, Ermakov, and Makhmut Gareev, the chief Soviet military adviser after the withdrawal, similarly noted the Islamic factor as a reason for intervention.[91] Although developments in Afghanistan and the post-Soviet space in the 1990s seem to have influenced their judgments, some in the military were already likely more attentive to Islam in 1979 due to personal and professional backgrounds. The same was true of some local party leaders in Central Asia.

Andropov also noted the threat of an Islamic Afghanistan for Central Asia after the intervention. He introduced an additional idea:

> We have a 2,400 km border with Afghanistan. If Amin were still sitting [in Kabul] and fomenting Islam with the support of the United States, this would be a highly dangerous abscess for us. Still today, the Central Asian Soviet Republics are not on par with Europe. There is still major religious influence there. Illegally working mullahs are very active. Until 1936 we were still fighting there with the Basmachi movement. Many of them went to Afghanistan. [If Amin had stayed in power,] we also would now have the United States with its signal intelligence right next to our border.[92]

Confirming the KGB's more acute awareness of Islamism, Andropov's quote illustrates one of this book's central arguments: The Soviets did not see the Islamic threat to Central Asia as an independent factor but as part of the larger concern streaming from a pro-American Islamic Afghanistan. The Soviets believed that the United States could foment instability in Central Asia by instrumentalizing Islam but not that the Islamists could do so on their own.

Brutents similarly linked Islamic fundamentalism and US foreign policy.[93] Gromyko's comments about the need to defend Tajikistan and Uzbekistan from "Muslim hordes" if the Soviets "lost Afghanistan" also echoed this idea.[94] Soviet understanding of Islamism changed little during the Soviet-Afghan War, even though their concern over the Islamist threat increased.

A final word needs to be said of two more justifications for the intervention, one that was prevalent in the 1980s and one that so far has seen little analysis. As we now know, there was no Soviet grand design to gobble Afghanistan and then push to get a foothold on the warm seas in the Persian Gulf. When Taraki and Amin floated the idea of attacking Pakistan, Moscow rebuffed it.[95] There is also no trace of the politburo ever discussing this idea before the intervention. By contrast, Adamishin noted one potential motivation not so far investigated. Kremlin politics may have played a role in triggering the intervention. As the politburo was preparing the struggle for Brezhnev's succession, the war in Afghanistan, expected to be quick and victorious, may have given "an additional ace" to Andropov and Ustinov.[96]

Finally, Andropov, backed by Ustinov and Gromyko, with the latter playing a secondary role, decided to intervene, leaning on an ailing and dysfunctional Brezhnev in November. By that point, the Andropov-Ustinov-Gromyko triumvirate ruled the USSR and faced little opposition. Brezhnev was not too keen on the whole affair and reportedly once openly blamed Andropov and Ustinov for "dragging him into trouble" in Afghanistan.[97] The triumvirate sidelined Kosygin, who was the main advocate of restraint and overruled the opposition of the General Staff who saw the intervention as impractical given Afghanistan's terrain and climate.

The plan was for Soviet forces to install Parcham's Karmal and then avoid engaging the insurgents while securing cities and routes and staying in garrisons. It anticipated that Afghans would greet the removal of Amin with relief given his repressive policies and that the entire operation would be over in a few months. On 25 December 1979, the USSR deployed its military to Afghanistan under the pretext of the existing Soviet-Afghan Friendship and Cooperation Treaty and Khalq's previous calls for intervention. On 27 December, Soviet Special Forces killed Amin who, until his last meeting with Tabeev a couple of weeks prior, was certain Brezhnev was about to receive him in Moscow.[98]

Khalq's Islam

It is important to highlight the characteristic aspects of Khalq's attitude toward Islam to serve as a counterpoint to analyzing Karmal and Soviet attempts at dealing with Islam in the 1980s. As we saw, Khalq's attacks on Islam usually came because of all-around radical reformism and anticlericalism and a lack of concern for hurting religious feelings. As Taraki and Amin, most PDPA cadres were not observant in matters of faith and had not been since their years at Kabul University, where they provoked the students of the Muslim Youth, the Islamist movement that emerged in 1969 inspired by Qutb's writing and that would serve as an incubator for Jamiat-e-Islami and Hezb-e-Islami. No PDPA leader, however, publicly declared that they would launch atheistic campaigns, close mosques, and execute mullahs.[99]

Suleiman Layeq, poet, son of mullah, and Parcham leader who became minister for tribes and nationalities under Karmal, asserted that there was an early split in the PDPA on Islam. Even if it was "not included in [the party's] program" and stated openly, "radicals wished to build their way separately from mullahs and mosques." To Layeq, this "position regarding the clergy and religious questions was a mistake," leading to distrust toward anyone who had any affiliation with Islamic leaders.[100] He suggested that such mistakes were prevalent across the PDPA, which had originally been structured around the tension between Islam and Western modernity, contrasting with the Muslim Youth's vision of Islamist modernity.[101] To different degrees, Parcham and especially Khalq, the more leftist faction, shared in a covert atheism while paying lip service to Islam.[102] Part of this legacy carried over into the Karmal period.

After the April Revolution, the PDPA claimed to respect Islam while leaving it out of policy speeches. At the same time, it told Islamic scholars not to meddle in politics and focus on praying.[103] Interestingly, the regime tried to co-opt some of the religious sentiment by declaring a jihad against the opposition, led, according to the Afghan communists, by the Muslim Brotherhood (Ikhwan-i-Muslimin), whom they called the "Brotherhood of Satan" (Ikhwan-i-Shayatin), borrowing Gamal Abdel Nasser's expression. Few Afghans took the PDPA's jihad seriously, particularly since communist leaders had rejected the title of Amir that could have made such a declaration vaguely legitimate. They had also foregone the religiously sanctioned ceremony associated with taking power.[104] The Islamists who had mainly relocated to Pakistan, meanwhile, also declared jihad on the "infidel, traitorous, communist Khalqis," leading Muslim diplomats to ironically comment that there were few precedents of jihads pitted one against another.[105]

Khalqis made attempts to show more respect for Islam, following Soviet advice, in late 1978. Taraki then promised that he would safeguard Islamic principles and protect Islamic scholars if they did not act against the revolution. This was a problematic message given the social role Islamic scholars had in Afghanistan. But to support his calls, Taraki participated in the ceremonies at the start of Ramadan. Likewise, he and Amin attended the Eid al-Fitr celebration at the end of the month-long fast and a *namaz* in a mosque in September.[106] The PDPA leaders also occasionally spoke about Islam in the foreign media. This, too, led to convoluted messages. To a Kuwaiti newspaper, Taraki was unable to say if it was possible to be both a communist and a Muslim. He was simply unable to meaningfully combine the PDPA's pervasive Marxist-Leninist ideology and Islam.[107] Karmal would face the same problem later.

For every modest sign toward Islam, the PDPA came out with statements directly out of the Marxist-Leninist playbook. On the Afghan New Year that coincided with the Herat revolt, Taraki praised the "red national flag that belonged to workers, [and] peasants," endorsed the communist motto "to each according to his need," confirmed the abolition of the bride price, and declared that the Afghan economy would follow a five-year plan. His speech promised to accelerate the pace of reforms, deploying a jargon that most Afghans certainly found unintelligible.

Taraki likewise repeated that the PDPA waged a "holy war" against the sheikhs and the Muslim Brotherhood who were "made in London and Paris," a multilayered reference to the prior exile of Ayatollah Ruhollah Khomeini, S. Mujaddidi's prior exile, and old images of British colonialism.[108] By equating the mujahideen with the Islamists, likely due to the legacy of opposition between the PDPA and the Muslim Youth, Khalq was putting in motion a self-fulfilling prophecy, boosting Islamist influence. In parallel, it blurred its message to Afghans. Denunciations of Islamists who used "religion for political goals" did not go well with claims that nothing had changed with Islam in Afghanistan, that people observed its rituals, maintained the mosques, and that *muezzins* read the call to prayer.[109]

In summary, Khalq alternated between paltry attempts to pay lip service to Islam and communist zeal. This was nowhere near enough to convince Afghans that the regime did not want to transform the country into a Soviet Central Asian republic. According to Abdul Darmanger, one of Taraki's aides and Khalq's vice minister of health, such was indeed Taraki's intention.[110] At various points, both Taraki and Amin explained to the Soviets that they envisioned changing their policies on Islam in the future. In Amin's words, "as soon as at least 20% of the population were alphabetized, [Khalq] would deploy a widespread antireligious campaign."[111] This no doubt explained why they had trouble producing a coherent narrative.

Under these circumstances, PDPA's attempts to counter accusations about its godlessness must have looked awkward to Afghans. Taraki's assertion that "*sharia* in [Afghanistan] was the workers' power" did not sound in line with Islamic theology.[112] It also helped little when the regime tortuously used Koranic justifications to back its reforms, notably on ending usury.[113] All it showed was how much of an afterthought Islam was at that stage. In classic Marxist-Leninist fashion, Khalq simply "wondered why Afghans did not see that its reforms were in their best interest."[114] Most important, the regime's blunders stood out to Afghans, including the red flag and disappearance of the Islamic preamble. Observers noted more such missteps. A mullah from eastern Laghman Province was so eager to praise the regime on the radio that he stated that Taraki was "the greatest leader of Islam in the last 1,400 years," so greater than the Prophet Mohammad himself.[115] In Kunar Province, leaflets airdropped by the regime again claimed it supported Islam but similarly missed the "Bismillah."[116]

The situation changed only in the summer of 1979 when the regime, due to increased Soviet pressure, expanded on its campaign to co-opt Islam, foreshadowing some of Karmal's future policies. The Soviet embassy noted with satisfaction that finally some steps had been taken; the work with Islamic leaders was now more coherent and centralized.[117] Taraki toned down his Marxism-Leninist rhetoric, regularly attended Friday prayer, and introduced his speeches with the Islamic preamble. A *jirga*—a traditional assembly of leaders and elders that decides by consensus according to the Pashtunwali, the Pashtun code of traditions and customs—then gathered the mullahs loyal to the regime in Kabul in August. These were mostly the so-called red mullahs, the lower ranks of Islamic scholars from the countryside, where there was some support for the PDPA. The *jirga* again declared a jihad to destroy the Muslim Brotherhood and promised support to the PDPA.[118] Official newspapers published photos of Taraki and Amin, along with other PDPA leaders attending the *namaz* for Ramadan. This was one of the last times the two leaders appeared together in public.

The next month a hastily formed Council of Ulemas (Jamiat-i-Ulama) declared its support for Amin while describing him as a "peaceful, patriotic and modest leader." However, it failed to say if Amin was a Muslim or not.[119] Because Amin was even more of a convinced communist, once declaring that Soviet Central Asia could not be a model for Afghanistan because it was not advanced enough, the Marxist-Leninist rhetoric came back in earnest while loyal Islamic scholars tried to build the regime's Islamic legitimacy.[120] This resulted in a cacophony of discourses.

Amin spoke of "a class war between workers and exploiters" in Afghanistan.[121] Such imported expressions in a country where the factory workers represented a fresh phenomenon that included seasonal migration between city and countryside and where the PDPA in Kabul had only 8 percent workers among its members made no sense to Afghans. Meanwhile, the communist leader timidly generalized some of Taraki's concessions, supporting a modest program to repair mosques and pay loyal mullahs.[122] The Council of Ulemas then sent a group of Afghans on Hajj, showing how these pilgrimages had become a state-managed event like in the USSR. Afterward, answering the "attacks by Ikhvanists" as put by the English-language *Kabul New Times*, the official media regularly wrote of the PDPA's respect for Islam. They described Amin as "a Muslim, born in a Muslim family" and quoted proregime demonstrators declaring that "[they] considered submission to [Amin] as Farz [Fard, a religious duty]."[123] The latter argument appeared after the Council of Ulemas declared Amin the Uli al-Amr, he who rules through the authority of God.[124] The title was akin to the divine rights of kings in medieval Europe.

These half-hearted attempts came though too late to make a difference. They had also been done unwillingly by Khalq who maintained its control over clergy activities, including in *madrasas* and mosques. As the Soviet embassy lamented, the PDPA was still set on excluding the clergy, including by reducing the size of Hajj delegations and the number of scholars in the Council of Ulemas and having no religious leader in the revolutionary council. In fact, even the pro-PDPA mosques were—in Amin's words—handled by "people most dedicated to the PDPA," whose job was to constantly control the mullahs.[125] Beyond this, Amin, as Taraki before him, "seemed unable to declare simply, like the majority of his countrymen: 'I am a Muslim.'"[126] According to the Soviets, few Afghans had thus illusions as to the real thinking of these leftist intellectuals who had "written books about the poor" like Taraki or "taught in lycées" like Amin and wanted to limit the traditional elites' power.[127] There was no foundation for compromise. Although Khalq claimed to only repress mullahs who tried to have a role beyond the mosque, no practicing Muslim could accept the authorities pushing Islam out of the social and political sphere, especially in education that both sides—as the Soviets during the Basmachi revolt—saw as critical to deciding the country's future.

The PDPA did not have to go around closing mosques and expropriating *waqfs* to seem un-Islamic. Neglect toward Islam, attacks on Islamic leaders' social and political roles, and the incapacity of PDPA's leaders to muster a profession of faith were enough. According to a KhAD head of department, the communists, aware that the country was Muslim, "did not try to explain everyone the theory of Marxist-Leninism" and "did not talk openly that it did not believe in God."[128] This was the maximum they managed under Taraki and Amin.

In addition to not convincing Afghans of the regime's Islamic credentials, Khalq's message undermined Afghanistan's position among Muslim countries. As the ambassador from Libya, a Soviet ally, ironically noted: "there is a big difference between a man saying that he 'respects' Islam and his saying that he is a Muslim."[129] This diplomat had also heard rumors in Kabul about the widespread executions of the jailed Islamists. This he saw as another sign of what he thought was the regime's "true color."[130]

Finally, Khalq's belated attempt to build a procommunist Islam was too modest to broaden the regime's base and had little effect in undermining the mujahideen propaganda. Khalq repressive policies created a problematic legacy that the following regimes struggled to overcome as they tried to build domestic legitimacy through Islam. Throughout the 1980s, PDPA leaders traded blame for the mistakes committed during that period.[131]

The year-and-a-half following the PDPA's accession to power and leading up to the Soviet intervention played a decisive role in the future of Afghanistan. It marked the moment when the PDPA, led by its radical wing, Khalq, antagonized the Afghan people. Because of its disorganization and arrogant drive to reform without considering the context, because of its sometimes intended and sometimes involuntary anticlericalism and because of its anti-Islamic policies, these "communist-amateurs" spurred a revolt that threatened its power. In parallel, Khalq, because of its factionalism, mismanaged its relations with the Soviet Union.[132]

Neither was Moscow nor its advisers in Kabul exempt from fault. The Soviets supported four Afghan regimes in two years—Daud, Taraki's Khalq, Amin's Khalq, and then Karmal. With such a lack of consistency, it was difficult to have Afghans profess loyalty to the regime of the day or the Soviets. What is especially striking is the extent to which the Soviets proved unable to steer the PDPA toward their preferred course of action from the start. Despite its massive economic and military support, Moscow could not force the Afghan communists to limit infighting and moderate their policies. Controlling the PDPA remained an issue and Afghanistan was only one illustration of the Kremlin's difficulties in dealing with its clients during the Cold War. Brutents recalled how Moscow had similar troubles imposing moderation on South Yemen in the 1960s and 1970s. Leaders in Aden were set on having a Yemen Socialist Party professing "the principles of scientific socialism."[133] As with Khalq, they did not want the Soviets to tell them they were not mature enough for real socialism.

At the same time, the Soviets had a preoccupation with Islam in Afghanistan which featured prominently in their advice to the PDPA and the KGB's analysis of the situation. Yet, Soviet policymakers did not fully understand the role played by Islam in Afghanistan and their recommendations were vague. These two factors also carried into the next period. The Soviets continued to have trouble with giving actionable advice on Islam to the PDPA while also espousing an ideological Marxist-Leninist approach to reforming Afghanistan through the dispatch of thousands of advisers.

Finally, the Soviets intervened in Afghanistan because they feared for their security if the United States were to establish military bases there and because ideology told them that the world was going their way. They feared what losing a progressive revolution to the Islamists or the United States would do to communism's image. Beyond this, parochial interests colored motivations for the intervention: Ustinov thought of Afghanistan as a testing ground for new weapons, the KGB was more concerned with Islamism and the United States, and Ponomarev wanted to show how a backward country could jump into socialism. All saw the intervention as a swift affair that would bring political dividends both at home and abroad. Among these secondary motivations, some Soviets, notably in the KGB, conceptualized the Islamist threat emanating from Afghanistan to Central Asia against the backdrop of the Cold War. They worried that an Islamist regime would be pro-American and that the United States would instrumentalize Islam against them. Islamism was thus connected to the Soviets' traditional security and ideological concerns.

CHAPTER 3

Ideology in the Karmal Era

From that [Afghan] war I brought back one, written already in the Bible, truth: "Do not hurry to make good!" It is impossible to make an entire people happy against its will. Each person should decide for himself how he should live.

—KGB Captain, 1981

We were obsessed with our messianic mission and blinded by arrogance. How could we have possibly hoped to teach the Afghans anything when we ourselves never learned to manage our own economy properly? In truth, we were exporting stagnation rather than revolution.

—A. Borovik, 1990

The Soviets quickly realized that the war was not going as planned. Karmal's regime was unable to fight the insurgency on its own while Soviet forces secured cities and communication routes. Following protests in Kabul and attacks on the Soviet embassy between 20 and 23 February 1980, and attacks on Soviet forces in other parts of the country, the LCST received instructions to begin military operations alongside the Afghan army. Karmal himself pushed for the Soviets to take over military operations showing how the relationship was, from the start, more complex than that of client and patron. Meanwhile, after discussions at the politburo that showed concern about getting bogged down, the Kremlin decided that a withdrawal was inadvisable until the situation was stabilized, including because of the growth of "Muslim extremism near the border of the Soviet Union."[1] This was, however, the last reason mentioned for staying in Afghanistan. Afterward, the war unfolded in three stages: the large-scale military operations by the LCST (March 1980, especially from 1982 to April 1985); the LCST at its peak in terms of strength and battle readiness but seeing reduced ground fighting while prioritizing air and artillery support to Afghan forces (April 1985 to January 1987); and the preparations for and the withdrawal of Soviet forces with limited Soviet offensive operations (January 1987 to February 1989).

On arrival, the Soviets put the Afghan government under supervision, sending thousands of party advisers to administer the country. They added to the engineers, teachers, builders, and other specialists who had worked in Afghanistan since the 1960s. Afghans had contrasted opinions of these people who were mostly present in the northern provinces of Balkh, Baghlan, Kunduz, and Takhar. Even though they appreciated their technical knowledge, Afghans also saw them through the lens of negative stereotypes. The Soviets were atheists and cardinally different from Muslim Afghans in many ways. The Soviet advisers' role after 1980 became to guide Afghans on the path to modernization. This sovietization enterprise was not simply the strength of inertia; there was in Kabul and Moscow the shared belief that Afghanistan could "jump" into socialism, proving Marxism-Leninism relevance. Soviet Central Asia was then to serve as a model for social and cultural modernization and industrialization but not—or not entirely—in the realm of Islam.

The Trap of Ideology

The belief in socialism's ultimate victory weighed heavily on the Soviet decision to intervene. It showed again when the Plenum of the CC CPSU validated the war in June 1980. Although the delegates had no choice but to accept the fait accompli, many praised the decision. Eduard Shevardnadze, Gorbachev's future minister of foreign affairs, was one of the most obsequious, presenting the war as necessary to defend the Afghan people and the Soviet southern border. The LCST's dispatch was the "courageous, only right, only wise step regarding Afghanistan that each Soviet person had interiorly waited for."[2] Speakers argued that the war had been unavoidable given the backdrop of the Cold War. Often repeated ideas about worldwide revolution and the victory of socialism, coupled with a shared educational and cultural background, formed the way of thinking about Afghanistan even among those who harbored doubts and later came to lead the perestroika. Ideological statements reinforced each other in a CPSU-wide groupthink.

Gromyko began his speech at the Plenum by analyzing the international context, arguing that all should see "the unstoppable consolidation of socialism's positions." The LCST was defending Afghanistan against foreign "reactionary" aggression. Gromyko was also quick to mislead the Plenum about the real situation, stressing that naturally fighting was "handled by the Afghan army," and the LCST was only helping. Summing up, he promised that, whatever happens, there will "be no return to old Afghanistan."[3] Gromyko's speech was symptomatic of how ideology, as incarnated in ill-defined tenets that had much less to do with Marx's and Lenin's writings by the 1970s, and propaganda never stopped in the Soviet Union. Its leadership had difficulties making objective assessments and formulating policy based on facts. When it declared that it was to be "building socialism" in Afghanistan, all it meant was that it would be reproducing bits and pieces of the Soviet system of the 1970s.

As information on Afghanistan was abundant but contradictory, policymaking was complicated and ideologized. A plethora of agencies sent reports to Moscow, including the KGB and its affiliates in Afghanistan and other countries, the 40th Army's commander, military advisers, the GRU, Soviet embassies in Afghanistan and other countries, and CPSU advisers. Analysts in Moscow then collated these reports and sent them to the Kremlin. Whilst information abounded, no one focused on Afghanistan in the politburo because all assumed it was for "a few months only."[4] This was part of the reason the politburo could wait for six months to get the Plenum's approval and distort information about Afghanistan.

No one would be able to assess the situation comprehensively, even by 1982. The Kremlin, the military, and the KGB talked of "bandits," "religious fanaticism," and the "counterrevolution" but, according to KGB's First Chief Directorate head Leonid Shebarshin, such "propaganda labels hindered the understanding of reality, limiting the analysis to convenient and comfortable stereotypes."[5] Few were able to admit that the Soviets were part of a civil war. In the politburo, beyond ideology, an acute perception of the East-West conflict and a hazy idea about the Islamic factor, there was little understanding of the context. In the words of a Soviet journalist, these "mossy" (*zamshelye*) politicians could barely tell PDPA leaders one from another; they did not and did not want to know about Afghanistan.[6] In 1981, Konstantin Chernenko, who would be general secretary in 1984–85, told Maiorov that all that he had to do was to reunify the PDPA. When Maiorov noted that this would be difficult, the old leader's response was that "Lenin's teachings are all-powerful" and that "the authority of Leonid Il'ich in the world is great."[7] What the Kremlin had was a surfeit of belief in the Soviet system and the final victory of socialism.

Against this background, ideology determined the worldview of the Soviets sent to Afghanistan, sometimes reluctantly. Advisers who had gone through the ideological school of Marxism-Leninism quickly occupied the country. Many were CPSU organizers who replicated what they knew, using Soviet methods and forms of political and social organization. They had little training besides a one-week course and operated based on in-country plans devised by the leading adviser in each group (chief military adviser, chief political ad-viser, etc.).[8] Beyond this, the advisers did not act based on any experience of working in Central Asia. Some tried to impose an atheistic propaganda that, even in 1970s Central Asia, would have been at odds with the growing accom-modation between Islam, tradition, and Marxism-Leninism. They were mak-ing the same mistakes as Khalq. This was ironic because the Soviets had supposedly replaced the "radical" Amin with the "moderate" Karmal whose job was now to set up a "national dialogue," build contacts with Islamic lead-ers, and "reduce the pace of socialism."[9] However, the advisers who arrived represented a country sure of its ideology and its system's superiority. The So-viets did not think of adapting anything to Afghanistan; rather, they pushed for sovietization.

Advisers' activism led to absurd situations as the Soviets organized "social-ist competitions" and "public readings of Brezhnev's books" and "set-up 'red corners' in remote *auls* (villages) and towns."[10] In a similar vein, Soviet CPSU members, who knew little of Afghanistan but a lot about Marxism-Leninism, prepared statements, and speeches for the PDPA in Russian. "They transferred to Afghanistan not only our experiences but also our errors and vices," noted Victor Polyanichko, the chief CPSU adviser from 1985 to 1988.[11] In an illus-tration, when setting up the office library, CPSU advisers in Kabul requested no books on Afghan culture or history but 300 books on Lenin, Marx, Engels, and related commentary.[12] Speaking with Mikhail Slinkin, the chief adviser in the PDPA International Department and one of the top Soviet experts on Afghanistan, Layeq noted that he was surprised by the "incompetence" of many of the advisers. He could not understand why instead of sending tech-nical experts, engineers, and people knowledgeable about Afghan culture and traditions, Moscow had sent so many intelligence operatives and party build-ers.[13] This was only partially true; technical specialists also went to the DRA, but Layeq's criticism was understandable. Even many of the Afghanists in the USSR were under the ideology's influence. Slinkin himself wrote in his diary that "an acute class struggle was ongoing" in Afghanistan in 1982, pitching pro-gressive forces against "bandits."[14] He, too, remained under the influence of the stereotypes. Few Soviets thought otherwise about the DRA.

Fikryat Tabeev, the ambassador who stayed until Gorbachev, embodied such Soviet ideologues. After heading the powerful Tatarstan republic, the Krem-lin sent him to Afghanistan because in part of his culturally Muslim back-ground but mostly because he was a successful party builder. He represented the paradox of Soviet engagement; he was a Muslim and once claimed that as a Muslim, he was well-versed in Islamic traditions and did not need anyone's advice, but he was also one of the biggest dogmatists that there was. Tabeev typically recalled how he expected Marxism-Leninism to find fertile ground in Afghanistan and came to help advisers implement CPSU methods.[15] He was part of this arrogant *nomenklatura*, along with many of the 316 CPSU advisers who worked with Afghan leaders in the 1980s, who took over the administration of the country. Tabeev became a man of endless outrageous quotes, often out-of-touch with the war. He once told a meeting of ambassadors from socialist countries that the Soviets "did not come to [Afghanistan] to leave" and, on another occasion, to the departing Soviet military, that the DRA was on its way to join the Warsaw Pact.[16]

The KGB suffered from similar issues, although not as acutely. An officer who trained KhAD, the Afghan KGB, operatives in Tashkent and went to Afghanistan pointed out that ideological jargon was common among the Soviets and, accordingly, among Afghan communists who tried to please the Soviets. Even some operatives in the KGB noted that this pushed away ordinary people.[17] For a long time, the KGB made no effort to adapt its training, language, and teaching material to Afghanistan, creating misunderstandings and tensions with the population. Some of its operatives' stories appear even amusing due to the disconnect they show with the population. One KGB Officer recalled how advisers in his area were unhappy about the regime suspending land reform and tried to preach about the negative influence of religion. They went around with slogans such as "Let's get rid of the influence of mullahs on people's minds!," "Give us kolkhoz!," and "Religion is the opium of the people!"[18] The Soviets were both prisoners of ideology and at risk of others using their relentless propaganda against them. Afghans were to turn this ambiguity to their advantage.

In retrospect, Vladimir Zagladin, theoretician of the perestroika, noted that the overreliance on Marxism-Leninism had led to "mistrust and even hostility between the local population, permeated by the ideas of the Koran, and the central authorities" in Kabul. Learning their Afghan lessons, Zagladin argued, the Soviets had to "without ideological dogmas consider . . . 'local socialism' that was certainly not scientific socialism, but was able to really ensure . . . countries' development, from a backward, tribal-kin structure, and excessive religious ideology, on the path to progress . . . (Though definitely not necessarily to Marxism)."[19] Otherwise said, the Soviets would accept that the Afghan society should be left to function according to local structures. They would abandon hopes that it may be entirely reforged but still astoundingly believe that—while the communist regime crumbled—they could salvage some socialism. After ten years, this would be the finale of the Soviet-Afghan War. Ironically, three years later, the USSR itself discarded scientific socialism. Tracing a parallel to the present, Zagladin comments also disturbingly echo the evolution of US thinking on Afghanistan from a belief that the Western democratic model could easily travel there to the recognition that Afghan society had its own rules.

One episode particularly helps illustrate the Soviets' approach to Afghanistan in 1980. As the International Department organized briefings for advisers, Ponomarev reported how he and his colleagues met Colonel Abdul Kadir Dagarwal, a leader of the April Revolution and Parcham-leaning communist arrested under Taraki. In a peculiar exchange of opinions, after Kadir suggested Afghans "had not been ready" for PDPA's reforms, the Soviets replied that such opinions were unacceptable. "Surely among the Afghan people, the working class was not numerous, not forged in revolutionary fights, but still the working class, the vanguard of the peasantry must inevitably support the revolution." Pressuring Kadir, the Soviets asked him: "If you knew that people were not ready for the revolution, then why did you take power in your hands?" To that, Kadir could only awkwardly respond that "[they] did not have another choice and that this resulted from circumstances."[20] Kadir was one of Moscow's loyal supporters and a committed communist. Yet, Ponomarev, the theoretician of Afghanistan as a testing ground for socialism, scolded him after he seemed to doubt the suitability of the communists' radical reforms. Such discussions cast a revealing light on many Soviets' mindsets. Knowing virtually nothing of Afghanistan, they told Afghans to stay the course of the revolution. The International Department especially saw Afghanistan through the prism of either Central Asia or Mongolia. As Rostislav Ulyanovsky, Ponomarev's deputy, once famously commented, "there was no country that was not ripe enough for socialism."[21]

Despite their earlier doubts about Afghanistan's readiness for socialism, the Soviets were now in-country and sure they would succeed in changing Afghanistan. It was only about selecting the right methods and tactics to minimize opposition and taking their time. Karmal's PDPA shared this delusion. Leaders in the Soviet politburo agreed that there was no rush in returning the LCST. It could stay in Afghanistan "for a year, maybe a year and a half, until the situation was stabilized," they considered.[22] Afghanistan was to stand first among Third World countries going the Soviet way.

Two other aspects about advisers confirmed the dominance of ideology. First, the Kremlin paid little attention to Asian studies experts, the "people who understood things about Afghanistan." The politburo seldom asked for the opinions of Primakov, Vladimir Basov, Yuri Gankovsky, and Vladimir Plastun from the Oriental Studies Institute.[23] Even when some of these people happened to already be in Kabul, they played little role in designing policy. Moscow even recalled Plastun and Basov home in 1980. This lack of interest in experts' opinions prevailed during most of the conflict. Plastun bitterly observed how ultimately "five years after the beginning of the war, [decision-makers] decided to consult the experts" as they invited him to a meeting on Afghanistan in Moscow.[24] Yet, the Oriental Studies Institute had worked on the "Islamic factor" and pre-1978 Afghanistan. While ideology and the lack of security clearances to deal with the DRA and Soviet Islam constrained its research, the Kremlin could assuredly have put Soviet scholars' ethnographic expertise and knowledge of Afghan languages to better use.

Second, as for the military preparations for the war, the Kremlin made the selection of advisers in a hurry and in secrecy. The military had no reliable maps of Afghanistan in 1980. They had little knowledge of the mujahideen or counterinsurgency tactics. Most had only a cursory knowledge of Afghan history, culture, and languages. The lack of translators despite the many Tajiks present was particularly an issue. Even elite KGB units lacked context analysts.[25] Coming to the DRA in 1985, one senior KGB officer noted how, after a two-year training course, he had "only the most general understanding about Khalq and Parcham." There were still few books dealing with post-1978 Afghanistan, and the Oriental Studies Institute published the first comprehensive monograph on the DRA only in 1984; only one copy was available at the KGB training center in Tashkent.[26] The Soviets gained knowledge about Afghanistan while already in-country.

Blissfully unaware of these failings, Soviet leaders believed that the issue with Marxism-Leninism was not that there was too much of it but too little. As Chernenko explained to his colleagues in February 1980, the PDPA did not do a good enough job with propaganda.[27] Soviet ideologues then made the same point in May while committing to support the PDPA's "ideological struggle" and adjusting their own propaganda. Slowly, they started to understand that standard Soviet propaganda, including the magazine *Soviet Woman*, may not be a good match for Afghanistan.[28] The fact that the Soviets had sent the magazine to Kabul in the first place was another example of how at all levels they reflected little on the practicality of their modernization enterprise. Adjusting somehow to the context, the Novosti Press Agency developed brochures in Dari and Pashto on the DRA's domestic and foreign policy. The Soviet "ideological work," however, continued to have no interest in Islam.[29] Propaganda tried to build the PDPA's appeal by highlighting the gains it brought to workers and peasants, communism's supporters according to the Marxist-Leninist canon, but said nothing of convergences between Islam and socialism.

Communists and mujahideen thereafter competed in shaping the narrative about the war, the latter being vastly more successful. Soviet advisers unanimously noted their propaganda's failure, claiming it was due to weak coordination and a lack of Afghanists, technical experts, funding, and equipment. While information in Afghanistan circulated orally through *jirgas* and Islamic figures' contacts with the population, the communists overrelied on print media and lacked the means to get their message across.[30] The Soviets also underlined how the PDPA, with its limited base, feared going to the countryside where many Afghans had no reliable information other than what the mujahideen provided.[31] Beyond this, the Soviets originally had considerable hope for radio propaganda but, because of poor equipment and power supply problems, this proved ineffective. "Radio waves were [instead] dominated by voices hostile to Kabul" from Pakistan and Iran. Things in this regard got better only by 1986. Even when they reached the population, the communists used a language that many Afghans did not understand. Finally, at the international level, Soviet and PDPA's failure to make their narrative about the conflict stick was similarly apparent, as we shall see in chapter 5.

The influence of ideology is central to understanding how from the beginning of the war the Soviets ended up conducting a policy that was at crosspurposes with its professed interests. No one in Moscow understood that engaging in sovietizing Afghan society by sending thousands of party builders was incompatible with a presence meant to be short-term and have modest objectives. According to one Soviet adviser, "we learned as we went. And, even only those who wanted to learn did so, but these were few." Meanwhile, "party advisers screamed that we needed to build socialism and the military pounded from all cannons and grenade throwers, it was all very primitive."[32] This dichotomy colored the ensuing Soviet experience and underlined how it was never clear what the goals of the Soviet presence were. As the Soviets struggled to change Afghanistan, they sent more advisers to the country, multiplying the problems noted above.

The Impossible Transformation

A *Pravda* journalist reported an especially dire picture of communist Afghanistan in late 1981. His report, which went directly to the CC CPSU, noted that Kabul "controlled less than 15% of the territory," "some 5,000 villages out of 35,000."[33] In addition to struggling to build support outside of cities and specific social groups, the communists waged a particularly brutal war. A French diplomat and aid worker argued at the time that Soviet warfare was nothing short of an "ethnocide."[34] Many Soviets admitted retrospectively that the communists' tactics in Afghanistan had been ruthless.[35] Indiscriminate airstrikes were meant to show rural communities that supporting the mujahideen had a cost. They depleted the opposition's resource base and pushed Afghans toward the cities. This brought them to work in governmental institutions and enterprises and made them more receptive to the regime's propaganda and dependent on the material benefits it provided. Yet, for all their mercilessness, the communists did not achieve much in two years.

For the *Pravda* journalist, the main issue was that two Soviet factions competed to make Afghan policy. The split was between the LCST's command, which focused on strategic military issues and believed that superior military power would win the day, and some of the CPSU and other advisers, probably including the KGB and some mid-ranking military officers, who lamented the lack of a "hearts and minds" strategy and an integrated political approach.[36] Soviet chief military adviser Maiorov and Sergei Sokolov, who headed the Ministry of Defense's Operations Group on Afghanistan, repeatedly formulated unrealistic assessments of when a victory would be achieved in 1980 and 1981.[37] As to the core tension over policy, it would only be resolved by the end of the war. Meanwhile, the *Pravda* journalist reporting to Moscow argued that only a "comprehensive politico-military and social-economic resolution" could ensure victory.[38]

The communists tried to build support among the population in the areas they controlled, establishing the PDPA's political authority there—the Soviets called it the *orgyadro* (short for "organization core"), a name reminiscent of the "government-in-a-box" attempted by the United States many years later—and distributing food, household items, farming implements, agricultural, and other products to Afghans and providing them with social services and benefits. This was, however, often done in a disorganized way, relying on corrupt Red Army and PDPA personnel who appropriated part of the aid.[39] Beyond this, villages deemed loyal were excluded from airstrikes. Testifying to the split in Soviet perspectives, this politico-military strategy was pushed by Tabeev while Maiorov claimed that the Soviet contingent was insufficient for such a seize-and-hold approach. More often than not, the situation was not stabilized and PDPA political authority could not be established in the areas retaken. Soviet garrisons had to either thwart mujahideen continuous harassment or make deals with them.[40]

By 1982, the Soviets effectively came to two conclusions. First, they reluctantly acknowledged that the mujahideen had built extensive support in the population, successfully debunking claims that they were bandits, thanks to their effective propaganda. Second, and PDPA leaders such as Karmal and Sultan Ali Keshtmand, the chairman of the Council of Ministers, shared this assessment, they understood that Afghanistan's stabilization would be a long-haul affair with or without the LCST.[41] A central reason was that the PDPA's policies were failing across the board. The *Pravda* journalist highlighted the issues with Karmal's land reform and nationalities' policy. His negative assessment was in line with that of the Oriental Studies Institute, which noted that the improvements made in extending the Kabul regime's base had been modest. In the Pashtun belt, tribes remained hostile to the communists. The regime's only success had been in stopping some of them from actively participating in the jihad. Even worse, the PDPA seemed in no hurry to address the issue. By June 1980, Karmal had still not met with any tribal leader. The Soviets either did not know how to improve the PDPA's effectiveness or did not care enough to act decisively. Instead, they launched their own transformative project, hoping it would boost support.

Soviet development and humanitarian assistance to Afghanistan have received considerable attention in the literature and among veterans and former advisers. One KGB officer contributing to this book sent a long letter detailing how many tractors, refrigerators, tons of iron, cars, and trucks the Soviets had provided to the DRA before discussing other aspects of the conflict.[42] In the 2000s, Moscow used that argument—highlighting that the Soviets had completed 142 major infrastructure projects—to deflect criticism about the Soviet-Afghan War and promote reengagement in Afghanistan. It is as if building factories, roads, and bridges could compensate for the thousands of deaths or as if the Soviets had built more than they had destroyed in Afghanistan. The latter is naturally wrong, but infrastructure building was indeed an important component of the intervention, as was the provision of technical assistance, material, and food aid. Integrating Afghanistan into their Council for Mutual Economic Assistance, the Soviets genuinely hoped that their development assistance would help stabilize the country.[43]

Such nation-building also increased the cost of the war. One estimate suggests that the Soviets spent some $7.5 billion total on the Afghan war between 1984 and 1987. While this was a relatively modest amount compared to the USSR's military budget of $128 billion in 1989, it was also a rough estimate that may not have included nonmilitary activities.[44] By 1988, the war's cost had increased to perhaps as much as $3.25 billion per year, apparently including the nonmilitary component.[45] Overall, the Soviet-Afghan War's cost, especially of its development component that often went through infrastructure building, remained difficult to quantify. The politburo repeatedly struggled to come up with a reliable number.[46]

Among the major projects built since the 1960s were the Naghlu Dam on the Kabul River, the asphalt factory in Kabul Province, Bagram Airport in Parwan Province, two other airports, the bakery, and a nitrogen fertilizer plant in Mazar-i-Sharif, 1,500 kilometers of highways and irrigation systems near

Jalalabad. During the 1980s, the Soviets completed more than fifty large-scale infrastructure projects.[47] This economic and technical assistance nevertheless suffered from structural issues and, ultimately, failed in modernizing the country. State-based industrialization and economic planning on the Soviet Stalinist model were not a good fit for Afghanistan, which had weak institutions, few technical cadres, no industrial base, and a corrupt government.[48] In retrospect, many Soviets recognized as much. The focus on providing Afghans with things they did not want—"products of an alien civilization" as put by an ethnic Russian general from Central Asia—while drawing them away from their rural homes was bound to fail. "This was the reason why [Soviet] material help never helped [the LCST] gain support."[49] As the Soviets withdrew, many projects remained unfinished and some of the industrial enclaves, notably in the gas sector, were shut down, depriving the government of already limited income. Until the end, as much as on military aid, Najibullah, Karmal's successor, would remain dependent on Soviet economic and in-kind assistance.

The Soviet transformative project helped little in raising the PDPA's profile because it did little to address the three stigmas attached to Karmal. Afghans saw him as simultaneously the heir to the cruel Amin, a Soviet atheist puppet, and the enabler of the LCST's brutal military tactics. The mujahideen called him Shah Shuja after the infamous ruler who had retaken the Afghan throne with British help in 1839 and that Afghans had learned to hate through stories about the First Anglo-Afghan War.[50] The Afghans naturally looked on the LCST as an occupation force akin to the British. Even people in the Kremlin had to acknowledge that the Soviet image in Afghanistan had deteriorated since the Khalq period.[51] The Soviets telling Karmal to break with that time and strengthen propaganda was of precious little help. Following shallow Soviet advice, the PDPA was struggling to make "the people believe in the ideals of the party."[52]

Disgruntled about that situation, Andropov, who had become the CPSU general secretary in 1982, had to motivate his politburo colleagues anew. Afghanistan was a "feudal country" where central power had never existed, he told them. They had to understand that things there could improve only slowly. The Soviet leader emphasized that the DRA was the Cold War's chief battlefield, extending the geostrategic thinking that had led to the intervention but also showing how Afghanistan was an ideological symbol. "American imperialism was making its stand [in Afghanistan], knowing full well that it had lost its positions in this area of international politics. For this reason, we cannot retreat." Meanwhile, in the Russian orientalist tradition, Andropov reminded his colleagues that sovietizing a backward Muslim country was always meant to be challenging. "Sometimes, we get angry with the Afghans

FIGURE 3.1.   A downed Soviet aircraft in the Panjshir, 1981 (Courtesy of Olivier Roy). The contrast was striking between rural Afghans' traditional lifestyles and the modernity—including regarding means of destruction—brought by the Soviets.

because they do not behave consistently, are slow in deploying work. But let's remember our struggle against the Basmachi. Almost the entire Red Army was concentrated at the time in Central Asia and the struggle against the Basmachi still lasted until the mid-1930s. Regarding Afghanistan, there is, therefore, the need to be both demanding and understanding."[53]

Andropov's underlying argument was that, as Central Asians, Afghans had been slow in awakening to the gains of progress, but he stopped his parallel at that point, not prolonging it, as Chernyaev would do in his diary, to note that Central Asia—the blueprint for Afghanistan—was still a special case in the Soviet Union. It had preserved its traditional customs and developed an accommodation between Islam and communism that was neither in line with Marxist-Leninist dogma nor approved by Moscow. Andropov's speech was emblematic of how the Soviet leadership continued to view Afghanistan through the lens of ideology. This was particularly surprising given how little the Soviets had achieved in transforming the country by 1983. Still, they believed that, almost by miracle, they, together with the PDPA, would eventually succeed.

Moscow meanwhile continued to form Afghan civilian and security cadres and send thousands more Afghans for training to the USSR.[54] The mujahideen saw that program as such a threat that they called on the Muslim world to provide its own quotas for Afghan students.[55] As boasted by Kryuchkov, now the KGB's head, the Soviet program also included hundreds of intelligence personnel—2,600 in 1983—from KhAD who were instructed at the special KGB center in Tashkent.[56] KhAD had then become the Soviets' flagship organization. Both the mujahideen and the independent Afghanistan Information Centre (AIC) in Peshawar recognized that it was their principal organizational success. It had mastered "subversive tactics" and was adept at "infiltrating the [mujahideen] groups."[57]

In parallel, advisers sovietized primary and secondary education in Afghanistan, including by promoting the study of the Russian language.[58] Education became an ideological battlefield between the PDPA and the mujahideen. Jamiat-e Islami, one of the two strongest insurgent parties, genuinely feared that this was how sovietization, including secularization, would spread.[59] It is, therefore, no surprise that the mujahideen often considered attacks on school staff to be fair game. On the other side, the communists hoped that state education would help in creating a new Afghanistan just as the replacement of the *madrasas* by state education had been a key tool in transforming the Caucasus and Central Asia for the Bolsheviks. Years later, the United States would also rely on education to shape a new Afghanistan.

Another issue that plagued the Soviet transformative project was the character of the Soviet-PDPA relationship. Andropov's assertion that the Afghans did not behave as they were told was an understatement. The relationship was one of endless disputes. There was an "inability of the Soviet leadership, despite Kabul's reliance on its economic and military support, [to] successfully impress its policies on the PDPA."[60] Soviet sources that have emerged since the conflict's end have confirmed as much. This presents a sharp contrast with Afghan and Soviet policymakers' repeated claims that the Soviets were managing everything.

The Soviets' most emblematic failure was indisputably their repeated inability to mend the Khalq-Parcham rift. The PDPA's wings did not want to cooperate, and there was nothing Moscow could do about it. It proved wholly unable to stop Parcham from purging prominent Khalqis in the bureaucracy and the army. Likewise, the Soviets proved, much as the United States did thirty years later, unable to curb nepotism and corruption among Afghan leaders. Those leaders knew that there was no one to replace them with and that any change would project a detrimental image of the regime and, by extension, of the Soviets. Some Afghans then plainly ignored the opinions and recommendations of the Soviet advisers, and even when they did follow Soviet advice, they had at least four tactics that they used to either interpret it in a way that best suited their own interests or get it reversed.

First, Karmal and others could criticize advisers while on visits in Moscow, accusing them of taking bribes and claiming that they had compromised themselves during the Taraki-Amin rule.[61] This was a convenient way of getting advisers removed when the PDPA opposed the policies the advisers advocated. Second, the PDPA could delay implementing policies. Despite Soviet insistence, the Afghans were, for example, "slow in developing a proper propaganda campaign to explain" the LCST's presence because they notably feared going into high-conflict areas and associating too closely with the Soviets.[62] Likewise, the Afghans often ignored Soviet calls to share power with other political forces, including in the post-Karmal era, and again, despite Soviet appeals, were reluctant to lead the fighting.

Third, given the few advisers knowledgeable about Afghanistan and the abundance of people like Tabeev who acted as if it was already the "16th Soviet Republic," Afghans had a vastly better understanding of the local situation than the Soviets.[63] This issue, which Moscow never fixed, considerably undermined Soviet effectiveness. Plastun, a leading Soviet Afghanist and adviser, recalls how a Parchami colonel explained to him how naive Soviets, "not knowing the specificities of the country, listened first to the people they were advising." "They were certain that they were the advisers but in reality, Afghans . . . directed their work into the most advantageous direction for them."[64] The turnover among the Soviets then exacerbated the problem as each new adviser had to learn about the context from scratch.

Beyond this, Afghans could also distort the information passed on to the Soviets. General Zabihullah Ziarmal, who led the Afghan military's propaganda department, once wondered if he should be telling the "entire truth" to the Soviet commanders even if he believed that they could do nothing about his issues. This added to the Soviets' own distortion of the information, often to make it seem more positive, before passing it to their superiors or Moscow. Such problems were also widespread in the KGB. Operatives struggled to gather information and had to rely on their Afghan colleagues. Yet, "during personal conversations, [those often] shared information that was predominantly advantageous to them personally, a given group of party bureaucrats or a faction."[65]

Fourth, Afghans played on rivalries among the Soviets. They could pit one group against another among the KGB, which had both formal and informal activities, the military, which also had informal activities through the GRU, CPSU advisers, and the embassy. The Soviets would then debate among themselves in terms of "our Afghans" against "your Afghans."[66] This compromised any chance at a comprehensive policy and left ample room for interpretation for the PDPA. According to Maiorov, infighting was so rife that it was not unusual for him to argue with Tabeev about policy in front of PDPA leaders.[67]

Two things then rendered intra-Soviet rivalry worse. On the one hand, tensions swelled because of Soviet agencies' competing preferences for either Khalq or Parcham. The military would call Parcham "Parcham-feudal" and blame its members for dodging the war while dismissing CPSU advisers.[68] The latter, Tabeev, and Andropov's KGB conversely pushed for the military's parchamization. In Tabeev's words, Parcham, unlike Khalq, at least "knew its Marxism-Leninism." Throughout the war, this issue remained, although the arrival of Varennikov as "super" chief military adviser and Polyanichko as well as the departure of Tabeev reduced tensions in 1985–86.

On the other, the splits in Kabul also paralleled those in the Kremlin. While the military wanted to run the show in Afghanistan, Andropov controlled the Kremlin. The fact that the entire military leadership, including Maiorov, Sokolov, the chief of the General Staff Nikolai Ogarkov, and, to a lesser extent, his deputy, Sergey Akhromeyev, opposed Ustinov, whom they saw as deferring to Andropov, compounded the issue. Between the lines, the question was about who had better access to Afghan leaders and the leaders in Moscow. In this, too, the Soviets were exporting to Afghanistan some of the worst features of their own bureaucratic model.

Islam Is Not a Soviet Priority

The Soviet neglect of Islam was the product of the ideological approach. Religion simply did not fit with how the Kremlin and its advisers saw the world. On religious policy, Soviet involvement in Afghanistan remained limited. There was consensus among Soviet policymakers that working with the population was "first the job of the Afghans themselves" and that it did not help when the Soviets came to Islamic scholars with talks of "freedom, brotherhood, and equality."[69]

Rahmatullo Abdulloev, a Soviet adviser with the Democratic Youth Organisation of Afghanistan (DOMA), the Afghan Komsomol, explained that the Soviets did not afford Islam any special importance. In addition to military and political training, Moscow educated advisers such as Abdulloev on Islamic theology before dispatching them to Afghanistan. This week-long training included talking to mullahs in Dushanbe's central mosque and learning about the fundamentals of the faith and its rituals. It was about "the essence of Islam; what aspects should a Muslim pay attention to; how to live and work among Muslims; how not to hurt people's religious feelings; how not to antagonize Muslims."[70] As is clear from Abdulloev's description, these were superficial cultural aspects. As we

FIGURE 3.2.   Young Mujahideen in a destroyed mosque in Herat Province, 1987 (Baz Muham-mad and Afghan Media Resource Center | Internet Archive). Karmal's Islamic policies had trouble compensating for the destruction the Soviet and Afghan communist forces brought to Afghanistan's mosques and holy sites during the war.

will see below, handbooks about Afghanistan for soldiers of the LCST adopted a similar approach. In short, Soviet advisers were not to blunder when speaking to Afghan Islamic scholars and believers.[71]

There was no attempt to understand what religion meant in the context of Afghanistan until the war's last phase. In fact, many Soviet policymakers, including Polyanichko and Alexander Yakovlev, one of Gorbachev's leading advisers, regretted this disregard for Islam by the end of the war.[72] This was one result of the few Afghanists involved in policymaking. Disregard for Islam was also the product of the enduring influence of orthodox communists in defining policy and of the military's belief in pacification by force. KGB officers noted that the Soviets "practically entirely ignored religious figures as [potential] ideological allies."[73] At best, Moscow continued to admonish the PDPA about the need to persuade tribal leaders and the clergy to help it build legitimacy at home and appease international Muslim opinion.[74] This disregard at the highest level did not mean that individual advisers could not intervene in matters of Islam. In one negative case, the editor of the Afghan journal *Life of the Party* complained that an adviser had rebuked the Afghan minister of Islamic affairs.[75] In a positive one, DOMA advisers organized the trip to Central Asia of an Afghan mullah to—apparently successfully—gain his support.[76] As was often the case during the Soviet-Afghan War, while policy was set in Moscow, Afghans and Soviets at all levels amended it even as they implemented it.

While not emphasizing Islam, the USSR started informing Afghans about the life of Soviet Muslims even before the intervention. In 1979, an exposition on Central Asia was organized at the embassy in Kabul. It had a booth devoted to Islam that distributed Korans, notoriously printed for foreign consumption only. Staffed by an Uzbek representative from the CRA, it was one of the most-visited parts of the exposition, including by Taraki and Amin.[77] In 1980, a photo exposition about Soviet Muslims opened in Kabul while the Soviet embassy discussed strengthening propaganda. Many proregime Islamic leaders visited it.[78] During the war, while Afghan media regularly reported about Central Asia, they focused on its industrial and economic development. Articles mentioned Islam only in passing. Likewise, there was characteristically no note on religion in the documents on cooperation between Central Asia and Afghanistan in the mid-1980s and little on Islam in the materials sent by the Novosti Press Agency to Afghan media between 1984 and 1987.[79]

People-to-people exchanges, including religious officials, added to the information about Central Asia. In 1980, the head of the Council of Ulemas reported that he had "visited Tashkent [in Uzbekistan], Tajikistan . . . with 15 mullahs." He claimed that the "respect shown to religious cults [in the USSR was] even greater than what [he] had witnessed in Saudi Arabia," a statement that likely gave true believers pause.[80] A milestone was the visit to the DRA of Ziyauddinkhan ibn Eshon Babakhan, SADUM's chairman, in 1981. Babakhan, already an old man by then, was the most influential Islamic authority in the Soviet Union and part of the state organ overseeing Islam. Afghans received him as a head of state as he toured mosques and met loyal Muslim figures and communist officials, including Keshtmand.[81] His visit even led to discussions about the dispatch of an adviser for religious policy that never came although the Soviets had dispatched advisers for everything else.[82] Visits by Afghan Islamic scholars to the USSR happened again in 1984, 1985, and 1987 while Soviet religious officials occasionally visited the DRA.[83] Beyond this, the Soviets opened two spots for Afghan students at the Imam al-Bukhari Islamic Institute in Tashkent, the main Soviet religious school. Even this modest program was, however, discontinued by the mid-1980s.[84]

Exchanges of Islamic officials were only ever modest in size. Those that did happen received limited attention, as is clear from the lack of reports about them in the Afghan media after 1982. "They never represented anything concrete" and were about "expressions of sympathy as to the ongoing war," a Soviet Afghanist explained.[85] Soviet Islamic leaders could not be trusted with something as sensitive as Afghanistan beyond the occasional ceremonial role of reading the *namaz* with Islamic leaders in Kabul. They typically had no presence at the University of Kabul theology faculty, which was the only faculty to receive neither Soviet advisers, nor support in 1984–85.[86] In a Soviet journalist's opinion, one reason was that the ideological people in the CC CPSU's Agitation and Propaganda (Ideology) Department, these "convinced Bolsheviks" like the latter's deputy head Vladimir Sevruk, and in the International Department could not accept mullahs defining policy in the DRA.[87]

This is a key point. Although many Soviets saw Central Asia as a blueprint for Afghanistan, the paradox was that few, particularly among the policymakers, knew much about Soviet Muslims. There was a break between what they thought the situation was in Central Asia—and what many advisers tried to transfer to Afghanistan—and what it really was. It is notable that despite Central Asians being held up as model Soviet Muslim citizens, few were senior advisers and none made policy on Afghanistan at the politburo. Out of the 300-odd CPSU advisers who passed through Afghanistan, only 69 were from Central Asia (including 47 from Kazakhstan, where ethnic Russians made up a large minority) and 5 from Azerbaijan.[88] The Soviet Muslims' absence from among senior policymakers then undermined their image among Afghan communists, recalling Amin's disparaging comments. As to the people in Kabul, Maiorov had this significant comment: "We thought we got rid of Islam on the territory of Soviet republics. How deeply and unforgivingly we were wrong!"[89] Afghanistan had put people like him in front of the contradictions on Islam that had existed in the USSR for a long time but had been hidden from view.

Ultimately, given how religion permeated the Afghan way of life, it was counterproductive for the Soviets to dwell on the situation with Islam in the USSR, an openly atheistic country. As one KGB officer put it, "why would you want to create additional problems by bringing it up?"[90] Confirming how an active engagement could backfire, Soviet Islamic scholars who came to Afghanistan, including Babakhan, were sometimes booed when they preached in mosques.[91] Another factor that played a role in limiting Soviet Islamic diplomacy was that, after Babakhan's death in 1982, SADUM lacked a leader with a similar level of Islamic legitimacy. Meanwhile, the influence of the Spiritual Administration of the Muslims of Transcaucasia and of its leader Sheikh ul-Islam Allahshukur Pashazadeh grew. Although Pashazadeh made trips to Afghanistan, the fact that he was a Shia complicated giving him a bigger role.

Nikolai Egorychev, the ambassador in Kabul in 1988, and Polyanichko noted that Soviet activism on Islam was also counterproductive to the PDPA, which had already to fend off the mujahideen's accusations of being "doubly infidel" for having first attacked Islam under Khalq and then brought in the Soviet atheists. Both men believed that Islam was the main factor working for the opposition alongside Afghanistan's difficult terrain.[92] Instead of debating the Soviets' complex relationship with religion, it was better for Kabul to focus on explaining that it was itself respectful of Islam and that the Soviets were there only temporarily to fight international interference.[93] This point was brilliantly made by Anahita Ratebzad, a member of the PDPA politburo and the most famous Afghan woman of the twentieth century. While commenting to Maiorov about Tabeev, she noted that "[Afghans] can handle *sharia* themselves, without a Muslim-communist."[94] Two senior PDPA cadres would make similar points.[95] Even among the Afghan communists, there was no interest to have Soviet Muslims come teach them about religion.

Other institutions dealing with Soviet-Afghan cultural exchanges similarly showed Islam's limited importance despite the Soviet embassy in Kabul's insistence on the participation of Afghan Islamic leaders.[96] In 1983, the 5th Conference of the USSR-Afghanistan Society of Friendship and Cultural Relations, although it saw the Soviet Union almost exclusively represented by Central Asians, entirely avoided Islam.[97] In 1984, the correspondence of the Soviet-Afghan Friendship Society (SAFS) similarly showed little interest in it. This was especially remarkable given that the SAFS included pro-PDPA Islamic scholars who traveled to the Soviet Union to be decorated.[98] The SAFS honored Abdul Wali Hojjat, the Afghan head of the Directorate for Islamic Affairs, and encouraged him to continue working for the consolidation of Soviet-Afghan friendship.[99] In his speech at the awards ceremony, Hojjat praised the Soviet-Afghan friendship reinforced by "the blood of Soviet and Afghan soldiers, defending the freedom and independence of Afghanistan." He remarked how he had been impressed by his trip but surprisingly did not say a word about Islam either in the DRA or the USSR.[100] The Soviets were treating Afghan Islamic leaders as cultural representatives and bureaucrats of Islam, which was how the Kremlin saw their role in Central Asia. Such a perspective was irrelevant for Afghanistan; no Soviet friendship prize could add prestige to Afghan mullahs. It was the contrary.

A photo exhibition on Central Asia staged by the SAFS across North Afghanistan also ignored Islam. Following its success, the SAFS noted that North Afghanistan, because it bordered the USSR, had many advisers who were "already actively engaging the local population," and had major infrastructure built by the Soviets, was the most promising place for future propaganda work.[101] The stress was on Soviet modernity, its technical achievements, and development aid. This was the same reason Moscow brought Afghans to study in Soviet technical institutes. Ultimately, the plan for the development of the SAFS for 1985–86 did not say anything about Islam. Moscow wanted to display Central Asians as cultural Muslims and their region as a model for industrialization. To increase effectiveness, the Kremlin called on Central Asian republics to develop direct economic and cultural links with Afghan provinces, leading to bilateral SAFS at the republic-to-province level and partnerships between Soviet and Afghan cities.[102] That policy led to renewed concern among the mujahideen who feared it was a step toward the sovietization of northern Afghanistan, a non-Pushtun region they too believed more prone to Soviet influence.[103]

The benefits of Soviet modernity were also what the Soviets focused on as they slowly developed a "hearts-and-minds" strategy. This illustrated the issues noted above, showing the Kremlin's lack of preparation for the war, the absence of a robust political strategy, and the primacy of Marxism-Leninism over realism and adaptability to the context. It is striking that, due to Soviet disregard for it, Islam ended up by default in the purview of the army's propaganda department, led by *agitprop* or special propaganda units—sometimes called "caravans of peace." As put by an officer in the LCST's information department, you had there "a bit more knowledgeable people" who were "more subtle in dealing with Afghans" and the clergy.[104]

There was no plan in 1980 to work with the population other than by relying on Soviet aid distributed through the PDPA. Colonel Nikolai Pikov, a senior special propaganda expert (*spetspropagandist*) who helped set up the political propaganda (*agitprop*), asserted that there were initially only a dozen people available for the "ideological support" of the LCST, in addition to individual units' political officers. There was no knowledge in the Red Army about what ideological propaganda even entailed.[105] Beyond this, the LCST command strongly opposed the *agitprop*'s deployment, arguing that its task was to fight the mujahideen and not talk to them. This changed thanks to the advocacy of senior officers, including Colonel Leonid Shershnev.[106] Still, the command's opposition explained why the setting-up of *agitprop* was painfully slow, with the first unit only appearing in the summer of 1981. The LCST then mainstreamed the program by the mid-1980s while the Afghan army adopted it only a couple of years before the Soviet withdrawal.[107] By 1988, there were thirteen *agitprop* units in the LCST while similar units apparently operated as part of KGB border guards from Soviet territory.[108] Given that the LCST numbered then more than 100,000 people, the *agitprop* was until the end a modest endeavor. As was often the case, it resulted from a lack of attention to nonmilitary aspects at the start of the war and the dominance of ideology. Soviet policymakers had no interest in the "information-psychological weapon," as they had little interest in PDPA politics and the context. They believed that the success of PDPA's reforms would ensure support as soon as they had defeated the mujahideen.

Managed by a Red Army, which was unprepared for the job, a typical *agitprop* unit had a speakerphone station, a bus, a medical car, and an armed escort vehicle. The latter remained a necessity due to regular mujahideen attacks. *Agitprop's* task was to distribute leaflets about the Soviet Union and explain the reasons for the LCST's presence, the PDPA's reforms, and negotiate ceasefires with the mujahideen. The units also provided medicine and food to remote Afghan villages, showed movies and organized concerts, brought doctors and dentists, collected complaints, and repaired infrastructure, including mosques.[109] The units were most efficient when they included PDPA cadres who could address the population's concerns. After 1986, *agitprop's* task became to build support for Najibullah's national reconciliation and prepare for the LCST's withdrawal. The units then increasingly went into mujahideen-held areas to offer truces.

In many ways, the *agitprop* remained a military endeavor. The units sometimes incorporated KGB operatives and conducted disinformation about the mujahideen. This ranged from the spreading of accusations against the opposition to the devising of jokes on political topics. In 1985, Pikov proudly claimed that some "50 jokes aimed at discrediting opposition leaders" had been prepared.[110] The LCST also occasionally tasked the units with retrieving Soviet soldiers' bodies in exchange for aid.[111] This awkward mix of humanitarian and covert military objectives, along with the Soviets' lack of familiarity with the context, may have ultimately limited *agitprop's* impact.[112] Nonetheless, Afgantsy usually accredit the *agitprop* units with a positive role.

By the mid-1980s, the *agitprop* units ended up incorporating Afghan mullahs as a sign of the concessions on ideology made in the second phase of the war. This showed how special propaganda became more sophisticated and better considered Afghanistan's specificities. As noted by Pikov, because of "the population's high religiosity," it became important "to skillfully use some provisions of the Koran." *Spetspropagandists* had to know Islam to connect with the population.[113] The Soviets were here though on safer ground by relying on proregime mullahs while they provided aid and showed photographs of Central Asia and movies such as *White Sun of the Desert* about the Basmachi revolt. In fine, the *agitprop's* story embodies the Soviets' incapacity to fully connect with Afghans and counter mujahideen propaganda. During the war, it was always predominantly up to the PDPA to win the population's support, including by highlighting how it was now respectful of Islam.

Karmal's Islamic Socialism

Soviet advice to the PDPA did not change following the intervention while the CC CPSU Department of Information discussed steps to build support for Karmal. Regarding Islam, it again intimated bringing the "middle and smaller ranks of the clergy" to the PDPA's side. Karmal was to attract believers by clarifying the party's stance on Islam "considering Afghanistan's specificities" and "establish regulated state relations with religion." Otherwise said, Moscow wanted Kabul to use its own bureaucratic model of state-Islam relations. In addition to Islamic leaders, the Soviets advised Karmal to tactically co-opt other "reactionaries."[114] Aside from such general policy recommendations, the Soviets themselves had no idea about how the Afghans were to tackle Islamic policy. This was a daunting task for Karmal, even more so since he had to account for Khalq's abuses and explain the Soviets' presence.[115] Still, religion became a topic on which his regime focused to boost its legitimacy. Relying on the radio, the television, the news agency Bakhtar and newspapers such as *Khakikat-e Inquilab-e Saur* (*Truth of the April Revolution*), the daily of the CC PDPA, *Kabul New Times*, the English-language daily, *Khivad* (*Motherland*) and *Anis*, it, as often as possible, paid respect to Islam. The media featured state officials and loyal Islamic scholars discussing Islam. They furthermore stressed Karmal's role in Afghan politics before 1978 to increase his political legitimacy and inscribe him into Afghan history.[116]

A discursive shift toward religion was noticeable immediately after Karmal's arrival. On 19 January 1980, Bakhtar published an "Address of the Presidium of the DRA to the Muslims of Afghanistan and the World" that asserted that the April Revolution was the "materialization of the will of the country's Muslim people toward the assertion of authentic social justice and a colossal step on the path to the materialization of the ancient aspirations of true Muslims." The April Revolution was no longer "proletarian," an Amin-era expression. The address presented it instead as part of a global Muslim struggle for liberation. It argued that the ideologies of the April Revolution and Islam converged around social justice, implying that the PDPA's program was indeed Islamic. Finally, it introduced an international angle by denouncing imperialist meddling and linking the April Revolution and the Islamic Revolution in Iran.[117] This argument served a double purpose: it drew on Iran's Islamic legitimacy to boost the PDPA's standing and pursued a policy of building a joint anti-American front with Tehran as explained in chapter 5.

A speech by Karmal on 26 January 1980 confirmed that the narrative toward Islam had changed. It introduced a new official Islamic language that marked a stark contrast with Khalq's era when officials often left talk about religion to proregime *ulemas*:

> The sacred religion Islam, our national traditions and the traditions of our ancestors [are] the precious heritage of our people and no one has the right . . . to oppose them. . . . Amin and his criminal band have per-

secuted a great number of spiritual leaders, mullahs . . . and elders of various tribes. . . . The Revolutionary Council . . . with all sincerity, declares again the complete freedom of cults, national customs and traditions, the complete freedom to follow these traditions and worship whatever believers are Sunni or Shia.[118]

After this Karmal continued to present the regime as a defender of religion. He would explain that "it was necessary in accordance with . . . the holy Koran and *sharia* to punish each person who dared to shamelessly violate the ideals of Islam."[119] His January speech also marked the start of a policy change as he made into law the measures supporting Islam. Religious figures were notably to regain their "offices, positions and assets" if they switched to the regime's side.[120] The Kremlin approvingly noted that this marked "definite shifts in the engagement with religious officials."[121]

Karmal then revised Khalq's policies that Afghans saw as especially un-Islamic. Some of his amendments were symbolic and tactical; others were major policy changes. Regarding the former, the regime now systematically celebrated Muslim holidays and festivals, such as Eid al-Fitr and the birthday of Prophet Muhammad (Mawlid), a practice that had been only irregularly present under Khalq. Karmal himself visited mosques, including when touring provinces as in Herat in 1982, and the whole "party and state leadership" participated in *namaz* on the Eid al-Fitr in 1985.[122] Maiorov hence noted how the Soviets often saw Afghan communists pray in public though professing atheism in private.[123] As noted by the US embassy, Karmal was making considerable efforts at convincing Afghans that he led an "Islamic government."[124] During Ramadan, the curfew was shortened to accommodate believers who wanted to attend morning and evening prayers at the mosque, propaganda about religion on television was increased, *sharia* courts run by *qadis* (judges)—though in greatly reduced numbers—were allowed to operate to deal with family and personal issues, and the school curricula now included three hours a week of Islamic education. In some provinces, classes were resegregated by sex and education was made voluntary for women. Afghan pioneers, a Soviet import, and PDPA youth "volunteered" to clean Kabul's mosques for the second plenum of the CC DOMA. Beyond this, the PDPA now provided fuel for mosques and restored the ones destroyed by the opposition. Between January 1980 and August 1985, it reportedly reconstructed 57 mosques and restored another 527 in Kabul alone.[125] It also paid stipends to loyal Muslim scholars, helped their families with accommodation, and financed pilgrimages to Mecca and holy places in Afghanistan.[126] While Amin had introduced some of these measures, Karmal had massively expanded the policies supporting Islam.

The Afghan communists, meanwhile, tried to identify the mullahs who could, in the words of a party bureaucrat, help in "building a new Afghanistan."[127] They organized national assemblies of Islamic scholars, a risky endeavor that at first led to criticism of the communists' policies. On the Soviet model, the scholars' support was then institutionalized through the creation of the High Council of Ulemas and the Clergy, instead of Amin's makeshift council, in June 1980, and of the General Department of Islamic Affairs at the end of 1980.[128] In 1985, the transformation of the General Department of Islamic Affairs into a Ministry of Islamic Affairs and Waqfs marked an important step in the institutionalization process.[129] The AIC underlined that this intensified the regime's "political and religious propaganda."[130] Hojjat, whom we encountered as part of SAFS, headed the new ministry.[131] Embracing the regime's new Islamic rhetoric, the change came in a decree that abundantly quoted the Koran, used the Islamic greeting, and interestingly announced the holding of a *loya jirga*, the legal grand assembly of elders and authorities conveyed throughout Afghan history to draft constitutions and provide leadership during crises. The regime was simultaneously attempting to prove its Islamic credentials, deprive the mujahideen of their justification for the war, and transform the political environment by creating political legitimacy for itself through the *loya jirga*. Yet, the problem for Karmal was that the Soviet presence delegitimized attempts at co-opting Islam and organizing political assemblies. Beyond this, the very creation of a Ministry of Islamic Affairs underlined that the regime itself, like some other leftist regimes in Muslim countries, was not intrinsically Islamic but needed a separate organ to deal with Islam. This illustrated how the Central Asian SADUM-CRA model was not adapted to Afghanistan.

As pro-Kabul Islamic institutions consolidated, the mujahideen started targeting them. Mohammad Yousaf, the Pakistani Inter-Services Intelligence (ISI)'s brigadier in charge of Afghan operations, noted that "Soviets, KhAD agents, government officials and their facilities" could be the focus of assassinations and attacks. "Educational institutions" were also "fair game" because they were guilty of "corrupting the youth of the country, turning them away from" Islam; and so were proregime Islamic scholars.[132] In 1984, Keshtmand reported that the mujahideen had killed more than 200 of them.[133] That campaign of violence demonstrated that in some areas, particularly in the North, the PDPA's work to attract Islamic figures to its side was seen as a threat by the opposition. Even Western observers noted that in the more secularized cities, PDPA's efforts on Islam were not fruitless.[134] At the same time, Keshtmand's number remained relatively small for a country with hundreds of thousands of religious specialists. This indicated that the PDPA still struggled to co-opt Islamic scholars.

Proregime Islamic scholars' functions included supporting political initiatives such as the National Fatherland Front (NFF). Created in 1981, it tried to give the impression of a growing popular base for the regime. It also played a role in religious policy by appointing some mosque imams and including among its leadership religious leaders, such as *Mawlawi*, a title given to a scholar who had completed his studies at a *madrasa*, Sayyed Afghani who would also head the General Department of Islamic Affairs until 1983 and *Mawlawi* Mohammad Salem Elmi. Elmi was the archetype of the Islamic leader supporting Kabul, a red mullah who went to opposition-held villages "with the Koran in his right hand and a Kalashnikov in his left."[135] He tried to garner support for the communists in areas of intense military activities, including in eastern Paktia Province during Operation Magistal', the last major Soviet operation of the war in 1987. However, even if someone like Elmi may have commanded respect in parts of Afghanistan, he and other possibly well-meaning Islamic leaders were mixed among Afghan and Soviet *apparatchiks* of the International Department in the NFF. This no doubt undermined their religious legitimacy.

In parallel, loyal religious leaders issued statements in support of the regime. Karmal would order them to explain "the government's positions about Islam" and expose "the lying propaganda of the enemies."[136] Following the adoption of the law on mandatory military service in 1981, they also used religious justifications to incite Afghans to join the army. Afghani would assert that it was "a holy duty" for each citizen.[137] In 1984, the party expanded that strategy by creating propaganda commissions of Islamic figures under the NFF who publicized the PDPA reforms in mosques and tried to boost conscription.[138] Although it now abstained from calling for jihad, the communists as the mujahideen were using Islam to mobilize Afghans for war.

The communists also recruited mullahs into the military to organize *namaz* and conduct propaganda activities. As recalled by a Soviet soldier from Uzbekistan, the Afghans he served with were practicing Muslims who once stopped almost mid-battle to pray.[139] Yet, testifying to the regime's struggle to find enough volunteers for a work seen as demeaning, the PDPA only managed to enlist some 200 mullahs by the mid-1980s.[140] This number grew modestly in Najibullah's time when Kabul gave more importance to Islam. By 1988, 203 mullahs served as officers and 127 served as soldiers, 63 of whom were in training to become officers at the Kabul University's Theology Faculty. To attract candidates, conditions were at that time made more advantageous, offering relatively high salaries and the possibility to avoid combat operations and, depending on the place, live at home. By the time of the Soviet withdrawal, an *agitprop* group of mullahs was even set up to organize celebrations and lectures and write handbooks.[141]

More fundamentally, Karmal reviewed some of Khalq's emblematic reforms. He replaced the all-red flag with the traditional tricolor that featured the color green, a *mihrab* (the semi-circular niche in the wall of a mosque pointing to the *qibla*, the direction of the *Kaaba* in Mecca), and a *minbar* (the pulpit in the mosque where the Imam stands when delivering sermons). The changes, as explained by Karmal, reflected the "objective realities of the Afghan society" and "[its] Islamic character."[142] They also immediately led to renewed tensions inside the PDPA as Khalq opposed Parcham's "moderation" and "respect for Islam designed to placate the hostile populace."[143]

In a similar perspective, the revision to Khalq's land reform was Karmal's most controversial, far-reaching, and symbolic measure. As in any leftist revolution, the land reform was the pivot around which Kabul wished to build its appeal; amendments to it questioned the Afghan communists' entire platform. At the same time, although the Soviets had a limited influence in piloting religious policy, Moscow and its advisers engaged extensively in designing the land reform. Significantly, the fact that Karmal still never got it right presented another vivid illustration of the limits of the Soviet recommendations.

The International Department formulated a summary criticism of Amin's policies and sent it to Tabeev in early 1980. The Soviets were especially unhappy with how Khalq had managed the land reform. The Afghan communists had rushed it and overlooked well-tested tactics to not antagonize landowners. Including army officers, Islamic scholars, and *waqf* lands in the reform had been an enormous mistake for the Soviets.[144] As the International Department noted, "the political importance of showing flexibility in maneuvering toward Islam, which was so strong and influent in the country, its traditional institutions and, accordingly, religious leaders did not need to be demonstrated." Yet "exceptions on that account in the reform's law were completely missing." Flexibility toward Islamic scholars was one of the three Soviet recommendations. The Soviets also advised the Afghans to be more cunning toward landowners by promising them compensations for expropriated lands that would, the report stated bluntly, not materialize—the Soviets pointed here to the example of Algeria—and exempting army officers from the expropriations. In many ways, this was about constituting a local privileged elite tied to the Kabul regime.

Despite the dire situation, the International Department believed that there was still time to adjust the land reform. Its advice then became the blueprint for Karmal's amendments in August 1981. The revised reform now stated that:

> Article 2. *Waqf* lands, belonging to holy sites of the religion of Islam, . . . cannot be seized and remain in the use of their custodians. Article 3. Surpluses of land areas included in the plots of religious scholars, imams

of mosques, . . . and leaders of other cults . . . cannot be seized and remain in their possession and use. These land areas cannot be sold or hypothecated by their current owners and are transmitted in heritage indivisibly to rightful heirs on the condition of the continuation of the corresponding religious office. Article 4. Surpluses of land areas included in the plots of chiefs, elders of tribes, who have contributed to the fight against the domestic and foreign counterrevolution . . . cannot be seized. Article 5. Surpluses of land areas included in plots of officers, who are serving in the armed forces, cannot be seized.[145]

The communists additionally decided that peasants would receive land for a symbolic amount of money instead of free.[146] These adjustments helped display the land reform as in accordance with the Koran and exemplified how the PDPA tried to rebrand its platform to appeal to and reward Islamic scholars, army officers, and tribal leaders. These groups were the ones whose support the regime desperately needed against the mujahideen. The PDPA would woo them until the end of the war. At the same time, the revisions exemplified how the Soviets, led by the International Department, provided advice that suggested integrating Islam only tactically, not hiding that, as soon as they pacified the country, another policy would be possible. No Islamic socialism was in the cards for Afghanistan.

The new land reform, however, did not assuage Soviet criticism. While praising Karmal's revisions in late 1981, the Soviet embassy remarked that distributing land on paper was not enough to gain support from the population. If the PDPA pursued the reform as is, it "may further worsen the domestic political situation." Up to now, the Soviets assessed, the reform had been a disaster, leading to "unjustified distribution of state lands and pastures, lack of an actual delimitation of the land parcels' borders . . . ; lack of a scientific approach to determining the parcels' size; ignorance of traditional, religious and national characteristics; cases of direct violation of revolutionary laws; [and] repressions of peasants, corruption, and bribery."[147] Some communist leaders and their families, the Soviets noted, had kept substantial land for themselves. Moreover, the PDPA had made no effort to devise water reform without which the land reform made little sense. The *Pravda* journalist encountered above also believed that the reform had failed. The PDPA returning lands to mullahs and army officers had sometimes led to new issues because senior military officers were often from rich landowner families, as were the tribal elders and some Parcham leaders. Many Afghan peasants did not understand these "corrections and their timing."[148]

In 1982–83, land reform remained the principal area of engagement for CPSU advisers who continued to call on the PDPA to better involve the Islamic scholars. According to Polyanichko, they even advocated for sending Afghan mullahs to Central Asia so they could see how agriculture was organized there.[149] Yet this only highlighted how the Soviets failed again to understand how their modernization model was not appealing in Afghanistan. The bottom line was that the PDPA struggled to pursue its radical transformative project while at the same time appealing to traditional authorities for political legitimacy. Conversely, the Soviets themselves seemed to be oblivious to this tension.

Ultimately, the land reform considerably hurt the PDPA. It broke the dependency structures between peasants and landlords without replacing them with new ones, leading to issues with water allocation and production tools' ownership. The Afghan communists did not try to fix these problems, being afraid that it may lead to even more opposition from traditional authorities. By 1982–83, the PDPA put the reform on hold and only used it as a counterinsurgency tool to reward or punish peasants based on their relationship with the mujahideen. In the Najibullah era, new revisions that raised the land ceiling rendered the reform largely irrelevant for 95 percent of Afghans. By then, peasants effectively received and cultivated only 15–20 percent of the country's land, mostly formerly state-owned.[150] While Karmal had dutifully adapted it to local Islamic realities, the land reform had failed due to both being flawed from the start and revised only ad-hoc to suit the counterinsurgency agenda. The same was true of the measures aimed at making the regime appear more Islamic.

One critical issue was with the backgrounds of the Islamic scholars recruited by the PDPA. Most had had no national role before 1980. Until his death in 1985, Afghani was the only Pashtun Islamic figure with a high-level Islamic education from Al-Azhar University in Cairo, the most renown center for Islamic education; Hojjat, the leader during the later years, was a Tajik with limited credentials. Jalil Yusufi, the head of the University of Kabul's Faculty of Theology, was an Uzbek educated at Al-Azhar whom the communists had deemed unreliable and kept for ceremonial purposes only. Overall, the PDPA had promoted many scholars through the ranks from unorthodox elements with early communist sympathies. Hojjat, for example, had been a Maoist early on. By 1984, however, even he had to concede that the regime's Islamic institutions had been unable to find representatives with proper credentials for all provinces. In parallel, the KhAD and KGB consolidated networks of support among the Shia clergy in the Hazarajat, a region in central Afghanistan. But even more than Sunni scholars originating from ethnic minorities, they had a limited national legitimacy.[151] Underlying the contrast, senior Pashtun Sunni

Islamic scholars who had survived Khalq's rule had reemerged in Pakistan, where they organized the mujahideen.

Testifying to Kabul's enduring distrust toward religion, KhAD's 7th Department closely managed the loyal Islamic scholars. It also monitored the activities of neutral and hostile mullahs. Thanks to KGB funding, it could reportedly support mullahs across 12,000 towns and 38,000 villages, and key "Muslim personalities" in cities between 1980 and 1982.[152] The KhAD 7th Department's work also involved infiltrating operatives among scholars to proselytize in support of the regime. The operatives tried to both defuse the idea that the war was about fighting godless communists and, interestingly, articulate a theological base for PDPA's policies.[153] A senior officer from KhAD argued, in hindsight, that their job was about "preventing a political interpretation of Islam and, on the opposite, [pushing] for [a] traditional view of Islam."[154] This sounded strikingly like Khalq's old approach to religion. The communists were still only ready to tolerate Islam if it stayed clear of politics; even better if it served the regime.

Beyond this, the sheer number of Islamic specialists in Afghanistan made it impossible to incentivize or even monitor them all, especially outside of communist-held areas. The Afghans' work with Islamic leaders even elicited occasional criticism in Moscow. The Soviets were, for example, dismayed that Kabul failed to support the families of Islamic scholars killed by the mujahideen, a fact that the latter unsurprisingly used in their propaganda. Likewise, a document about Afghan policy at the CC CPSU noted that Karmal, contrary to all Soviet advice, had conducted repressions against the clergy and tribal authorities until the very end of his rule.[155] Such contradictions and oversights demonstrated how, despite the Islamic facade built for the regime, the PDPA under Karmal remained a Marxist-Leninist party that often denigrated Islam.

During the war, the AIC and the mujahideen naturally played on these limitations to dismiss Karmal's Islamic policies. After noting that, as compared to Khalq's rule, a major shift had been the adoption of an "open pro-Islamic stance" by the PDPA, the AIC rightly argued that it was not enough to have loyal Islamic scholars "find religious justifications" for communist policies. Kabul, it argued, would struggle with its "Islamic propaganda" "as long as Islam [was] not proclaimed as the official religion of the state" and "well-known religious personalities in the resistance [had not] confirmed the legitimacy of the regime."[156] The mujahideen meanwhile intoned the same tune. "The communist regime," they noted, "tried to show that it was respecting Ramadan but hypocrisy revealed itself" and "people did not attend the congregational prayers led by the so-called mullahs on government payroll."[157] In a society that valued

FIGURE 3.3.   A Mujahideen propaganda poster about Karmal (Hi-Story | Alamy Stock Photo). The Mujahideen saw Karmal as trying to speak the language of Islam while being a supporter of the Soviets and communism at heart.

linage and long-established ways of acquiring Islamic legitimacy, the PDPA could not boost the standing of its Islamic scholars simply by appointing them to high posts. Another problem was that the Islamic rhetoric continued to be lost among the Marxist jargon that infused the PDPA leaders' speeches. The AIC thus sarcastically remarked that "the Afghan villager" still "[did] not know what 'imperialism,' 'chauvinism,' 'feudalism,' 'proletariat,' etc. mea[nt]."[158]

Such was the issue with the communists' strategy: The PDPA was ready to review measures unacceptable to believers but not to forsake the socialist ideal. Many party cadres remained anticlerical. In a representative case, an official summarily dismissed a mullah wanting to join the PDPA.[159] The mujahideen's propaganda similarly made a huge deal of the fact that, despite the regime's Islamic rhetoric, party cadres "hurt the sanctity of the month [of Ramadan] by eating in public."[160] They and, as we will see, Karmal personally, were not observant in religious matters. Likewise, anti-Islamic propaganda, despite the Islamic education in schools, crept into the higher education system. According to a defector, the PDPA conducted a "de-Islamization in military academies." "Religious subjects were simply removed and replaced by 'Principles of Marxism-Leninism' and 'Political Economy,'" leading to resistance from students.[161] In other words, there was still no coherent strategy on Islam by the mid-1980s.

The PDPA officially argued for convergence between Islam and socialism, but under the dominance of the latter and with freedom of worship and equality between Sunni and Shia Muslims. Instead of devising a symbiotic relation with Islam, it insisted on the positive changes brought by the April Revolution. Such a message came short of most people's aspiration to see Sunni Islam return to its central place in Afghanistan and become part of the way of life again. When proclaiming the PDPA's action plan in 1982, Karmal claimed that the April Revolution's drive to establish "social justice and equality" was "one of the main values, of the main traditions of the holy religion of Islam." He took the examples of Algeria, Syria, Libya, and South Yemen to back his argument: "revolutionary transformations" did not contradict "the social content of Islam" in these countries.[162] Yet no one could describe their leftist regimes as "Islamic." They could not represent an acceptable model for Afghans even if they knew enough about them. In 1984–85, Karmal's speeches only made cursory mention of religion. This became typical of how party leaders treated Islam as they tried to instrumentalize it to build the PDPA's religious legitimacy. As noted by a Soviet adviser and an Afghan official in DOMA, many in the PDPA leadership did not "know the language of the people" of Afghanistan and understand Islam.[163]

"To the Soviet Soldier about Afghanistan"

Soviet Soldiers initially had little understanding of the Afghan context, although Central Asians slightly helped in filling cultural gaps. To address the problem, the Soviet military authorities disseminated handbooks about Afghanistan to the LCST. Interestingly, instead of the Afghanists, the same military advisers who dealt with *agitprop*, including Shershnev and Gennady Arzumanov, authored the handbooks. This explained why these, too, served as an example of the Soviet ideological approach. The handbooks had to be both informative, helping the Soviet soldiers survive in Afghanistan, and propagandistic, maintaining the well-established Marxist-Leninist tropes. Throughout the war, they navigated this thin line. Their evolution over time demonstrated some of the issues faced by the LCST when dealing with the Afghans and the changing Soviet policy on Afghanistan.[164]

Edited by the Political Directorate of the Turkestan Military District, one of the first handbooks in 1981, entitled *Sovetskomu voinu ob Afganistane (To the Soviet Soldier about Afghanistan)*, was fifty pages long and comprised sections about Afghanistan's history, territorial administration, political regime, civil society organizations, population, social structure, national and tribal relations, Islam, customs and traditions, economy, transformations under the communists, media, and the army. The final sections examined political issues: the nature of the opposition to the PDPA, the "Achievements of the April Revolution," and Soviet-Afghan relations. The handbook then concluded with recommendations to Soviet soldiers and maps of Afghanistan.

While the handbook provided wide-ranging basic information about Afghanistan, Marxist-Leninist jargon and dogma permeated its pages. The handbook called the PDPA the "vanguard of the working class" and argued that, thanks to the April Revolution, "power had passed from a small feudal grouping, making only 5% of the populace . . . to the revolutionary-democratic forces." As most Soviet soldiers could figure out, such statements were disingenuous; there were few workers in Afghanistan and the PDPA led by the Parchamis was a diverse group that included some of the previous elites. Still, the handbook upheld a class-struggle perspective, typically complaining that the Afghan peasantry's lack of "class consciousness" explained the PDPA's lack of support.[165] Again, Soviet soldiers, painfully aware that Afghans operated using different concepts, probably quickly came to doubt such statements.

The handbook also showed how Moscow had refined its justifications for the conflict as compared to 1979. First, it explained that the Soviets had come to support "brotherly" Afghanistan because "imperialism had started an undeclared war" against it. This had, in turn, "created a direct threat to the [Soviet Union's] southern border's security" that "forced [the USSR] to provide the military help demanded by a friendly country."[166] The argument combined internationalism and patriotism but said nothing of US soldiers allegedly already being in Afghanistan at the intervention's start. Second, the handbook stayed clear of PDPA politics and strangely did not criticize Amin. Perhaps the Soviet policymakers saw the topic as too subtle; they may have believed that it was better for Soviet soldiers not to raise these problematic issues with their commanders or the Afghans. Meanwhile, the handbook adamantly upheld the official line: Karmal and his supporters had removed Amin in an outlandish coup before the Soviets' arrival. Confronted with the daily manifestations of the Khalq-Parcham split, Soviet soldiers may have here too quickly understood that something was amiss in the PDPA.

On religion, the handbook reflected the traditional Soviet limitations; it failed to well-explain Islam's spiritual, cultural, and social roles in Afghan society including, for instance, even the difference between Sunnism and Shiism. It also painted Islam as mostly hostile to the April Revolution. Noting that there were some 250,000 Afghan mullahs, the handbook asserted that "a considerable part of them were fighting the revolution." After a summary on the mujahideen, the handbook noted that "the Reaction was trying to cover its aggressive actions . . . with the flag of religion, calling itself 'zealots' of Islam, 'defenders of the faith against the godless communist government.'" Soviet soldiers could not but understand that Islam was against them and vice versa. This was a short-sighted message to disseminate. The handbook's half-hearted attempt to nuance it by quoting Lenin's statement that "the communists were showing respect for the religious beliefs" of Muslims and that "liberation struggles could be waged under the banner of Islam" made little difference.[167] In short, the handbook adhered to the old Bolshevik idea that Islam may be a step toward socialism in "backward" countries. Yet, in Afghanistan, which was on its way to modernity, it only hindered progress.

The handbook also used Lenin's quote to explain the PDPA's Islamic policies, including the incorporation of mullahs into the army and the creation of mosques near Afghan garrisons. These aspects seemed to contradict earlier statements and likely added to the Soviet soldiers' confusion, especially since their leaders meanwhile told them that religion and socialism were, in the long run, mutually exclusive. The handbook continued to stumble on Islam by immediately nuancing the impact of Karmal's Islamic policies. "It would be wrong to overestimate the positive transformations in the mindsets of the Muslim clergy," it argued, and "underestimate the still remaining threat . . . of conspiracies and machinations from . . . extreme right clerical circles."[168] This was the idea in 1981. Islamic scholars, save for a few exceptions, were with the counterrevolution and, therefore,—the enemy. As to Lenin's liberation struggles, there was the need for a considerable stretch of the imagination to apply that label to the PDPA backed by Soviet bayonets. Maiorov's noted this paradox as he heard the PDPA "pray" for "Allah to punish . . . the infidels." While the LCST was in-country, who could seriously think that the infidels were the mujahideen?[169]

The handbook gave considerable practical advice to soldiers on how to behave near holy places, about the necessity to respect Islamic holidays and
prayers, not to hail women in the street, be respectful when visiting Afghans'
homes, and not ask women to remove their *chadaree*.[170] Attesting to these cultural aspects' importance, the military command distributed a handbook spe-
cifically about them in 1984.[171] It added information on the importance of
respecting village elders, the system of compensation for offenses, the blood
feud, the ceremonies accompanying burial and weddings, and Afghan super-
stitions. Pilgrimages to holy places were listed in this last category as a sign of
how the Soviets saw such practices. As remarked by a Kazakh veteran, the practical recommendations constituted the handbook's most useful part because
the Soviets received little information before departure. Central Asians, he argued, "coming from Muslim countries [*sic*] knew a bit, how to interact with
women, that it was forbidden to address women in *paranja*," but "fellows from
Russia, Ukraine—they read these books, because they had to know about
that."[172] The recommendations remained supplemented by essentializing re-
marks on Afghans' behavior and way of life, picturing them as "cunning but
freedom-loving people." These were the traditional stereotypes Russians attached to "Easterners" and "Southerners" such as the Basmachi. Vividly, they
would similarly transpire in assessments of Karmal.

The Soviet soldiers received another edition of the general handbook in
1987. As compared to 1981, the changes were not in the basic information on
Afghanistan but in the sections on communist policy and ideology. The new
handbook showed the modest influence of Gorbachev's wish to withdraw and
of Najibullah's attempts at changing his regime's platform. Much stayed the
same. The handbook still presented the clergy as mostly hostile to the regime
while Marxist-Leninist tropes permeated the text. It typically claimed that the
PDPA's policies "had helped the growth of class consciousness." However, the
handbook noted, "that process was encountering great difficulties . . . due to
the century-old humiliation and backwardness of peasant masses, additionally backed by the Muslim clergy's resilient influence."[173] This was the message the Soviet policymakers shared with the LCST while at the same time
Najibullah, with their support, would launch a policy to co-opt Islam and scrap
Marxism-Leninism. The 1987 general handbook hence trailed the changing
strategy in Afghanistan. On Islam, it was more critical than a book for the general Soviet audience released in 1984. The latter at least argued that, while the
"higher clergy" was against the communists, its lower and middle ranks had
"started co-operating with the new organs of power."[174] The principal reason
for that discrepancy was likely that propaganda on Afghanistan in the USSR
needed to concern itself less with reflecting the reality. By contrast, the hand-

books had to reconcile propaganda with an imperative to help soldiers inter-act with the population, build support for the LCST and, ultimately, survive.

In each company, the *zampolit*, a portmanteau word meaning deputy com-mander for political work, played a role in educating the soldiers and dissemi-nating the information from the handbooks. One such officer in a KGB border guard unit on the Soviet-Afghan border recalled how he organized classes on Afghanistan and Soviet domestic and foreign policy in-between operations. The unit's fighters had then to write essays based on these lectures. Although things were certainly laxer in the LCST, this showed the weight given to hav-ing the soldiers know their Marxism-Leninism and the handbooks' informa-tion.[175] As recalled by a Kyrgyz conscript, the *zampolit* in their unit, occasionally seconded by the KGB, rehearsed with them how to behave with Afghans, mak-ing them learn sentences in Dari. He though talked about Islam only rarely beyond explaining that "[Afghans] did *namaz* five times a day . . . and that was why everything went quiet and that they had an Islamic republic while [the Soviets] had atheism."[176] This demonstrated how soldiers often had to fill the gaps about religion on their own.

The *zampolits* relied on special handbooks issued by the Political Director-ate of the Turkestan Military District. These were often both more ideologi-cal and transparent regarding Soviet thinking than the general handbooks. They typically prepared the LCST to interact with Afghans and fight the mu-jahideen. One handbook from 1985 was titled *Knowing and Respecting the Tra-ditions, Morals, and Customs of the Afghan People, While abroad, Keeping High the Honor and Dignity of the Soviet Soldier.*[177] It provided material for in-Afghanistan lectures and better explained Islam's multilayered role in Afghan society while repeating the same practical recommendations to Soviet soldiers. A similar handbook from 1987 dealt with Afghan customs and traditions as part of a course that had sections on the global arms race, the handling of personal weapons, and new recommendations describing how Soviets soldiers had to mind their behavior and stay clear of drugs in Afghanistan.[178] Repeating stan-dard ideas about Afghan "backwardness" and Soviet internationalist support, that handbook was notable for its very existence. Soviet policymakers deemed by then context knowledge to be important enough to come together with ideological preparation.

By contrast, a special handbook from 1985, evocatively titled *Actual Prob-lems of Creating among the Contingent the Understanding of the Goals and Tasks of the Presence of the Soviet Forces in the DRA, Class Hatred toward the Afghan Revo-lution's Enemies,* clarified the reasons for the Soviet presence. The LCST was, first, to help the PDPA and its revolution and, second, to defend the Soviet Union. The handbook developed that second part by arguing that because the

United States, following the loss of Iran, had wanted to establish bases on the Soviet border, "the [Soviet] authorities" had made the "decision to send the LCST to the DRA."[179] The handbook explained this in one paragraph after ten pages on the April Revolution, the made-up story of Amin's removal, and internationalism's meaning. It was as if the handbook's authors believed that the second justification for the intervention would be more understandable to the soldiers than the first. As opposed to the general handbooks, this one mentioned the US's disruptive role in Afghanistan. Yet, it gave little evidence of its activities. It is not clear to what extent that argument landed in the LCST, given the absence of US soldiers and long even US-made weapons. In many ways, embracing the Cold War paradigm and Marxism-Leninism seemed to be more a matter of faith for the Soviets.

That handbook was remarkable for what it said about US propaganda. It warned the LCST about the US-backed *Radio Kabul* that claimed that the Soviets had come to destroy Islam in Afghanistan and attacked the Soviet "way of life."[180] To neutralize the first argument, the handbook encouraged political officers to invite Afghan communists to conduct lectures on Soviet-Afghan friendship. It is unclear if this helped in defusing the idea that the Soviets were against Islam and the population given that the PDPA itself visibly struggled with building popular support. The second point was even more interesting. It betrayed the concern that rather than Soviet Muslims being contaminated by Islamism in Afghanistan, the Kremlin feared that the LCST would be exposed to classic Western capitalist propaganda.

Ultimately, two special handbooks dealt with religion. The Soviet policymakers believed that they needed to explain the USSR's take on Islam to the LCST, especially since it had become the main discursive signifier in mujahideen propaganda. A handbook from 1982, titled *Islam in Modern Afghanistan, The PDPA's Policy toward Religion* explained why Karmal's Islamic policy was unavoidable. After repeating Lenin's classic quote on Islam, it noted that "Islam had become the flag of the counterrevolution and mullahs its main supporters." For this reason, the PDPA was working to "attract the wide masses of Muslims." Yet, it encountered difficulties because: "The events happening now in the DRA were objectively undermining the social roots of religion, bringing considerable corrections to the clergy's role. Islam's positions however remained and would continue for long to remain quite strong. It is enough to say that among the overwhelming majority [of Afghans], religious consciousness still dominated over class consciousness . . . Islam was for believers a way of thinking and behaving."[181]

It was crucial to remember, the handbook noted, that "mullahs remained a privileged class." Few among them supported an idea akin to "Islamic so-

cialism." "Most in the clergy were for an 'Islamic way of development' without the inclusion of the concept of socialism; [they] would not even accept
the word 'socialism' in combination with Islam."[182] This meant that Karmal
was failing in promoting Islam's convergence with the April Revolution. The
mujahideen's targeting of pro-PDPA Islamic scholars further undermined his
Islamic policy. The handbook did not hide that it postulated an opposition between Marxism-Leninism and Islam in Afghanistan. It underscored how Islam was the glue holding the mujahideen together. Mullahs, it noted, led
Islamic committees that administered villages while mosques represented
"strongholds" in mujahideen-held areas.[183] This could only mean, although the
handbook did not say so openly, that the Soviet soldiers had to eliminate the
Islamic leaders.[184] Such an uncompromising narrative was surprising to find
in a handbook that was intended for LCST training. It again showed how the
Kremlin prioritized an ideological approach to Afghanistan. How could the
Soviet soldiers then not see all Islamic scholars as enemies?

The handbook also discussed at length the mujahideen's propaganda. It
noted that they accused the Soviets of being "servants of the devil" and claimed
that the PDPA was "illegitimate according to the Koran." Similar attacks targeted the LCST in mujahideen journals. Likewise, the handbook noted that
mullahs threatened villagers with the "godless and communist idea of collec-
tivism," telling them that "as long as Soviet soldiers were in the Holy Afghan
land, Allah would not accept their prayers." This "reactionary clergy," the
handbook argued, wanted a return to "medieval norms"—opposing mixed
schools, secular education, and unveiled women.[185] The mujahideen's accusations demonstrated that Khalq's social-economic reforms had deeply undermined the Afghan Islamic way of life and remained controversial even following
Karmal's readjustments.

Remarkably, far from acknowledging any mistake, the handbook argued
that the principal problem was with the PDPA's poor information work. Indeed, the mujahideen had succeeded in their propaganda because of Afghans'
"low level of political and class consciousness, illiteracy, and incapacity . . . to
with all clarity see [its] inimical content." Afghans were just unable to fathom
the progress brought by the April Revolution. The handbook followed this note
with an exposition of Karmal's policies. It showed no sign that even part of
the mujahideen's criticism—some of it formulated by the Soviets themselves—
may be legitimate. The handbook listed their accusations for information,
but mostly it presented a picture of enduring ideological opposition between
Marxism-Leninism and Islam. At best, it warily suggested that Karmal's "use
of religious argumentation" to defend the April Revolution was not just "instrumentalization" and "tactic" but that, at the present stage, Islam needed to

be part of policy.[186] This was only to say that the communists could not oppose Islam outright. That was the bottom line of their attitude toward religion under Karmal.

The handbook's final section listed recommendations on how to counter enemy propaganda that were to be either shared with the Afghan army or followed by the Soviets. The LCST was to tell Afghans that "eliminating insurgents did not bring sin and was in accordance with the Koran" because the PDPA was the lawful ruler and, in line with the *sharia*, had invited the LCST and implemented the land reform. Beyond this, the Soviet soldiers, the handbook advised, had to emphasize that they respected Islam and explain that the USSR had just organized an international conference of Islamic scholars in Tashkent. Here, the Soviet soldiers were also to explain that Muslims in the Soviet Union observed the rituals and precepts of Islam and that Afghan Islamic scholars who had traveled to the USSR found that "many socialist ways of doing things . . . were the realization of Prophet Muhammad's dream." Once again, one could wonder what Afghans made of such comments coming from atheist LCST officers through translators. Soviet Muslims in the LCST may also have had mixed feelings, to say the least, when hearing such propaganda. In any case, Afghans were to know that even though the "USSR was not a Muslim country; its government gave Muslims such rights and opportunities that were inaccessible to Muslims in Muslim countries."[187] This was a convoluted way of saying that what was important to Soviet Muslims was economic and industrial development. The Soviet Union was offering the same development package to Afghans: they could live as Soviet Muslims. There was a lack of understanding that Afghans may not be interested in the benefits of Soviet modernity.

That handbook on Islam was a fascinating document that demonstrated the early Soviet efforts at defusing the "Islamic factor" and instrumentalizing religion in support of the PDPA. It unwittingly exemplified the ideological heavy-handedness of the Soviet arguments to counter the mujahideen and the approach to religion in the Karmal era. The communists believed that it would be possible to trick the Afghans into accepting the PDPA as sufficiently Islamic. The handbook candidly made that clear in its conclusion:

> Refusing in principle the idea that it is possible to solve with the help of Islam all social-political problems, the PDPA in parallel considers that given the population of Afghanistan's deep religiosity, the low level of political consciousness of a considerable part of the workers, the country's extreme backwardness, it is impossible to fight for the masses from openly atheistic positions. The PDPA is struggling for Islam,

which continues to be used against the revolution by its enemies, to become a means of mobilization of the masses for social justice and progressive changes in the Afghan society, which had taken a course on the socialist orientation.[188]

This paragraph was a prime example of double-speak. It betrayed the idea that, in the future, when the Soviets had pacified the country, a more aggressive PDPA policy against Islam would be possible. The handbook hence epitomized the Soviet Union's disregard for the context and religion, ideological approach, and support for the PDPA's radical reformist agenda. Afghanistan was to "jump into socialism."

Finally, another special handbook from 1987, titled *The Real Essence of the Islamic Holy War for Faith*, saw the Soviets try to discredit the idea of *jihad*. Some twenty pages long, it featured a dense Marxist-Leninist argumentation. Beyond Soviet party workers, it is difficult to imagine who among the PDPA, Afghan Islamic scholars, or even other Soviet advisers and military could have even understood such a document. Still, the Soviet military released the handbook showing that late into the war Moscow started paying more attention to Islam in Afghanistan, including at a high theoretical level. Without going into the details, the handbook, as expected, concluded with a critique of jihad's pan-Islamic nature. Jihad, it argued, "gave the military efforts of countries for the spread of Islam the form of an above class, pan-national task, independent from the actual character and goals of the wars and military conflicts, from the actual social context of the military violence."[189] Here emerged the old Soviet concern with pan-Islamist ideas that may eventually, although the handbook did not say so, spread to Soviet Muslims.

Central Asians' Higher Loyalty

Central Asian soldiers originally dominated the LCST because recruits mostly came from the Central Asian army reserve and not because, as a Russian *zampolit* claimed, "they had more children."[190] At the intervention's start, Central Asians, with 32,000 soldiers, particularly from Tajikistan, Uzbekistan, and Turkmenistan, represented slightly less than half of the strength of the 40th Army. As many as 65,000 soldiers, including 25,000 in active combat units, passed through the Soviet-Afghan War from Uzbekistan alone.[191] By comparison, some 620,000 Soviets served in Afghanistan, including 520,000 in the military.[192] More strikingly, Central Asians suffered proportionally the most casualties. They recorded 65 killed per million population, as compared to 51.1 killed per million for

Russians and 53.5 on average for all Soviets.[193] The Kremlin's reliance on Central Asians indicated that it did not see them as a liability in Afghanistan despite their kinship and religious ties with the mujahideen and, accordingly, had little fear that they could be a conduit for Islamism spreading to Central Asia. Rather, the Soviet policymakers and ethnic Russian officers in the LCST trusted the Central Asians would bring Afghans to the Soviet point of view. In addition to their "regular job" as "translators, engineers, party activists and university teachers," the Central Asians had "to demonstrate the ability of the system they represented to combine respect for national culture with progress and equality."[194] A soft-power tool, they embodied the end result of what they advised. Many Central Asian veterans recalled that they too assumed they had been selected because of their familiarity with the context, being aware of the recommendations presented in the handbooks, and purported facility in convincing Afghans to embrace communism. Afghanistan was less exotic for them than for Russian conscripts. Far from raising suspicions, this knowledge made Central Asians feel "respected" and "valued" in the LCST.[195] Meanwhile, Central Asia itself, after having long been on the USSR's margins, changed status as it transformed into the Soviet-Afghan War's rear-base.

After mid-1980, the proportion of Central Asians in the LCST decreased. The Bennigsen school and US policymakers interpreted the shift as displaying Soviet fears regarding an Islamist contagion spreading from Afghanistan to Central Asia. This concern played only a limited role.[196] There were few protests during war mobilization in Central Asia and only isolated cases of Central Asians' fraternization with the mujahideen.[197] Other factors explained the Soviet change of mind. As noted by astute Western observers relying on interviews with Soviet veterans, many Central Asians were not in active combat units and were largely absent from elite units. Although a few were part of airborne forces and the two elite "Muslim battalions" linked to the GRU, many served in construction, police, and other support units, and as conscripts. This made them both more visible to external observers and closer to the population.

The main issue with Central Asians was their unpreparedness. The decision to rely on the army reserve—called "partisans" by career military—also testified to the Kremlin's short-sighted approach to the intervention. One veteran recalled how he saw an underequipped unit of Central Asian soldiers, averaging well over forty years old, struggle to deploy in the harsh Afghan winter.[198] This gave a poor image of the Red Army and undermined its effectiveness. The situation was dismal; the LCST command assessed that over 70 percent of reserve officers were incompetent.[199] In this context, the efficient dislocation of the Red Army across Afghanistan in December-January 1980 was indeed an achievement. Then, as the LCST's goals changed, the military command had to replace reserve units with regular ones. If in 1979 the premise was that Afghan forces would handle combat operations, it was clear by the spring of 1980 that the Soviets would do the fighting.[200] By 1982, the LCST's multiethnic composition, equipment, and training had therefore become no different from the Red Army in other places.[201] Beyond this, another problem was that the dispatch of Central Asians had led to ethnic tensions in Afghanistan. Pashtuns were not thrilled to see thousands of people representing Afghan minorities arrive. This again highlighted the extent to which the Kremlin had not thought out even seemingly evident aspects in advance. It simply did not appreciate the importance of national and religious factors.

Another point debunking the myth of Central Asians' untrustworthiness was the limited number of defections among them. A Soviet journalist, who participated in repatriating Soviets personnel who were Missing in Action (MIA) and Prisoners of War (POW), indicated that of the 300 Soviets MIAs and POWs by war's end, only a proportion of this group—perhaps half—were defectors half of whom were Central Asians.[202] Interestingly, in most cases, it was the horrific living conditions and abuse in parts of the LCST and not the ideological aspects or ethnic and religious solidarity which triggered the defections. The Central Asian soldiers who did defect, particularly in the non-Pashtun north, had, nevertheless, an easier time adapting to life in Afghanistan. The Afghan population also generally treated them better than other Soviets.[203]

The mujahideen occasionally called on Central Asians to defect, including in leaflets. During one of the Panjshir offensives, "the *dukhi* [spirits] in the mountains," as recalled by a Kyrgyz soldier, "broadcasted on speakers to 'come, join [them],'" saying they would "'not touch [Central Asians] because [they] were Muslims,'" that they would "'only fire on the Christians, the infidels, the atheists.'"[204] The Kyrgyz soldier, however, made it clear that he did not know anyone who might have been taken in by such calls and that they did not register with him, as probably with other Central Asians, because he "never went to the mosque." He thus saw Afghanistan as a result of his Soviet experience that was characterized more by the social and economic progress and secularization in public life of the 1970s than by the fading memories of the Basmachi. To Central Asians, as highlighted in *zampolits'* lectures, Afghanistan was a backward country whose living standards were nowhere near Central Asia's.

Many Afghan descendants of the Basmachi had likewise been impressed by Central Asia's development when the USSR allowed them to visit their relatives in the 1970s. While some lamented Islam's disappearance from the public sphere—but not from people's homes—and the loss of traditional customs, others highlighted modernity's benefits, including running water, electricity, and the education and healthcare systems.[205] The Soviet advisers in the northern Badakhshan, Herat, Baghlan, Parwan, Kunduz, and Kabul provinces that most benefitted from Soviet infrastructure projects told a similar story. The Soviet development model had appeal in parts of Afghanistan.

Regarding Central Asians' relation to Islam, some soldiers assuredly grew more religious during the Soviet-Afghan War. One Afghan journalist told the story of how a Central Asian soldier begged a mosque in a mujahideen-held village to give him a Koran, telling Afghans that he had sworn to his mother to bring one back home.[206] Although critical of the Soviets, the journalist suggested between the lines that Central Asians were some "lost Muslims." Given the difficulty of procuring a Koran in the USSR, his story is not implausible but it does fantasize about Islam's mass appeal to Central Asians. By contrast, most of them conceptualized religion as a cultural and not a spiritual attribute. They were the products of Marxism-Leninism that presented Afghanistan as a Cold War battlefield and of decades of sovietization. They shared a generational bond through socialization and "military-patriotic" education in the USSR.[207] "You know it," a Kyrgyz soldier said, "at the time we were all atheists." It was odd to him that someone could think anti-Soviet Islamism might appeal to Central Asians. Other Central Asian and Russian Afgantsy gave similar answers. In a focus group discussion involving a Russian *zampolit* in a Central Asian combat unit and two Central Asian veterans, suggesting otherwise was insulting to them. "We did not fight Islam" in Afghanistan, the *zampolit* argued. "If I told [my unit] that we fought Islam, they would have probably shot me first. Every one of them was a Muslim from childhood."[208] Although the question had not been about whether the Soviets had fought Islam, the answer embodied the often-unconscious way in which Central Asians saw Islam. They were atheist Muslims; Islam was for most of them a cultural factor.

The focus group's comments are evocative of how Ambassador Tabeev presented himself to the PDPA and of how other Soviets saw Soviet Muslims. The *spetspropagandist* Pikov hence recalled a significant story about one "clever and competent artilleryman" who was, judging by his name, a Caucasian Muslim. This man once told Pikov: "What *namaz* in the daily agenda of the unit are you talking about? Has there not been a revolution here?" Such comments testified again to the limits of communist Islamic policies and to the Soviets' neglect of Islam but, in this case, Pikov's judgment is as interesting as the Caucasian man's brash statement. Indeed, he reflected that "[this man]—a Muslim—did not understand the meaning of religion in a Muslim country." This was not an isolated case, Pikov argued.[209] He hence equated Soviet Muslims' lack of knowledge about Islam to them not knowing about their republics' history and culture. Pikov wanted them to be both Soviet and Muslim.

Central Asian veterans who participated in a multicountry oral history project on the Soviet-Afghan War expressed similar ideas. More than seventy soldiers were interviewed as part of the project and noted that their loyalty to the USSR and their soldier's duty easily trumped Islamic solidarity in Afghanistan.[210] They saw themselves as both Muslim and Soviet or even, paradoxically, Muslim and atheist. One veteran explained that he was then a "Kazakh, a Muslim," although he "obviously did not know the Koran at the time." His fellow soldier noted that "the Soviet Union was the country of atheism. Religion came to [the Kazakhs] at the beginning of 1990."[211] A third Kazakh veteran explained that "[the soldiers] were all atheists."[212] Veterans from Uzbekistan made similar comments. One bluntly noted that "in the 1980s, it was the highest level of atheism. Religion did not have an impact on Soviet troops."[213]

Even in Tajikistan, a republic where religiousness was more widespread, veterans did not see fighting the mujahideen as connected with Islam. One Tajik veteran explained that he did not pay any heed to the rising religiousness.[214] A fellow soldier remarked that "religion did not have an influence on the [Soviets]."[215] It is remarkable how downplaying Islamic solidarity was common among the veterans' responses, even more so since the post-independence Islamic revival in Central Asia should have made it improper to profess atheism. Most interviewees stated that they had since become practicing Muslims, but only a few declared that Afghanistan had played a role in changing their worldview. One Tajik interviewee noted, in one such rare acknowledgment, that in Soviet times "it was forbidden to call for Friday Prayer on speakers, but in Afghanistan, [Central Asians] heard it five times a day, accordingly, their feelings for religion awakened."[216] It may have shaken some of their professed scientific materialism. More, nonetheless, likely subscribed to the view of one Kazakh veteran who explained: "I could not even imagine that [Islam could lead to conflicting loyalties]. I have been myself reading *namaz* for seven years now. When you stand in the mountains at the given point [for the operation], looking down you see a *kishlak* [village]. You hear from there when the call for prayer is happening, but we knew they were Muslims, that we were Muslims. At that time the military service was more important to us, we defended our country."[217]

Central Asians saw loyalty to the LCST as towering over kinship and religious ties with the mujahideen. Because the practice of Islam was considerably more prevalent among elderly people, the fact that many soldiers were young conscripts also led them to downplay religion.[218] Given the pressure to conform inside the LCST, even the few who had been more observant such as one Tajik son of a mullah who initially refused to eat pork had to fall in line either because there was no other option, in this case for food, or due to the *zampolit's* ideological education.[219] The latter kept "a close eye" on Soviet Muslims so that they would not even think of engaging in Islamic rituals.[220] Seeing that Soviet Muslims were not observant then undermined the Soviet claims that they were as Muslim as the Afghans. It was another vivid illustration of the USSR's contradictory approach to Islam in Afghanistan.

Overall, three things are striking in Central Asians' accounts. First, they stressed their good relations, as compared to other Soviets, with the Afghans due to religious and sometimes linguistic and ethnic proximity. Second, they downplayed the "Islamic factor." Few veterans saw it as an issue that their enemies were Muslims and none questioned his loyalty because of that. It seems that the same was true for Caucasians.[221] Third, Central Asians tended to see Russians as more likely to convert in captivity and defect to the mujahideen, even though, they argued, defections were rare. Many noted the influence of the film *A Muslim* released in 1995 in popularizing this issue in Russia. *A Muslim* recounted the story of a Russian POW who had converted to Islam in captivity before returning years later to his village in Russia. Although fictional, the movie was inspired by Soviet soldiers who had stayed in Afghanistan after the war.

Ultimately, despite their religious and ethnic links with the Afghans, the Central Asian soldiers upheld their loyalty to the USSR during the Soviet-Afghan War. This aligns with the historian Tasar's argument about the convergence that existed between Islam and the communist state in Central Asia by the 1980s. By contrast, the historian Timothy Nunan's story of a Tajik translator, who felt that he was an "insufficient Muslim" as compared to the Afghans, seems to have been either an exception or, at least, shows that such feelings among Central Asians did not challenge their loyalty.[222] Beyond this, the Central Asian soldiers' disregard for Islam suggests that it had little chance of undermining the Soviet state in Central Asia. It helps explain why the Kremlin paid little attention to the Islamist threat. The Central Asians' story also shows another facet of the Soviet failure to connect with the Afghans. They were not the ambassadors of Islamic communism; they were the products of a situation where communism had won and pushed Islam to the private sphere where it survived. They described themselves as Muslims but did not practice the pillars of the faith and saw Islam as a cultural factor. This was unacceptable to most Afghans who did not want to trade their Islamic way of life for that type of modernity.

The Karmal Problem

By the mid-1980s, the Soviets were bogged down in Afghanistan, unable to pacify the whole country or to have the PDPA effectively administer the areas which the communists controlled. Regarding Islam, Karmal's half-hearted reforms and the Soviets' ideological approach had annihilated any chance of building religious legitimacy for the regime or of challenging the mujahideen's propaganda. To the Soviets, a major reason for the stalemate was Karmal himself. They notoriously saw him as lazy, duplicitous, and a drunk.[223] At various times Andropov, Kryuchkov, and other Soviets tried to have him cut down on the drinking but, as in many other respects, to no avail.[224] Meanwhile, Afghans inside and outside the PDPA saw Karmal as a Tajik, the ethnicity of his father, despite his Ghilzai Pashtun mother. This further compromised his capacity to federate the country or the party, especially among the Khalqis.[225] Finally, Karmal was a dogmatic Marxist-Leninist. While this had served him well when the Soviets had come to Afghanistan with Marxism-Leninism in hand, it was bound to become a liability as they began exploring a more flexible approach.

Karmal's radicalism was especially obvious with regard to Islam. An early communist but, unlike Amin and Taraki, coming from a wealthy background as his father was a major general and the Governor of Paktia Province, Karmal was only able to gesture toward religion. His record on Islam was problematic long before 1978. In 1970, Parcham's journal published a poem to celebrate the centenary of Lenin's birth that used for the communist patriarch the benediction reserved for the Prophet ("*dorud bar* Lenin").[226] The episode spurred street protests by mullahs who had traveled to Kabul and led to the closing of the journal.[227] Like Amin, Karmal even had trouble pretending to pay attention to Islam. One rumor, likely false, even accused him of burning a Koran while a member of the Afghan parliament in the 1970s.[228] Another story, this time true, had him refusing to say the "Bismillah" before a speech at the parliament, leading him to be unanimously condemned by fellow deputies, including Amin.

Given his record, it is no surprise that Karmal tried to subsume Islam under his Marxist-Leninist project when he came to power. Speaking to *Newsweek* in 1984, he argued that the PDPA's goal was not "to get rid of religion but to organically integrate it into the revolution."[229] When asked by *Spiegel*, a German journal, in 1985 if the fact that he now prayed at the mosque was meant to appease the conservative population, Karmal only answered that "the April Revolution had guaranteed respect for Islam." Pressed further, he again was unable to, as Amin before him, muster a profession of faith and say that "yes, he was a Muslim."[230] The communists believed that showing respect for Islam by offering economic incentives to mullahs and rebuilding mosques would be enough to deflate most Afghans' belief that the PDPA was godless. This quickly proved a misconception.

Because the Afghan situation was deadlocked, increased Soviet scrutiny of Karmal was unavoidable.[231] Karmal's main value, Ustinov argued at the politburo in 1984, was that there was no one to replace him with. Victor Chebrikov, who had become the KGB's chief after Andropov's promotion, noted, in a comment that recalled Russian orientalist stereotypes about Muslims and Asians, that, while he continued to refuse to take responsibility for Afghan policy, Karmal had become more "cunning" (*khitrit*) with the Soviets, having "got used to being the head of state."[232] In this context, the politburo under Andropov had been reassessing its Afghan strategy considering Karmal's passivity and the impasse on the ground. Voices in the Kremlin had been calling for that since 1982. Vadim Kirpichenko, Kryuchkov's and then Shebarshin's first deputy in the KGB's First Chief Directorate, had contended that it was apparent that "Soviet military, economic and other help to Babrak Karmal would not save his regime and bring stabilization."[233] Many KGB operatives on the ground and military leaders shared this assessment.[234]

Both at the time and in retrospect, the KGB, the military, the International Department, and the MID have blamed Karmal for the Afghan disaster. It was his fault that the intervention got stuck, that the Afghans turned against the Soviets, that the PDPA had been unable to gain popular support, that it abused Marxist-Leninist jargon, and that it did not follow Soviet advice.[235] Varennikov criticized Karmal for pushing for large-scale military operations in 1984–85, which achieved little, while only a few pages later profusely praising the 40th Army's commanders. He remarked: "Karmal—himself an Afghan, should have perfectly known the people, the traditions, the social, and moral rules, the unwritten laws, the views on various societal events and as a politician, operating on a national scale, should have and must have conducted a policy considering these specificities. But everything was done the other way around. Yet the mistakes of Taraki and Amin were obvious. It seemed: just take them into account. But no! He did not only purse these mistakes, but increased them by imposing the '*orgyadro*.'"[236]

Varennikov's criticism could be as much, if not more, applied to the Soviets themselves. His assessment is nonetheless representative of the dominant view among Soviet veterans and former advisers. Some even came to blame Karmal for the intervention itself, arguing that he had influenced his friends in the KGB while in Moscow in 1979.[237] By contrast, Karmal—while in exile in Moscow in the late 1980s—would be eager to explain to visiting journalists that he never had any authority.[238] The same mechanism was at work: he too wanted no responsibility for the Afghan disaster. In many ways, this blame game bears similarities to the one the United States will be having with the Afghan authorities in the 2010s.

Varennikov's narrative was especially convenient for the Soviets because it made Karmal the scapegoat for the failed policies. It also strikingly contradicted the story of the Soviets managing the Afghan government that is often emphasized in the Soviet and Russian historiography. In reality, the USSR was as ideological as the PDPA, had no idea how to adjust to the context, and did not have a plan for stabilizing the country other than through force. Accordingly, the Kremlin's advice to the PDPA was superficial and its implementation difficult to monitor. As to the nature of decision-making in Afghanistan, it was one of mixed responsibility. Given the Soviets' lack of information, it could not have been any other way around. Several senior Soviet advisers and Afghan leaders recognized as much while noting that the Afghans' significant autonomy was a source of tensions with the Soviets.[239]

Such was the background to Gorbachev's rise to power following Chernenko's death in March 1985. Although the young Gorbachev brought a wind of renewal as the head of the USSR, he remained impregnated by the same ideology that had legitimized the intervention.[240] He thus did not immediately reverse course on Afghanistan and left the military to manage the situation. The Soviet Union, he argued, "would not abandon its [Afghan] brothers in dire straits."[241] It was only by the end of the year that his perspective changed. Meanwhile, as was clear from Polyanichko's superficial briefing before his departure for Kabul in the spring of 1985, the Soviets wanted things to change in Afghanistan but were unclear about how to proceed and what to do with Karmal.[242] In mid-October, Karmal secretly flew to Moscow to meet the politburo which had forced him to bring Najibullah along for the trip.[243] In a tense discussion, Gorbachev scolded him for his lack of progress in broadening the regime's base. He told Karmal to make "a U-turn back toward free capitalism, Afghan and Islamic values, to share actual power with the opposition and even currently hostile forces," reflecting little on how the Soviets' policies had been part of the problem so far.[244] The new recommendations were an ultimate attempt at pushing Karmal toward a more active policy before the Soviets replaced him with another leader.

By then, the Soviet politburo increasingly felt that Karmal was not up to the job. His coming to power, thanks to the Soviet intervention, had forever tainted him in the eyes of the Afghans. He was a weak organizer and part of the old PDPA guard that was out of touch with the new situation. Karmal's incapacity to adapt to the new Soviet course eventually determined his removal. As noted by one of Najibullah's supporters, Karmal's faction held a grudge against those in the PDPA who had installed Najibullah with Soviet support, but Najibullah "did not remove Karmal, changes in Soviet policy did. Gorbachev needed someone to support the Soviet withdrawal and this was a very risky move to support."[245] During his visit to Moscow Karmal vehemently opposed the LCST leaving. "If you leave now, next time you would have to send a million soldiers" to prevent the United States from establishing a presence in Afghanistan, he

FIGURE 3.4. Last meeting between Babrak Karmal, Mikhail Gorbachev, and Andrei Gromyko (to Gorbachev's right) in Moscow, 1985 (Courtesy of the Gorbachev Foundation). The meeting went poorly as Gorbachev forcefully enjoined Karmal to make a U-turn in his policies to salvage his rule in Afghanistan.

told Gorbachev. More than anything else, this signed his end. On 17 October, the day after meeting Karmal, Gorbachev announced at the politburo that the Soviets should prepare to leave Afghanistan. He had already "stunned" Karmal with the news, he told his colleagues. Karmal had been "sure that the Soviet Union needed Afghanistan more than he did" and expected that the LCST "would be there for long, if not forever."[246] This had been his mistake. It was also telling of his state of mind and reminiscent of Taraki's belief that Afghanistan would join the USSR.

Gorbachev explained to Karmal and the politburo that he expected Afghans to defend themselves by late 1986. In practice, this meant that they had to "forget thinking about socialism" and implement his new recommendations, including raising the salaries of army officers and proregime mullahs.[247] This marked an inflection in Soviet policy, being an open admission that sovietization was not working. The ensuing adjustments were to reverberate across the PDPA, the apparatus of Soviet advisers, and the LCST. In November 1985, back from Moscow, Karmal proclaimed a new plan of ten goals for the Afghan government that included, as point eight, the support of religious education and religious scholars who did not support the mujahideen. This, however, would be too little too late.

Marxist-Leninist ideology was crucial to the Soviet approach in Afghanistan, it colored the politburo's view and influenced the Soviets on the ground. Because they knew little about the context and the intervention saw considerable improvisation, the advisers could not but rely on ideological tropes and familiar models of organization. They leaned on ideology as on a crutch while the Red Army fought the war it had been trained for. The handbooks distributed to Soviet soldiers and *zampolits* exemplified this approach. They folded the complicated Afghan reality into the familiar concepts of Marxism-Leninism while providing some practical advice to the soldiers. The advice was useful to the LCST, but the rest was wishful thinking. The Soviet leaders almost irrationally believed that Afghanistan would espouse their modernization project and, for this reason, did not bother to design an actual policy.

Even among the Central Asian soldiers, living embodiments, in the USSR's view, of how Islam could coexist with communism, there were at the same time facilities to adapt to the context and deal with the Afghans and a perception of the Soviet-Afghan War that was no different from their compatriots. The type of young, "modern" Muslims they represented—not practicing and having only a cultural attachment to Islam—did not appeal to the Afghans and did not challenge the mujahideen propaganda about godless communists. In this context, contra other analyses, this chapter demonstrated the Soviet neglect of Islam in Afghanistan during the Karmal era. This was the most blatant example of its disinterest in the context and of ideology's dominance in its decision-making. The Soviets were glad to leave the task of gaining the population's support and dealing with religion to the PDPA.

Like the Soviets, the Afghan communists trusted in Marxism-Leninism. They were certain that their reforms would gain popular support once the Soviets had pacified the country. Islam was a secondary issue—an afterthought. Karmal's regime professed and displayed its respect for religion to placate the Afghan populace, but only on a superficial level. The Afghan communist leaders were not even ready to publicly say that they were Muslims and continued to present themselves as communists and atheists in private. Their goal remained to build a society in which Marxism-Leninism would overtake Islam. This instrumental relationship to religion limited the appeal of Karmal's policies to co-opt some of the religious sentiment, though it is unknown if a different approach might have had more success as long as the LCST was present.

By 1985, it was clear that the Soviets had reached an impasse in Afghanistan amid mounting casualties. "The bet on the fast resolution of economic, political, and social issues by the revolution ended up being wrong. But to understand that, we had to make that mistake," Polyanichko concluded upon arrival to Kabul.[248] The repeated changes at the USSR's head only exacerbated the problem as each new leader took time to adjust to the situation. In this context, Gorbachev's rise finally consolidated power in the Kremlin and allowed for a reassessment of Afghan policy, building on preexisting aspirations for change. This, in turn, determined the changes to come in Afghanistan. The PDPA had to switch course and Karmal had to go.

CHAPTER 4

Najibullah's Islamization

> In the course of the politics of national reconciliation,
> [the PDPA] will even more actively support and
> develop the Muslim people [of Afghanistan's]
> respectful relation toward Islam. Our commitment to
> Islam shows in the state's emblem and flag; it is clear
> in the restoration of Islamic values, and the creation of
> the conditions for the free practice of religion.

> —M. Najibullah, February 1987

The Najibullah Solution

Najibullah, long known by his moniker Najib, became the PDPA's general secretary in May 1986. Testifying to their difficulty in managing PDPA politics, the Soviets had to stage a protracted campaign to cajole Karmal into leaving peacefully. The decision to get rid of him was a difficult one for many Soviets. Despite his flaws, Parcham's old leader was a believer in the communist ideal. In a blasphemous way, he would tell Kryuchkov that: "A believing Muslim reveres God, his Prophet, and the first righteous caliphs. My feelings for the Soviet Union, its leaders are close to that reverence. This is the directive principle of my life."[1] If any Afghan outside of the PDPA had overheard that declaration, he would have been more than ever convinced that Karmal was not a Muslim.

The choice to remove Karmal, backed by the politburo and by the senior advisers in Kabul, was especially controversial among some of the Soviet experts and parts of the PDPA. Slinkin, who tried to convince the Kremlin to either stick with Karmal, or go with Layeq, argued that Najibullah's problem was that he had limited support in the PDPA and the wider population because he was, at under forty years old, too young by Afghan standards.[2] Darmanger, who disliked Karmal for jailing him in the Pul-e-Charkhi Prison, also believed that Najibullah's legitimacy was dubious. Many in the PDPA shared his and Slinkin's opinion while, until the end, the party harbored a large pro-Karmal faction. This made replacing the PDPA leader a tense and complex affair.

Interestingly, one Afganka—a Soviet female nurse—remembered that Karmal's ousting led to several days of protests in Kabul. The capital was full of women angered and afraid, the nurse remembered, that Karmal "would be stripped from power and might get killed, like Amin had killed Taraki."[3] The authorities showed restraint in dealing with the situation and things soon normalized. The protests still vividly showed how Karmal, often seen as a Soviet puppet, had political legitimacy in procommunist areas. Supporting the PDPA did not mean for the Afghans to passively subscribe to all directives coming from Moscow. Polyanichko, who was then Karmal's adviser, tells a similar story while noting many people feared a return of the Khalqis.[4]

Nonetheless, Najibullah and the Soviets fully maneuvered Karmal out of power by late 1986 and sent him into exile to Moscow. In the Kremlin's view, pacifying Afghanistan required an ideologically flexible leader dedicated to an inclusive policy and with a reputation for toughness. Being the KGB's creature, Najibullah was the man for the job despite being tainted by his years of running KhAD. His promotion also sent the signal that the Kremlin was still behind Parcham.[5] Najibullah was a notorious opponent of Khalq while rumors circulated that his and Sayed Muhammad Gulabzoi's, the minister of interior and leading Khalqi, operatives were killing each other in Kabul.[6] In the long term, this proved a crucial issue as Najibullah was never able to quell the infighting in the PDPA. At the same time, while some in the Red Army saw Najibullah as duplicitous and too close to the KGB, his promotion reinforced the tensions among the Soviet agencies.

Darmanger, a Khalqi who knew Najibullah before the war, believed that his arrival meant both continuity and change in Moscow's course. The Kremlin wanted to put its yes-man in charge to be fully in control while coordinating the withdrawal.[7] This proved a misconception. As Kirpichenko reflected years later, faith in Najibullah and KhAD's dependability likely delayed the Soviet withdrawal. It made the Kremlin believe that it could reproduce the organizational success achieved with KhAD on a country-wide scale and that stabilization would eventually pick up.[8] However, Najibullah proved to not be as pliable as the Soviets had thought.

Najibullah also had other factors going for him. Unlike Karmal, a man of mixed ethnicity with support mostly in northern Afghanistan, Najibullah was a Ghilzai Pashtun, one of the two main Pashtun tribes, from Paktia Province, which is a strategic region bordering Pakistan. His father had been Kabul's consul in Peshawar in charge of maintaining good relations with the Pashtun tribes on both sides of the border. Although some of his kin rejected him after he became the PDPA's general secretary, his networks in southeastern

Afghanistan remained strong. Najibullah could also rely on the kin by marriage as his wife was descended from the royal line of Abdur Rahman Khan.
When appealing to the mujahideen, Najibullah used his tribal legitimacy, including symbolically by receiving tribal representatives in traditional Pashtun
garments.[9] Two prominent Soviet experts even argued that his Pashtun nationalism was so strong that it conflicted with his loyalty to communism.[10]
Yet, this was exactly what the Soviets needed. Inside the PDPA, Najibullah's
Pashtun background was more appealing to Khalqis. Najibullah was also a
more acceptable Islamic leader to many Afghans while his lower profile before the war was, in some respects, an advantage. Meeting French president
François Mitterrand after the withdrawal, Gorbachev would revealingly argue
that "Najibullah was not at all a Marxist or a socialist, he was a nationalist" by
contrast to the "cultist (*sektant*)" Karmal.[11]

Najibullah's promotion also stemmed from the changes in the Kremlin.
After his disenchantment with Karmal, Gorbachev publicly voiced a negative
assessment of the Soviet-Afghan War and made clear his wish to bring back
the LCST in early 1986 at the 27th Congress of the CPSU. Because of the
"counterrevolution and imperialism," Afghanistan had become a "bleeding
wound" for the Soviets.[12] Following protracted negotiations with the United
States, Gorbachev finally announced in February 1988 that the withdrawal
would soon start. Only two months later, the USSR and the United States
signed the Geneva Accords. The Soviets then conducted their withdrawal in
two phases between 15 May 1988 and 15 February 1989 with half of the LCST
leaving by August 1988 since the Kremlin had agreed to front-load the withdrawal. Meanwhile, from 1986 to 1988, Moscow tried to reach a settlement
that would secure the Afghan communist regime's survival. This meant having an Afghan leader who took the Soviet intention to leave seriously and acted
accordingly. Najibullah was one of the few in Kabul who did so even though
he tried his best to delay the departure.

While charting their new course, the Soviets tried to change how they in-
teracted with the Afghans. They now believed that sending too many CPSU
advisers and not adjusting their development model to Afghan specificities had
been their two original sins. Back from Kabul, Egorychev underlined that the
"sending of party advisers in big groups . . . led to dependency . . . a deficit of
responsibility and even freeloading on the advisers' activities."[13] He, too, had
realized that ideology had led to an impossible policy of sovietizing Afghanistan.
Accordingly, Gorbachev advised Najibullah in virtually every conversation not
to rely too much on Soviet advisers. The politburo drastically cut their number, estimated by then at some 9,000 people. By 1987, out of the 240 CPSU

FIGURE 4.1. A meeting between Mohammad Najibullah, Mikhail Gorbachev, Eduard Shevard-nadze (to Gorbachev's right), and Anatoly Chernyaev (to Najibullah's left) in Tashkent, 1988 (Courtesy of the Gorbachev Foundation). Relations considerably improved between Soviets and Afghans after Najibullah's arrival, even though the PDPA had difficulties accepting the Soviet withdrawal.

advisers present in 1985, only four would be left.[14] It was time to "let the Afghans handle their country," Gorbachev noted.[15] In late 1986, the Kremlin shared another call to be more proactive with the PDPA.[16] Telling Afghans to ignore the advisers appeared easier to do for the Soviet leaders than transforming their own people's mindset after years of indoctrination. The "forces of inertia were still present" among the advisers, a Soviet report noted.[17] Gorbachev again called on Najibullah to "act independently" in 1988.[18] The Soviet leaders indeed had faith in their protégé. Without the LCST and its army of advisers, they were bound to have less control over the Afghan situation.

Downplaying the Soviet influence and propping up Najibullah's importance became a staple of communist propaganda.[19] The Soviets now saw statements that showed the Afghans' deference toward the CPSU as a problem. In Gorbachev's team, Chernyaev remarked that, while Najibullah's speech at the 19th Plenum of the CC PDPA in 1986 had been fine, the Afghan leader proposing to personally report to Gorbachev was an issue. "One of the factors of the breakthrough in Afghanistan, the broadening of the regime's social base was the demonstration of the 'sovereignty' of the new authorities' decisions and adopted policies," he noted.[20] Presenting the PDPA as fully independent had been part of the reason for Karmal's removal. Nevertheless, having

Chernyaev take the word sovereignty in quotation marks testified to his limited knowledge about decision-making in Afghanistan. Even in Karmal's time, Soviet control over the PDPA had been imperfect at best.

At the Plenum of the CC CPSU in 1988, Gorbachev went a step further by linking the withdrawal with Najibullah's rise to power. "Although the politburo had been looking for ways to leave" Afghanistan since 1985 he argued, the "capacity to solve that issue only came at the end of 1986 after the arrival . . . of the truly national forces headed by Najibullah." This was helping Afghanistan become an "independent, neutral, and nonaligned" country, Gorbachev remarked.[21] While these three adjectives soon became the new Soviet motto for Afghanistan, Gorbachev's statement was especially significant for how it suggested that backing Karmal for so long had been a mistake and, more controversially, that he had tried to withdraw the LCST as soon as he came to power. It also showed that he had invested considerable political capital in Najibullah. Acutely aware of that, Najibullah did not miss a chance of playing it up, once pointing out to Gorbachev that national reconciliation in Afghanistan was also "part of perestroika."[22] For better or worse, the Kremlin would be now stuck with Najibullah until the end.

Ultimately, what was surprising was not that the Soviets selected Najibullah—a young, dynamic Pashtun with an adequate family background—but that they had originally bet on Karmal, an atheist Tajik, and Keshtmand, a Hazara. This, too, showed how ideological rectitude trumped other aspects in the Kremlin's minds. Beyond this, Najibullah's promotion was only a half-hearted attempt at a new course. Grachev explains it best by observing that it: "was not a signal that [the Kremlin] conceded anything to the Islamists. [Najibullah] was a man of the security agencies; a 'traditional Muslim leader,' perhaps, but one from before the Islamic Revolution, the era of Nasser, of Assad the Senior, people who were often at loggerheads with Islam."[23]

The choice of Najibullah signaled that, despite its talk of compromises, the Kremlin was not yet ready to scrap everything it had tried to build in Afghanistan. There was to be a combination of a political solution on Moscow and Kabul's terms and of toughness when dealing with the mujahideen. The last two years of the Soviet presence would show how this policy both allowed for some stabilization and reached its limit.

National Reconciliation in Islam

Gorbachev's intention to leave Afghanistan meant that the task of building support for the PDPA had become more urgent. It did not, however, become easier. Sergey Akhromeyev, now chief of the Soviet General Staff, plainly noted

دولت ج . د . ۱۰ ملکیت دهقانان و سایر زمینداران را مطابق به احکام

قانون محترم شمرده و تضمین میکند .

FIGURE 4.2. A PDPA propaganda poster of a man with his land ownership document received from the government (Archive Collection | Alamy Stock Photo). The PDPA long tried to sell Afghans on its land reform despite its many limitations.

that a military solution was no longer possible. "[The communists] had lost the battle for the Afghan people," he claimed.[24] Najibullah similarly acknowledged that the PDPA had failed to gain the peasantry's support because its land reform had been unsuccessful. In fact, "the peasantry's situation in government areas was in some respects worse than in areas controlled by the counterrevolution."[25] This was the miserable outcome of five years of sovietization.

Under the new circumstances, the communists needed a bolder political strategy to improve the regime's standing. This assessment paved the way for Najibullah's national reconciliation program that was meant, at least in the Soviet view, to offer political concessions and economic incentives to the opposition in exchange for support. According to Polyanichko, the new policy had to be based on local and international precedents of political compromises, Gorbachev's New Political Thinking, Afghan tribal and kin-based conciliation systems, and the rejection of the "forms and dogmas of revolutionary transformation" that had proven foreign to Afghanistan.[26] Islam was to serve as a conduit for the new policy. In his first week as general secretary, Najibullah went to the Ministry of Islamic Affairs and Waqfs. He told Islamic leaders that the party saw the "patriotic clergy as a cornerstone of the revolutionary state" and that he counted on them to help end the war.[27] This message paralleled the PDPA Propaganda Department's calls to not underestimate "the sacred banner of Islam." It was the communists' role "to wrestle it away from the hands of the counterrevolution" because "Islam's calls for freedom, justice, and equality were close to party slogans."[28]

Najibullah prepared his national reconciliation program in September 1986, putting it under the moribund NFF. Presented in a televised speech in early 1987, it included a ceasefire and three measures to bring insurgents to the regime's side: national and local coalition governments, amnesties for fighters who disarmed, and the promise of the LCST's withdrawal after the situation was stabilized.[29] As to the first measure, so-called *jirgas* of peace were to incentivize support for the government by offering material and economic incentives relying on Soviet aid and technical support, including in irrigation and healthcare, to the population to achieve "areas of peace." In such areas, local authorities could mitigate the regime's most unpopular policies, notably on conscription, and people could circulate more easily.[30] The program's overall goal was to find common ground with Islamic and tribal leaders, monarchists, and other groups amenable to negotiating with the PDPA. Najibullah and the Soviets hoped to drive a wedge between such "moderates" and the Islamists, the "irreconcilable, fanatical part" of the insurgents who sought a military victory.[31] Najibullah's national reconciliation built on Karmal's attempts to broaden the regime's base by strengthening its Islamic credentials, but it went further in all aspects. Where Karmal wished to instrumentalize religion, Najibullah gradually developed a new platform for the PDPA.

Calling on the mujahideen, Najibullah claimed that the belligerents had to focus on what united them instead of on their differences. All Afghans had "a shared belief in Islam, [a] shared motherland," he noted.[32] Thus, Islamic scholars had to become mediators in the war. They were to join grassroots national reconciliation commissions and play a role in government. One planned measure was for the insurgents to recommend representatives to the Ministry of Islamic Affairs and Waqfs through their Islamic Committees. This was meant to establish "another channel of communication with various groups of counter-revolutionary forces."[33] In 1988, the regime released a brochure titled *The Role of Ulemas in the Invitation to Peace* that publicized these arguments and explained that because Afghanistan was an Islamic society, *ulemas* should use their influence to mobilize the people in support of national reconciliation.[34] Such statements and publications were part of what the AIC labeled a "massive domestic propaganda campaign" for national reconciliation that also saw the regime conduct "subversive and propaganda" activities in Pakistani refugee camps to encourage Afghans to return.[35]

Compared to Karmal, Najibullah was better at highlighting the Islamic and nationalist credentials of the communist regime while keeping the Marxist-Leninist rhetoric for party meetings and the Soviets.[36] After he became general secretary, he dropped the nickname "Najib." Afghan media and the Soviets now referred to him as Dr. Mohamad Najibullah, both a more Islam-appropriate name and one that emphasized his medical degree.[37] By all accounts, Najibullah was a more charismatic and effective leader than Karmal. Although he was stained by his years running KhAD, he was still able to highlight that it was the most efficient of the regime's agencies, a fact even acknowledged by his enemies.[38] Beyond this, Najibullah was a gifted orator, able to speak the language of the Afghan people both literally—he was fluent, unlike Karmal, in both Dari and Pashto—and figuratively—he was comfortable talking about nationalism and Islam. Frequently and properly quoting the Koran, including at party meetings, he was confident in blaming the insurgents for their "unrighteous war against [Afghans'] belief, against [their] country, tribes, and native land."[39] His oratory skills were crucial in a country where the information traveled orally. It was likewise a considerable change compared to Karmal's awkward attempts to explain the party's respect for Islam and tendency to leave the talk about religion to affiliate institutions such as the NFF.

This helped Najibullah convincingly promote the talking points that the PDPA had been developing since 1980. At the 20th Plenum of the CC PDPA in 1986, he argued that the April Revolution and Islam had "one common rationale"—the country's "hardworking Islamic people." It was the role of the "patriotically geared mullahs to serve their revolutionary people."[40] Najibullah's approach was to reframe the message about convergence between socialism and Islam more boldly, recognizing that it was essential to be an Islamic authority to remain in power in Afghanistan. In 1987, he stressed that "the PDPA fought for the interests of the Afghan people, the overwhelming majority of whom historically practiced the religion of Islam." The party had to admit, he noted, that it "did not have another social base."[41] Najibullah was even more candid when reaching out to tribal elders and traveling to Afghan holy sites such as the Hazrat Ali Maza in Mazar-i-Sharif immediately after he became general secretary. There he admitted mistakes on the PDPA's side, and said that he, too, was Muslim and respected *sharia*.[42]

In Kandahar, where Najibullah came to pray at the Shrine of the Cloak, one of the holiest sites in Islam because it contains the cloak that the Prophet had purportedly worn, local leaders told him that no national reconciliation would be possible until the Soviets left.[43] Still, his visit once again attested to Najibullah's keen understanding of Afghan mythology and Islam, and of the legitimacy that he could derive from both. A little less than ten years later, Mullah Omar would don the cloak in that same spot, claiming legitimacy for himself and the Taliban.

In addition to the new rhetoric, Najibullah expanded PDPA's policies in support of Islam and Islamic leaders. By 1986, the regime claimed to have restored 1,026 mosques, financed the construction of 231 new ones (mostly in Kabul), and provided 147 *ulemas'* families with housing. This was both significant and modest given that Afghanistan had tens of thousands of Islamic leaders and mosques. At the start of national reconciliation, Najibullah nevertheless boasted that his regime was "building more mosques, than [the mujahideen] had time to destroy."[44] The communists further expanded their support to Islam, including twice raising the salaries of Islamic scholars. According to one KGB estimate, the regime supported 10 *madrasas*, 10 Koran readers' houses, 134 Shia praying houses, some 2,500 mosques out of a total of 15,000, and 87,500 Islamic leaders in the areas it controlled, including 11,500 with salaries.[45] Meanwhile, the regime had increased the number of mullahs in the Afghan army to try to have one per company and broadened their role and privileges.[46] There had therefore been substantial positive changes in the support to Islam as compared to the Karmal era, even though there were both economic and logistical limits to it. Islamic leaders' salaries, for example, continued to represent only a fraction of what they got in insurgents' Islamic committees and less than what some civil servants and military personnel received.[47]

The increased funding to Islamic institutions and leaders showed how the regime's priorities were shifting nationwide. In a meeting with the Ministry of Islamic Affairs and Waqfs, Najibullah plainly explained that party committees "had been strictly instructed to pay special attention to the needs of mosques and the clergy."[48] Not mere propaganda, such comments marked a change in the narrative inside the party and a challenge to the PDPA's lingering anticlericalism. Actively looking to co-opt Islamic leaders by offering them

growing political, material, and economic incentives was different from paying occasional rhetorical respect to Islam. Surprisingly, the historiography often underestimates this remarkable break with the Karmal era.

Financial support to mullahs and mosques was only one aspect of the evolving relationship with religion. At the start of national reconciliation, Islam's
place in the DRA had already changed. The University of Kabul had a thriv-
ing theological faculty; the authorities opened a new Islamic Study Centre in
Kabul and Najibullah attended its inauguration; they held regular conferences
of Islamic leaders; newspapers were not published on Islamic holidays; *Kabul
New Times* featured articles about Afghan *madrasas*; the television had religious
programming; and Kabul hosted an international Koranic reading competition, which Najibullah personally promoted, with participants from pro-Soviet
Muslim countries.[49] The PDPA leadership meanwhile collectively participated
in *namaz* for the end of Ramadan and attended Friday Prayers that encouraged national reconciliation and called for an agreement on Afghanistan to be
found in Geneva. The PDPA officials in other provinces did the same and
organized meetings after Friday prayers upon Najibullah's injunction.[50] By the
war's end, Kabul was even giving the honors of martyr, in the Islamic sense,
to officers killed fighting the mujahideen.[51] Unlike before, the goal was to demonstrate to the population that the PDPA not only respected religion but was
truly Islamic and had the support of Afghanistan's Islamic authorities.

As disapprovingly noted by an enemy, the regime was even "giving a new
shape" to "educational affairs to deceive the nation." While religious subjects
used to be taught three times a week in schools, they were now taught six times
a week.[52] Attacks against Islam even disappeared from lectures on Marxism-
Leninism.[53] The change in education was the clearest sign that the regime had
transformed its matrix. Originally, the PDPA had planned through education
to form a new generation of Afghans who would be secularized and open to
socialist ideas as the Bolsheviks had done in the Caucasus and Central Asia.
Karmal had claimed to the Soviets that he hoped that state education and
DOMA, the Afghan Komsomol, would in time help prepare 80% of the PDPA
recruits.[54] That the PDPA would alter the Afghan social fabric by "brainwash-
ing" the youth was also one of the mujahideen's main concerns. They feared
the youth would start leading a more secularized life, that its values would
change in a country without *madrasas* and *sharia* courts.[55] By returning *en force*
to Islamic education beyond Karmal's token steps, the PDPA was jeopardizing its future.

Najibullah summed up his Islamic policy in early 1987 and emphasized the
Islamic scholars' new political role in a milestone speech to the Special Commission for National Reconciliation:

The very word "Islam" in translation from Arabic means "living in peace" . . . [During] national reconciliation, [the PDPA] will even more actively support and develop the respectful relation that the Muslim people [of Afghanistan] have toward Islam. Our commitment to Islam is enacted in the [country's] emblem and the state's flag; it is apparent in the restoration of Islamic values and the establishment of the conditions for the free practice of religion. Our enemies cannot silence such undeniable facts as the election of 750 mullahs into our local organs of state power and the nomination into the revolutionary council of 12 representatives of the clergy. [The] Afghan people and the clergy are convinced: Islam is in danger not from the April Revolution's side. Islam is threatened by the enemy of the Muslim world's liberation movement—the international imperialism headed by the USA.[56]

The circumstances certainly forced Najibullah to embrace Islam. The shift nonetheless showed how the PDPA had recognized that Marxist-Leninist rhetoric and symbols were not gaining any supporters. Beyond the NFF, loyal Islamic figures now played a political role, even though they remained subservient to the PDPA. In a significant concluding remark to his speech to the Special Commission for National Reconciliation, Najibullah noted that the party needed to understand "that mass work with the population was conducted in mosques."[57] At odds with Taraki's infamous promise to empty them, they were to be centers of PDPA activity. The climax of Najibullah's Islamization of the party was that the April Revolution itself became connoted religiously: it "had happened by the Will of Almighty Allah."[58] This was a major challenge to the party's ideology and one that triggered negative reactions from Soviet and Afghan hardliners. Still, Najibullah, with Moscow's support, would take it one step further and institutionalize these changes, re-forging the PDPA and the DRA in the process.

The Soviet Blessing

The Soviets undeniably inspired and supported the PDPA's national reconciliation. Although its launch led to an immediate intensification of mujahideen attacks, in Moscow's view it returned the political initiative to Kabul as the latter tried to expand its popular base. The policy was the translation of the Kremlin's new thinking as to Islam's role in Afghanistan. As colorfully put by Plastun, national reconciliation "was proclaimed when they came to their senses in Moscow." It, however, came too late, Plastun believed. "Many Islamic leaders in

Afghanistan could not forget . . . the elimination of the 'reactionary Islamic clergy' under the Taraki-Amin regime."[59] This was Khalq's dire legacy.

Polyanichko and Yuli Vorontsov, the influential Soviet deputy minister of foreign affairs, brainstormed the core ideas of national reconciliation in Kabul in the fall of 1986. They were at times joined by Primakov from the Oriental Studies Institute who, Polyanichko noted, provided important background information. They took this plan to Moscow, where the Kremlin and the PDPA leadership, which came in December, hammered its details in small working groups, and validated it.[60]

In line with Gorbachev's reassessment of Afghan policy, the Soviet media had though already began presenting a changed narrative regarding Islam in Afghanistan since late 1985. Telegrafnoe Agentstvo Sovetskogo Soyuza (TASS), the USSR's central news agency, published, for example, a long article titled "The Afghan Counterrevolution and Islam" that exemplified the new thinking:

> After the revolution of 1978, the clergy opposed the political and socio-economical changes in Afghan society's life; it became the counterrevolution's principal weapon. The religious fanaticism of most of the population presented a fertile ground to attract it to counterrevolutionary activities. The Islamic slogans used by the counterrevolution were to some extent more comprehensible for [the population] than many others. . . . The population of Afghanistan, not receiving any tangible positive results from the April Revolution, was to some extent in confusion at the time. . . . The mistakes committed during the implementation of the land reform likewise damaged the revolutionary authority's credibility . . . [Yet] the DRA's new leadership from January 1980 onward put as a cornerstone of its actions to right the mistakes committed. . . . Today the Afghan Muslim finally clearly realizes who is a friend and who is an enemy, who respects religion and who, so to say, uses Islam for his own ends.[61]

The article confirmed Soviet continued support of the PDPA's more inclusive Islamic policy. Soviet policymakers had gradually stopped seeing Afghanistan as a testing ground to build socialism. As noted by Egorychev, the Soviet ambassador, "many made parallels between the current [Afghan] situation and the history of the Civil War and of the socialist changes in Central Asia, [Soviet] internationalist help to the People's Mongolia and the Spanish Republic" but this was not the same situation.[62]

In Afghanistan, some among the Soviet advisers, military and KGB also grew better at understanding the country. As noted by one KhAD officer, "they now followed the rules that would not lead to more rejection of the Soviets and the PDPA."[63] They became skilled at dealing with tribal questions, using

Islam in *agitprop*, and generally "considering the specificities of a Muslim country."[64] Meanwhile, the Kremlin had told some of the senior Soviet advisers arriving to Kabul that the policy in Afghanistan may be about to change. Gorbachev remarkably told Polyanichko, who had studied the Basmachi while in Moscow and believed the parallels with the mujahideen to be extensive, that he had to start thinking about reconciliation in Afghanistan when he dispatched him to advise Karmal in March 1985.[65] These had though all been small steps.

The TASS article set the ground for Najibullah's push to Islamize the regime. It was aimed at Soviet advisers who had to prepare to see the Afghan communists dilute their Marxism-Leninism. The handbook on jihad for Soviet political workers discussed in chapter 3 similarly reflected the new perspective. Its authors argued that although the insurgents' jihad only served imperialism and was hence a foreign import, the "majority of [Afghan] religious figures now supported the PDPA's religious policy" and were not part of the opposition.[66] Although this was far from the truth, it is significant that it became the official line. Like Najibullah, the Soviets would eventually make the argument that two competing "Islams" were crystallizing during the conflict, hoping that in time it would be more than just propaganda. Accordingly, the general handbook for Soviet soldiers released in 1987 emphasized Gorbachev's "bleeding wound speech" and Najibullah's national reconciliation program.[67]

Following national reconciliations' start, the Kremlin continued to insist on the religious factor's centrality in it. Discussing Najibullah's initiatives in 1987, the politburo, after noting their "modest" success, repeated that there could be "no Afghanistan without Islam." The Soviets, therefore, advocated for a more "realistic approach" that would entail, "if the name of the [PDPA] was kept," to add "the word 'Islamic'" to it. It was time to "add some 'Islamization' to the image of the party," Kryuchkov noted.[68] There was no dissonant voice: pragmatism had to dominate. On this, Moscow and Kabul were on the same line. Najibullah would shortly thereafter propose considering a "more accurate name for the PDPA."[69] Still, what remained striking was how superficial the Soviet advice was. Making the PDPA appealing to Afghans was more complicated than adding the word "Islam" to its name. This confirmed, however, the end of ideology in Afghanistan. Chernyaev noted that there could be "no talk about socialism there" anymore. The country after the Soviet withdrawal was to be nonaligned and neutral without Soviet military bases but also without US ones. The PDPA leadership needed to concede 50% of official positions to the opposition and try to have the king return in a "Father of the Nation" role. This would be as unacceptable to Islamist mujahideen parties as to Najibullah.

The influential Oriental Studies Institute similarly suggested concentrating on Islam in Afghanistan, recommending measures that went further than what the politburo was ready to consider. Yuri Gankovsky, the leading expert on Afghanistan, argued for the PDPA to move entirely into the background. An organization tentatively named "The Popular Islamic Party of Afghanistan" could then replace it. In addition to building support among Afghan minorities, Gankovsky then suggested considering replacing Najibullah.[70] As we will see, this illustrated a tension at the core of national reconciliation. How could the new policy at the same time broaden the base of the regime and consolidate it around the PDPA? While the Soviets tried to juggle this contradiction in 1987, it became evident that it would be the policy's main limitation. Making the regime more representative would have weakened it in the short term and made withdrawing the LCST a nightmare. For this reason, as put by Shevardnadze, "the most important [for the Soviets] was not to allow Najibullah's regime to fall!"[71]

A new awareness of Islam's importance also spread to the Soviets in Kabul. Plastun recalled a characteristic incident from late 1987. An officer from Varennikov's staff approached him because his boss urgently needed Plastun to answer questions about: (a) the differences between Sunni and Shia Muslims; (b) the possibility of building mosques for Shia Muslims to gain their support; (c) how ranks among Islamic leaders corresponded to ranks in the Christian clergy; (d) Ismailism; (e) the importance of Islam in the relations with Iran and Pakistan; and (f) how Islam could be used to pacify Afghanistan.[72] This episode showed both the ongoing lack of awareness of the Islamic factor among Soviet commanders and their interest in it. Varennikov's last question clearly echoed Najibullah's national reconciliation program. At another level, the fact that Plastun, a civilian adviser in the military, had to answer such questions seems to confirm the lack of Soviet Islamic advisers.

Embracing Islam was indeed the Soviet advice to the PDPA, according to General Kim Tsagolov, Varennikov's political adviser. Tsagolov, who claimed to have had a hand in writing Najibullah's speech on national reconciliation, explained that the clergy had to promote the new policy because the "PDPA had discredited itself as a political force."[73] Moscow's hand was certainly visible in many aspects of national reconciliation. The policy was to start on 1 January, a date selected based on the Gregorian and not the Islamic calendar, and the authorities had scheduled ceasefires forgetting that the Afghan working week started on a Saturday.[74] The Kremlin, the military, the KGB, and the Soviet advisers, including Tabeev and Polyanichko, often debated in advance the measures that Najibullah would adopt.[75] Beyond this, the USSR even made symbolic gestures in support of Islam in the DRA. It hence helped finance the Islamic Study Centre in Kabul to highlight that Soviet aid was "not only in the areas of economics, culture, and technical development but also religion."[76] It also gifted Kabul a plane specially dedicated to taking pilgrims to Mecca.[77]

Although they have been eager to dissociate themselves from the Karmal era, many Soviets have, by contrast, claimed national reconciliation's authorship. Yet the Afghans had shared thinking with the Soviets that could have led to a policy akin to national reconciliation as early as 1981. Layeq and Karmal's father tried, for example, to convince Maiorov to push for the LCST's withdrawal because it was impossible to win against the mujahideen and because the Soviets did not know how to deal with Islam.[78] This is not to say that the Kremlin did not set national reconciliation's goals but to note that it stemmed from the Soviets finally recognizing Islam's political importance of which many Afghans had been aware. Beyond this, there was a difference between deciding on a new policy in Moscow and making it work on the ground.

There are examples of senior PDPA workers advising the Soviets to be more flexible on ideology. Commenting in retrospect, an Afghan politburo member claimed that there had been "serious calls" in the party to leave "radical positions" by the mid-1980s. Nevertheless, the "Soviet military presence," he argued, rendered that complicated.[79] Likewise, a PDPA worker in charge of Kabul's 10th district approached Plastun to discuss the communists' propaganda in 1987. The man wanted the Soviets to support the propaganda work in mosques because this was where the PDPA could reach the most people. As he explained, "in a 30 min speech [in a mosque], he would spend 27 min talking about Allah, the Prophet, and the Koran, and 3 min in conclusion to say, 'you see that all of Allah's precepts, as transmitted by the Prophet and reflected in the Koran, are followed by our party [as part of] national reconciliation.'" These arguments, the PDPA worker contended, were more productive than the Marxist-Leninist rhetoric that angered the Afghans who thought the PDPA wanted to "look cleverer than them."[80] One other example had the PDPA general Nabi Azimi engineer stabilization in Herat by speaking with believers in mosques, an endeavor rendered easier by the fact that Azimi was a practicing Muslim.[81] Both stories were indicative of the difficulties of setting up national reconciliation and representative of how many Afghans were aware of how best to reach the population. There was nothing complicated or especially new about national reconciliation.

Beyond this, the Afghans could still adjust national reconciliation in their preferred direction by continuing to play on the tensions among the Soviets. While the military ran the show in Afghanistan, the KGB and the MID did so in Moscow. Together with Kryuchkov, Shevardnadze boasted about how he handled Afghan policy under Gorbachev.[82] As to the KGB, while its influence peaked under Andropov, it always had a special relationship with Najibullah due to the latter's KhAD background. While the tensions among the Soviets in Kabul subsided after Varennikov arrived in 1985 as a "super" Chief military adviser, they never entirely disappeared. Still, Varennikov led decision-making while establishing a close working relationship with Polyanichko.[83] In parallel, the Kremlin finally removed Tabeev. In May 1986, the Soviet ambassador told Najibullah that "he had made him General Secretary." After that, the exasperated Gorbachev concluded that it was time to recall Tabeev because he conducted himself as a "governor-general" in Afghanistan.[84] Pavel Mozhaev replaced him in August and stayed until March 1988 when Egorychev arrived. In late 1988, Vorontsov arrived as the ambassador and played an important role. The shuffling of ambassadors, however, testified to the remaining dissensions between Soviet agencies and between Moscow and Kabul.

In this context, much as about Karmal, controversies abound in the historiography about Najibullah's political agency. Slinkin wrote that a sign of the Afghan leader's lack of independence came in a letter from prominent Khalqis in 1988 suggesting that Polyanichko took all the decisions. Even if there was truth to it, and others criticized CPSU advisers for similar reasons, one cannot but wonder to what extent such letters to Moscow were meant to boost the standing of one or the other of the PDPA factions.[85] Afghans were keenly aware of the advisers' shortcomings and there is no doubt that Najibullah, who had direct access to Gorbachev, knew how to maneuver them, something he would prove by only taking what he wanted from Soviet plans for power-sharing with the opposition.

Beyond this, infighting was so rife in the PDPA that it made it difficult for the Soviets to monitor the policies' implementation and hold the Afghans accountable. Following Shevardnadze's mission to Kabul in early 1987, Vorotnikov recalled that there was even questioning in the politburo about who Moscow's main supporters in the PDPA were between Najibullah, Keshtmand, Gulabzoi, and Abdul Wakil, the new minister of foreign affairs.[86] This was a sign of the Kremlin's difficulty in keeping track of the mushrooming PDPA factions. This confusion meant that there was ample room for reinterpreting Soviet advice and adjusting policies as each faction felt best.

The national reconciliation program was overall the product of a joint effort between the Soviets and the Afghans. The fact that some advisers downplayed the Afghans' role by pointing out that the decision to switch political platforms came from Moscow is inverting the policy's most important components. The point was not about arguing that Islam was important for the PDPA; as noted by Soviet analysts, this had become inevitable by then and, as this book shows, the Soviets had certainly not been prescient about it. Rather, it was about being able to maneuver efficiently in Afghanistan and sell the idea that the communist regime had changed. That was something that Najibullah did well in 1987–89 and even more so after the Soviet withdrawal. By that time, the Afghans did feel in charge of "day-to-day decisions," a KhAD officer reported.[87] In fact, Najibullah was so efficient as to gain respect from his opponents. Calling him a "simple implementer," as Slinkin surprisingly does, misses that point.[88] To be fair, contra to how Karmal is often assessed, more Soviets, especially Polyanichko and Egorychev, gave credit to Najibullah for transforming, for better or worse, the blueprint set for him in the Kremlin.[89] The bottom line is perhaps given by Anatoly Adamishin, the Soviet deputy minister of foreign affairs, who felt that what was happening in Afghanistan then was that "Najibullah was conducting an intelligent policy, not [the Soviets] through Najibullah, but himself; many people understood his policy of national reconciliation."[90]

The fact that Gorbachev often discussed national reconciliation with Najibullah also testified to the latter's importance. In July 1987, their exchange dwelled upon Islam. Gorbachev advised the Afghans to "not forget about the religious aspect." "In the end, [the communists] will establish peace, for people to peacefully labor their land. This is the decisive factor that does not contradict the Koran," he noted.[91] Like the Oriental Studies Institute, Gorbachev pointed to other aspects of national reconciliation, particularly its measures for nationalities and among Pashtun tribes. Under Najibullah, the PDPA worked to boost the national consciousness of national-ethnic groups such as the Hazaras, Tajiks, and Uzbeks, creating a double national affiliation on the Soviet model.[92]

Following his mention of religion, Gorbachev volunteered advice on how to work with Islamic leaders based on the Soviet experience of dealing with—surprisingly—the Orthodox Church. Although he was glad that it "supported the party's politics," Gorbachev admitted that the CPSU would have to celebrate the 1,000th anniversary of Russia's Christianization. This was an obvious concession. Yet "all of [the religious sentiment] had to be considered. Because politics constructed outside of reality are not viable, doomed to be shaky, lead to disappointments," he explained.[93] The message to Najibullah was clear; if even the CPSU had to co-opt religious sentiment, what was there to be said about PDPA? This was an interesting parallel that showed that Gorbachev was starting to also reassess ideology at home. It was, however, striking that the Soviet leader could not think of an example involving Islam, an apparent sign of his limited knowledge of Soviet Muslims. Such exchanges of opinions continued afterward. In the spring of 1988, Gorbachev told Najibullah that they "had devised [national reconciliation] together." The Soviet leader, as his advisers focused on perestroika, believed at that time that the program

FIGURE 4.3. A meeting between Mohammad Najibullah, Mikhail Gorbachev and Raisa Gorbacheva, Eduard Shevardnadze, and Rafiq Nishanov, the first secretary of the Uzbek CPSU in Tashkent, 1988 (Courtesy of the Gorbachev Foundation). For better or worse, Gorbachev and his team would be saddled with Najibullah until the end of their Afghan adventure.

would lead to the PDPA sharing power. "Next to the PDPA there would be mujahideen," he argued.[94] This proved to be a pipe dream.

Gorbachev meanwhile passed the message about the importance of national reconciliation to the rest of the PDPA, including the most influential Khalqis, Gulabzoi and Minister of Defense Shahnawaz Tanai. He explained to them in 1988 that "in a situation where all the country's population was enmeshed in the war, purely military solutions could not be effective." The Afghans had to find "a political settlement."[95] Given the PDPA's fragmentation and concern over losing power, it was no surprise that the Soviets had to help Najibullah talk other Afghan leaders into backing the new policy. It had, from the start, encountered widespread opposition in the PDPA's politburo. However, Gorbachev's invectives would not prevent most Khalqis from opposing national reconciliation until the end. As Polyanichko recalls, it was difficult for leading Afghan communists not to see national reconciliation as an ideological defeat.[96]

Soviet hardliners opposed the new paradigm in 1988 for the same reason. An embassy adviser openly complained that the PDPA did not understand Marxist-Leninist theory. It "had no answer [to] the level of development of the Afghan society" and could not explain its goals. The adviser did not believe that the PDPA could hold after the withdrawal. Its problem, he maintained, was the "irreconcilable fight waged [against it] from class positions" by the mujahideen who wanted a "fundamentalist Islamic regime." There was, therefore, "no reason to place particular hopes in . . . national reconciliation." The only solution, the adviser contended, was for Khalq to take over and return to "building a socialist society."[97]

Clearly, not all Soviets were on board with scrapping ideology and leaving. They could not accept an approach that was in dissonance with years of indoctrination and the situation in the USSR where, despite perestroika, changes were slow to come at the lower levels of Soviet power. Egorychev similarly noted that the embassy's staff found it difficult not to impose their views on the Afghans, and many continued to bring the unfiltered Soviet experience to the DRA.[98] One adviser recalled how the Soviets still had to attend lectures on Marxism-Leninism despite being in the process of Islamizing the PDPA.[99] Ideology did not disappear overnight. The fact that the new advisers coming from Moscow were in the middle of rethinking their worldviews in the context of perestroika further complicated things.

At the same time, there were limits to the extent the Soviet military was ready to change its modus operandi to adapt to national reconciliation. Their initiatives were sometimes misguided, as when Varennikov called for deserters and their families to be cursed by army mullahs during *namaz*. Given how many Afghans evaded conscription, this was a recipe for disaster.[100] In another illustrative example, a senior military adviser in Varennikov's team once told his Afghanist colleague in response to him arguing that there was no need for a military operation near Kandahar because national reconciliation was ongoing there: "To hell with national reconciliation! Warriors receive decorations on their chest, get stars on their epaulettes, and are paid money not for reconciliation but for running military operations! This is what you, expert, did not understand!"[101]

This was not an isolated incident. After six years, violence was feeding violence on both sides. It was difficult to stop the bloodshed with political measures. In southeastern Zabol province, national reconciliation could not stop GRU units from "destroying all that they saw," apparently following orders from their superiors Kabul. As for the senior military adviser above, their "kill count" measured their efficiency, leading to attacks on civilians when they lacked insurgents to fight.[102] The same was true of the mujahideen. Many could not contemplate reconciliation following years of killing and while the Soviets were still present.

In many cases, simple inertia explained the Soviets' difficulty in changing. Ziarmal, the Afghan general encountered before, complained about how military advisers still duplicated mobilization strategies inherited from the Second World War. He had been unable to explain to them that Afghans coming from ethnic and religious minorities in northern and central provinces could not understand calls to fight in Pashtun areas away from home in the name of the April Revolution or the PDPA. They were nowhere near that level of political or national consciousness, Ziarmal argued.[103] According to *spetspropagandists*, this was an issue for national reconciliation itself. It did not register among the "popular masses," in the Soviet jargon, because no such thing existed in Afghanistan. The *agitprop* units had learned to speak to specific social, religious, and ethnic groups, making them somewhat effective. Najibullah would also be able to do this after the Soviet departure, but this was too much to ask from the entire LCST.

Finally, opposition to national reconciliation also existed in Moscow. In a letter to Gorbachev in 1987, a Marxism-Leninism professor at the Frunze Military Academy and a veteran of the Soviet-Afghan War blamed Afghanistan's problems on Parcham that had, unlike Khalq, "never truly supported the revolutionary power."[104] The Afganets asserted that Karmal, relying on the LCST, had "eliminated more than a million Afghans." Even worse, Karmal "had made it look like it was done . . . under the Soviet Union's guidance." This had led to "no less than 90–95 percent of Afghans being anti-Soviet," the author claimed. If true, this meant that no two parties could reconcile in Afghanistan as long as the Soviets were present. While blaming Karmal as other Soviets did, the professor extraordinarily also criticized the LCST and, consequently, the politburo's policies. He concluded by noting that national reconciliation could not work because it was nothing new compared to Karmal's policies. Most remarkably, he gave voice to the Soviets, who considered that the original ideological approach had not been radical enough. Some former advisers also made the claims that, besides the Soviets not dutifully studying the context, the main issue was that some advisers were not "sincere communists," people who did not really espouse Soviet values.[105] Soviet Muslims were often among those considered by other Soviets and Afghans as too prone to compromise on ideology; for example, Slinkin noted how the PDPA always asked for advisers "to come 'preferably from the Russian Federation' (meaning Slavs)."[106] This also used to be Amin's opinion.

Months later, the same Afghanistan veteran sent another letter to Gorbachev. His argument remained along the same lines, criticizing national reconciliation for being a "social class reconciliation." The Afganets was appalled that Moscow wanted to make it look like: "the 'blame' for what had happened in Afghanistan [was] on the truly progressive forces who had been too hasty in raising the red flag in Central Asia . . . in 'imposing' socialism from above in its 'non-Afghan,' 'non-Islamic' form that insulted traditions, led to violence and abuses."[107] Instead, the author contended, the Soviets had made too much of the Afghans' "immaturity" and "religiousness" and their "incapacity" to move past "their traditional way of life." The real issue was that "no one had really attempted to build socialism" in Afghanistan. His was a traditional hardline view, with the military's inclination toward Khalq, but also one that fascinatingly summed up the new Soviet thinking by contrast. In conclusion, even this convinced Marxist-Leninist paradoxically noted that it was still necessary to rename Afghanistan as the Islamic Democratic State before restarting the whole sovietization enterprise.[108] This showed that even hardliners felt that the religious aspect of the conflict had been mismanaged; the tension was between those who thought that Islam needed to be only tactically integrated and those, like Gorbachev and Najibullah, who were increasingly ready to scrap ideology altogether. Among the latter group, some wanted actual power-sharing while others pushed for the rebranded PDPA to stay solely in charge.

Without doubt, Moscow fully backed Najibullah's new policy, as evidenced by its direct advice but also symbolic aspects. The Soviet media, for example, translated the new thinking into a new language. Instead of calling the mujahideen "bandits," "*dushmans*," "*basmachi*," and "counterrevolutionary forces," they now called them "the Islamic parties" and "the military forces of the opposition" because, as candidly explained by the Sekretariat of the CC CPSU, "it was inappropriate to speak of national reconciliation with bandits."[109] Despite some relapses into the old terminology, this was a clear break. A journalist with the LCST then noted that things had changed on the information front in 1986–87: "There was less atheistic propaganda, the advisers who used to 'not recommend to read *namaz*' in the Afghan army had disappeared."[110]

In fine, while the Soviets gave Najibullah their blessing to integrate Islam, this was easier done at Gorbachev's level than at that of the mid-level advisers or the military, people who came from Western Russia and believed that religion had all but disappeared in the USSR. Still, the strategy of devising a new Islamic platform for the PDPA continued, with the Soviets sometimes even going ahead of the Afghans. By late 1988, some senior advisers even floated the possibility of creating an Islamic Council, more *sharia* courts, and a school to train judges for such courts.[111] Najibullah meanwhile intensified the Islamization of the state institutions as an additional component of national reconciliation, preparing for after the Soviet withdrawal.

The PDPA's Conversion to Islam

Political reforms transformed the DRA into an Islamic-looking, if not truly Islamic, state in late 1987. During the summer, the PDPA changed the law on political parties. The new law's first article stipulated that "parties had to treat the holy religion of Islam with respect."[112] By fall, it created a Popular Islamic Party of Afghanistan in a transparent attempt at challenging the opposition with its own Islamic party. The new party's name was deliberately consonant with those of the insurgents in Pakistan. It also launched *Islamic Guidance (Ershad Islami)*, a weekly journal published by the High Council of Ulemas and the Clergy and whose avowed goal was to "unite Afghan Muslims for peace and national reconciliation."[113] Interestingly, the Soviets devised these measures together with the Afghans.[114]

The regime then prepared a new Afghan Constitution that proclaimed Islam as the state religion and set out the national reconciliation program's principles. Before its adoption, the regime circulated 7 million copies in five languages—displaying its attention to minorities—of the draft across Afghanistan. The TASS correspondent in Kabul interestingly reported ordinary Afghans' selected feedback on the draft. Some people protested that the Constitution's preamble did not mention the April Revolution, while others believed that the statement about Islam being Afghanistan's religion should have gone into the preamble.[115] This exemplified the tension even in regime areas between those who believed that the PDPA had already gone too far in transforming the DRA and those who felt that it needed to do more. In any case, the Constitution served as a nation-wide propaganda prop and a way to consolidate the regime's turn in favor of Islam. As to the Soviet role in preparing the Constitution, the Afghanist Gankovsky claimed that Soviet advisers wrote it.[116] This was probably largely true but paradoxically not the most important thing about it. Much as for other aspects of national reconciliation, the Constitution's importance was less in its compliance with purported international standards than in how the regime used it to gain popular support and highlight its new platform. Remarkably, as with the rest of Afghan policy, there was no unanimity among the Soviets on the Constitution. Some Soviet diplomats contended that it went too far too quickly in changing the PDPA's platform.[117]

The adoption of the Constitution instead of the *Fundamental Principles* of the DRA, a de facto Constitution introduced by Karmal, came as the culmination of the process of institutional Islamization in November 1987. By that time, Gorbachev had made up his mind about the need to start the withdrawal. Najibullah was under pressure to give the opposition tangible concessions on symbols and ideology. These included a change to the country's name. Instead of the Democratic Republic of Afghanistan, it became the Republic of Afghanistan. In another reworking of the country's flag, the symbolic red star was dropped. The Constitution introduced new legislative and executive bodies. Instead of the Soviet-style Revolutionary Council appeared a parliament, the National Council. The country's leader was now called the president instead of the general secretary. An advisory council of Islamic figures was created by his side. According to Polyanichko, the council's job was then to discuss and approve all the new measures.[118] The Constitution's preamble did not mention the April Revolution, but its second article stipulated that "the religion of Afghanistan [was] the holy religion of Islam."[119] The new Constitution truly did not leave much of Khalq's Marxist-Leninist revolution.

After the Constitution's adoption by a loyal *loya jirga*, Najibullah swore that "as President of a Muslim country," he would "protect Islam's positions in the spiritual life of the people."[120] Before parting, the traditional assembly repeated that the "patriotic clergy," the Council of Ulemas, had to help Najibullah's "historic peacebuilding mission [under] Islam, the heavenly precepts of the Koran."[121] Such reliance on traditional assemblies was a strategic policy for the regime. The Council of Ulemas' role was to make PDPA's policies "ostensibly conform to Islam" and find examples to back them in the Koran.[122] Unlike in the Karmal era, the PDPA took this aspect seriously. At the same time, traditional assemblies played a role in politically legitimizing Najibullah's reforms and the new Constitution. The regime, therefore, continued to hold elections and *loya jirgas* and convey Islamic assemblies afterward. In some areas, that strategy helped it consolidate popular support by presenting itself as the guarantor of stability and security.

The regime adopted more measures aimed at highlighting the country and the party's Islamic character by 1988. The Islamic Centre in Kabul had by then 450 students while 7,000 more were in government *madrasas* and Koranic schools.[123] Although there are questions about what type of Islamic education was provided in such institutions—two Swiss ethnographers who visited the Islamic Centre noted that it looked like a Soviet orientalist import where religion was treated like a form of knowledge among others and handled by *apparatchiks* who had been sidelined from the PDPA—their growth showed the genuine investments made by the regime into, even though not always successfully, integrating Islam.[124]

In some provinces, this drive went even further than in Kabul. Visiting Jalalabad with Kryuchkov, Shebarshin noted how the LCST's withdrawal—effective by then there—had affected Nangarhar Province on the Pakistani border. Interestingly, the local situation had significantly improved after Governor Wakil Azam Shinwari, who had fled Afghanistan after tensions with other insurgents before returning following a governmental amnesty, had implemented policies perceived by the population as in accordance with Islam's values and rules. Shinwari had gained popularity after forbidding brothels and shops selling alcohol, even raising concerns in Kabul over his independence. In Shebarshin's assessment, this was the success of a man who had understood that Afghans were tired of the "difficult to understand political-ideological incantations" of the PDPA.[125] To be fair, though, the Soviets had clearly made the same errors.

Taking stock of the new situation, the AIC similarly wrote of "the regime's program of Islamization," emphasizing its expansion since the Karmal era. It highlighted that Afghan national identity cards once more carried a column stating the holder's religion, that the regime had made it "compulsory for high-ranking party members to attend prayers [at] the mosque," and that the Afghan communists had dropped the title "comrade" for "honorable" and "dear" in official communications.[126] These three measures were highly emblematic and visible, affecting party members and ordinary Afghans alike. Najibullah was therefore transforming the social fabric of the PDPA and Afghanistan. He made compromises not only on symbols but also on ideology to retain power while the LCST was leaving. Forced by circumstances, his policies translated the understanding that Marxism-Leninism was effectively dead as a mobilizing force in Afghanistan. There could be no more talk of displaying the April Revolution's benefits.

The changes introduced by Najibullah angered many PDPA hardliners who thought that he was selling out the revolution while integrating "reactionary mullahs" into the government.[127] Some party workers started asking why the party no longer commemorated the death of Mir Akbar Khyber, the Parchami leader—also respected by the Khalqis—whose assassination in unclear circumstances had sparked the April Revolution.[128] Khyber was part of the PDPA's mythology that Najibullah had now discarded. This tension between the communist ideal and the resurgent traditions and Islam would continue to fracture the PDPA and the Afghan society even after the Soviet withdrawal. The April Revolution had been the product of long-standing social tensions for a generation of Afghans who had looked at forms of Western modernity while remaining constrained by the rigidity of Afghan social structures.[129] Many Afghans, notably in urban areas, had then sincerely fought to bring Soviet-style modernity and progress to Afghanistan, becoming accustomed to a different lifestyle and espousing new values in the process. Influenced by state education, travel to the USSR, and service in the military, they had supported the social and economic changes brought by the PDPA. To these people, Najibullah's compromises felt like a retreat.

The tensions over national reconciliation permeated the PDPA, serving as a background for its leaders' personal ambitions. Still split between Khalq and

Parcham, the party saw each politburo member develop his clientele. Najibullah conducted another series of purges to consolidate the party in late 1988, but the PDPA never appeared as a unified entity. Karmalism—support for Karmal—was, for example, rife in KhAD due to the rejection of Najibullah's "traitorous policy." This resulted both from ideological opposition to national reconciliation and fear regarding personal well-being. As a Soviet KGB officer confessed, "many [KhAD] collaborators who had been at the forefront of the struggle against the armed opposition, . . . had effectively cut themselves a way back to any kind of reconciliation." Given the violence KhAD had leveled on the population, many of its operatives were too compromised to make peace with the mujahideen. Because of that, the agency's effectiveness declined after 1987, the KGB officer complained.[130] Significantly, opposition to national reconciliation had spread because concessions on symbols and ideology had endangered the PDPA's internal cohesion. It had happened while the PDPA had made no meaningful attempt to politically integrate opposition forces. Accordingly, the PDPA's weakness put at risk the Soviet withdrawal strategy.

The Kremlin's advice for the need for the PDPA to share power was in any case half-hearted. Gorbachev had a limited capacity to bend Najibullah to his will and gave priority to withdrawing in good order. The MID's Kornienko would bluntly state at the politburo that "Najib understood 'national reconciliation' under the framework—'the PDPA is the leading force'" and not as a coalition government with the PDPA's participation. Gorbachev, too, believed that 50 percent of all positions should have gone to the opposition and that the rest was idle talk (*govoril'nya*). The problem was that if the Soviets told the PDPA that it would not have the leading role, "[the Afghans] would simply all run away in different directions," Gorbachev lamented.[131] Kryuchkov's and Shevardnadze's line of unyielding support to Najibullah, therefore, had to dominate to keep the PDPA together. As seen by an officer in the LCST, this meant that reconciliation "could only be done on Kabul's conditions."[132] Najibullah hence continued to seek a dominant role for the PDPA and himself. To the Soviets, he made it clear that he had no intention of relinquishing power. The fact that in the meantime Mohammed Hassan Shark, a neutral politician from the prerevolutionary era, had become prime minister did not change the situation. Despite garnering approval from the Kremlin, Shark remained hostage to the PDPA, lacking tangible personal support. By late 1988, even Varennikov had become disillusioned with Najibullah's clinging to power.[133]

Soviet and Western observers had a mixed assessment of national reconciliation in 1987–88. Following the established trope, Gromyko blamed the Afghans for misleading the Soviets about the policy's successes.[134] Tsagolov, Varennikov's adviser who would later proudly claim to have been central in devising national reconciliation, forcefully denounced it in a letter to Dmitry Yazov, Gorbachev's minister of defense. Stating that "it was necessary to let go of socialist illusions," he argued that national reconciliation had been rejected by the mujahideen and the Afghan people.[135] Tsagolov's assessment was most notable for its rehashing of existing measures, including calls to create a made-up Islamic party, rename the country, and negotiate with the mujahideen. Polyanichko, more softly, noted that it was a shame that national reconciliation never became all it could have been because the Soviets were never able to entirely let go of the legacy of the war. The policy became mostly about the Geneva Accords.[136] There was an enduring blindness among the Soviet policymakers about the fact that there was nothing more that could be done regarding national reconciliation while the LCST was in Afghanistan. In the West, Roy, a prominent Afghanistan expert, similarly noted that national reconciliation had not so far worked. The mujahideen had rejected the PDPA's offer of "peace of the braves." Marking the policy's struggles, few refugees had returned from Pakistan despite the PDPA's using coercive means to incite returns, and the ceasefires were only on paper.[137]

Most important, the PDPA's Islamic policy long struggled to make a difference. One reason was that Kabul was often unable to protect the people who moved to its side. The mujahideen killed three successive Islamic leaders in charge of Kandahar's national reconciliation commission until the authorities could not find anyone to take the job.[138] Overall, the mujahideen assassinated the leaders of national reconciliation commission in at least seven provinces. They similarly harshly retaliated against the tribes that accepted the government's ceasefires.[139] A second was that the regime's reforms and support to mosques and Islamic leaders, though appreciated, lagged what most Afghans wanted as to Islam's place. Widespread corruption and lingering ideology also diminished these measures' effectiveness. One cunning shopkeeper in Kabul had, for example, managed to go on Hajj three times thanks to governmental subsidies.[140] Other PDPA leaders and mullahs made entirely inappropriate parallels during sermons between going on Hajj and visiting the USSR.[141] Although Moscow stepped up humanitarian aid and infrastructure reconstruction on its way out, including to mosques, their distribution and implementation by PDPA committees with little oversight was a problem.[142] In addition, there was a long way between distributing aid and preaching in mosques and building enough support for Afghans to enlist in the army. During national reconciliation, conscription remained the most hated governmental policy and desertion remained rife. Kabul long failed to translate adherence to its Islamic policy into concrete support.

Finally, the main issue was the Soviet presence that made the PDPA look like a puppet authority, especially among refugees. It was now less about Islam and the PDPA's reforms and more about the continuation of a discredited regime that had brought in the Soviets and waged a brutal war against its people. In 1988, Najibullah himself half-joked about it to the Soviet politburo. Reporting on his meeting with Hekmatyar's Hezb-e-Islami, the most radical of the mujahideen Islamist parties, he claimed that they told him that "in Islamic issues [he] had gone so far that they could give [him] a membership card in their party."[143] By then, the stalemate was clear for all sides, preventing national reconciliation from building traction for the time being.

While the new policy had helped Kabul gain support in mostly non-Pashtun areas by giving local strongmen—over 350 field commanders controlling 140,000 people according to a Soviet estimate republished by an Afghan scholar favorable to the mujahideen—autonomy and economic incentives, it did not lead to actual power-sharing.[144] It crucially did not immediately increase disinterested support for the regime. The PDPA co-opted only a handful of influential mujahideen commanders while discarding its most emblematic reforms, including the land reform, women's literacy programs, and bride price limitations.

As the Soviet withdrawal accelerated, national reconciliation, nevertheless, gained momentum. After another mission to Afghanistan in late 1988, a French diplomat and aid worker reported that even though national reconciliation did not lead to the expected results, it had "sent politically the ball back to the resistance." Its limitation was that the regime did not always keep its promises, including on ceasefires. However, the Frenchman significantly noted that the regime's Islamic propaganda was taking hold: "Islam introduced in Article 2 of the Constitution removed another communist veneer from the regime that did not stop trying to hide it underneath nature. This reference to Islam and Najibullah's incongruous shows of piety at Friday prayers may trouble some people's spirits that end up wondering if they should not pretend to take the hand extended to them to then get rid of this reviled regime from the inside instead of being caught up in radicalization that Pakistan is trying to promote and that is only meant to serve its interests."[145] At the international level, the United Nations Special Rapporteur on Human Rights missions to Kabul similarly lauded the improvements in the human rights situation, including the free practice of "religious manifestations" in PDPA areas.[146]

Even among the mujahideen, Najibullah's religious offensive led to concerns that, against the backdrop of the LCST's withdrawal, the PDPA's support may increase as we will see later in this chapter. Meanwhile, the opposition's infighting and Islamist radicalization spurred by the arrival of Arab fighters started to repulse some Afghans. The same poll that showed a rejection of national reconciliation in Pakistani refugee camps also showed the mujahideen leaders' discredit. Instead of mujahideen rule, some 70 percent of the interviewees wanted a return of King Zahir Shah.[147] The background in Afghanistan was hence set for recomposition to happen based not on ideology but rather on ethnicity and tribe.

These evolutions set the stage for after the Soviet withdrawal when the PDPA would be able to claim more convincingly that it was a bulwark against the arrival to power of the fundamentalists who wanted to fight "social progress" and return Afghanistan "to practices of the Middle-Ages."[148] The formerly communist regime would hence picture itself as a bastion of "traditional Islam." The AIC remarkably noted the risk for the opposition that such propaganda may succeed. It feared that the communists may go even further along the Islamic road, replacing Najibullah with "a simple Muslim puppet" and calling "the country the Islamic Republic of Afghanistan." This, the AIC believed, would have "confused the nation."[149] As this chapter has shown, the Kremlin chose another strategy when it selected Najibullah. It adopted a middle course between a more acceptable traditional Muslim leader and a product of the PDPA system. This was Najibullah's limit and the reason the reservations of some of the Soviets about him not going far enough in sharing power seem disingenuous in retrospect.

The Mujahideen and the Soviets

The Mujahideen parties' development and ideology and their leaders' background are well-covered in the literature on the Soviet-Afghan War. Considerable scholarship also exists on how the United States and some Arab countries channeled support to the most radical groups through Pakistan's intelligence agency, the ISI. By claiming that they were less active against the communists, the ISI sidelined traditional and non-Pashtun leaders who often supported the deposed king to back the Islamists who were more receptive to its own goal of creating strategic depth in its confrontation with India. Prioritizing the Islamists was also Saudi Arabia's and the American Central Intelligence Agency's (CIA) policy. Riyadh saw Afghanistan as a religious issue and deferred most of its handling to its Islamic establishment and political entrepreneurs such as Osama bin Laden. Like the ISI, the CIA preferred Hekmatyar's Islamists, believing them to be the best fighters among the mujahideen.[150] By 1984–85, Arab volunteers, guided by the Saudis and their allies, started arriving in the wake of the Palestinian preacher Azzam to join the jihad.

FIGURE 4.4.   Ronald Reagan receiving Mujahideen leaders at the White House, 1983 (Courtesy of the Ronald Reagan Presidential Library). The United States publicly supported the Afghan Freedom Fighters. It, however, channeled most of its aid to the most radical Islamist groups.

Beyond this, suffice to say that seven parties in Pakistan and eight in Iran were part of the jihad against the communists. The groups in Iran were only active in the majority Shia regions of central Afghanistan and were less important. They were controlled by Tehran and did not play a prominent role during the Soviet-Afghan War. By contrast, the "Peshawar-7" that consolidated in the first years of the war in Pakistan dominated the jihad. It controlled the multitude of groups inside Afghanistan, distributing the weapons and funding provided by the ISI. This control was tighter or looser based on the party and the region. Coordination remained notoriously complicated among and within parties and infighting was frequent. Soviet and Western observers separated these Pakistani-based mujahideen between Islamist or fundamentalist and moderate Islamic or traditionalist wings.[151] In both, it is striking how the leaders' profiles contrasted with those of the Islamic scholars the Kabul regime had brought to its side. Virtually all mujahideen leaders had a greater Islamic legitimacy than the head of the state ministry dealing with Islam.

The Islamists included the Hezb-e-Islami (Islamic Party)—a party that since its inception had been influenced by the Muslim Brotherhood—of Hekmatyar who, despite his radicalism, had the weakest Islamic credentials.[152] They also included its offshoot the Hezb-e-Islami of *Mawlawi* Younas Khalis and the Ittehad-e-Islami bara-ye Azadi-ye Afghanistan (Islamic Union for the Liberation

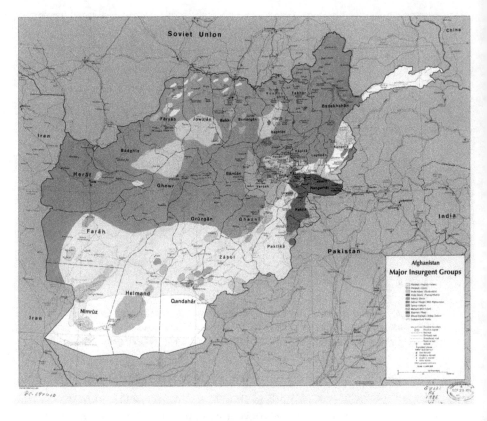

MAP 4.1. Historical map of areas controlled by Insurgent Groups in Afghanistan produced by the CIA, 1985 (Library of Congress, https://www.loc.gov/item/85697410/).

of Afghanistan) of Abdul Rasul Sayyaf, an Islamic scholar who had studied at al-Azhar University and was close to the Saudis but had the fewest forces fighting inside Afghanistan. More toward the center, the Jamiat-e Islami (Islamic Society) of Burhanuddin Rabbani—a former professor at Kabul University, graduate of al-Azhar University, and adherent to the Naqshbandiyah Sufi order—and its partly independent branch the Shura-e Nazar (Supervisory Council of the North) of Massoud were non-Pashtun dominated and arbitrated divergences with the traditionalists.

The traditionalists were made up of: the Mahaz-i-Milli-ye Islami-ye Afghanistan (National Islamic Front for Afghanistan) of Pir Sayyid Ahmed Gailani, the head of the Qadiriyyah Sufi order in Afghanistan whom the Soviets had hoped to co-opt in 1979; the Jebh-i-Nejat-i Melli (National Liberation Front) of Sibghatullah Mujaddidi, a member of the most prominent family of Islamic scholars and leaders of the Naqshbandiyah Sufi order in Afghanistan who had studied at al-Azhar University; and the Harakat-i-Inqilab-i-Islami (Islamic Revolution Movement) of Mohammad Nabi Mohammadi, an Islamic scholar from eastern Logar Province who had been a member of the parliament in the 1960s, clashing, including physically, with Karmal.

Islam was central to the mujahideen's cohesion and emphasized at all levels, up to the name "Islamic committees" used for their local government councils inside Afghanistan. It shaped the meta-narrative for the war that had been a jihad even before the Soviet intervention. *AFGHANews*, the English version of Jamiat-e-Islami's journal, made it clear that "only good Muslims" could join the mujahideen. The "secular elements," "anti-Soviet leftists," "undisciplined loose liberals or blind nationalists" were not welcome.[153] The dominant binary narrative opposing believers and infidels masked that the claim to Islamic legitimacy was different among the mujahideen. It was least obvious for the Islamist intellectuals who had studied abroad and lacked the influence of hereditary Sufi leaders such as Mujaddidi and Gailani, or of well-known local leaders such as Nabi and Khalis. The war allowed Hekmatyar, Sayyaf, and Rabbani to gain influence by altering traditional power structures and how Afghan society negotiated Islamic legitimacy. Previously, "the authority conferred by literacy and religious knowledge was offset by other considerations, such as ancestry, land ownership, marriage ties, and connections to state offices and officials."[154] This changed with the conflict.

The Soviet-Afghan War made Islam a national integrating factor, even though the mujahideen parties' recruitment long remained regional and ethnic, and changed how Islam shaped the Afghan way of life.[155] Islam's political importance had eroded in many provinces and customary law was as vital a factor of legitimacy as Islam before the war in Pashtun areas. However, the mujahideen remade Islam into the main legitimizing factor of power, countering secularizing trends that had been ongoing since Amanullah Khan's reign and intensified under Daud.[156] The war helped the Islamists recapture some of the influence lost by the traditional Islamic leaders in previous years.[157] Through education in Pakistan, and hence in competition with the communist project, this also prepared Afghan society to embrace a more rigorist interpretation of the Islamic texts. The end process of this transformation would be the Taliban.

By 1987, the most important aspect for the Soviets was to separate the mujahideen ready to negotiate with the PDPA from the so-called irreconcilables.[158] The hope that the PDPA, with or without Najibullah, could remain at Afghanistan's helm as part of a coalition government was likewise at the center of pre- and postwithdrawal Soviet negotiations with the United States as they continued to back their respective Afghan clients. The Soviets believed that the traditionalists, who were the ones eager for the king's return, may at least have been amenable to a coalition with the PDPA. They were especially hopeful that Gailani and Mujaddidi may compromise, although neither saw a major role for Najibullah after the war.[159]

There was, however, a crucial reason for the traditionalists to move closer to the Kabul regime. As Victor Spolnikov, the former KGB head in Kabul, pointed out in his analysis of the Afghan opposition, Mujaddidi and Gailani needed a political settlement "before the traditional bases of their influence were destroyed" and Hekmatyar and Rabbani sidelined them.[160] Hence, the Soviets had an astute enough grasp of the context by the late 1980s to play on the conflict among the mujahideen. Unfortunately for the communists, though, none of the mujahideen leaders, including Massoud, whom the Soviets also saw as prone to compromise, could strike a separate peace deal with Najibullah while the LCST was still present. They "could not let go of the Islamic slogans that had long guaranteed the effectiveness of their fight," a Soviet general argued.[161] This meta-narrative about the war and corresponding party discipline only started to erode after the war against the Soviets ended and the PDPA, the other side of the ideological duopoly, shed its Marxist-Leninism. Beyond this, the mujahideen were also on the winning side, opposing a regime expected to fall soon. In post-Soviet Afghanistan, Najibullah's resilience would further challenge Islam's role as an integrating factor among the mujahideen. Hezb-e-Islami, Jamiat-e-Islami, and other parties would then try to attract defectors from the PDPA and increasingly fight each other.

Because of the proximity of his Panjshir base to the USSR's border, Massoud was the mujahideen leader with whom the Soviets dealt the most. While they conducted as many as nine offensives against Massoud, the Soviets also signed regular local ceasefires with him, gaining respect for the brave Afghan leader over time.[162] The Soviets, "after they became more flexible and started to better understand Afghanistan, learned to deal with him, organizing ceasefires and prisoners' exchanges," a Soviet journalist who met the Panjshiri leader noted.[163] The LCST command would at times ally with Massoud against his opponents in Hezb-e-Islami. Meanwhile, the Soviet policymakers in Kabul and Moscow would clash over whether they should deal with Massoud through negotiation or military action. In late 1988–89, this would lead to considerable tensions between the military command and the Najibullah-Shevardnadze-Kryuchkov group. To Varennikov, the issue was with Najibullah's "pathological hate" of the Tajik leader.[164] Ultimately, the Soviets would never manage to engineer an understanding between Massoud and Najibullah. Illustrating the ambiguity of the Moscow-Kabul relation again, the Kremlin under the PDPA's influence would instead force the LCST into conducting a series of militarily futile airstrikes against Massoud-held territory in the last weeks of the withdrawal.

Despite its radicalism and US backing, parts of the PDPA and the Soviets moreover courted Hezb-e-Islami as we will see in chapter 6. Composed mostly of Pashtuns, Hezb-e-Islami had ethnic and kinship ties with some of the Khalqis. In parallel, it increasingly professed anti-American positions. For these two reasons, some in Moscow and Kabul believed that striking a deal with it was not the worst option.

Jamiat-e-Islami and National Reconciliation

Jamiat-e-Islami, the party of Rabbani and Massoud, was particularly important for the Soviets. Examining its assessment of the communist Islamic policies helps better understand their effect in Afghanistan. Over time, Jamiat-e-Islami's communication became more sophisticated while its bi-weekly *AFGHANews* became professionalized. In 1985, the journal's unnumbered issues featured only short reports about military engagements, presenting a roughly typed text on bad quality paper. By the war's end, *AFGHANews* was a full-fledged information journal with analytical pieces, occasionally by invited Western experts, professional text editing and page layout, pictures, caricatures, and editorials. Many Soviets bitterly highlighted the quality and complexity of the mujahideen propaganda, believing that they were losing the information war. Egorychev and Polyanichko, for example, saw the communist propaganda's inefficiency in the countryside as a key explanation of the Soviet difficulties.[165]

AFGHANews, like other mujahideen journals, denounced the LCST and the PDPA for going against Islam, accusing them of "humiliating mosques, shrines and religious books."[166] It similarly charged the Kabul regime for being "godless" despite its professed support to loyal Islamic leaders and mosques. Remarkably, *AFGHANews* also wrote of the persecution of Muslims in other pro-Soviet countries, reinforcing the idea that communists attacked Islam everywhere.[167] What was striking was how the denunciations of the Afghan communists' attacks on Islam and the PDPA's Islamic policies grew over time. Marginal in 1985, they took on considerable importance in the Najibullah period.

One reason for this evolution was that the mujahideen, as indeed the PDPA, had a limited understanding of propaganda's importance and of how to conduct it effectively, especially in English. As the Soviet-Afghan War progressed, they learned to use photographs and produce elaborate articles on complex topics by mobilizing professional writers.[168] Another was that the mujahideen

FIGURE 4.5. Ahmad Shah Massoud talking with a mullah in the Panjshir, 1981 (Courtesy of Olivier Roy). One of the leaders of Jamiat-e-Islami, Massoud played a key role in the mujahideen's victory against the Soviets. He also came to be respected by the Soviet military.

took time to assess the importance of extensively talking about Islam. They may have perceived the issue to have long been obvious to *AFGHANews'* international audience given that the meta-narrative for the war as one between believers and infidels went uncontested. Karmal's regime was visibly not Islamic and there was no need to dwell on that. Their new focus on Islam was a response to the success of Najibullah's Islamization policies.

In an interview for the BBC in 1987, Rabbani tied the issue of the Kabul regime's lack of Islamic legitimacy to the Soviet presence and quickly dismissed the whole thing: "When the Russians and Russians' agents faced a defeat vis-à-vis the decisive determination of the people, they put on such false masks. But this was only temporary. If they felt that the critical stage has passed, they would reveal their Satanic faces again."[169] This was a keen observation and certainly true in the Karmal era, but by 1987 the communists had engaged on a course that would lead them to abandon Marxism-Leninism altogether.

The mujahideen had been slow in recognizing that an actual shift was happening and that it may challenge how ordinary Afghans saw the conflict. They detected it only after national reconciliation was in full swing. *AFGHANews* then dedicated substantial attention to countering the PDPA's Islamic policy, an indication it was concerned that it could work in propping the regime's domestic and international legitimacy. In 1987, it published an editorial that extensively tackled the problem. After contending that the "communists had found Islam a major obstacle on their way to impose an alien way of life on Afghans" and had therefore "declared a total war against it," the editorial's author argued that they had now changed strategy. The PDPA's "new tactic [was to] destroy Islam with Islam," he claimed. He followed this assertion with a comprehensive list of the regime's measures to appear more Islamic. Then, remarkably, he betrayed his concern as to the policy's impact: "The easiest target for their campaign was the common man who has a shallow understanding of Islam. Communists thought that by talking about religion, whitewashing the mosques, and participating in congregational prayers they could win the hearts and minds of the people . . . This explains the purpose of all religious propaganda launched by the regime. Holy Quran is recited each morning on the state-controlled radio . . . After the national reconciliation program, the religious propaganda launched by the regime was intensified."[170]

Although the editorial predictably concluded by saying that such propaganda would not sway the Afghans, its author was obviously concerned about the regime's Islamic policies. It is salient how the condescending image of Afghans he presented was reminiscent of Soviet claims about their backwardness, which made them unable to appreciate the benefits of modernity. The mujahideen deployed the same rhetorical argument by suggesting that ordinary people were not clever enough to see through the regime's propaganda. This again testified to how all conflicting parties were always eager to speak in place of the people while advancing their agendas for post-conflict Afghanistan.

The editorial also dwelled on the situation in Soviet Central Asia to argue that communism and Islam were incompatible. This was another indication that behind the PDPA's Islamic policy, Jamiat-e-Islami feared an attempt to make the Central Asian model acceptable to Afghans, especially as the USSR had strengthened links between Central Asian republics and Afghan provinces. Another article in the same volume contended that Islam was experiencing a revival in Central Asia, challenging communist ideology, in line with the arguments of the Bennigsen school.[171] It was a transparent attempt to heighten Soviet fears of an Islamist threat coming from Afghanistan.

AFGHANews continued to attack the PDPA's national reconciliation and Islamic policies thereafter. It maintained that makeshift adjustments such as introducing a fake multiparty system where all parties were loyal to the PDPA and renaming the country, would "not bring the regime any good at home."[172] The journal similarly complained that the April Revolution and the Soviet invasion had disrupted the religious and traditional life of the people and that only a mujahideen rule could restore the Afghan way of life. As an article in

AFGHANews asserted, the "puppet regime which [had] brought all this trag-edy to the country [now] tried to exploit" Ramadan to boost its legitimacy by announcing "the release of some prisoners in honor of Eid." The mujahideen ultimately enjoined Afghans not to forget that the PDPA's leaders were "com-munists and did not believe in religion" even though they "participated in the congregation prayers." Their only "purpose was to deceive the people who are Muslims."[173]

Jamiat-e-Islami no doubt rejected national reconciliation but, unlike Kar-mal's policies, discussed it extensively. This was the clearest sign that some-thing new was happening in Afghanistan against the backdrop of the Soviet withdrawal which, although it weakened the regime militarily, was about to remove its main liability in terms of popular perception. In this context, *News of Jihad*, Jebh-i-Nejat-i Melli's journal, published a remarkable editorial on na-tional reconciliation, showing that other mujahideen parties also debated the policy.[174] Opposing it for the same reasons as Jamiat-e-Islami, Jebh-i-Nejat-i Melli argued that the fundamental issue with national reconciliation was that it postulated that the Soviet-Afghan War was a civil war. Yet accepting such a proposition was unacceptable for the mujahideen because it meant changing the meta-narrative about the conflict and legitimizing the Kabul regime.

Be that as it may, the mujahideen had to answer national reconciliation unless they wanted to appear to be prolonging the war. In 1988, according to Soviet intelligence, Massoud argued in a speech in the Panjshir that they had to take the policy as a serious challenge. The mujahideen had to increase their propaganda and ideological work, including regarding Islam. "It was unaccept-able to move into the background the idea of the Holy War" against the com-munists, Massoud claimed.[175] Such statements must be seen in the context of the tensions among the leaders in Peshawar, the infighting among the muja-hideen inside Afghanistan, and the increasing temptation of some to reexam-ine Najibullah's offers after the Soviet withdrawal.

AFGHANews articles and Massoud's speech confirmed that the PDPA's drive to integrate Islam into the regime's platform had helped it gain support. The policy was becoming troublesome for Jamiat-e-Islami in the context of the LC-ST's departure. The PDPA, *AFGHANews* admitted, had been "partially suc-cessful in [its] previous propaganda moves like 'cease-fire' and 'national reconciliation,'" leading it to "add a new element to it—purchase of arms from [the] mujahideen."

According to Jamiat-e-Islami, Najibullah aimed his new measures as much at a domestic audience as at undermining support for the mujahideen abroad, trying to change the content of UN and OIC resolutions.[176] This, Jamiat-e-Islami complained, occasionally produced results. Some countries now argued that national reconciliation could be good for Afghanistan, *AFGHANews* lamented.[177] As the next chapter shows, Najibullah's foreign policy toward Muslim countries was gaining traction at the same time.

Moscow changed its strategy in Afghanistan in the wake of Gorbachev's rise to power. This led to the replacement of Karmal by Najibullah and ultimately to the national reconciliation program. Encountering modest success while the LCST was present, national reconciliation's achievement was in preparing for the Soviet withdrawal while setting the stage for post-Soviet Afghanistan. Meanwhile, the PDPA, originally a vanguard Marxist-Leninist party, modified its message and platform to raise its support among the population and retain power. By 1989, it had done away with Marxism-Leninism and taken measures that unambiguously supported Islam. After the LCST's departure, this strategy brought Najibullah and the PDPA even more dividends.

The PDPA's transformation happened with Moscow's sanction. This was both remarkable and not at all surprising. Despite Soviet propaganda's talk of internationalism, ideology was not the sole reason for motivating the intervention. The LCST's deployment responded to traditional geostrategic concerns. Moscow likewise had no problem backing other regimes with dubious Marxist-Leninist credentials. However, Afghanistan was not Angola, Libya, or Ethiopia. By accepting for the PDPA—a party it had groomed since the 1960s and that had received in its socialism building enterprise unprecedented support—to discard Marxism-Leninism for Islam, the USSR was admitting that communism was not a mobilizing factor in Afghan society. In this sense, while many see the Soviet-Afghan War as having contributed to the Soviet collapse by the economic burden and the negative domestic coverage it generated, the conflict also contributed by showing that the ideological appeal of the USSR and its type of modernity had run out of steam. It stimulated "Soviet disillusion in internationalism" and questioned the "idea of a transition to socialism in the Third World on which the whole system rested."[178]

While Moscow had initiated and sanctioned this policy change, this chapter has again shown the interconnections between Soviet and Afghan decision-making, deflating the idea that Najibullah was the passive implementer of national reconciliation. Even more than Karmal, he altered the Soviet course of action, leading to a relationship where both parties ended up unsatisfied. However, he managed the bigger feat: to get the PDPA in line for Soviet withdrawal. This was no small achievement. Prompted to comment on Najibullah's importance, Gorbachev would emphasize that point: "Don't Forget Kabul. Remember that Karmal headed the Afghan government. He was a very particular personality and he had his own agenda. In view of this, I am afraid

that even with the backing of the United States we would have had a very difficult time [leaving Afghanistan]. With Najibullah it was different. I don't
think the world has appreciated what he did in bringing around his colleagues
to accept my view [about the need to withdraw]. A person of lesser ability
would not have been able to do it."[179] This admission vividly confirmed both
Karmal's and Najibullah's agency during the Soviet-Afghan War.

CHAPTER 5

The USSR, Afghanistan, and the Muslim World

> But you know it is easier for all of us to fly off together to another galaxy than for the Arabs to agree among themselves.
>
> —M. Gorbachev, February 1987

> The United States has directed Afghanistan against us. It helped them coalesce with the Muslim world and make it forget about the things Israel was doing in the Near East.
>
> —A. Adamishin Interview, August 2019

Condemnation among Muslim Countries

Nonalignment had been the defining principle in Afghan foreign policy even before the emergence of the movement of the same name. Khalq's ascendency marked a stark departure from that course. At the Non-Aligned Movement (NAM) Conference in Belgrade in 1978, Amin's position on international questions had been indistinguishable from those of Moscow and Havana.[1] Following the Soviet intervention, most countries saw Karmal's Afghanistan as even more subservient to the USSR. The rejection of Soviet imperialism went far beyond Moscow's Cold War enemies, spreading to the Third World, communist parties in Europe, and even Romania.[2] Aside from Soviet allies, India was the only country with which Afghan relations would prosper due to their mutual opposition to Pakistan. With the West and most of the Muslim world, the PDPA faced opposition throughout the 1980s.

At the UN General Assembly in November 1980, 111 countries voted for a resolution that called for the "immediate withdrawal of the foreign troops" from Afghanistan. The vote came as a stinging rebuke to the USSR. Only 19 countries, including communist Afghanistan, supported its intervention, while others either abstained or did not participate in the vote. Among pro-Soviet Muslim countries, the tally was especially preoccupying: Syria and South

Yemen had opposed; Algeria, Chad, Guinea-Bissau, and Mali abstained; and Iraq, Libya, and the Yemen Arab Republic did not participate.[3] Even pro-Soviet Algeria and Iraq criticized the intervention.[4]

Another vote on Afghanistan a year later proved even more damning as 116 countries condemned the Soviets while only 20, including communist Afghanistan, opposed the Resolution. Libya had joined the opposing ranks while Iraq, a country with which Moscow had a Treaty of Friendship and Cooperation like the one with Kabul, voted for the Resolution.[5] This show of Muslim solidarity surprised the politburo and showed its limited awareness of the rising cohesion of the Muslim world. Suddenly, Grachev remembered, Moscow's "traditional and favorite allies among Arab countries had joined the camp of its critics."[6] These were the countries on which the USSR had relied in the Middle East since Khrushchev's time. That the United States got a parallel publicity boost among Muslims for their support for the mujahideen after years of being disparaged for aligning with Israel only made things worse for the Soviets.[7]

The opposition of Muslim countries, some of which sent notes of condemnation to the Soviets, led to the diplomatic ostracism of Afghanistan.[8] As Gromyko told Shah Mohammad Dost, his Afghan counterpart, in January 1980, "Saudi Arabia intended to get six countries bordering it to break off diplomatic ties with the DRA" because of its anti-Islamic regime.[9] Although except Saudi Arabia and Egypt, Muslim countries only downscaled diplomatic relations instead of breaking them, this testified to Afghanistan's isolation. Accusations of atheism against the PDPA also justified the support of Pakistan, Iran, Saudi Arabia, and Egypt for the mujahideen and drove support to the insurgents inside Afghanistan. In the view of a KhAD operative, "the United States had successfully raised the issue of the defense of Islam, culture, traditions against the USSR. To implement its strategy, it had chosen Pakistan, providing it with big money." With Muslim countries' help, the Afghan operative argued, "[the United States] had persuasively colored [the war] in religious tones."[10] This was a crucial point that both sides recognized: the international framing of the Soviet-Afghan War had become problematic for the communists; it was between good and evil, Islam and atheism, Afghans and invaders. Over time, Muslim countries' support for the mujahideen expanded and calls to defend Islam took on a special meaning as Arab fighters flocked to Afghanistan.

The Soviet-Afghan War's negative fallout undermined years of Soviet backing for causes important to Muslims. As put by the High Sunni Council in Beirut, although "the Soviet Union's support for the Arabs' struggle against Israel received high appraisal . . . what was now happening in Afghanistan [could] only be described as an intervention against a Muslim people."[11] The blow to Soviet influence in the Muslim world was more critical because the latter had already been struggling for some time. Moscow had been unable to secure Muslim political objectives in the Middle East and answer Egypt's rapprochement with Israel.[12] Things were now getting worse. The Institute of the Economy of the World Socialist System (IEWSS) underlined the hit taken by Soviet influence in the Third World, "especially among Muslim countries," in a paper sent to the CC CPSU. The IEWSS contended that the intervention had allowed Islamic fundamentalists to increase propaganda among the Afghan population and helped unify Islamic insurgent groups and the Muslim world against Moscow.[13] In an instant, it shelved Soviet hopes of improving relations with pro-Western Saudi Arabia and Jordan. The Soviets had to satisfy themselves that the authorities in Morocco and Kuwait kept the criticism of the Soviet-Afghan War under control.[14] The Soviet intervention was a defining moment for Muslim countries. It fostered the cohesion of a Muslim world that remained extremely diverse in terms of political regimes, language, and culture. It also led to the emergence of new leaders.

Egypt was one of the countries that stood at the forefront of political support for the mujahideen. It was a unique opportunity for Cairo to reverse the ostracism it had experienced following the Camp David Accords signed with Israel in 1978. The Palestinian Liberation Organization (PLO), Iraq, Libya, and Syria—the pro-Soviet faction in the Muslim world—had obtained drastic sanctions against Egypt just months previously, including the recall of Arab ambassadors from Cairo, its expulsion from the Arab League, and the end of Arab economic aid. Now, it was Egypt's turn to get back at them. Its People's Assembly rapidly condemned the Soviet intervention and called it "anti-Islamic." Scholars from al-Azhar appealed to Muslim countries to confront it with jihad.[15] In January 1980, demonstrations in Cairo against the USSR gathered more than 10,000 people with banners reading "Soviets, Kabul will be your grave" near the al-Azhar Mosque. A representative of the Muslim Brotherhood addressed the crowd.[16] Egypt then continued to lead the international condemnation. In November, Sadat spoke at the People's Assembly to criticize those Muslim countries that had offered a muted response on Afghanistan.[17]

Like Egypt, Pakistan "stood to gain enormous prestige with the Arab world as a champion of Islam and with the West as a champion against communist aggression," a Pakistani intelligence chief recalled.[18] The Oriental Studies Institute in Moscow similarly pointed out that Islamabad had taken advantage of the PDPA's anti-Islamic policies by capitalizing on its own Islamic image. Hence, Pakistan's "Islamization of the domestic life of the country and its foreign policy directed at the multifaceted development of contacts with Muslim countries, [and] in particular Saudi Arabia" had garnered support in Afghan tribal areas and had helped consolidate Pakistani influence. Islamabad now included representatives of the tribal belt from the Afghan side in its Hajj delegations. Pakistan had been indeed wise in stressing Muslim rather than Pashtun solidarity to boost its influence in Afghanistan, the Oriental Studies Institute argued.[19]

Against this background, the Kabul regime's anti-Islamic image was an issue that it worked to correct throughout the conflict, but it was as much the product of the legacy of Khalq's policies as of the presence of the Soviet atheists. Although it could not easily fix these two perception problems, the PDPA tried to highlight its support for Islam to broaden its popular base at home and to undermine international support for the mujahideen. To achieve the latter objective, the PDPA under Soviet leadership concentrated on two aspects. It organized an information campaign in domestic and foreign media to present its domestic pro-Islamic policies and supported international causes important to all Muslims. In addition, it tried to establish diplomatic relations with Muslim countries and secure endorsements from influential Muslim leaders.

The Information Campaign

The CIA had been discussing setting up a covert program of "book production and distribution" to denounce Soviet atheism targeted at Soviet Muslims since the 1970s but had difficulties finding approval in the US Department of State.[20] This changed following the April Revolution and the Soviet intervention in Afghanistan. In November 1979, the National Security Council (NSC) discussed measures to "increase public diplomacy and expose Soviet's 'tawdry' record toward Islam."[21] Afghanistan was a rare opportunity for Washington to denounce the Soviets and counter its bad image among Muslims worldwide. The NSC quickly decided to "step up broadcasting to [the] Moslem [sic] world, including Soviet Central Asia [to] publicize the Soviet intervention, stressing the anti-Islamic element, particularly among countries of [the] Middle East." Its goal was to portray Karmal's regime as "a Soviet puppet and Soviet action as anti-Afghan and anti-Muslim" while stressing America's "common interests with the Islamic world."[22] In 1980, the United States engaged with Egypt and Saudi Arabia to see if it could lease "radio transmitters to broadcast Radio Liberty programs targeted at Soviet Muslims."[23] Cairo was reluctant, but Riyadh was ready to help.

Between the propaganda organized by the United States and the Muslim world's hostile reaction, Moscow and Kabul faced an uphill battle in countering accusations of attacking Islam. They had to show the PDPA's respect for

religion, with the ambiguity this expression involved, and sidestep the problem of Soviet atheism. They undertook to address these issues through articles and interviews with PDPA officials and Afghan proregime Islamic figures
in domestic and foreign media. In parallel, they diverted attention from the
Soviet intervention to the US role in supporting the mujahideen against the
PDPA and other issues important to Muslims worldwide.

The Kremlin took the lead in organizing this information campaign. As
noted by the politburo, it aimed at NATO and Western countries, and the NAM
using the resources of Cuba and Vietnam. That latter aspect particularly worried the United States.[24] Testifying to the special attention paid to the Muslim
world, the campaign concentrated on opposing "the hostile activity of the USA
and its allies regarding the Islamic countries of the Middle and Near East, particularly Pakistan and Iran, and also such influential countries of Asia as India."[25] The Soviets also mobilized other leftist parties, including in Muslim
countries, in support of the DRA. Their avowed goal was to counter US attempts "to reorient Islamic fanaticism into an anti-Soviet direction." Here,
Moscow also considered Iran, which it wanted to steer into an "anti-imperialist,
primary anti-American" direction and prevent from "inspiring antigovernmen-
tal demonstrations in Afghanistan on a Muslim basis." By contrast, the Soviets planned to contain Pakistan's support for the mujahideen and push it to
limit their activity on its soil through "special channels," meaning KGB and
KhAD undercover activities and behind-the-scenes diplomatic pressure.[26]

Although the Soviets formally adopted them only a couple of weeks later,
Gromyko had probably already conveyed the main points of that strategy to
Dost in advance of the UN General Assembly. Thanks to Soviet materials concerning "American military bases," Afghans were to answer uncomfortable
questions about the deployment of the LCST. They had to deflect criticism
by exposing the aggressive politics of the United States. In New York, Vasili
Safronchuk, an adviser from the Soviet embassy in Kabul, accompanied the
Afghan delegation and helped it, behind the scenes, with the diplomatic response. Throughout 1980, the Kremlin devised additional measures to support
propaganda on Afghanistan. The Sekretariat of the CC CPSU discussed such
activities in July, October, and December. Using TASS, the Soviets supported
the PDPA and the DRA's news agency Bakhtar in the "deployment of ideological work."[27] Throughout the war, the Afghan media remained accordingly
dependent on the Soviets for articles dealing with regional and international
issues.[28]

Karmal's support for Islam at home and the communist support for Muslim
causes around the world structured the information campaign on Afghanistan.
As reported by Grachev, who spent the 1980s dealing with propaganda in the

CC CPSU, the campaign had two stages. From 1979 to Gorbachev, it was "classic Soviet counterpropaganda that emphasized American interventionism, [and] how it funded and armed insurgents in Pakistan." The idea was that the USSR "needed to rebuild relations with the Muslim world and basically weather the storm." Presenting the DRA as more Islamic helped with that goal. The problem, according Grachev, was that it "was a dead-end also in terms of propaganda because [the Soviets] could no longer hide [their] losses" and the impasse in Afghanistan. There was no plan beyond the feeling that the Soviets needed to hold and hope for things to improve in Afghanistan. Then, with Gorbachev, the situation changed. "It quickly became clear that one of the main tasks that the new leader had set for the USSR was to leave Afghanistan, so [the propaganda] needed to prepare that." The job became to "sell that change in [the Soviet] position, the readiness to leave Afghanistan without getting advantages" and to promote Najibullah's national reconciliation campaign.[29] In broad strokes, this summed up the evolution of Soviet thinking on Afghanistan.

During the campaign's first stage, the Novosti Press Agency published a brochure in English titled *The Truth about Afghanistan* with speeches by Soviet officials, articles from the Afghan and foreign press, and testimonies from Afghans and foreigners about the "real" situation in Afghanistan.[30] To counter the mujahideen's propaganda about the "godless" PDPA, the brochure featured an interview with an Afghan Islamic scholar in the Spanish daily *El Pais*.[31] The Islamic leader praised Karmal's support for religion and argued that Moscow did not seek "to start any atheistic propaganda" in Afghanistan. He also claimed to have appreciated the respect shown to Islam in the USSR. Statements by Soviet Islamic scholars in the Soviet and foreign press supported such claims, even if one may wonder to what extent they had much of an international impact.[32] The brochure also republished Karmal's "Address of the Presidium of the DRA to Muslims of Afghanistan and the World" discussed in chapter 3.[33] The PDPA's ideology now supposedly converged with Islam as both wished for social justice. The Address also denounced Chinese and American policies against Muslims and associated the April Revolution with the Islamic Revolution in Iran, allowing Kabul to draw on the latter's Islamic legitimacy.

The Truth about Afghanistan also republished pro-DRA articles from newspapers in Muslim countries, including *Al-Shaab* and *Al-Kifah al-Arabi* in Lebanon, *Millat* in Pakistan, and *Indonesia Merdeka* in Indonesia.[34] These articles presented the same series of pro-PDPA arguments. One typical article in the newspaper *Al'-Muvazzaf* in Tripoli in 1980 explained that "American imperialism and international reaction had tried to divert the attention of the Arabs and Muslims" using Afghanistan. The article then criticized the Arab leaders who "forgot about the problems that stood in front of the Arab countries" to

FIGURE 5.1.   Ronald Reagan signing Proclamation 5621 that designated 21 March 1987 as "Afghanistan Day," amid US and Afghan policymakers (Courtesy of the Ronald Reagan Presidential Library). The Soviets tried to counter the information campaign conducted by the West and most Muslim countries in support of the Mujahideen.

attack the USSR. Conversely, it described the Soviet Union as Muslims' true friend and truly respectful of Islam.[35] The planting of such articles in the foreign press was usually part of KGB's active measures to sway public opinion abroad, including in Southwest Asia and in the Palestinian press in Beirut.[36] Similarly, the KGB distributed cassettes, pamphlets, and brochures hostile to the mujahideen in Pakistan, including in refugee camps. Moscow meanwhile tasked the MID and the Soviet ambassadors abroad to conduct counterpropaganda events on the official Afghanistan Day declared by the United States and other pro-mujahideen countries on 21 March after 1982.[37]

Similar pro-DRA articles appeared during the 1980s. The Egyptian newspaper *As-Siyasi* explained in 1986 that the PDPA respected Islam as testified by "the regular meetings of B. Karmal with religious actors."[38] That same year, the Kuwaiti daily *Al'-Watan* published an interview with Karmal. Catering to local audiences, he explained, clearly overestimating its role, that "Israel was playing the central role in the undeclared war against Afghanistan." He also declared that the DRA gave "particular attention to strengthening relations with brotherly Muslim and first of all Arab, countries."[39] Western newspapers, including *Newsweek* and *Spiegel*, interviewed PDPA cadres who spoke about Islam.[40] Such efforts likely had a limited effect in the Muslim world, but they were another sign of the importance the communists gave to building a positive international image and debunking the idea that they were atheists.

As the conflict progressed, Afghan and Soviet media increasingly focused on all-out support for national reconciliation—Grachev's second stage in the information campaign. They discussed the mujahideen who had signed truces with the regime, Najibullah's propositions for peace, and the Soviet withdrawal. Afghan and Soviet leaders' declarations in domestic and foreign media dealt with similar themes.[41] There was concern by then among the mujahideen that the regime's propaganda was starting to register internationally. *AFGHANews* wrote that Najibullah had, in the eyes of some Western media, become "a reasonable, innocent, rational, and religious person who was concerned about the safety of the civilian population and was the only guardian of peace in the country."[42] The mujahideen would similarly fear the PDPA propaganda's effect in Muslim countries.

An interesting aspect of the communist information campaign was its limitations. Pro-DRA articles featured limited criticism of the Arab countries that supported the mujahideen. Saudi Arabia was notably spared a part of the blame unlike the United States, Pakistan, and, after 1983, Iran. Probably because it was home to most Islamic holy places, it was important for Kabul not to seem entirely at odds with Riyadh in a context where it was trying to send more pilgrims on Hajj and uphold its Islamic credentials. Likewise, there was limited talk in the Afghan media about the Arab fighters among the mujahideen after the mid-1980s. It looked as if no one wanted to highlight that fighting the godless PDPA had become attractive to Muslims worldwide.[43]

Ultimately, while its practical impact should not be overestimated, especially since mainstream media in the Muslim world produced a different narrative, the pro-DRA information campaign was still notable in its scope. The communists genuinely believed that it might be possible to change the world's perception of the DRA.

Soviet Islamic Diplomacy

As the international relations expert Fred Halliday noted, there were three external and one mixed internal-external dimensions to Soviet relations with Muslim countries: (a) support for leftist movements fighting colonialism and imperialism; (b) outreach by Soviet Islamic institutions and leaders to their counterparts abroad; (c) state-to-state relations with Muslim countries; and (d), the mixed dimension, measures to deal with the potential fallout of pan-Islamic movements among Soviet Muslims.[44] The third aspect was by far the most important for the Soviets, including regarding Afghanistan. The Kremlin also mobilized its Islamic diplomacy (b) in support of Kabul. That Islamic diplomacy related to the mixed dimension (d) as Soviet concerns over the Islamist threat grew in the late 1980s, as we shall see in chapter 6.

Soviet Islamic diplomacy has been most intensive from the late 1950s to the mid-1970s, registering modest successes. The Kremlin believed that it could "create an effective divide between its attitude to Islam at home and abroad" to secure allies in the Third World, attributing to Islam "a positive role in countries of a less 'progressive' character."[45] This policy had started changing by the early 1970s as visits of foreign Islamic delegations did not bring clear gains. The USSR then reverted to a tougher stance toward Islam at home amid concerns regarding the Iranian Islamic Revolution and the troubles in Afghanistan.

Soon, however, the USSR had more than ever to publicize its respect for Islam because of the Soviet-Afghan War. In 1979, the *mufti* of Tashkent, for example, made two radio speeches extolling "the Soviet policy of religious freedom and the state of Islam in the USSR."[46] Months before the intervention, the Pakistani minister for Islamic affairs and Minorities toured the USSR and came up with positive statements about the situation of Islam in the country that the Soviets circulated.[47]

As the Afghan war progressed, the USSR engineered large-scale initiatives to correct its negative image among Muslim countries. In September 1980, it organized an Islamic Conference in Tashkent that focused on Afghanistan. The fact that only delegates from pro-Soviet countries attended and the criticism that even they formulated regarding the intervention in Afghanistan undermined its effectiveness.[48] Yet, the *agitprop* units in the LCST still highlighted the Tashkent conference when talking to Afghans. Testifying to its disinterest for Islam in Afghanistan, the USSR put further such initiatives on hold in the Karmal era, receiving only occasional delegations of Islamic scholars from Soviet Muslim allies with which it talked about Afghanistan. It was only after Gorbachev's arrival that Soviet Islamic diplomacy picked up traction again.

Its goal then became to secure international support for the national reconciliation that Najibullah articulated around Islam. In October 1986, the USSR organized a landmark Islamic conference in Baku titled "Muslims in the Struggle for Peace." The choice of the location marked the importance of the Spiritual Administration of the Muslims of Transcaucasia in Azerbaijan and of its leader, Pashazadeh.[49] The Baku conference was the largest such event ever to be organized in the USSR. At least 189 delegates from 59 countries attended. Since the event focused on Afghanistan, it is no surprise that, with fifteen people, the DRA's delegation was the largest after the USSR's.

The conference was, according to the Soviets, meant to "bring to the attention of representatives of the Muslim world information on the settlement of the situation around Afghanistan." This was to happen along with talks of "militant (*voinstvennogo*) Islam."[50] The use of that new expression contrasted with the usual talk of Islamic fundamentalism and showed that the Soviets had some awareness of the evolution that Islamism was undergoing against the background of the Soviet-Afghan War. Interestingly, as is clear from the conference's preparatory documents, Moscow was also ready to see the foreign delegates discuss the situation of Soviet Muslims.[51] The Soviets hence acknowledged that they could not separate that issue from Afghanistan.

During preparatory talks at their embassy in Kabul, the Soviets instructed the Afghans to be ready to carry out propaganda and information measures during the conference. The Afghans, startlingly represented at these talks by a secretary of the PDPA International Department, were to organize a photo exposition and show movies that "explained the April Revolution's conquests and the PDPA and the DRA policies in the religious domain and exposed the counterrevolution's crimes perpetrated under the slogan of the 'defense of Islam.'"[52] The Baku conference was also to see "press-conferences, interviews with members of the Afghan delegation, the organization of meetings and discussions with foreign Muslim delegations." The Afghan Ministry of Islamic Affairs and Waqfs and the High Council of Ulemas were to use these contacts to "broaden and strengthen ties with Muslim organizations in foreign countries."[53] The Afghans responded that they would dutifully prepare for the conference and asked the Soviets to assist them in securing an invitation to another international Islamic Conference, this time in Tripoli. So far, they had received no response from the Libyans.

This exchange was remarkable in several ways. First, it confirmed that by late 1986, the Soviets were paying attention to Islam in Afghanistan. Boosting the DRA's international Islamic credentials was part of their new Afghan strategy. Second, they continued to go about it in a typically communist way as the Soviet embassy in Kabul and the PDPA International Department handled the preparations for the conference. No Islamic scholar was involved on either side at that stage, again confirming how their role was marginal in Soviet-Afghan relations. Third, the PDPA's complaint about not receiving an invitation to the Islamic conference in Tripoli was embarrassing. Libya was a Soviet ally and one of the few Muslim countries where Kabul had an embassy. Yet even Libya did not take the DRA seriously on Islam. This disregard of the Islamic scholars supporting the Kabul regime conditioned the limited effect of the Baku conference. While the latter was a success in terms of organization and representativity, the DRA's relations with Muslim countries did not expand right afterward. The conference remained a Soviet-managed event in which the Afghans may have struggled to appear as independent actors.

In the following years, the DRA's religious institutions nevertheless continued their outreach to their perceived counterparts abroad with Soviet support. The Soviets hence invited the Afghans to a new Islamic conference in Tashkent in 1990.[54] As with national reconciliation, the DRA encountered more success in its Islamic diplomacy after the Soviet withdrawal. The Soviet embassy in Kabul in 1991 was keen to highlight to Moscow the Afghan scholars' increasing links with Islamic leaders in Iran, Libya, and Turkey, and the Saudi-based Muslim World League (MWL) and Pakistani-based World Muslim Congress (WMC). Building on the re-assessment of Islam in the Soviet Union in the late Gorbachev era, it then suggested that Soviet Islamic institutions encouraged such links as they could help with national reconciliation and stabilization in Afghanistan.[55]

In 1986, however, the Baku conference's summary report written by a CPSU apparatchik, testified to the Soviets' enduring ideological approach to Islam. The communists had to tactically co-opt Islam to weaken support for the mujahideen, the report's author contended. With that in mind, he assessed the conference's effect positively. The foreign delegates had been satisfied with their tour of Central Asia, their meetings with Soviet Islamic scholars, and having Arabic as the conference's working language.

Some delegates, the CPSU apparatchik asserted, had meanwhile claimed that "the founder of Islam Muhammad and his Koran [had had a] paramount role [in the] development of most of the positive historical and universal values that constituted the foundation of communist ideology." This was a positive thing even though "in the global sense . . . neither Marxism-Leninism, nor religion hid that their materialistic and idealistic foundation were irreconcilable." "Being irreconcilable as ideologies [Marxism-Leninism and Islam] could co-exist, act together, cooperate only as political factors."[56] Otherwise said, temporary tolerance for Islam should not preclude the long-term victory of Marxism-Leninism's tenets, including atheism. If such was the Soviet thinking at home: it explains why it was almost impossible for the Kremlin to have advisers in Afghanistan see national reconciliation as anything else than a retreat. At the juncture of the Karmal and Najibullah eras, such reports demonstrated how the Soviets' position on Islam in Afghanistan had not yet crystallized across the CPSU.

Finally, the CPSU apparatchik examined the rise of pan-Islamic ideas. The call "Muslims of all countries unite!," an expression vividly betraying his ideological bias, had emerged, he noted. Such a call could be positive only if it "was filled with pro-Soviet, pro-socialist and anti-American, anti-imperialist content." The fact that Soviet Muslims also heeded it was an issue that the Kremlin needed to address promptly but the Baku conference, despite its "indisputably positive influence abroad," had regrettably also "stirred up the mind of some Muslims circles . . . contributed to some extent to the strengthening of religion, [and] created a more difficult situation for atheistic propaganda," the CPSU apparatchik complained. The USSR, therefore, had to take control of pan-Islamism to raise its influence in the Muslim world and orient its goals. If successful, this strategy would "relieve [the USSR] from the need to somehow isolate Soviet Muslims from the unwanted effect of this Union [of all the Muslims] if it fell into the hands of circles dependent on the USA."[57]

The report never mentioned Afghanistan, but it was clear, particularly since the entire conference was about it, that some Soviets had started to think about an Islamist threat to the USSR in the context of the Soviet-Afghan War. However, as in 1979, they linked this threat to the United States as part of the geopolitical and ideological struggle of the Cold War. The Soviets did not see the Islamists as independent actors who could spread their ideology to Soviet Muslims. This assessment would remain remarkably consistent until the end of the Soviet-Afghan War.

Diplomacy in the Muslim World

Following Khalq's arrival to power, most Muslim countries expressed doubts regarding the new regime's Islamic legitimacy. Answering critics in a Kuwaiti newspaper, Taraki criticized the "disregard religious leaders in other Muslim countries have had for the masses" as he claimed that Afghanistan's "toiling people" would "themselves preserve Islam."[58] One exception was Saddam Hussein who was keen on having the PDPA visit Baghdad in 1978. Keshtmand, more pragmatic than the Khalqis, then told the Soviets that he was ready to go because a visit to an Islamic country would help counter the Muslim world's accusations about the PDPA's atheism. Yet, after the promising visit of the Iraqi minister of foreign affairs to Kabul, Keshtmand's arrest by Taraki and Amin shelved the plan amid Iraqi repressions against local communists.[59]

Khalqis' brash anti-Islamic statements and attitudes naturally did nothing to raise the DRA's Islamic profile, and even the Soviets and their allies wondered why Khalq operated at cross-purposes in its foreign policy by, for example, needlessly antagonizing Pakistan. Puzanov, the Soviet ambassador, believed that Kabul, instead of outright opposition, should have tried to exchange support for Islamabad's bid to join the NAM for it curtailing Islamic propaganda among tribes on the Afghan-Pakistani border and support for the mujahideen.[60] As in other matters, Soviet advice remained ineffective in changing Khalq's policies. Taraki only reluctantly agreed for an Afghan delegation to attend an OIC Council of Foreign Ministers (CFM) in Morocco and offer other Muslim countries to send representatives to the DRA to examine Khalq's attitude toward Islam.[61] Even before the Soviets' arrival, the PDPA was doing poorly in its diplomatic endeavors, unsurprising given its ideological approach to policymaking.

On the Soviet side, diplomatic aspects had also not been thought through. Although Gromyko had his advisers thinking about how to justify a deployment to Afghanistan from early December 1979 as a matter of contingency planning, the official line remained long unclear, and the MID was unprepared to carry counterpropaganda immediately after the intervention.[62] A senior diplomat thus recalled how he struggled to explain it to the French ambassador on New Year's Eve.[63] Still, the USSR called on allied countries and leftist parties and on the international forums it sponsored such as the Afro-Asian People's Solidarity Organisation (AAPSO) and the World Peace Council to support Karmal's regime. Both international forums had already issued statements supporting the DRA in mid-1979.[64] At the meeting of the secretariat of the World Peace Council-linked International Committee for Solidarity with the Arab People and their Central Cause—Palestine based in Tripoli, the Soviet delegates also explained the reasons for the intervention in Afghanistan.[65]

With its troops now in-country, the Soviet goal was to improve the DRA's international recognition. As Gromyko told Dost, they had to organize meetings with ambassadors from Iraq, India, and other nonaligned countries to explain the events that had taken place in the previous weeks.[66] The Soviets placed special emphasis on Afghanistan's neighbors Pakistan and Iran and other Muslim countries. Vladimir Vinogradov, the Soviet ambassador in Iran, went to see Khomeini in Qum on 28 December 1979. He reminded the Iranians that the Soviets had supported them politically against the United States but was told that "there could be no mutual understanding between a Muslim nation and a non-Muslim government."[67] Then, in early January, the Kremlin instructed Soviet diplomats to explain to Muslim governments that "the deterioration of the situation in Afghanistan must be viewed as a direct result of the events in Iran" and to blame Amin whose "disregard for the slogans and principles of the April Revolution had deprived him of the support of influential Muslim circles in Afghanistan."[68] Getting Muslim countries to maintain diplomatic relations with the DRA was a challenge. Even Soviet-leaning Algeria declared that it would not be opening an embassy "as long as there was a single foreign soldier on Afghan soil."[69]

The 1980s, nonetheless, were a time of modest diplomatic expansion for the DRA in what the communists increasingly saw as an interconnected Muslim world. The PDPA sent notes to various Muslim leaders for religious holidays and in times of tension with the West. Telegrams of support, for example, reached Muammar Gadhafi in 1981 and 1986, calling for an end to US "state terrorism."[70] In response, however, Karmal and Najibullah only received notes from Syria's Hafez el-Assad, particularly praised by the Soviets for his "resolute support" to Afghanistan, and Hussein.[71] Syria and Iraq were the two countries with which there were intensive bilateral contacts, including Afghan visits to Damascus in 1985 and 1987 and to Bagdad in 1985, 1986, and twice in 1987.[72] The latter two confirmed Iraq's support for the DRA which the mujahideen strongly denounced.[73] Afghan-Iraqi relations had meanwhile developed following Soviet disillusionment with Tehran and an Iraqi delegation came to Kabul in 1985.[74] Moreover a South Yemeni delegation visited Afghanistan in 1987.[75] Finally, Libya accredited an Afghan ambassador in 1985, although he could not secure Afghanistan's participation in the Islamic conference in Tripoli.[76] Even if that list is not exhaustive as lower-level contacts existed, the lack of contacts with most Arab countries testified to the DRA's isolation. Even with Soviet clients, relations fluctuated because leaders in Libya, Iraq, South Yemen, and Syria did not always follow Moscow's instructions.[77] Beyond this, the fact that Assad, the main communist ally, was an Alawite, a Shia sect that many Muslims saw as heretical, who had crushed a domestic Sunni Islamist revolt in 1982 did not help the PDPA's attempts at using him to boost its standing in the Muslim world. Contacts with Assad may have been in fact counterproductive as they created a parallel between two repressive regimes fighting Islamists.

After 1987, Kabul registered more diplomatic success. As agreed between Najibullah and Gorbachev, it launched an all-out diplomatic offensive by sending "67 delegations to various Asian, African, and Latin American countries to conduct explanatory work" about national reconciliation, also relying on the support of the socialist countries.[78] The Soviets and the Afghans considered it afterward a breakthrough when Wakil, the DRA's new foreign minister, visited Libya, Syria, Jordan, and Kuwait in 1988. The trip's significance was reinforced by the fact that Saudi Arabia and the United States, in a show of tensions in the pro-mujahideen camp, had advised Amman and Kuwait City against receiving Wakil. The communists saw Wakil's trip as crucial for two reasons. First, it allowed Kabul to make its case to the Western-leaning Muslim countries that were most open to better relations with Kabul before another OIC summit. Second, the Soviets had hopes that a closer relationship between Kabul and Tripoli, including economically, could become a conduit for the DRA to develop its relationships with other Arab countries.[79] After the Soviet withdrawal, Afghanistan's diplomatic outreach grew modestly and some embassies opened in Kabul and Najibullah visited Turkey and Iran.[80]

Throughout the 1980s, however, the DRA's diplomacy in the Muslim world struggled to expand, sometimes registering important setbacks. Afghanistan hence lost its mission in Saudi Arabia in a sign of the latter's support to the mujahideen, complicating the sending of pilgrims on Hajj. Overall, the DRA's isolation remained mainly due to its actual and perceived lack of independence from Moscow. Because of the lack of local diplomats and specialists in international affairs, advisers, unlike in domestic policy, fully controlled foreign policy. In the PDPA International Department, Mahmoud Baryalai, the department's head, transferred the de facto lead to Slinkin in 1982. Slinkin then shaped Kabul's position on a series of international issues.[81] He notably advised the PDPA not to react negatively to political issues in Turkey, concerned that this may lead to a break in relations with yet another Muslim country. While Baryalai boasted that some thirty foreign delegations visited the DRA in 1983, these were not from Muslim countries, and his claim that the DRA had now relations with over one hundred communist, worker, and leftist parties further highlighted its international alignment on the Soviet bloc.[82]

Accordingly, the improvement in relations between the USSR and some Muslim countries in 1987–89 had implications for the DRA. The perhaps overly enthusiastic Brutents from the International Department claimed at that time that "the influence of the Soviet Union in the Near East had again reached its peak" thanks to Gorbachev's "de-ideologization" of foreign policy.[83] Kuwait and the Soviet Union moved closer together in 1987 following the leasing of three oil tankers to Kuwait by the Soviets.[84] In 1988, Saudi foreign minister Saud al-Faysal visited the USSR, showing also the potential for better relations.[85] Soon after, a Soviet envoy went to Riyadh. Soviet relations similarly improved with Egypt and Jordan. After Gorbachev announced that the Soviet withdrawal would start in May 1988, Soviet envoys in Arab countries and Iran also actively promoted Najibullah's national reconciliation.[86] Gorbachev's New Thinking in foreign policy had allowed the DRA to expand its diplomacy in the Muslim world leading to Wakil's trip. Yet, it also underlined its diplomatic dependence on the Soviets.

At different moments, the PDPA also used pro-Soviet international forums to boost its international and domestic legitimacy. Its goal was often to publicize its Islamic policies. In 1981, the Lebanese Independent Nasserite Movement came to Kabul to meet with pro-PDPA Islamic scholars. Both parties condemned what they saw as Israeli aggression and praised the solidarity between the Lebanese and Afghan people. Back home, the movement's delegates informed Lebanese religious leaders about the "false character of the imperialist propaganda about Muslims and Islam" in the DRA.[87] Likewise, AAPSO delegations regularly visited Kabul. In 1984, one such delegation participated in a conference of pro-PDPA Islamic scholars and another that same year, led by the Director for Mosque Affairs of the Ministry of Waqfs of Egypt, met with Afghan Islamic leaders.[88] AAPSO delegates asserted that "the Egyptian people had never doubted that Afghans were proponents of Islam" and that "Islam was upheld in the DRA not only in words but also in deeds," and the Afghan communists informed them about the 40 mosques they had built in Kabul since 1980.[89]

For the same reasons, the PDPA invited Islamic scholars and Muslim leaders from South Asia to Afghanistan, probably under Soviet inspiration; on the advice of the Oriental Studies Institute, the Soviets had used a similar strategy at home to boost their own international Islamic credentials.[90] In 1982, an Imam from Karachi denounced in Kabul the "military regime of the junta in Islamabad."[91] In the mid-1980s, the PDPA intensified its links with leaders in the Pakistani Federally Administered Tribal Areas and the North-West Frontier Province who opposed Islamabad, receiving visits from Khan Abdul Ghafar Khan and Khan Abdul Wali Khan.[92] The latter particularly infuriated the mujahideen.[93] Wali Khan, the most influential Pakistani tribal leader to support the PDPA, had traveled to Kabul for the *loya jirga* aimed at consolidating the PDPA's political and Islamic legitimacy. For the same reason, a representative of the *ulemas* of the Khyber and Mohmand districts participated in the high-profile conference of Islamic figures in Kabul in 1987.[94]

Indian Muslim leaders were similarly mobilized. In 1985, a delegation of Islamic leaders from Madhya Pradesh made a joint declaration with the High Council of Ulemas in Kabul which condemned the "intervention of international imperialism headed by the USA and its minions, in particular, Pakistan," in the DRA.[95] Another delegation of Indian Muslims came in 1986. However, such visits provided little in terms of actual Islamic legitimacy to the DRA. India, on which the Soviet Union relied to balance Pakistan, had no influence in the Muslim world, being markedly excluded from the OIC. Beyond this, advocacy by tribal leaders and Islamic scholars could not offset condemnation from Saudi Arabia, Iran, Pakistan, and the OIC. Such initiatives nevertheless catered to a domestic audience and fed the Soviet information campaign on Afghanistan.

Failed Expectations in Iran

Afghanistan's relationship with Iran was a special case of its diplomacy toward the Muslim world because Iran was its neighbor and because its patron, the USSR, had ambivalent feelings about the Islamic Revolution. The Kremlin was worried about the spread of Islamic fundamentalism to Soviet Muslims, particularly because Iranian media and leaders played up that threat.[96] As the US embassy in Moscow pointed out, while Soviet Muslims seemed content with the cultural freedom and economic development they enjoyed, there was still moral solidarity in Azerbaijan and other Muslim regions with Iran.[97] In this context, Soviet concerns over Islamism were twofold: (a) as to its independent ideological appeal for Soviet Muslims and (b) as to Iran or another power's instrumentalizing this ideology and spreading it in the USSR. While these concerns were linked, the second one was preponderant in the Kremlin's mind.

The Soviets' first problem was that they had, like the United States, misread the situation in Iran. The US embassy in Tehran was thrilled to report that the Soviets, too, were dismissing the mullahs in 1978. Vinogradov, the Soviet ambassador, then argued that "religion was a thing of the past" and that "people wanted no return to the dark ages of Islam."[98] According to the United States, the Soviet embassy was sure as of December 1978 that the shah would be able to reassert power by force. Supporting this view, one can see that the Soviet media took time to acknowledge that the mullahs were indeed winning.[99] Still, what was most striking in Vinogradov's talk—even in the unlikely case it was disinformation—was his disparaging view of religion. Having the Soviet ambassador in a Muslim country speak of Islam in such a manner was unwise, to say the least. It again demonstrated how few in Moscow saw religion as an important factor at the critical juncture of the 1970s and 1980s. Politicians and academics spoke of an Islamic factor but few seriously believed that it could ever be an issue in the USSR. Rather, they expected religiousness to eventually decline in other countries. The Oriental Studies Institute reports on Iran in 1979 and 1980 consequently could not predict the future evolutions of the regime, cautioning the Soviet leadership not to be overoptimistic but also failing to assess Islam's actual influence.[100]

The Islamic Revolution was also a foreign policy victory for Moscow. Grachev, then in the International Department, recalled how it had "created delight" in the Kremlin because it was "the crash of the American system of strategic encirclement of the USSR."[101] Along with such geopolitical considerations, finding common ground with Tehran was meant to stabilize the Soviet southern border, limit support for the mujahideen in Afghanistan, and protect Soviet economic interests. As Gromyko said in 1980, the USSR "supported [Iran's] anti-imperialist direction against primarily American imperialism" despite its "religious fanaticism."[102] The comment was again telling of Soviet condescension toward the Islamists and their ideology.

Beyond this, as Grachev explained, Moscow believed that Iran "would be taking the road of Europeanisation more than Islamization," led by Abolhassan

Banisadr, its president from February 1980 to June 1981.[103] Leonid Shebarshin, then the KGB station chief in Tehran, likewise asserted that, while seeing it as a priority, the Kremlin understood the situation in Iran poorly. With Vinogradov, it overestimated the shah's importance, refusing to believe KGB reports that the "monarchic idea was dead."[104] Welcoming Tehran's anti-Americanism, Moscow hoped that it would join the Soviet camp after losing some of its radicalism. Unlike Pakistan, which it planned to contain by relying on India and Afghanistan, the Kremlin tried to assuage Tehran by avoiding confrontational language. *The Truth about Afghanistan*, therefore, said nothing of Iran's support for the mujahideen while the Soviets enjoined the PDPA to also keep a positive attitude toward Tehran.[105] For the Soviets and the Afghans, Iran was also the more important regional player compared to Pakistan or Iraq.

Moscow also hoped for more favorable developments in Iran. The People's Party of Iran (Hezb-e Tude-ye Iran, known as Tudeh), the Soviet-aligned communist party, now had a political role in the country. Its leader, Iraj Eskandari, plainly explained that Tudeh welcomed the fact that Islam had been "playing an important role in the mobilization of democratic and national forces against the . . . pro-imperialist regime" and called for union with the Islamists.[106] This position was also the Soviet one, offering a stark contrast with Khalq's anticlerical policies in Afghanistan during the same period. After the consolidation of the Iranian regime, Tudeh remained in close contact with the Kremlin while the KGB provided training to its activists.[107] Its position in Iran, nevertheless, gradually weakened after the Soviet-Afghan War began. Protesters chanting "Death to Russia" and slogans in support of the mujahideen even captured its office in Tehran in July 1980.[108] Moscow had again misjudged the situation in Iran, overplaying the communists' role in the revolution and pushing Tudeh to back Khomeini without guarantees from his side.[109]

Given its high expectations regarding a potential anti-American alliance and still aware that many Iranians did not trust the atheist USSR, Soviet policy toward Iran unsurprisingly focused on propaganda.[110] In 1980, the politburo noted that its objective was to maintain Iran's anti-US orientation to divert its attention from Afghanistan.[111] The Soviets passed measures aimed at improving the USSR's image including increasing radio broadcasts in Farsi from Azerbaijan, having the Novosti Press Agency and the Oriental Studies Institute prepare brochures in Farsi and Arabic about the Soviet Muslim republics, inviting Iranian journalists, and having the CRA translate its journal *Muslims in the USSR* into Farsi for circulation in Iran. The Soviets did not intend these measures to undermine the Iranian regime but rather to make the USSR look better. A Soviet memo, however, pointed out that Tehran had so far been successful in limiting Soviet propaganda.[112]

After a period of relative quiet, relations between Tehran and Kabul soured in 1979 following the revolt in Herat, the protests in Kabul's Hazara neighborhood, and Khalq's repressions against the Hazaras.[113] Afghanistan and Iran afterward expelled respective diplomatic representatives and the Iranians deported some 7,000 Afghan workers. In response, Afghan media stepped up anti-Iranian rhetoric, accusing Tehran of supporting the mujahideen. Acting again at cross-purposes in its foreign policy, Khalq appeared eager to provoke what it branded as the "clique of made-in-Paris mullahs," ignoring Soviet attempts to placate Tehran.[114] As the US embassy ironized, there was "no love being lost between Kabul and Qom" while each side accused the other of exporting its revolution across the border.[115] Amin then astutely cautioned the Soviets that Iran may become one of DRA's major antagonists and that Tudeh was wrong in dealing with Khomeini.[116] Still, the tensions remained mostly rhetorical while the Soviets made attempts a mediation. There was little real Iranian support for the mujahideen and even the Soviet intervention did not see condemnation in Iran on the scale seen in other Muslim countries.[117]

As in other aspects, Kabul's policy took a sharp turn after Parcham replaced Khalq. Days after Khomeini came to power, Karmal wrote to him heeding Soviet advice. Addressing the Ayatollah, the Afghan communist was keen to sound as Islamic as possible, opening his letter with "in the name of Allah, the Almighty and the Merciful to the great brother Imam Ayatollah Khomeini." Karmal blamed Afghan-Iranian problems on Amin, whom he said was perhaps even "worse" than the deposed shah and claimed that, together with "American imperialism," they had been preparing an "offensive policy" against "the liberating Islamic Revolution."[118] Beyond this, Karmal insisted that the Afghans wanted "friendly, brotherly, Islamic relations" with Iran, "unity of each of the two directions of the sacred Islamic religion" and were ready to provide Tehran with security guarantees in light of the Soviet presence. He also proposed a personal meeting with Khomeini. As elsewhere, Karmal associated the April Revolution and the Islamic Revolution. This was another way of upholding the DRA's Islamic credentials and a departure from Khalq's line. On a domestic level, good relations with Iran remained important in quelling protests among the Hazaras and returning the refugees who had fled there. The millions of Afghans abroad were also undermining the PDPA's legitimacy at home.[119]

This appeasing letter went unanswered. Instead, Iran debunked Afghan calls for solidarity. *The Voice of the Islamic Revolution*, the official Iranian radio, condemned the Soviet intervention and praised the anticommunist forces.[120] These rebuttals did not, however, stop the Afghans from keeping to their narrative. The PDPA, like the Soviets, genuinely believed that it could find an understanding with the Iranians.[121] Throughout 1980, Karmal denounced in the domestic press and in the Lebanese weekly *Al-Watan al-Arabi* "the imperialists" who tried to "undermine" the Afghan revolution and afterward "deal a fatal blow" to Iran.[122] On a visit to India, Dost told journalists that he "was sure that Iran's rulers would, in the end, understand [Afghanistan's] true motives and goals."[123] The same could have been said by the Soviets. Remarkably, Karmal was even comfortable discussing Iran in an interview with *Spiegel* in June 1980. The Iranian revolution had "an antimonarchic and anti-imperialist character. It was and remained Islamic. It had been supported and would continue to be supported" by the DRA, he argued.[124] The Afghans then made other gestures to please the Iranians, including the appointment of a Shia cleric who had studied under Khomeini as deputy head of the High Council of Ulemas, and the release of Iranians imprisoned under Amin.[125]

In response, Iran only strengthened its anti-DRA rhetoric. In an interview with the Lebanese daily *An-Nahar Al-Arabi Wad-Duvali* in March, Banisadr argued that, contrary to Karmal's claims, the Islamic Revolution had "provoked a second revolution in Afghanistan" that forced the USSR to "intervene to repress it." The Iranians now threatened to provide the mujahideen with weapons. Beyond this, Banisadr claimed that Iran's revolution had "created problems in the Soviet Union among Muslim populations that professed [Iran's] religion and culture," echoing Soviet concerns with Islamism, and that the Russians were the Iranians' historic enemy. "If the Soviet forces reached Pakistan, then Iran would be their next target," he claimed. In a final blow, Banisadr revealed that Yasser Arafat, whom the Afghans were at the time courting, had told him that he too condemned the Soviet intervention.[126] The Iranian president had thus methodically debunked Soviet and Afghan talking points. He had done so in Beirut where sympathies for Moscow ran higher.

Increased confrontation with the United States in April 1980 did not change Iran's attitude. Ghotbzadeh challenged Soviet claims that Moscow had anything to do with the failure of the US operation to rescue the American hostages captured at the US embassy in Teheran.[127] Answering Karmal's message shortly thereafter, Mohammad-Ali Rajai, Iran's new prime minister, bluntly wrote that the Iranians "were taken by compassion because of the suppression of the fight of [their] Muslim Afghan brothers . . . [by] the colonizers."[128] Officials in Iran hence competed to come up with the strongest condemnation of Kabul.

Likewise, Iran's position did not change at the start of the Iran-Iraq War in September. This was surprising to the Kremlin since, despite its Treaty of Friendship and Cooperation with Baghdad, it had suspended arms deliveries to Iraq.[129] According to Shebarshin, the fact that Soviet-built planes were bombing Iran did little to increase the Soviets' popularity in Tehran.[130] In 1981,

Tehran rejected direct negotiation with the PDPA, again being harsher in its attacks on Kabul than the OIC. It also announced that it would call for the NAM to replace Karmal's regime with the mujahideen. Tehran, moreover, became tougher in its criticism of the USSR. In April, Khomeini asserted that there was a core Soviet hostility toward the Islamic Republic, predicting that if Tudeh and the Soviets came to power "they would destroy Islam, as the foundation of [Iran's] unity."[131] Clearly, the Soviets had failed to improve the USSR's image in Iran and Tehran's leaders now postulated a direct opposition between Islam and communism. Given Iran's influence, this complicated Kabul's Islamic and traditional diplomacy across the Muslim world.

By late 1980, Moscow began tiring of Tehran's unresponsiveness to its overtures while the failure to reach an agreement on Iranian gas transit through the USSR also soured relations.[132] A *Pravda* article denounced Iran's support for the mujahideen and Ghotbzadeh's anti-Sovietism, but there was still hope for an Iranian turnaround in the Kremlin.[133] Moscow allowed Iranian products to transit through the USSR to Europe following the US blockade in late 1980 and, at the highest level, Brezhnev explained in February 1981 that a "liberation struggle" could develop "under the banner of Islam" in more "backward" countries and that the USSR wanted to develop "good relations" with Iran.[134]

Meanwhile, Kabul, following the Soviet lead, continued to disregard Tehran's criticism. While the Afghan media mentioned it as among the countries supporting the mujahideen, they often shielded Iran from the extensive blame that rained down on Pakistan, China, and the United States. As in Moscow, there were lingering hopes for an improvement in Iranian-Afghan relations. In late 1981, Dost explained that the DRA had had "a wise policy" toward Iran. Despite Iran's lack of "reciprocity," it expected that Tehran would, in time, change its mind and understand Afghan sincerity. The Soviets could have made the same statement. The PDPA meanwhile downplayed the Iranians' role in supporting the mujahideen by noting that the incursions of fighters from Iran were nothing compared to the flow from Pakistan.[135] Likewise, while calls for the unity of revolutions had been toned down, an article in *Khakikat-e Inquilab-e Saur* in early 1982 still typically contended that "the common enemy of the Afghan and Iranian people" was imperialism.[136] An additional reason for this continuing positive attitude, claimed a PDPA official, was that after the removal of Ghotbzadeh in August 1980 and Banisadr in June 1981, Tehran had toned down its criticism of the DRA, allowing for a temporary modus vivendi.[137]

This situation changed dramatically in late 1982, and soon anti-Soviet opinions became so strong in Tehran that KGB's Shebarshin had to leave in a hurry.[138] A key factor was the rapprochement between Baghdad and Moscow and accordingly between Bagdad and Kabul in the context of the Iran-Iraq War.

As Iran gained the upper hand in the conflict, Moscow restarted arm shipments to Iraq in July 1982 before expanding assistance in 1983–84. The domestic factor was similarly important. Authorities in Iran suppressed the pro-Soviet Fedayin-i Khalq and Tudeh parties while Khomeini asserted ideological and political control over the regime.[139] The Islamic Revolution was to be the vanguard of the *ummah*, contesting Saudi leadership and calcifying Iran's opposition to the Soviets in Afghanistan. By 1984, Tehran had increased its hitherto limited support for the Shia mujahideen groups.[140] In 1985, Moscow retaliated by withdrawing some 1,500 technical experts from Iran, officially because of the risk of Iraqi bombardment.[141]

The Afghan media reflected this change of attitude. If in 1980 they presented a neutral analysis of the Iran-Iraq conflict, they no longer did so in 1983. *Khakikat-e Inquilab-e Saur* featured one of the first articles that attacked Iran for its leading role in supporting the mujahideen.[142] Criticism of Iran intensified in 1984 as *Khakikat-e Inquilab-e Saur*, for example, explained that Iran had for years nurtured plans to militarily intervene in the DRA. Many articles now alleged that Afghan refugees were sent to fight on the Iraq front or were kept as hostages in refugee camps.[143] At times original themes emerged with one article fascinatingly discussing the "oppression of women" in Iran, a topic that seemed to come in dissonance with the renewed emphasis on Islam and traditional values in Afghanistan.[144] Logically, the denunciations of Iran came in parallel to the consolidation of Kabul's relations with Baghdad. A note in the press in 1984 celebrated a bilateral agreement that allowed Hazaras to make pilgrimages to the holy city of Karbala. Diplomatic contacts with Baghdad then intensified.

The deterioration of Iran's image in the Afghan media led to the reactivation of a sectarian argument. Tehran was trying to drive a wedge between "Shia-Iranians and Sunni-Afghans," the PDPA argued.[145] In this context, Karmal continued to meet the Hazaras, whose loyalty was in doubt. He warned them in 1985 that Afghans were in no need of "the export of the Islamic Revolution."[146] As always, the DRA's Islamic institutions were mobilized to explain that Kabul's regime was itself a bona fide Islamic one. The High Council of Ulemas condemned Tehran's "machinations" and its role in "arming and coordinating" the mujahideen's subversive activities. It accused it of "fermenting religious strife," thus hinting at the sectarian argument, while covering its "vile political goals with Islam."[147] As usual, the *ulemas* later listed the PDPA's measures in support of Islam. In the DRA's propaganda, Tehran had taken its place among the principal enemies.

Criticism of Iran continued until the Soviet withdrawal, even though most attacks remained focused on Pakistan and the United States. *Khakikat-e Inquilab-e*

Saur evoked the arms sales deal at the center of the Iran–Contra Affair in 1987 and disparaged Tehran for its ties to Washington.[148] It was a rare opportunity for the Afghans to turn the argument of the defense of Islam on Iran. Nevertheless, because Iran's support for the mujahideen was considerably less than Pakistan's, because the Iran-Iraq War had mobilized Iran's resources, and because Tehran's international isolation limited its options, Iran was less of a problem for Kabul.

Eventually, a new shift in the USSR's attitude toward Iran under Gorbachev also forced the Afghan communists to reassess their position. An early sign that things were evolving came following the Kremlin's decision to decrease propaganda in support of Tudeh in 1986, acknowledging that that party had disappeared as a political force.[149] This though initially did not yield Moscow any goodwill from Teheran. Amid discussions about a withdrawal, the Kremlin was dismayed in November 1987 that Iran's position on Afghanistan was close to that of Pakistan: it wanted no role for the PDPA in the future.[150] Similar criticism of Iran was voiced by Gorbachev in his negotiations with the United States. For both superpowers, it was unacceptable to have Tehran engineer "a fundamentalist government" in Afghanistan, especially in tandem with the Pakistanis.[151] Gorbachev was just then starting to worry about the consolidation of an Islamist belt along the Soviet Union's southern border. As discussed in the next chapter, Tehran was one country that the Soviets believed could instrumentalize Islamism against them.

Only months after this apparent stalemate, Tehran's attitude however evolved as the reality of an actual Soviet withdrawal from Afghanistan profoundly changed the strategic environment. Moscow now believed that Tehran wanted "a strategic alliance against the United States." The Iranians, the Soviets thought, still pushed for the fundamentalists to take power in Kabul, but the regime they envisioned had to be anti-American first.[152] Iran's shift was a welcome change given Pakistan's continuing hostility to Najibullah. It also showed how sharp ideological divergences between the Soviets and the Iranians did not prevent a rapprochement that was bound to marginalize the Sunni mujahideen. Here, Islamic solidarity had reached its limit. According to Akbar Hashemi Rafsanjani, Iran's soon to be president, Iran was now looking at the future and concluding that the United States was the bigger regional problem than the USSR, much to the mujahideen's displeasure.[153]

After the withdrawal, the rapprochement between the USSR and Iran continued. Khomeini sent a letter to the Soviets offering to "fill the vacuum of religious faith in [their] society" with Islam. Although Gorbachev politely declined, this opened the way for Shevardnadze's visit to Tehran in February.[154] While the talks there went awkwardly—Shevardnadze trying to sell Khomeini on Gorbachev's New Thinking and Khomeini wishing to hear an answer to his spiritual message—both parties agreed to spin it as a breakthrough in relations. Meanwhile, some mujahideen feared that Moscow had persuaded Iran that they had to jointly oppose US meddling in Afghan affairs.[155]

In the summer of 1989, a Soviet politburo meeting concluded that Tehran had indeed adopted a more "constructive position" following the talks between Gorbachev and Rafsanjani in Moscow. Iran was now close to accepting a role for the PDPA in an Afghan settlement. Rafsanjani was negotiating with Kabul, an official in the PDPA confirmed, although he had to make it look like Iran was not reneging on its support for the mujahideen and refusal to recognize Najibullah.[156] In turn, the Kremlin believed that it needed to prop up Iran through propaganda and secret channels to have it play a larger role in Afghanistan.[157] The hope was that it would mitigate the influence of Pakistan which remained opposed to talks with Najibullah. In October 1989, the Iranians cut their support for the Shia mujahideen and told them to find an understanding with Kabul.[158] In November, Najibullah gave an interview to the Iranian daily *Resalat* confirming the improvement in relations but also showing how Afghan diplomacy was again in tow to the Soviets.[159]

This shift in relations which showed how Tehran was ready to have geopolitics take precedence over Islamic solidarity came though too late and was not decisive enough to significantly boost the PDPA's international or domestic standing. The Soviets were leaving, and their allies in the Muslim world were gradually abandoning the PDPA. In parallel, Iran's influence in Afghanistan was by then negligible and having an Iranian-influenced government in Kabul was unrealistic. As a KhAD senior operative resentfully noted years later, the Iranians had "'played' [with the PDPA] during the war," but "in the end, they had tricked Kabul and did not go for anything. They had obtained what they wanted and became a regional power."[160]

The Palestinian Cause

The DRA's focus on the Arab-Israeli conflict came at the intersection of the PDPA's two other drives to uphold its Islamic legitimacy. The Afghan media and the PDPA leaders' speeches denounced Israeli and US policies in the Middle East to divert attention from the Soviet-Afghan War while the PDPA tried to build ties with the PLO, which Khomeini's regime also supported, to draw on its legitimacy in the Muslim world. According to a KhAD operative, the PDPA was interested "in a close relationship with the PLO and was ready to host Palestinians refugees in Afghanistan."[161] That the USSR was a long-time supporter of the Palestinians helped Afghan endeavors.

Even though the PLO had posted a representative in Kabul during Taraki's time, its relationship with the DRA remained complicated at many levels.[162] Amin hence complained to the Soviets that he was tired of declaring his support to Palestine but hearing nothing from Arafat. It is like we are having a "one-sided love affair" (lyubov' bez vzaimnosti), he joked to Soviet embassy staff.[163] In fact, the attitude to adopt toward the DRA was creating real tensions in the PLO as a member of the Democratic Front for the Liberation of Palestine (DFLP), one of the PLO's leftist parties, complained to the Soviet ambassador in Ethiopia.[164]

After the Soviet intervention, the Afghan media regularly mentioned Israel as helping the mujahideen and PDPA leaders denounced its policies in the Middle East. When a delegation of the Popular Front for the Liberation of Palestine (PFLP), another leftist party of the PLO, visited Kabul in 1980, Dost pledged DRA's "full support for the right cause of the Arab people of Palestine . . . against Zionist aggression" and Keshtmand, during a visit to Beirut, announced that Afghans and Palestinians had "one common enemy—international imperialism, world Zionism, and Reaction."[165] After the Israeli invasion of Lebanon in 1982, Kabul witnessed demonstrations in support of the Palestinians and the Afghan Red Crescent Society donated humanitarian relief.[166] Pro-PDPA Islamic scholars made calls to condemn the attacks on the Al-Aqsa Mosque and the Sabra and Shatila massacres in Lebanon aroused widespread indignation in Afghanistan, leading to multiple mentions in the local media. In his message on the International Day of Solidarity with the Palestinian People in 1983, Karmal referred to them while denouncing Israel's "occupation of Lebanon aimed at destroying the PLO."[167] In 1984, a PDPA minister attended a gathering in memory of the victims in Kabul.[168]

Increasing contacts with the PLO were sought by the DRA, but both sides had to tread carefully. The PDPA wanted to be on friendly terms with the Palestinians, but its relationship with them was dependent on that of the USSR and the Soviets had issues with parts of the PLO in the 1980s. After the Camp David Accords in 1978, the PLO and the USSR had moved closer together and Arafat had personally led a delegation to Moscow, showing that even the PLO's more centrist Fatah was reorienting toward the Soviet Union. Following the talks, the Kremlin agreed for the first time to declare the PLO as the "sole legitimate representative of the Palestinian people."[169] The intervention in Afghanistan, however, tested this rapprochement. Other developments, including a closer relationship between the USSR and Syria that had tried to promote Arafat's rivals to head the PLO and Fatah's leadership's attempts to work more closely with pro-Western Jordan and Saudi Arabia and to talk to Western officials also complicated relations in 1981–83.

Moscow had to be cautious not to antagonize Syria, its main ally in the Arab world. Following the Syria-Israeli conflict in 1982, which had led to tensions over the Soviets' lack of support, the Kremlin had agreed to transfer advanced air defense systems to Syria and even man them until it could train local personnel.[170] This though did not lead to greater Soviet control over Syrian foreign policy.[171] In 1983, Gromyko argued that the Kremlin should not allow Assad "to stir up infighting in the Arab world" amid troubles in Lebanon. To that, Andropov replied that if Moscow "went to Assad with advice about leaving Lebanon, it was risking a lot."[172] Subsequently, while the USSR remained committed to its alliance with the PLO, it increasingly leaned toward the PFLP and DFLP. It was crucial for the USSR that both unequivocally backed its policies in Afghanistan and were not at loggerheads with Syria.

For Kabul, the irony was that the conflicting and arcane politics within the USSR-Syria-PLO-Lebanon relationship limited the possibility of relying on Soviet Arab allies for diplomatic support. It was not until Gorbachev became general secretary that Moscow rekindled its relationship with Arafat and brokered an understanding between the PLO and Syria. Nonetheless, even in 1988, Arafat remained an annoying ally to whom, as a collaborator advised, Gorbachev should not give too much weight by meeting him personally, including to not anger Syria.[173] By that point, the value of Palestinian support had in any case diminished for the DRA while the Soviets searched for a way out of Afghanistan.

For the PLO, the DRA was a troublesome ally because much of the Muslim world had condemned the Afghan communists. Supporting them put the Palestinians at odds with the mujahideen and with Riyadh and Tehran, its own sponsors, as Amin had already astutely noted in 1979.[174] Along with the Iran-Iraq war, the Soviet intervention in Afghanistan undermined the Arab unity achieved following Camp David. It similarly tested the PLO's.

Farouk al-Kaddoumi, one of Arafat's future opponents in Fatah, declared that "Soviet help" to Afghanistan was an internal Soviet-Afghan affair in January 1980.[175] Later, a delegation of the PFLP visited Kabul, and Arafat met Dost in Beirut in April 1980 and again in 1981.[176] In 1981, while in Kabul, the PFLP's Tayseer Qubba'ah expressed his "solidarity with the Afghan people" and denounced "imperialist propaganda against the DRA," declaring that the "DRA's leadership treated the religious feelings of its citizens with respect," a dissonant statement coming from a leftist leader.[177] Up to this point, only the PFLP and DFLP had, however, expressed support for Kabul. The messages Karmal had sent to Arafat and that the Afghan press publicized had received no response from Fatah. In 1981, a typical letter from Karmal explained that the "DRA always stood on the side of the heroic Palestinian people," condemned Camp David, and declared the PLO to be the "sole lawful representative of the Arab-Palestinians."[178] Yet, at the same moment, a *Time* interview embarrassingly quoted Arafat as saying that the USSR was trying to establish control over Middle Eastern oil by invading Afghanistan. TASS answered that claim by publishing Arafat's statement that it was a "gross distortion."[179] Still, the episode showed Fatah's unease with the DRA.

A shift in the PLO's attitude toward Kabul only occurred after it resolved its internal conflicts and Fatah renormalized its relationship with the USSR. In 1983, after the invasion of Lebanon and the PLO's relocation to Tunis, the Afghan media finally published a message from Arafat to Karmal. The Palestinian leader nevertheless only thanked the DRA for its support at the Conference of the NAM in New Delhi.[180] It was not until 1984 that Arafat's messages to Karmal became more cordial. One of them noted that the "PLO's goal [was] to reinforce the ties of brotherhood and solidarity between the Arab people of Palestine and the people of revolutionary Afghanistan."[181] Contacts between the DRA and the PLO remained afterward friendly while an important delegation led by Talaat Yacoub, one of the PLO's hardliners, visited Kabul in 1986.[182] Along with delegates from Islamic and communist countries, the Palestinians also attended the conference marking the launch of national reconciliation.[183]

Exemplifying his now favorable attitude toward the Afghan communists, Arafat personally attempted to mediate between the regime and the mujahideen in Islamabad in 1989. According to *AFGHANews*, he was by then known as a "pro-[Kabul] regime and pro-Soviet politician . . . In all international forums in which [the] PLO had had a voice it had opposed the mujahideen."[184] Because of the importance of Palestine for the *ummah*, no one could, however, simply dismiss Arafat. Like the Afghan media, Jamiat-e-Islami had published articles supporting the Palestinians.[185] Arafat was important enough to meet the Pakistani prime minister and Mujaddidi, the head of the mujahideen's dysfunctional Afghan Interim Government assembled under US and Pakistani pressure in Peshawar.[186] Beyond this, Arafat was a channel for the mujahideen to Moscow and pro-Soviet Arab states. They hoped that they might agree to pressure the Kabul regime into more compromises as part of post-withdrawal negotiations on a coalition government and on Soviet prisoners of war. Arafat also attempted to mediate between Kabul and the mujahideen during talks in Libya, Tunisia, and Iraq in 1989–90.[187]

Securing the PLO's support allowed the DRA to draw on its and Arafat's fame to strengthen its Islamic credentials and political legitimacy. The PLO provided Afghanistan with much-needed diplomatic backing throughout the decade, including at the OIC as we will see below. Yet, the considerable time it took Arafat to openly support the DRA, the PLO's dependence on the USSR, and the bickering among Soviet allies diminished the value of the PLO's support. By the time Fatah unequivocally backed the PDPA, the context had already irremediably transformed: Moscow was leaving Afghanistan and rapidly losing influence in the Arab-Israeli conflict. Domestically, the PLO's support was similarly important for the PDPA's propaganda. At the same time, because most Afghans remained illiterate, had only a limited knowledge of international affairs, were exposed to competing Iranian and Pakistani propaganda on the radio, and—most crucially—had their own war and suffering to worry about, its importance should not be overestimated.

The Mujahideen's Reaction

Kabul's diplomacy toward Muslim countries and hosting of friendly Pakistani tribal leaders and ulemas angered the mujahideen because they feared that it could undermine their jihad.

After national reconciliation started, AFGHANews increased its criticism of such visits in an article that attacked the Pakistanis who went to Kabul to legitimize the PDPA's Islamic policies. It ordered such "traitors [to] rejoin their Muslim brothers in support of the Afghan mujahideen."[188] A year later, another article denounced the PDPA for trying to "put up an Islamic face by inviting 'Islamic delegations' for the 'International Islamic Conference' in Kabul." The mujahideen noted that most of the delegations came "from Islamic organizations of communist countries or so-called Arab radical states" to "pass resolutions endorsing [the] 'National Reconciliation Program' of the regime."[189] Be that as it may, the pro-Soviet Arab countries were still eminent parts of the Muslim world and the presence of their delegations brought diplomatic recognition and Islamic legitimacy to the Kabul regime.

The mujahideen regularly focused their attacks on these countries that, according to AFGHANews, "called themselves Muslim but did not support the [Afghan] jihad." In the mujahideen's view, they were breaking the unity of the Muslim world in the Soviet-Afghan War by compromising with the atheists in Moscow and Kabul. In 1986, following the opening of a Soviet embassy in Abu Dhabi, AFGHANews emphasized that point by noting that the USRR had always fought Islam, not only in Afghanistan but also in Central Asia, North Iran, and Turkey. For this reason, there should be no Soviet embassies in the Muslim world. There was a risk, AFGHANews contended, of the Soviets "brain-

THE AFGHAN MUJAHID

**BY THE
GRACE OF
ALLAH WE
SHALL
OVERCOME**

الَّا إِنَّ حِزْبَ اللّهِ هُمُ الْمُفْلِحُونَ ۝

The Party of God that
Will achieve Felicity.

PUBLISHED BY PRESS AND INFORMATION COMMITTEE LONDON
ISLAMIC ALLIANCE OF AFGHAN MUJAHIDEEN
BM BOX 2084 LONDON WC1N 3XX. TEL: (01) 208 0763

FIGURE 5.2. Front page of a Mujahideen Journal (*The Afghan Mujahid* [June 1988]). One of the multiple English-speaking publications produced by the mujahideen, it built support for the mujahideen in the West and emphasized the centrality of Islam in the conflict.

washing" young people by sending them for education to the USSR. This was the return of the mujahideen's old fear that sovietization through education may jeopardize the Islamic way of life in Afghanistan in the long run.[190]

In 1988, a milestone article in *AFGHANews* developed a more structured criticism of the pro-Soviet front in the Muslim world. These were the "Muslim brothers," a remarkable title that showed that no one doubted these countries to be truly Muslim—especially Libya, Syria, and South Yemen, who had supported Moscow despite the "godless [Soviet] communists'" attack on Afghanistan. These countries "had strong links with the puppet-regime in Kabul" and "lobbied for Soviet causes in international forums," *AFGHANews* argued.[191] Besides these staunch DRA backers, it criticized all the Muslim countries who had wavered in supporting the jihad to not anger the Kremlin. Algeria had hence "failed to support even the weak resolution on Afghanistan passed by the UN" and Iraq's "position had fluctuated throughout the past eight years. Sometimes it supported the resolution and sometimes [it] abstained." North Yemen had kept making contradictory statements during the war, and finally, there were the "oppressed Palestinians" who instead of standing by the mujahideen remained close to the "Soviet invaders who have always played a double game in the Middle East." For *AFGHANews*, these countries had divided the Muslim world and prolonged the occupation of Afghanistan.[192]

Yet, *AFGHANews* maintained that, despite their avowed support for Kabul, these Muslim countries' representatives still said that they had "open and secret positions" and that in "[their] hearts they were with the [mujahideen]." Such double language was not enough, *AFGHANews* claimed, but it did suggest that circumstances and not ideology determined support for the DRA in the Muslim world. Save for perhaps South Yemen, whose leading party shared many of the PDPA's characteristics, there were no true communists among Soviet Muslim allies. As the USSR's international influence declined at the end of the Cold War, it would be increasingly difficult for Najibullah to rely on them.

The Impossible Understanding with the OIC

The idea of a Muslim world has been reinterpreted in different historical contexts since the time of the Prophet. Following the Second World War, Karachi hosted two world Muslim conferences in 1949 and 1951. They led to the emergence of the WMC with its secretariat in Pakistan. The WMC, which had adopted a declaration stipulating that it would treat aggression against any Muslim country as an aggression against the "world of Islam," however, did not lead to an immediate reinvigoration of pan-Islamic mobilizations.[193]

One exception was the creation of the MWL in 1962. The MWL was a Saudi-funded nongovernmental organization that remarkably accepted SADUM, the Soviet official organization policing Islam in Central Asia, as a member in 1980. While it provided the Soviets with an indirect connection to the Saudis, SADUM's membership mostly resulted in the MWL criticizing Soviet policies abroad and toward Muslims at home. The organization was, for example, markedly more vehement in its opposition to the Soviet-Afghan War than the OIC. The MWL also offered to conduct seminars on Islamic theology in Central Asia in 1981, promising at the same time to stay clear of Soviet politics. The Kremlin naturally rejected the proposal, which it saw as a transparent attempt to influence Soviet Muslims but, significantly, SADUM had originally recommended the CRA move forward with it, arguing that it could help in neutralizing hostile propaganda about Soviet atheism and pave the way for diplomatic relations with Riyadh. This suggested that, on SADUM's part, there was little concern that it might be unable to control the Islamist mullahs coming to Central Asia.[194] The episode again testified to many Soviets' disregard of an Islamist threat.

Created by the Saudi king Faisal in 1969, the OIC, and not the WMC or MWL, became, however, the main international Muslim forum. It conjured the idea that Muslims were a "unified religious—and presumably politic—body transcending ethnic, linguistic, cultural, and national boundaries." It helped deal with the traumas of the Caliphate's disappearance and the Arab-Israeli conflict.[195] The OIC's creation marked the ascendency of Saudi Arabia as the leader of a nascent Muslim world after socialism and Third World internationalism had failed to secure Muslim political objectives.[196] During the Soviet-Afghan War, the OIC became the forum where supporters and critics of the DRA confronted each other, debating over if the DRA's authorities were Islamic enough and *in fine* legitimate.

Days after the Soviet intervention, an Extraordinary Session of the OIC CFM condemned the USSR and called for "Islamic solidarity" with Afghanistan. As noted by the Pakistani Sharifuddin Pirzada, the OIC's future general secretary, it was the first time "the intervention of a super power in the internal affairs of a member state of the OIC" had prompted such a reaction.[197] Importantly, the OIC suspended Afghanistan's membership, a ban that it had so far only applied to Sadat's Egypt. When the OIC similarly excluded the DRA from following sessions, the PDPA denounced it for "covering the anti-Islamic crimes and conspiracies of imperialism and Zionism" by focusing on the Afghan War. Kabul nevertheless still explained that it would be ready to rejoin the OIC if allowed to.[198]

This ambiguity would mark the attitude of the DRA toward the OIC throughout the 1980s. The reason for it was twofold. First, membership in the

OIC considerably helped uphold a state's Islamic credentials and political legitimacy at home and abroad. Because of its suspension, those of the DRA were in doubt. The Soviets then feared that if the mujahideen got the DRA's OIC seat, it would be the first step toward their broader international recognition.[199] Second, the DRA could argue in OIC forums for Muslim countries to reduce financial, military, and political support to the mujahideen. Given its limited diplomatic contacts with most Muslim countries, the OIC forums would have represented a unique opportunity for the PDPA to make its case.

The 11th OIC CFM in Islamabad came after the failed attempt to free the American hostages. That event stole the spotlight from the Soviet-Afghan War and gave more prominence to the Iranian delegation. Tehran, while criticizing the United States, was also tough on the PDPA and even brought to the conference five mujahideen leaders.[200] The session's resolution then urged for the "unconditional withdrawal of all Soviet troops" and the respect "for the sovereignty, territorial integrity and political independence of Afghanistan," as well as for its "non-aligned status" and "Islamic identity."[201] The support the DRA received from the Steadfastness and Confrontation Front, a group formed by pro-Soviet Arab states after Egypt's "capitulation" to Israel, mitigated that criticism. Gathering Syria, Libya, Algeria, the PDRY, and the PLO in Damascus, the Front condemned the United States, pledged support to the USSR and, confirming the Soviet bloc's ambiguity toward the Islamic Revolution, solidarity with Iran. Its goal was to divert attention from Afghanistan to other Muslim causes.[202] In Kabul, Karmal enthusiastically thanked these "heroic and truly Islamic countries" in his speeches.[203] This was again an example of how diplomacy toward Muslim countries translated on the domestic stage. Iranian delegates, in turn, complained that "some friendly countries took the position of nonalignment because of their relations with Soviet Russia."[204] Ironically, at that time, Iran itself had still not broken up with the Soviets.

Before the Islamic Summit Conference of Heads of States (ISCHS) in Mecca in 1981, the DRA again called on the OIC to stop wasting time with the "Afghan question." The OIC adopted in response a resolution denouncing the violations of Afghans' rights in similar terms as in 1980, as well as noted that Afghanistan preoccupied "the entire Islamic World." However, the rest of the resolution was mild in its criticism of the DRA. It replaced the call for Soviet withdrawal with one for the withdrawal of all "foreign troops." The resolution also abstained from calling for "jihad" in Afghanistan while using the term in its call to fight the "Zionist enemy."[205] In toning down the resolution, Agha Shahi, the Pakistani foreign minister from 1978 to 1982, supported the pro-Soviet front. He would be the only Pakistani politician to seriously explore a negotiated solution to the Soviet-Afghan War.[206] Ultimately, the resolution came short of the unequivocal support the mujahideen hoped for. It showed the disagreements among the Muslim countries as to the Soviet-Afghan War's importance. Iran even noted that the OIC had still spent too much time on Afghanistan, ironically echoing the PDPA's argument.[207]

The DRA was undoubtedly satisfied with OIC's focus on Palestine given its engagement with the PLO. The tension between Palestine and Afghanistan was by then so evident that Habib Chatty, the OIC's general secretary, had to emphatically address it at the CFM in Baghdad in 1981. He underlined that the OIC needed to "find the right balance between Islamic principles and relations with [the USSR]." However, "the support of the Palestinian question by [the USSR] did not mean that [the OIC] would give it away the land of the Afghan brothers."[208] Still, Afghanistan was deemphasized in Baghdad, while the OIC focused on the Iran-Iraq War and Jerusalem.[209]

In this context, the emergence of Iran as an alternative pole of attraction in the Muslim world was an issue for Saudi Arabia and its US ally. It also became the OIC's role to contain it. Coupled with the support provided by Soviet allies, it explained why OIC resolutions adopted at CFMs in Niamey in 1982, Dhaka in 1983, and Sana'a in 1984, resulting from compromises, remained restrained in their criticism of the DRA. After the session in Dhaka, the OIC held its 4th ISCHS in Casablanca. The latter produced another resolution on the Afghan War in the same mold.[210]

The stalemate achieved at the OIC did not provide the PDPA with tangible legitimacy gains or a reduction in Muslim countries' support for the mujahideen. Kabul therefore continued to both denounce the OIC for its "reactionary and anti-Muslim actions" and argue its readiness to reintegrate into the organization. The DRA wanted no one to scold it on Islam and saw itself as "an important member of the world Muslim community."[211] In 1984, the High Council of Ulemas and the Directorate of Islamic Affairs issued a joint call to the OIC to protest the United States and its allies' strategy "to undermine the positions of the DRA in the Islamic world." The call detailed the PDPA's Islamic policy, including the subventions for Hajj, the building and reconstruction of mosques, the salaries paid to imams, and the subventions to *madrasas*. Eventually, proregime Islamic scholars even asserted that "justice in the DRA was rendered according to Islamic principles," a statement that was especially disingenuous.[212] Still, the PDPA was ready to do whatever it took to prove the Islamic character of its regime internationally to boost its legitimacy at home. Recognition by the OIC could have indeed been a major propaganda victory for Karmal, compensating for the limitations of his Islamic policy. After Najibullah's accession to power, the calls to the OIC intensified in parallel to the further Islamization of the PDPA's platform.

Kabul's appeals left the OIC indifferent. The arrival of Pirzada as general secretary in 1984, a development that marked, in his own words, "a recognition of Pakistan's role" in the organization, also did not help Kabul's cause.[213] For Islamabad, the Soviet-Afghan War was more important than Palestine. It was the reason for the massive US military support and the chance to establish a client regime in Kabul. As its opponents gained prominence and tensions between Lebanon and Israel subsided, allowing efforts to be refocused on Afghanistan, the tide turned more resolutely against the DRA in the OIC. In 1985, Pirzada declared to the Egyptian daily *Al Akhbar* that "the membership of Afghanistan in the OIC [had been] suspended, because its ruling regime was not considered Muslim."[214] Denial of the DRA's belonging to the Muslim world in a mainstream Muslim journal overshadowed Kabul's own information campaign, highlighting how the Afghan communists struggled to get rid of the atheist label.

The 16th OIC CFM in Morocco in 1986 confirmed the OIC's tougher stance against the backdrop of increased Soviet military operations in Afghanistan in 1984–85. Its resolution, for the first time, praised the mujahideen's "heroic struggle." It also included what was simultaneously an incentive and a warning to Moscow, stating that the "withdrawal of [Soviet] forces from [Afghanistan]" would "remove a major obstacle in [its] relations [with] the Islamic Countries."[215] Afghanistan continued nevertheless to divide the Muslim world according to the Cold War paradigm. That divide also paralyzed the OIC. The latter was, conspicuously, still not talking of jihad. This was ironic given that the mujahideen, the MWL, when remarkably writing to Soviet institutions dealing with Islam, the Saudi king Fahd at a Hajj greeting, and Pakistan abundantly used the term.[216] As to the mujahideen, they again complained that the OIC conference had been side-tracked. This time it had concentrated on the US attacks on Libya while the "Afghan issue was not given its proper importance." Besides, the mujahideen complained, pro-Soviet "radical Arab" states had claimed that Afghanistan "undermined the importance of the Palestinian problem." However, "the massacres of Sabra and Shatila by Zionists were as painful as the massacres of the people of Afghanistan by the Red Army."[217] Western observers similarly noted the OIC's tepid resolutions on the Soviet-Afghan War.

It was indeed a paradox that the mujahideen who fought for Islam against an atheistic power could not get a seat at the OIC while the PLO, a laic and nationalist movement, represented Palestine. In truth, the OIC and the *ummah* continued to be Arab-centric despite Arabs being a minority in the Muslim world. This explained why Afghanistan remained on the OIC's sidelines while many states valued Soviet support for Arab nationalism and the Iran-Iraq conflict concentrated attention.[218] At the same time, the DRA's effective courting of the PLO had helped it gain a voice on the most important cause for the Muslims. It had forced the mujahideen to argue that their fight was as important as that of the Palestinians.

The deadlock in the OIC eased only after Gorbachev came to power and the USSR changed gears on Afghanistan. In late 1986, Pirzada visited Moscow, taking advantage of the favorable atmosphere created by the Baku conference, and declared that "the problems around Afghanistan [would] be soon resolved."[219] Both parties were ready to help a Soviet withdrawal. In parallel, Najibullah spoke positively of the role that the 5th OIC ISCHS, which was about to start in Kuwait, could play on Afghanistan and reached out to it with a letter about national reconciliation.[220] At the CC PDPA Plenum launching national reconciliation in December, he explained that he hoped that the OIC, along with the NAM, the UN, and "Islamic countries" could help in bringing peace to Afghanistan.[221] Gorbachev, in turn, sent a formal greeting to the OIC in advance of the ISCHS, a stark contrast after years of Soviet leaders' labeling it a reactionary forum.[222]

The resolution adopted by the OIC in 1987 reflected this new situation. It, on the one hand, still celebrated the mujahideen's "heroic struggle" but, on the other, welcomed national reconciliation which, it noted, "reflected the will of the people of Afghanistan and their Islamic character."[223] The nod to national reconciliation was a strong positive sign for Najibullah and Gorbachev. Finally, the resolution repeated that leaving Afghanistan would help Moscow improve its relations with the "Muslim world," a term the OIC now used. This was the closest the organization would ever come to accepting the DRA.

In Kabul, Bakhtar and other Afghan media praised the OIC's and progressive countries' support for the "efforts at national reconciliation."[224] While on a trip to Czechoslovakia, Najibullah rejoiced that the "extremists" had not received Afghanistan's OIC seat.[225] He was also pleased that the OIC had this time invited the regime's journalists.[226] Satisfaction was also clear in Moscow. According to a former KGB head in Kabul, the OIC had finally displayed objectivity on Afghanistan. The "covert intrigues of the leaders of the Afghan opposition, present at the conference as observers, their attempts to obtain from the OIC their reconnaissance as 'lawful representatives of the Afghan people' had proven futile," he exulted.[227] For Kabul and Moscow, this was proof that Muslim countries were increasingly ready to recognize Najibullah's regime as representing the Afghan people. They believed that the OIC and the United States might then agree for Najibullah to stay during a transition period after the Soviet withdrawal.[228]

The mujahideen, by contrast, vehemently denounced the OIC's new tone. It was clear, *AFGHANews* claimed, that Moscow used Pirzada for propaganda as it used "trips by religious figures, international organizations, and even sport." Pirzada's visit was exclusively meant to "improve [Moscow's] relations with the Muslim world," while Gorbachev said "beautiful words" to the OIC, it noted.[229] This was a representative moment. The OIC's general secretary had tried to take on a mediation role in the Soviet-Afghan War, but the mujahideen denounced him for it. To them, the OIC's job was to support their jihad. This ambiguity was present throughout the decade: it was unclear if the OIC could be an independent forum on the Soviet-Afghan War, as Kabul and Moscow seemed to believe.

AFGHANews, meanwhile, listed Jamiat-e-Islami's reproaches to the Kuwaiti conference. "The Amir of Kuwait [had] personally read Gorbachev's message to the conference," "the conference [had] reluctantly allowed the mujahideen representative to speak . . . and only then at improper times, . . . [it had] passed the weakest resolution about Afghanistan ever, the [United Arab Emirates] and Oman [had] established diplomatic and economic relations with the Soviet Union."[230] For Jamiat-e-Islami, the OIC was too afraid of Iran, and the USSR was using that fear to boost its influence. The OIC was "the real target of Soviet penetration." In addition to the friends it had there, Moscow could rely on Kuwait, who was "afraid to make the Soviets angry" because it needed them to protect its oil tankers. Some Muslim countries were ready to "ignore an invasion and the suffering of millions of Muslims" to advance their own interests, the mujahideen complained.[231] Interestingly, a letter by Rabbani to Pirzada followed the article in *AFGHANews*. Rabbani then shared his concern that Kabul's approaches to Muslim countries may be working, particularly regarding Iraq. He wanted Pirzada to warn Baghdad against increasing its ties with Kabul as if the OIC's general secretary should have acted on behalf of the mujahideen.[232]

In the meantime, the prospect of a Soviet withdrawal promised such sweeping changes that the OIC believed that it needed to encourage them. The ongoing tensions in the Middle East also made its members worry about jeopardizing their relations with Moscow. This meant that OIC's overtures targeted the USSR more than they did the DRA at a moment when it looked like the USSR would shape a future coalition government in Afghanistan.[233] However, the Soviet side did not understand that. In a note to Gorbachev's team, the Afghanist Gankovsky argued that replacing Najibullah with someone outside the PDPA would help the OIC accept the DRA.[234] This, however, would have been unlikely. Saudi Arabia and Pakistan had little interest in dealing with another Soviet-backed leader unless forced to by a Soviet military victory. When it appeared that the Soviets would leave without a deal over the future of Afghanistan and that the PDPA's positions were weakening, they saw no reason to be soft on the DRA. In late 1987 while negotiations between Moscow and Washington entered their final stage, the OIC shared its "grave concern" that Soviet and PDPA forces had intensified attacks against the mujahideen. The organization now claimed that the Afghans had "rejected" the Kabul regime's "so-called national reconciliation [under] Soviet occupation," a sharp turn compared to its earlier tone.[235] Its communiqué put pressure on Gorbachev to publicly commit to a withdrawal.

The Soviet leader would do so after King Hussein of Jordan's landmark visit to the USSR in February 1988. For the Soviets, the support of Muslim countries and the United States was vital to leave Afghanistan on honorable terms.[236] As noted above, Wakil then went on a trip to Kuwait and Jordan, hoping it could be a "step toward the restoration of Afghanistan's membership" in the OIC.[237] Although Moscow and Kabul likely understood that this would be complicated, Wakil was at least to obtain a reduction in anti-DRA statements and the OIC's support for the Soviet-American negotiations on Afghanistan by relying on countries most favorable to the USSR in the Western-leaning group. Increasingly, to Kabul's probable displeasure, the diplomacy toward Muslim countries had become about helping the Soviets withdraw from Afghanistan.[238]

The 17th OIC CFM in Amman in 1988 marked a new take on Afghanistan. Its resolution, while welcoming Gorbachev's commitment to a withdrawal, showed greater support to the mujahideen. Declaring for "the Geneva Proximity Talks," the OIC announced that it would keep Afghanistan's seat open "until the complete withdrawal of foreign forces," "the return of the Afghan refugees, and the formation of a government acceptable to the people of Afghanistan."[239] This meant that the DRA would not be part of the organization anytime soon. It moreover showed that the OIC increasingly looked forward to a mujahideen victory.

Interestingly, the belligerents had mixed assessments of the Amman conference. The Soviets were glad that the mujahideen did not obtain recognition for their interim government despite sending fourteen representatives to Amman. Jordan had here backed the Soviet allies. The KGB saw that as not the worst of outcomes given that an OIC recognition might have had a domino effect in the Muslim world and the West.[240] The Soviets hence still took the OIC seriously and hoped that the situation on the ground might eventually force it to recognize Najibullah.

Yet, the Amman conference really marked the beginning of the mujahideen's victory and foreshadowed a shift in the OIC's stance. The following year, only four weeks after the last Soviet soldier left Afghanistan, the OIC conference in Riyadh saw the Saudi and Pakistani positions finally triumph. The

OIC threw its full support behind the mujahideen as they launched an offensive on Jalalabad with Pakistani support. In a shorter resolution, the OIC then used for the first time the term "jihad" in relation to Afghanistan. After praising the April 1988 Geneva Accords, it furthermore invited the mujahideen to occupy Afghanistan's seat.[241] This settled the matter: The window of opportunity when it seemed that the PDPA and the Soviets could leverage increased acceptance from the OIC into political legitimacy in Afghanistan had closed. It was now obvious to all, including pro-Soviet countries, that the communists would end up on the losing side of the war.

Throughout the Soviet-Afghan War, the Soviets and the Afghan communists put considerable effort into strengthening the DRA's Islamic credentials on the international stage. Moscow mobilized its Muslim allies, integrated Afghan Islamic scholars into its Islamic diplomacy and used the KGB and pro-Soviet forums to improve the DRA's image among Muslims. In their endeavor, the Soviets and the Afghan communists relied on the support of Soviet Muslim allies—Syria, Libya, Iraq, South Yemen, and the PLO—and leveraged the Soviet influence on the Arab-Israeli conflict. By legitimizing the DRA internationally, they hoped to reduce political, financial, and military support to the mujahideen. The PDPA was to be the legitimate ruler of Afghanistan, recognized by other Muslim countries and international forums such as the OIC. In the same way as they hoped to wait out the mujahideen's opposition in Afghanistan, the Soviets and the PDPA believed that the Muslim world would eventually have to accept the DRA. As shown by their success in blocking the mujahideen's international recognition, including by the OIC, which had remarkably recognized the secular PLO, that strategy encountered some success in the 1980s.

Building international support in the Muslim world also mattered domestically. The PDPA leaders used international successes to present themselves as legitimate rulers in Afghanistan. By stressing their contacts with the PLO and with Muslim countries, Karmal and Najibullah equated themselves with well-known Muslim leaders such as Arafat, Assad, and Hussein. By republishing positive articles from the foreign press, they wanted to show that they had support and recognition abroad. By comparing their revolution to Iran's, they suggested that both had anticolonial roots. By taking advantage of Soviet Islamic initiatives, they bolstered the pro-PDPA Islamic scholars. To use Max Weber's terms, they channeled their international contacts into domestic rational and traditional Islamic legitimacy and boosted their own charismatic legitimacy.[242]

Unfortunately for the communists, the strategy to build the DRA's Islamic credentials had limits. First, it relied entirely on the USSR and made the DRA appear as a passive actor. Second, it yielded only mixed results even among Soviet Muslim allies. Those remained a disparate group which backed the DRA in exchange for incentives from the Soviets. During the Afghan War, organizing their steady support for the DRA proved challenging and diminished their impact. Perhaps if Moscow had been able to muster the PLO and Iraq's full backing for the PDPA in 1980, it would have helped it reintegrate the OIC and fill in its enormous legitimacy deficit in Afghanistan.

After the Soviet and the Afghan communists had become bogged down in their fight with the mujahideen in the mid-1980s, the Soviet allies' support mattered less. By then, the Soviets had decided to leave and the PDPA had discredited itself by waging a brutal war in Afghanistan. In this context, the improvement of relations between the DRA and Western-leaning countries and Iran was not the product of their believing that the PDPA would prevail but testified to these countries tactically maneuvering to get the USSR out. The OIC's position testified to that irony. While it seemed to welcome Najibullah's national reconciliation in 1987, it reversed course the moment Gorbachev announced the withdrawal. With the Cold War out of the way, the Muslim world, with the notable exception of Shia Iran, which focused on regional geopolitics, finally saw Islamic solidarity prevail over Cold War realpolitik.

CHAPTER 6

Moscow's Islamist Threat

> Our opponents—the Afghan opposition and Pakistan
> and the USA—have not yet entirely opened their cards.
> I agree with you that they are interested in a consolida-
> tion of the positions of Islamic fundamentalism not
> only among the people of Soviet Central Asia but
> among all Soviet Muslims.
>
> —M. Najibullah to M. Gorbachev, 1990

The Shuravi Have Left

On 15 February 1989, Gromov, the LCST's 40th Army's last commander, declared that there were no Soviet, or Shuravi as the locals called them, soldiers
left in Afghanistan as he crossed the bridge over the Amu-Daria River. Najibullah meanwhile continued his national reconciliation policy, stabilizing his
regime thanks to the mujahideen's dissensions and Moscow's continuing support. He hence managed to remain in power until April 1992 when a mujahideen offensive, the end of Soviet support, and a coup inside the regime finally
forced him to seek shelter in the UN headquarters in Kabul. Four years later,
the Taliban would gruesomely execute Najibullah after taking Kabul from the
mujahideen. Exposing Najibullah's mutilated body for all Kabulis to see, they
would send the message that there would be no mercy for people who had
been on the "wrong side of jihad."[1] The Taliban hence drew a line under years
of civil war.

Najibullah regime's survival for more than three years after the LCST's
withdrawal was an unexpected achievement. Tsagolov, the military adviser
who had helped engineer national reconciliation, had bluntly stated in the Soviet press in 1988 that the PDPA would have to relinquish power. The Kabul
regime had discredited itself and failed to co-opt the clergy, he noted. Tsagolov's view was the dominant one in Moscow, Kabul, and among the mujahideen and their supporters.[2]

According to some of the PDPA's leaders, "Najibullah was stressing in
discussions with members of the politburo that 'half of the Soviet military

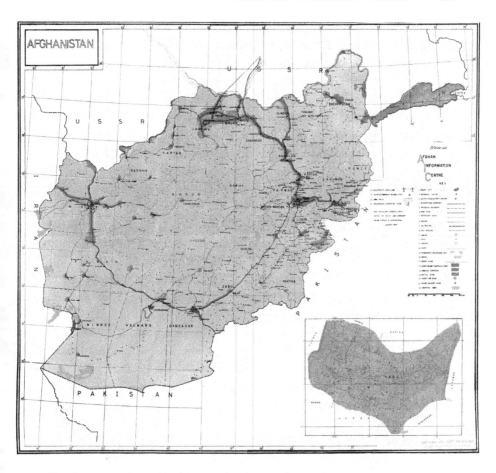

MAP 6.1. Areas of control in Afghanistan between Soviet and Afghan communist forces (in dark) and the Mujahideen, 1988 (*Monthly Bulletin of the Afghan Information Center*, no. 94 [1989])

contingent needed to stay, otherwise [the regime] was doomed.'"[3] Many Afghan communists were preparing to emigrate while the Soviets in Kabul observed how the mujahideen were already retaking areas in districts along the Pakistani border.[4] Liberal-minded policymakers in Moscow such as Zagladin argued that the Kremlin had to let go of the Afghan communists.[5] Gorbachev candidly told the Soviet republics' heads that it was impossible to "understand who [the Red Army] was fighting [in Afghanistan]. By day, there was one authority on some territory, by night—another." The bottom line for him was that no one was "expecting a miracle" and the USSR "did not need a pro-Soviet regime in Afghanistan. And it was unlikely [it] would be able to keep one." The Soviets had lost the war; this "regime could not be saved."[6]

The Kremlin's minimum objective was to avoid a replay of America's withdrawal from Vietnam. The LCST was to make an orderly and honorable retreat—a phrase dear to all defeated colonial powers—avoiding the humiliation of seeing the regime fall immediately after its departure. While concerns ran high as to how Soviet allies, including among Muslim countries, would see the PDPA's collapse, even this minimum goal seemed out of reach. The Kremlin at most cautiously assessed that if Najibullah were to hold on through the summer of 1989, he could begin consolidating. Throughout 1989–90, concerns over his imminent collapse were so high that Shevardnadze, Kryuchkov, and Yazov, the Soviet hardliners, repeatedly pushed to reintroduce troops to Afghanistan or at least conduct airstrikes from Soviet territory. To them, the withdrawal fostered by the Geneva Accords that Wakil, the Afghan negotiator in Geneva, had vehemently opposed had been rushed and did not allow the Kabul regime time to consolidate its position. Interestingly, some mujahideen and Pakistani decision-makers were, on the contrary, unhappy about the Accords because they left the communist regime in charge and allowed for continued Soviet support.[7]

The Soviets had also started negotiating with the mujahideen. Brokered by the UN, the first encounter between the enemies happened in November 1988 in Islamabad at the Pakistani Ministry of Foreign Affairs. Saudi Arabia then hosted a higher-level meeting the next month between a Soviet delegation led by Vorontsov, now the Soviet Ambassador in Kabul, and a mujahideen one led by Rabbani, Mujaddidi, and Hekmatyar's representative. More talks took place in Pakistan and Libya.[8] In parallel, members of the PDPA met with Gailani in Baghdad in 1988 and representatives of Hekmatyar and other mujahideen in various places. The PLO helped arrange some of these meetings. These many encounters testified to the growing Soviet and Afghan flexibility regarding what they called the "irreconcilable opposition," but also showed the cracks in both coalitions. It was clear that no one could speak for all the mujahideen and that Moscow and Kabul's objectives diverged. The Soviets wanted to organize a coalition government in Kabul, but this was unacceptable to all sides. Short of that, they wanted a commitment that the mujahideen would not target the LCST on its way out, progress on returning Soviet POWs, and hedge against the possibility that the PDPA would lose power. The ex-Afghan communists, by contrast, were only ready to help the mujahideen to power while retaining a leading role for themselves.

The Kabul regime's ability to survive by relying on only a limited number of Soviet advisers and military and humanitarian support came as a surprise to Moscow. Unlike the mujahideen, Najibullah had no foreign fighters on his side, despite calling on "a series of countries, especially Muslim" for help.[9] The consolidation of his regime was instead due to the continuing of national reconciliation after the LCST's departure. As reported by the AIC, Najibullah stuck to the same precepts but now unapologetically doubled down on them: "[Najib] started calling the same terrorists and bandits—"'heroes.'" He asked mujahideen not to resort to subversive activities and instead to occupy cities and centers peacefully. In his words, they can choose governors, judges, and security officers between themselves for those areas. He admitted to some of his mistakes in a humble tone and was ready for compensation. He was asking for Islamic amnesty and tried to show he was a devoted Muslim. The Marxist ideology was abandoned and instead, Najib started preaching Islamic values and national interest."[10]

Following the LCST's departure, Najibullah's political legitimacy undeniably increased. Declaring a "war on Wahhabism," in the AIC's words, he used the fact that many Afghans saw the mujahideen as controlled by foreign powers, full of foreigners, and dominated by Hezb-e-Islami's radical brand of Islam to change the perception of his regime.[11] Najibullah's Islamic and nationalist rhetoric now sounded different to Afghans, especially since many of them continued to experience mujahideen attacks but not Soviet airstrikes. This in turn led the mujahideen to worry about losing the political initiative and support in Afghan cities. The Soviet withdrawal had marked a shift in the war and in the meta-narrative about it. Against this backdrop, the mujahideen's failure to retake Jalalabad in eastern Afghanistan in April 1989 despite US backing and direct Pakistani military support reinforced the regime and led to a decline in fighting. It showed that the mujahideen's victory was not a foregone conclusion.

The AIC's reporting, in parallel, showed increasing frustration with the mujahideen, who allowed Najibullah to instrumentalize their dissensions and score more propaganda victories as they failed to agree on an interim government. The former KhAD chief maintained that he had asked the LCST to leave because the PDPA was strong enough to fight the mujahideen on its own. By co-opting the themes of ethnicity, nationality, family, and patriotism through national reconciliation, his regime expanded its support, especially among Afghan minorities.[12] Monumental wall paintings appeared in Kabul showing a woman in a *chadaree* who was sending her son to war, not for communism or the party, but for the fatherland. Many Afghans were indeed ready to turn the corner on the communist period.[13] The war had divided their country and many families had members who had fought on opposite sides. Each camp had seen countless splintering and conducted horrific abuses. By 1992, this would mean that no group could claim the higher moral ground, a situation that was

FIGURE 6.1.   A mural poster in Afghanistan in the late Najibullah era, 1989 (Muhammad Moqimand Afghan Media Resource Center | Internet Archive). Najibullah abandoned talk of communism and emphasized instead Islam and nationalism to mobilize support for his regime, as the inscription indicates.

conducive to more violence and score-settling but that also allowed many former communists to seem no better or worse than former mujahideen.

The conflict had become about taking power, not defending Islam or fighting invaders. Najibullah had partially delegitimized the jihad and sapped the mujahideen's cohesion by Islamizing his regime. In 1989, a *fatwa*, a nonbinding opinion on Islamic law, by proregime Islamic scholars argued that with the LCST's departure, there was no more reason for war. Another *loya jirga* in Kabul conveyed the same point. Najibullah then fully embraced his Islamic persona, no longer separating his official image from his private dealings with the Soviets. Following the Jalalabad debacle, the advisers who came to discuss military support found him to be arrogant and changed. The ex-communist told them that "he could not offer them food or drinks because it was now the time of Ramadan," one of the Soviets reported.[14] To the Soviet newspaper *Izvestia*, Najibullah would explain that Afghanistan was an "Islamic nation" and that Islam guided the Afghan revolutionaries.[15] Although Soviet support remained both a necessity and a political liability for the regime, Kabul made increased efforts to dissociate itself from the USSR. This was the key to Najibullah's success, and, as recalled by a KhAD officer, many in the PDPA felt that they might be close to victory against the mujahideen in 1990.[16] This breakthrough also showed to what extent the Soviets' original approach of disregarding Islam and pushing Marxism-Leninism was wrong. If only the Kremlin had been more pragmatic and staged an early national reconciliation of sorts, the Soviet-Afghan War might have gone a different way.

Exacerbating his dissociation strategy, Najibullah soon blamed Marxism-Leninism for the Afghan tragedy. In April 1990, weeks before taking the symbolic move of renaming the PDPA into the Hezb-e Watan (Homeland Party), the now-declared party of peace and Islam, he announced he was abandoning socialism. It was now about "the fight for national reconciliation" that integrated Islam and traditions.[17] Only "believing and practicing Muslims" could join Hezb-e Watan. Soon after, another reworking of the Constitution "prohibited laws repugnant to *sharia*," created a multiparty system, and downgraded Hezb-e Watan's role. The ex-communists had officially made Afghanistan into an Islamic state while also finally abandoning the hated land reform. The last remaining issue with Islamization was the Kabul regime's ongoing inability to co-opt influential Islamic leaders from the mujahideen, while even some Islamic scholars in regime areas criticized Najibullah.

The situation in Afghanistan had changed. Najibullah's political legitimacy had increased and nationalism now often worked against the mujahideen. The regime was adept at claiming that negotiations among their leaders about the interim government elected by a *loya jirga* in 1989 happened abroad and focused on refugees and not on the Afghans in Afghanistan. The Pakistani role and the Arabs' influence dissatisfied many opposition commanders in Afghanistan, leading them to negotiate with the Kabul regime.[18] Najibullah never failed to insist on this point in his speeches, claiming that "while the Shuravi [the Soviets] were long gone, the Pakistanis, and the Arabs had stayed."[19] On such occasions, he, as always, spoke from memory and quoted the Koran and the *hadiths*. He also criticized the now-distant Soviet Union and some Afghan operatives who had been especially close to the Soviets started to disappear.[20] Stressing his independence, Najibullah would end up asserting in a speech in 1991 that the first day of the LCST's withdrawal was Afghanistan's "day of national liberation." The claim angered some in Moscow, whereas most Soviet policymakers accepted it as another necessary concession. Such was the bitter but logical end of Soviet discredit in Afghanistan. The Kremlin had anyway less and less interest in Afghanistan by then.[21]

The mujahideen's fabric was also becoming more problematic because of sectarian conflicts fostered by the influx of thousands of Arab fighters.[22] As reported by the AIC, the Afghan Arabs preached a radical form of Islamism. They opposed not only the Soviets but also Muslims they considered having drifted away from pure Islam. Their presence led to tensions as they tore down "the flags flying over the graves of martyred mujahideen" and accused other mujahideen of "polytheism."[23] Beyond this, the Arab Afghans often executed captured Afghan communists, harassed Western aid workers, journalists, and even CIA operatives, and used suicide attacks. Such attitudes were problematic for most of the mujahideen and increasingly for the CIA.[24] According to the AIC, "the increasingly visible role of Arab volunteers, distributing . . . huge sums of money [and] propagating the alien Wahhabi sect of Islam, had . . . increased resentment." In an illustrative story, a mujahideen commander in Jalalabad had "rejected Arab offers of money in return for following their ways." Arabs, he complained, "thought jihad was a business, where [Afghans] sold [themselves] for the highest price."[25] In this context, the regime's accusation that foreigners perpetuated the war while it labored for peace and moderate Islam registered among Afghans despite being grossly exaggerated. The deep-rooted historical enmity between Arabs and Afghans helped the regime spread its message.

The Soviets also encountered Arab Afghans, noting the role private entrepreneurs such as bin Laden played in their arrival, but generally paid them little attention.[26] They pictured them as mercenaries, as another weapon the inspirers of the Afghan jihad—the United States and Pakistan—used against them. A Soviet *zampolit* would typically recall that "these mercenaries fought for money . . . There was then in Afghanistan no [fanatics] fighting for Islam."[27] The politburo discussed the Arab Afghans in the summer of 1989 but only noted that these "mercenaries" clustered near the Pakistani border, being part of the "irreconcilable" opposition.[28] The Soviets had nothing more to say about them.

The Soviet embassy in Kabul meanwhile noted with admiration the expansion and success of Najibullah's Islamic policies. As best as it could, it supported it, helped by the relaxation of antireligious policies in the USSR, establishing links between Afghan and Soviet Islamic scholars, and multiplying information sessions on the USSR's new religious policies, exhibitions about Islam in the USSR, and movies' presentations. At the difference of the 1980s, it was now open for CRA and SADUM to actively engage with Afghan policy, including restarting the exchanges of students between Soviet Islamic education centers at the Mir-i Arab *madrasa* in Bukhara and the Imam al-Bukhari Islamic Institute in Tashkent and the University of Kabul, at the Afghan Islamic scholars' request.[29]

A new reality had taken hold in Afghanistan. Many Afghans feared that a mujahideen takeover may mean "Arabs running around, shooting and destroying" and imposing an alien form of Islam as had happened after the Kabul regime had lost cities in Kunar, Takhar, and Kunduz provinces.[30] Even among the mujahideen in Afghanistan, there were increasingly questions as to the jihad's goals. The Pakistani operatives handling the mujahideen were similarly worried about the situation. The call to arms against the Soviets had been "the major unifying factor" among the mujahideen, a Pakistani intelligence officer noted.[31] Now, infighting was rife. Hekmatyar, with ISI support, had moved to wipe out other groups as a "mafia don taking over the territory of his rivals," analyzed a CIA operative.[32] A new meta-narrative had replaced the Cold War paradigm and the Kabul regime had skillfully taken advantage of the blurring of lines.

The clearest indication that equilibriums had shifted came in March 1990 when Tanai, the hardline Khalqi minister of defense, unsuccessfully attempted to seize power together with fellow Pashtuns from Hekmatyar's Hezb-e-Islami.[33] Tanai's coup was criticized by all parties to the conflict. Jamiat-e-Islami called it no less than a "blow to the popularity of jihad," arguing that the mujahideen should focus on overthrowing the "godless" communists instead of making alliances with them.[34] The AIC pointed out how radicals from both sides were able to come together but not the moderates.[35] The failure of Tanai's coup further consolidated the Kabul regime that even recovered some of the areas lost to the mujahideen the previous year. In parallel, the Khalqi debacle allowed Najibullah to intensify national reconciliation that had now become about erasing the few remaining symbols of the communist era. The regime hence no longer celebrated the April Revolution in 1991.[36]

Tanai's coup ended up shattering the mujahideen's claim that the war was about getting rid of communism and restoring Islam. It was a watershed event. Although it passed a resolution claiming that the "jihad [would] continue unless an Islamic government replaced the infidel and atheistic regime in the country," the Afghan Interim Government, painfully assembled by the Pakistani from among the Peshawar-7, could not mask its disarray.[37] Lust for power and ideological and ethnic divergences about the government's composition divided the mujahideen and prolonged the war. By 1991, the AIC had become understanding of the regime's policies and critical of the mujahideen. It acknowledged the regime's success in imposing its narrative about the conflict. Thanks to KhAD's "skillful propaganda . . . the people forgot their sacrifices and the crimes of the regime," the AIC contended.[38] The regime made deals with the mujahideen as shown by Tanai's coup, had a foreign policy, no longer relied on the LCST, and got rid of communism. This considerably boosted its political legitimacy, but it soon stopped mattering.

In June 1991, Karmal's return to Afghanistan, an event that remains shrouded in mystery, intensified the infighting in Hezb-e Watan, reinvigorating his supporters. Many formerly communist Afghan leaders believed that Najibullah had either gone too far in his concessions or needed to leave to allow for a comprehensive deal to arise with the mujahideen. This tension and a shift in the Kabul regime's military fortune that saw it lose the town of Khost on the Pakistani border marked the beginning of the regime's end. Not even Najibullah's desperate attempts to give far-reaching concessions to either Hekmatyar or Massoud saved the situation.[39]

The final blow came from Moscow. Kryuchkov promised more support to Najibullah in April 1991, but the failed August 1991 coup against Gorbachev discredited him and the other hardliners. In the aftermath, as Gorbachev ended up on the losing side of a battle for power with Boris Yeltsin, there were no supporters of the ex-Afghan communists left in the Kremlin. Andrei Kozyrev, Russia's minister of foreign affairs since October 1990, could now openly state that "everything was ready for a settlement in Afghanistan, the only problem left was the Soviet support to the 'extremists' led by Najibullah."[40] The comment showed how Islamism was not being taken seriously by the liberals around Yeltsin. In September 1991, the USSR and the United States agreed on a "negative symmetry deal," committing to stop supporting their respective Afghan clients while leaving Islamabad a free hand to support the mujahideen.

In November 1991, Rabbani led a mujahideen delegation to Moscow amid tensions over leadership in the Peshawar-7. In the talks that included representatives of the Central Asian republics, the mujahideen secured a new pledge from Russia to end all support to Najibullah and recall its advisers in exchange for help in recovering Soviet POWs and MIAs.[41] Despite the success of his policies, this was the end for Najibullah. The Soviets would cut military support and fuel supplies for the Afghan army's planes, tanks, and artillery.[42]

For many Soviets from the military and KGB, former advisers and policymakers, this was Moscow's final betrayal of its Afghan friends. It was also the logical result of the Soviet disengagement from Afghanistan.

Soon after, infighting in Kabul in the wake of Karmal's return, the loss of support of the Uzbek militias by Najibullah after the end of Soviet financial backing, and a push—coordinated with these groups—by Massoud on Kabul led to the end of Najibullah's regime. On 13 April 1992, Najibullah personally accompanied the last seven Soviet advisers to Kabul airport. One month later, Kozyrev would be visiting Kabul to meet the "moderate" mujahideen—Mujaddidi, Rabbani, and Gailani—now in control, telling them that Russia was ready to discuss military cooperation with them.[43]

Mujahideen Operations in the Soviet Union

The KGB border guards, an elite force with an in-depth vetting process, worked as much to prevent infiltrations from abroad as to keep people inside the Soviet Union. They were like a "hoop on a barrel."[44] The border guards were especially attentive along the most exposed borders with China, Iran, and Afghanistan. They were mobilized at the start of the Soviet-Afghan War to operate in an area of 150 kilometers into Afghanistan and counter mujahideen incursions into the USSR. This was a considerable change as compared to before the conflict when border guards seldom crossed the Amu Darya River.[45] In the 1980s, the border guards would be at the forefront of the Soviet preoccupations with the Islamist threat.

Diffuse concern among Soviet policymakers over violence and Islamism spilling over from Afghanistan to Central Asia had been present since before the Soviet-Afghan War. It intensified as the fighting moved to Badakhshan and Kunduz provinces near the Tajik border and Balkh Province near the Uzbek border in 1980. Maiorov's perhaps retrospectively inflated assessment was that the mujahideen's leaders wanted to "ignite . . . a holy war against the infidels," meaning the LCST and the authorities in Central Asia. They relied for that on the Basmachi's descendants, he believed.[46] The KGB's chairman Victor Chebrikov likewise acknowledged in 1983 that insecurity may be spilling over into Soviet territory. The border guards had to hence "carry out with honor their international duty to help" Afghanistan, he noted. They had "to push back on those who had the audacity to attempt to trench on the sovereignty of [the Soviet] border."[47]

Yet, despite such concerns, the Soviet-Afghan War had little impact in Central Asia, leading to only a handful of protests. While newspapers in Tajikistan, Uzbekistan, and Turkmenistan, unlike at the union level, paid attention to issues connected to Afghanistan—referencing the Basmachi, the border guards, and fundamentalist Islam—this was not mainly a response to the mujahideen gaining support among Central Asians.[48] Attention to such themes was instead part of the traditional Soviet atheistic propaganda, reinvigorated in the late 1970s because of the Kremlin's wish to recapture the revolutionary ideal and diffuse long-standing concerns with pan-Islamic ideas in the context of the troubles in Iran and Afghanistan.[49] The Soviets aimed this propaganda preventively.

As chapter 3 showed, there was no pervasive sympathy toward the mujahideen among Central Asian soldiers. The same was true for their families. Because of its proximity to Afghanistan, Central Asia more than the rest of the USSR witnessed the stream of "cargo 200s," the code name for the transportation of killed Soviets. The region also hosted hospitals for wounded and diseased soldiers and stories of the mujahideen's cruelty accompanied the arriving casualties. This does not absolve the Soviets of their abuses in Afghanistan but explains their hostility toward the mujahideen. Central Asia also saw a considerable number of Afghan communists come to study, reinforcing the negative feelings about the mujahideen.

A CIA assessment based on a 1986 poll noted that "support for the [Soviet-Afghan] war had increased markedly, while opposition has only grown marginally" in Central Asia. Many among the urban and educated classes believed that the Soviet modernization model was better than the "alternative posed by the Islamic fundamentalists."[50] Although attitudes were less clear-cut in rural areas which witnessed an Islamic revival in the 1980s, there was a significant difference between hostility toward the meaningless conflict, rising religiousness, and support to the mujahideen. If the first was generally true across the USSR and the second true in many parts of Central Asia, the third was the wishful thinking of the Bennigsen school and some Western policymakers.

Condemnation of the Soviet-Afghan War in Central Asia on religious grounds was rare. Muhammadjan Hindustani, a scholar influenced by the Muslim Brotherhood and who was at the center of the burgeoning Islamist study and teaching circles in Tajikistan, had for example supported it.[51] In Tajikistan's Kulyab Province, an unregistered mullah claimed, by contrast, in 1983 that it was "forbidden to bury Soviet soldiers killed in Afghanistan according to Muslim rites [because] they had fought against true Muslims."[52] There were likewise reports of mullahs inciting the population to "not serve in the Soviet army," including because of Afghanistan, and Tajik Islamists staging two protests in 1986 and 1987.[53] Islam's strength in Central Asia was nevertheless disconnected from the Soviet-Afghan War, predating the crises of the late 1970s. Its contestation potential in the region was thus both subdued and endogenous. The KGB reported "a possible danger to local security from Islam" in Tajikistan in the 1960s. However, it was not clear to what extent that danger was internal, "given the vitality of Islam in Tajikistan and the physical inaccessibility of so many of its strongholds" or related to Afghanistan.[54] The same was true of the 1980s. Religiousness was high in rural Tajikistan but independent of mujahideen activities. A sign that this assessment dominated in the Kremlin and the KGB was in the general lack of additional measures taken against the "unregistered clergy" during the Soviet-Afghan War aside from collecting information on Sufi orders' attitudes to the conflict and increasing atheistic propaganda.

The mujahideen represented a limited security threat to Central Asia. Their cross-border incursions swelled only at the end of the Soviet-Afghan War, taking advantage of the porosity of the mountainous border between Tajikistan and Afghanistan. In 1986, a Tajik newspaper had the local KGB head complaining that Islamic propaganda was coming from abroad and some undefined foreign forces tried to use the "Islamic factor" to undermine stability. Other KGB operatives made similar assertions retrospectively.[55] The Soviets assessed the mujahideen's activities in Central Asia to be part of the CIA and ISI's Program-M. Sources from KhAD and the Soviet military opined that Program-M had started in the mid-1980s and remained active as late as 1991.[56] The Soviets, therefore, saw Islamism as a weapon that their enemies could use at will. As summed up by a senior KGB operative, the "Islamic factor" was "a concept constructed artificially and skillfully in the context of the cold and then armed war for the remaking of the world order."[57] In Afghanistan, the KGB believed that Islamism's nuisance potential would diminish after the Soviet withdrawal and that the Soviets could keep it in check by dealing with its sponsors. Few in Moscow worried that Islamism might appeal to Central Asians.

While the Peshawar-7 did not conduct large-scale operations in the USSR, fighters affiliated with Jamiat-e-Islami, Hezb-e-Islami, and smaller groups carried out sabotage, diversion, and propaganda activities. The Soviets attributed some of these attacks to a group named Ittehadiya Islami-ye Wilayat-i Shamal (Islamic Union of the Northern Provinces, Ittehadiya) which rose to prominence in 1987 and was allegedly headed by Azad Beg, a Pakistani-born son of a qo'rboshi. Although Ittehadiya was small, its declared goal was to "liberate Soviet Central Asian republics from communist domination and create along the Soviet-Afghan border a 'Great Turkestan,'" something that worried Moscow.

At the time of its emergence, the Soviet and Afghan communists saw Ittehadiya as enough of a threat to have a KhAD unit monitor its activities. By 1990, the MID assessed that Beg had a training center used to send agents into the USSR. It claimed that Ittehadiya was then looking to recruit Central Asians across the Amu Darya River to oppose the Soviet authorities while smuggling drugs, weapons, and books into the USSR.[58] Soviet concerns with

Ittehadiya went all the way up to the Kremlin, while the KGB and the military saw the threat it represented to be largely about foreign powers meddling in Soviet affairs. Varennikov called Ittehadiya a pan-Turk organization and blamed its rise on the CIA and ISI. Ittehadiya, he argued, had transit bases and weapons caches along the border to supply "extremists" in Uzbekistan, Turkmenistan, and Tajikistan.[59] In line with KGB and MID's assessments, Varennikov collated nationalist and Islamist threats in Central Asia while denying groups such as Ittehadiya any agency.

These Soviet assessments are in line with what is now known from Western and Pakistani sources. As noted in chapter 5, the CIA had tried to intensify Islamic propaganda in the USSR from the 1970s, inspired by the Bennigsen school. After the Soviet-Afghan War's start, the CIA authorized operations that saw ISI-recruited mujahideen carry Korans to Central Asia.[60] Remarkably, Pakistan had pushed for the smuggling of Korans while the CIA initially believed that the mujahideen should be smuggling books about Central Asian culture and the history of Soviet abuses against the local people, a fascinating indication of the different perceptions of Islam's potentially disruptive role in Central Asia between the two. The ISI had pushed some 5,000 Korans into Central Asia by 1985, some of which had been intercepted by the KGB, and then with the CIA's approval decided that, in addition to propaganda, it would stage diversion and sabotage operations.[61] The CIA provided equipment for these operations but remained concerned about what would happen if the Soviets intercepted one of the teams sent to Central Asia. This ISI-CIA drive to sponsor guerrilla warfare on Soviet soil was indeed unprecedented since the 1950s, and the CIA had become increasingly apprehensive about its involvement in these operations by 1986, according to an ISI operative.[62]

As the ISI pushed for brasher operations, thirty mujahideen in three teams went into Central Asia in late 1986. The following spring, one hit an airfield near Termez in Uzbekistan, another "equipped with rocket-propelled grenades and antitank mines [set-up] violent ambushes along a border road," and the last one conducted a barrage of some thirty "high-explosive and incendiary rockets" on a factory twenty kilometers inside Tajikistan.[63] According to the US embassies in Kabul and Islamabad, which seemed to be in the dark as to the US role in these operations, the mujahideen were conducting guerrilla operations in Central Asia for "two or three months at a time" by that point.[64] However, these last series of attacks came as a turning point. The Soviet Ambassador went to see the Pakistani minister of foreign affairs the day after the attacks in April 1987. Whatever transpired during that meeting, it appeared the Soviets had threatened military reprisals on Pakistan if attacks continued. They passed the same warning to Washington, leading to considerable nervousness. The bulk of the attacks were immediately stopped, and the CIA told the ISI to "not start a Third World War."[65] The remaining incidents were of a limited scale in 1987, and Hezb-e-Islami claimed at least one of them.[66]

The attacks inside the Soviet Union were modest but had highlighted the mujahideen's reach and the Soviets' vulnerability. The ISI argued that the attacks had made Moscow "concerned not so much with the actual damage [they] caused," but with their effect in boosting the local Muslim population's opposition to the authorities.[67] This was ISI and the mujahideen's wishful thinking. Few Central Asians had sympathy for armed men who rained down rockets on their factories and roads. If anything, the attacks reinforced support for the Soviet-Afghan War and upheld Moscow's argument that the LCST defended the fatherland in Afghanistan. The dissemination of Islamic propaganda in Central Asia was probably more concerning to the Soviets, although again it had only a marginal impact in boosting contestation. More problematically for the Kremlin, the mujahideen's attacks challenged the domestic narrative about the Soviet-Afghan War, undermined Soviet prestige—including because Iranian media that were also eager to allege Central Asian support for the mujahideen reported them—and were the clearest illustration of how the LCST had become bogged down in Afghanistan.[68]

As to Ittehadiya, the Soviets continued to monitor its activities after 1989 but without ISI support, its disruption potential was modest. Soviet reports suggested that Beg, together with Tajik and Uzbek mujahideen, was still smuggling books and weapons into Central Asia in 1991. Soon though, the USRR's collapse would alter the regional geopolitical landscape. Mujahideen activities in Central Asia would then come in the context of the upheaval in Tajikistan. To former KGB and Red Army officers, this was the Soviet-Afghan War's legacy. The KGB's chief in Dushanbe would again blame ISI's Program-M, aimed "at destabilizing the social-political situation in the Central Asian republics and creating the conditions of them leaving the USSR," for the "strengthening of Islamic fundamentalism" in Tajikistan.[69] Varennikov would in turn lament that the threat represented by Program-M had never seriously worried the Kremlin and the national authorities of the Central Asian republics.

Beyond this, the reports about the mujahideen's attacks were an important part of the propaganda battle that went parallel to the military one. Moscow used them to highlight that the Soviet-Afghan War was not only about internationalist help, a point also made in the handbooks distributed to soldiers. Chebrikov visited Tajikistan to honor the border guards who had died in April 1987. Although the episode was not immediately publicized nationwide, it helped demonstrate within the security forces that the war was also about defending the USSR.[70] A month later, testifying to glasnost rise and the Kremlin's new Afghan strategy, *Literaturnaya Gazeta*, a union-level newspaper, finally published an article about the attacks while noting that the mujahideen had even tried to recruit Soviet citizens.[71]

On the mujahideen's side, Jamiat-e-Islami took pains to deny that it sponsored large-scale operations in the USSR.[72] The USSR, it claimed, instrumentalized the few incursions to conduct massive retaliation and have its border guards operate in Afghanistan.[73] Likewise, *AFGHANews* downplayed the attacks' importance. One article in 1987 noted that Soviet reporting of them was meant to "give the impression that [the USSR's] invasion of Afghanistan was an act of self-defense."[74] At the same time, Jamiat-e-Islami was keen to express solidarity with Soviet Muslims. *AFGHANews* hence explained that Soviet policies "did not eliminate the love of Islam from the hearts of Muslims" in Central Asia.[75] While again downplaying the cross-border attacks, it argued that the Soviet-Afghan War was bound to have "an indirect effect on Central Asia" where Muslims were to rise against the Soviet system.[76]

By then, *AFGHANews* was increasingly commenting about Soviet Muslims. It claimed the Central Asians supported the mujahideen because, according to an alleged Uzbek writer, Moscow had failed to "de-Islamize" Turkestan.[77] It also reported that a Tajik mullah had been arrested for criticizing the Soviet-Afghan War and the Soviet authorities within his "religious discussion group." The journal, however, never provided evidence as to the importance of pro-mujahideen attitudes. It made the same mistakes as the Bennigsen school, first, by equating increased religiosity with support for the mujahideen and readiness to fight against fellow Soviets and, second, by confusing national and religious factors. Instead of widespread support for the mujahideen as a whole, there was considerable sympathy in Tajikistan for Jamiat-e-Islami's Massoud. Many Tajiks saw him as a national hero.[78] This is the context in which one should see Jamiat-e-Islami's claim that by 1983 it had 2,500 card-carrying members in Tajikistan, a number that was impossible to ascertain.[79]

Ultimately, the mujahideen walked a thin line between downplaying the cross-border attacks to not provoke the Soviets into retaliation and to keep international public opinion on their side and implying that the Soviet-Afghan War had led to an Islamic awakening among Soviet Muslims. In truth, the mujahideen were even apprehensive about such an awakening. *AFGHANews*, for example, feared that if the "spirit of jihad" spread across "the Muslim territories of Russia," Moscow might decide to sever North Afghanistan to create a sixteenth Soviet republic to make it easier to stabilize Central Asia.[80] The Kremlin would hence deal with "the effect of a lost war on the Muslim people in Central Asia" by creating a buffer.[81] This was unacceptable to the mujahideen. Beyond questions of Islamic solidarity, their priority was always Afghanistan.

India's Triangular Diplomacy

Already in 1979, the Soviets had primarily conceived of the Islamist danger from Afghanistan as directed at India. An Oriental Studies Institute's report remarked that Islamabad could decide to use the "Islamic fundamentalism" that had crystallized among the mujahideen against it.[82] This indicated Soviet awareness of Islamism's disruptive potential, but they did not articulate the Islamist threat in the context of Central Asia. Later, the Soviets tried to play on Indian fears. Tabeev, a man with a seemingly endless appetite for scheming, would once tell the Indian ambassador that the Indians may want to consider intervening in Kashmir while the Soviets were in Afghanistan, a suggestion New Delhi considered carefully.[83]

India had a heightened awareness of religion's importance in its struggle with Pakistan, rendered more acute by the Bangladesh Liberation War of 1971. The Pakistani angle dominated all other considerations and determined New Delhi's tolerant attitude toward the PDPA. It also explained Prime Minister Indira Gandhi's muted response to the Soviet intervention in Afghanistan.[84] India loomed large in the Soviet-Afghan War's background while Pakistan welcomed the renewed military cooperation with the United States that the conflict had brought and made efforts to emphasize that it faced a regional Indian-Afghan-Soviet alliance. Muhammad Zia-ul-Haq, the Pakistani leader, would tell the CIA in 1982 that the Soviets had gone into Afghanistan as much to protect against the Islamist threat to Central Asia as to prepare an attack on Pakistan and Iran.[85] The underlying claim was that they would do so with India's support. The Soviet-Afghan War, Zia asserted, was part of a "pan-Islamic revival" directed against India but that would also "one day win over the Muslims in the Soviet Union."[86] As Islamism consolidated and Pakistani influence among the mujahideen grew, India tried to raise awareness over the Islamist threat through talks with the Soviets and the Americans.

US president Ronald Reagan wrote a letter to Rajiv Gandhi, Indira's son and India's prime minister, in March 1987. He confirmed that the United States supported Soviet withdrawal plans even though they still doubted Gorbachev's intentions. The Americans were pushing India to lean on Moscow to solve the Afghan issue "urgently" and "realistically" and to get rid of Najibullah.[87] Only three months later, Gandhi met Gorbachev. The Soviet leader explained that "the Afghans had freed themselves from leftist slogans . . . from the idea of transitioning from a tribal system directly to communism," confirming that there would be no more ideology in Afghanistan. The PDPA and, one may add, the Soviets were now being more realistic, although only to a certain extent. Gorbachev still wrongly believed that Najibullah was prepared to share power with the mujahideen. He hoped that national reconciliation would create "more favorable conditions" for a coalition government with, among other groups, "the Islamic clergy."[88] The conversation testified to the Soviets' openness with the Indians as to their Afghan strategy. Gorbachev had made India the cornerstone of his Asian foreign policy and visited it soon after assuming power.[89] Gandhi came to the USSR three times between 1986 and 1988. The personal sympathy Gorbachev felt toward Gandhi reinforced the Soviet-Indian relationship. According to Kryuchkov, there was a complete understanding between the Soviet Union and India.[90]

Following his talks with the Soviets, Gandhi briefed John Gunther Dean, the US ambassador in India, in July 1987. The prime minister first catered to Americans' views, noting that he too found the Afghans to be "so divided that it would be difficult to find a political solution to the imbroglio" while dismissing national reconciliation. Then he introduced the religious angle. Gandhi noted that he "found [Gorbachev] to be more concerned about the strengthening of fundamentalism than about [the] increased influence of moderate Afghan leaders who enjoy the support of the West."[91] This was a striking assessment and one that seemed to more express the Indian view than the Soviet. Although a full record of the Gorbachev-Gandhi talks is not available, it is unlikely that the Soviets found radical Islam to be so high on their agenda. They wanted to stabilize Najibullah's regime by any means possible, including by dealing with Islamist mujahideen groups. Likewise, Gandhi was aware, as future conversations showed, that it was not only the moderate mujahideen who enjoyed Western support. Therefore, Gandhi was to some extent playing the Americans, trying to show that he agreed with them on some points while pushing his own line. Meanwhile, he drew attention to Islamic fundamentalism in both Washington and Moscow.

Within the USSR-India-US triangle that had emerged in Afghanistan, Moscow was aware that India had its own agenda. Gorbachev's talks with Najibullah in July 1987, right after his talks with Gandhi, touched on his perceptions of Islamism and India. After stating India's position that Afghanistan should not end up under US influence as a "good base for cooperation," Gorbachev stressed the limitations of New Delhi's support: "The Indians are concerned that the normalization of the situation in Afghanistan would lead to that Pakistan would direct subversive activities against India. It is possible to feel, . . . that the Indians are interested for the USSR to not hurry up with the withdrawal of its troops from Afghanistan. But in this position of India, only the interests of India are considered at one-hundred per cent. But the interests of Afghanistan and the Soviet Union, perhaps, [only] at twenty per cent."[92]

The Soviets saw the threat of "subversive activities" by the mujahideen as a weapon Islamabad may use against India after the Soviet withdrawal. The danger such groups represented for Central Asia was secondary. The Soviets did not see the Islamists as independent forces but as a tool engineered in and directed from Islamabad with US support. Moscow, Kabul, and New Delhi were well aware that Pakistan's strategic gaze was on Kashmir, not on Tajikistan or Uzbekistan. This seemed like the reemergence of a Great Game mindset.[93] The Soviets assessed that India and Pakistan already imagined the post-Soviet period in Afghanistan and considered ideology as largely irrelevant. Moscow believed it would exert indirect influence in the region regardless of who held power in Kabul. Concluding this part of the conversation, Gorbachev noted to Najibullah that, even with this caveat, the "core interests of the USSR, India, and Afghanistan in what concerned international questions and the situation in the region were aligned." On his side, the Afghan leader floated to Gorbachev the idea of joint military action—"a preventive, some form of demonstrative strike"—with India against Pakistan.[94] Gorbachev gently rebuffed the proposition, but it marked the start of the Afghans' attempt to raise Soviet concerns over an Islamist threat.

Another round of USSR-India-US exchanges happened in November 1987. New Delhi was again talking simultaneously to both superpowers without it being clear if Washington and Moscow knew how candid it was with each of them. Dean reported on a striking conversation he had with Rohen Sen, Gandhi's diplomatic adviser, who had come to brief him on Gandhi's conversation with Nikolai Ryzhkov, chairman of the Soviet Council of Ministers. The Indian prime minister had told Ryzhkov that "the victory of fundamentalism in Afghanistan would affect adversely the Muslim areas of Soviet Central Asia."[95] He also admitted that it would be an issue for Kashmir. Gandhi contended that it was Soviet and Indian interest that whatever government emerges in Kabul after the Soviet withdrawal, the Islamic fundamentalists should not dominate it.

It is unclear if this was also the Soviet assessment or if the Soviets were so concerned about Islamism's effect on Central Asia. It may have been here again more the Indian view while it was clear that New Delhi was making efforts to influence the Kremlin on that issue. Meanwhile, the Soviets told Gandhi that they were negotiating with all the mujahideen groups.[96] This confirmed that the need to find support for Najibullah trumped their concern over the Islamist threat. At that stage, the Soviets believed that their best bet was to return Zahir Shah, the former Afghan King now in exile in Italy.[97] This did not mean that the Kremlin could not accept other options as long as the regime that emerged in

Afghanistan was not anti-Soviet. Finally, Sen's briefing to Dean was again remarkable for how it catered to US perceptions. Sen emphasized that New Delhi did not think that national reconciliation had a broad popular base.

A month after the Dean-Sen conversation, Gandhi wrote to Reagan that "it was in [India's] interest and [that of the United States] to avoid [the] fundamentalist elements gain[ing] an upper hand in Afghanistan."[98] New Delhi was, as the Soviet-Afghan War wound down, working to make Moscow and Washington mindful of what an Afghan government dominated by the likes of Hekmatyar and under Pakistani influence may mean for the region and its own security. Even more than the Soviets, the United States was dismissive of Indian warnings. Reagan answered without reference to Islamism and reiterated that the Soviets should simply let go of Najibullah and accept "the need for a fresh start."[99] In his response letter, Gandhi, after meeting Najibullah in New Delhi, contended that the Afghan leader was more than Moscow's puppet. "Najibullah and the PDPA were showing greater flexibility in approaching the political issues involved," he argued.[100] This was the start of India's departure from its earlier more skeptical assessments of national reconciliation.

The White House dismissed India's warnings in February 1988. Although he claimed to understand New Delhi's concerns that a "Khomeini-like fundamentalist regime takes over in Kabul," Reagan maintained that "Afghan historical and cultural experience, along [with] the fact of a small Shi'a minority, argued strongly against such a development."[101] This was a paramount statement that embodied US thinking and showed how many observers saw radical Islamism at the time: It was not associated with Sunni Islam and countries like Saudi Arabia and Pakistan. The United States assessed that the Afghan opposition was mostly moderate, a judgment they saw as confirmed by the mujahideen's "ties to conservative Islamic governments." There was little awareness—at least to the extent the White House shared it with New Delhi—that more than a liberation struggle went on in Afghanistan. Washington's conviction was that a Soviet withdrawal would solve everything, creating a popular regime supported by large swathes of Afghan society. This was to reduce "the influence of extremist elements," Reagan argued.[102] There are certainly limits to the extent it is possible to assess US thinking based on diplomatic exchanges, but they do suggest that Washington did not take Sunni Islamism seriously. As for the Kremlin, this ideology was for the White House circumscribed to the Soviet-Afghan War.

By early 1988, the United States found Indian activism in shaping post-Soviet Afghanistan "distinctly unhelpful." There was no patience for either India's claim that there was more in Afghanistan than a Cold War confrontation or its argument that they had to control Pakistan.[103] The only one who took India's concerns seriously was Dean.[104] He again met Gandhi in June 1988, and the Indian prime minister told him that the United States should be mindful that the Soviet withdrawal was not the end of all things Afghanistan-related and to reassess its support to the mujahideen. Gandhi also confirmed his reviewed assessment of Najibullah. The PDPA's general secretary was "committed to keeping the fundamentalists like Hekmatyar from taking control of the government in Kabul," he argued. This was why New Delhi was backing him "not as a leader" but as a bulwark against the fundamentalists.[105] Hence, India's criticism of the United States had grown in parallel to its concern that Hezb-e-Islami would replace the PDPA. It also showed the success regarding India of Najibullah's new platform. He had effectively switched to stressing how he was the better alternative to the Islamists, even though he was negotiating with them at the same time. There is little doubt that the talks between the Indians and Soviets also featured discussions of Islamism.

In parallel to the Dean-Gandhi talks, the Pakistani chairman of the Joint Chiefs of Staff, General Akhtar Abdur Rahman, and the vice chief of the Army Staff, General Mirza Aslam Beg, met Arnold Raphel, the US ambassador to Pakistan. In addition to their support to the mujahideen, opposition to national reconciliation, and strategy to block—as the Kabul regime rightly claimed—the Afghan refugees' return, the Pakistanis outlined their far-reaching plans for Afghanistan. "Of all the possible outcomes in Kabul," they argued, "the one which the Soviets feared most was an Islamic republic."[106] India and the USSR's common interest was to prevent it, they said. This remarkable statement showed that Islamabad wrongly assumed the Soviets saw Islamism as necessarily a vital threat to them.

Moreover, the Pakistani delegation also volunteered the controversial opinion that an "Afghan Islamic Republic" if it were to emerge after the PDPA's demise could "join with Pakistan, Turkey, and Iran . . . in an Islamic economic and political bloc which could serve as a barrier to regional Soviet ambitions." Such talk confirms how South Asian powers were then preparing to have a reconfiguration of alliances and assumed others were two. Islamabad and New Delhi assessed that Islamic solidarity, supported by Islamic forms of government—though it is unclear how Turkey with its secular regime and Shi'a Iran fit into that paradigm—would play a central role in the new alignments. As Raphel noted, "clearly the Paks felt that a new phase has started in the perennial Great Game."[107] Interestingly, Gorbachev mentioned to Schultz in April 1988 the same idea of a "union of Islamic countries" spearheaded by Iran and Pakistan, showing how he was aware of Islamabad's thinking. Yet, the Kremlin remained skeptical of Islamism's disruptive potential for the USSR despite Indian warnings.

By mid-1988, India's position had crystallized into supporting Najibullah while the United States was, according to one of Gandhi's advisers who came to brief Dean on new meetings in Moscow, having "no role for Najibullah now or later." The Indians maintained that the PDPA was trying to "keep extreme fundamentalists out of Kabul."[108] The countries were now at odds. It was remarkable how Najibullah and Gorbachev's new policies, coupled with US unchecked support to Pakistan and Islamist mujahideen, had made the PDPA appealing to New Delhi. India continued supporting Najibullah after 1990, providing refuge to the Afghan leader's family.

As to Gandhi's adviser's answer to Dean, one may again wonder to what extent this was the Soviets' and PDPA's position. One hint it was less of an issue for Moscow comes from an exchange between the Indian defense minister and Gorbachev in February 1988. New Delhi appealed to the USSR to do something as part of the Geneva Accords about the weapons stockpiles accumulated in Pakistan during the conflict and that it feared the mujahideen would use against it. While the Soviets recognized the problem, leaving was more important and Gorbachev explained that there was nothing he could do.[109] The Kremlin, while concerned with the "irreconcilable opposition," did not believe that the crucial aspect was the Islamist threat. Najibullah needed to integrate Islam to make his regime more appealing to the population. The communists, meanwhile, liaised with all the mujahideen parties and, as we have seen, Najibullah even claimed to Gorbachev that Hezb-e-Islami was ready to find a deal with him in 1988. Although in that same conversation Gorbachev and Najibullah, in the words of the former, agreed that Afghans "would not support the fundamentalists," they believed that it was no problem having them together in government with the PDPA.[110] Two years later Hezb-e-Islami would find an agreement with the Khalqi Tanai behind Najibullah's back.

Gorbachev again visited India in November 1988. Even though the Soviet leader was keen to stress afterward the "unique level of their relations," this visit marked the beginning of strategic disunion. At the politburo, Gorbachev noted that "India now had a great power policy," centered on creating its own sphere of influence in South Asia and not on playing second fiddle to the USSR. As to Afghanistan, the meeting confirmed that Islamic fundamentalism was less of an issue for the Soviets than for the Indians. Gorbachev reported that "Rajiv stressed the gravity of the threat of Muslim fundamentalism. Pakistan, Afghanistan, Iran, Turkey are for him a headache."[111] Nothing was said of it being one for the Soviet Union. This was in line with previous assessments—

the Soviets were glad to have India directly engage Najibullah, including dealing with the Islamist threat.[112]

India, after it was sidelined from the Geneva Accords, was further marginalized on Afghanistan while Moscow, having already made progress with Tehran, thought of ways of improving its relations with Islamabad. The USSR
suggested to the Indians that they do the same. In February 1989, Shevardnadze went on a trip to Pakistan but it gained the Soviets nothing. The ISI participated in the Jalalabad attack and the Soviets were no closer to retrieving
their POWs and MIAs or having the mujahideen agree to a coalition government. The trip undermined USSR-India cohesion while Gandhi struggled politically at home amid a corruption scandal and the fallout from the intervention
in Sri Lanka. In a final effort to play a role in Afghanistan, he fantasized about
either a joint Indian-Soviet war with Pakistan or even Indian military support
to Najibullah.[113] Neither option was in Moscow's interest on the eve of the
LCST's withdrawal.

As 1988 drew to a close, the Indians again tried talking to the United States
to alert them to Islamism.[114] Meanwhile, Robert Oakley, the new ambassador
in Pakistan, reported that Beg, now the Pakistani army's chief of staff, had denied that there would be "a fundamentalist government" in Kabul.[115] He also
said that the "new [mujahideen] leaders (such as Hekmatyar and Rabbani) were
not traditionalists or tribal leaders and they would not cede power to others
who had not fought the Soviets." As noted in chapter 4, the war had seen the
emergence of the Islamists who did not anchor their claim to power and
political legitimacy in traditional tribal or religious structures. Considering that
its mujahideen had won the war, Islamabad wanted to see a government in
Kabul aligned with its interests. Finally, Beg repeated to the United States that a
"strategic consensus" was emerging between Pakistan, Afghanistan, Iran, and
Turkey. It was a "grand design," he argued, that should help create "a new regional power equation and provide the US with new options for dealing with
India, the Soviet Union, and the Mideast."[116] The Pakistanis made no secret of
their intention to prop their influence through Islamism, vindicating India's
fears.

Considerations of regional stability were nevertheless not high on the US
agenda. Shortly thereafter, the White House confirmed that it would continue
backing Pakistan and had no interest in an Afghan coalition government.[117]
Reflecting on these events many years later, Dean pondered whether the US
main objective was not really "to place a pro-Pakistani and pro-American government in Kabul, which would be, above all, anticommunist." It seemed
that Washington—even if it could not direct them against the USSR—

considered that, on its side, it had nothing to fear from the Islamists.[118] The risk of them taking power in Kabul was secondary to the Cold War's objectives. In the words of Zbigniew Brzezinski, who stood at the origins of the US support to the mujahideen under President Jimmy Carter: "What was more important in world history? The Taliban or the collapse of the Soviet empire? Some agitated Moslems or the liberation of Central Europe and the end of the Cold War?"[119]

The same tenets governed the George H.W. Bush administration. A National Security Directive reaffirmed US support for the mujahideen and detailed the objectives in post-Soviet Afghanistan. "Working in concert with Pakistan," the United States was to "(1) promote Resistance cohesion; (2) promote a peaceful political succession, rather than support any individual or faction; (3) avoid a civil war and (4) prevent the emergence of a new Afghan government that was pro-Soviet, pro-Iranian, or messianic-Islamic."[120] Preventing the creation of a "messianic-Islamic"—a peculiar term—state was last on the US priority list. By 1991, Peter Tomsen, the US special envoy to Afghanistan, noted that preventing a "Muslim extremist victory" dropped even further as he was unable to have it included among US priorities in Afghanistan.[121] By that point, as vividly recalled by the former CIA chief in Pakistan, George H. W. Bush would once ask about Afghanistan: "Is that thing still going on?"[122]

Between 1987 and 1989, the Indians and the Pakistanis, operating at cross-purposes, better understood what was at stake in Afghanistan beyond the Soviet withdrawal. New Delhi had emphasized the Islamist threat to both Moscow and Washington, overplaying the Soviet concerns with it to the United States. With both superpowers, India's concerns failed to register as the bigger picture of the Cold War and Najibullah's future, not as a bulwark to Islamism but as the incarnation of a surviving ex-communist regime, dwarfed them. Najibullah's parallel attempt to make a similar argument about Islamism to the Soviets also struggled to register.

A Slow Reckoning

Mujahideen attacks in Central Asia and India's triangular diplomacy came in parallel to Soviet-American negotiations on the Geneva Accords, rising nationalist contestation in Central Asia, Soviet talks with Najibullah, and Gorbachev's new foreign policy in the Muslim world. These latter four factors that are detailed below shaped the Soviet perceptions of Islamism, building on diffuse concerns present since before the Soviet-Afghan War. These perceptions remained, however, ill-defined as was the understanding the Soviet elites had of Islam. It was the religion most alien to them and one that did not fit into their world-views dominated by Marxism-Leninism. In Gromyko's words, "was there another religious cult that could compare with Islam in the power of its magnetism. Would anyone dispute that Islam, therefore, created the most fanatics?"[123]

Regarding the first factor, Moscow increasingly saw Islamism as connected to US policy in South Asia and the Middle East. While preparing to leave Afghanistan, Gorbachev wanted Washington to pressure the mujahideen into embracing national reconciliation. The Soviet-American negotiations at that time seldom touched on Islamism, but it remained in the background as the superpowers haggled over Afghanistan's future. Robert Gates, the CIA's deputy director, for example, noted that the Soviets raised the issue informally with the United States. In late 1987, Shevardnadze apparently asked Shultz, in confidence, for "American cooperation in limiting the spread of 'Islamic Fundamentalism.'" This did not provoke a reaction from the United States, leading the journalist Steve Coll to argue that this showed how the Soviets were mindful of the Islamist threat while the United States discarded it.[124] This was, however, only partially true. What Moscow wanted most was an Afghan regime that would not be pro-American, while the Cold War paradigm dwarfed the Islamist problem for the Kremlin as it did for the White House. Indeed, Gorbachev was then himself very much a cold warrior.

The Soviet hardliners appeared mostly willing to point to the Islamist threat to secure US support for Moscow's coalition government in Kabul. In parallel to Gorbachev's visit to the United States in December 1987, Kryuchkov would tell Gates about the danger that fundamentalist Islamic groups would rise to power in Afghanistan, founding a Sunni equivalent to Shia Iran. "You seem fully occupied in trying to deal with just one fundamentalist Islamic state," Kryuchkov joked to his US counterpart, while arguing that Islamism threatened both the USSR and the United States.[125] Kryuchkov then still saw Islamism as a state-based phenomenon on the Iranian model.

Meanwhile, Vorontsov and Michael Armacost, the US under secretary of state for political affairs, met in late 1987 to prepare the Shevardnadze-Shultz talks about the Geneva Accords in early 1988 and the Gorbachev-Reagan summit in Moscow in June. Two things stood out. First, the Soviets alleged that Oakley had met the three Islamist mujahideen leaders—Hekmatyar, Sayyaf, and Rabbani—to discuss "propaganda and military measures" to compromise national reconciliation and prevent contacts with the Kabul regime "under penalty of Islamic Law." Armacost countered by saying that Vorontsov's account was "full of misrepresentations" but did not deny it. Second, both sides disagreed as to Najibullah's policies and the importance of the changes—the renaming of the country and the constitution—he had introduced.[126] This exchange provided

FIGURE 6.2.   Ronald Reagan, Mikhail Gorbachev, and other policymakers in the Oval Office, 1987 (Courtesy of the Ronald Reagan Presidential Library). The Soviet and US leaders talked about arms control and other global issues. On the margins, Shevardnadze and Kryuchkov discussed Islamism with their US counterparts.

another indication that the mujahideen and their backers took national reconciliation seriously enough to design countermeasures. It moreover showed that the United States was in close contact with the Islamist mujahideen.

The Shevardnadze-Shultz talks later dealt with the Soviet withdrawal from Afghanistan. They made no mention of Islamism in February 1988.[127] In March, Shevardnadze was equally focused on having Schultz agree to an end to US military support to the mujahideen after the Geneva Accords. He then underlined that US support for Hekmatyar, "a fundamentalist, a person of extreme views" who could not even deal with other mujahideen, made an Afghan settlement more complicated.[128] In reality, the Kremlin did not see the problem to be so much with Hekmatyar's ideology. If he found a deal with the PDPA or at least guaranteed that the United States would have no military bases in Afghanistan, even Hekmatyar could be an acceptable partner. More than about Islamism, the Soviets worried that pro-US armed groups would take Kabul.

The second factor to influence the Kremlin's assessment of Islamism was the rising protests in Central Asia in the late 1980s that had nationalist and religious undertones. Up to that point, Moscow had believed that the mujahideen's cross-border attacks and the limited activity of the Central Asian Islamist elements represented the Islamist danger. Islamism did not represent an ideological challenge to the Soviet system. The new popular contestation crystallized the Kremlin's awakening to a potentially broader Islamist threat for the Soviet system. Gorbachev expressed his new understanding most clearly in a discussion with Najibullah in April 1988. As to "Islamic fundamentalism," he argued, "the Americans were trying to throw that topic at [the Soviets], in Uzbekistan."[129] Gorbachev, therefore, saw a religious matrix in the protests in Tashkent while the United States' supposed role in engineering these protests made in his mind the connection with Afghanistan and the Cold War.

Gorbachev's claim to Najibullah demonstrated how he had been rethinking Islam for the previous two years. Following a report by the Department of Propaganda in 1986, Gorbachev noted that "the influence of Islam was rising" at the politburo. In response, it was crucial to strengthen atheist propaganda. However, it should not appear as "a struggle against Islam," Gorbachev contended, but as one against "the anti-Soviet consequence of religious extremism . . . It was important to attempt to decrease the religiosity, transfer this longing [*potrebnost'*] into another direction" and fight "political [and] social isolation [which] was the environment for religion," Gorbachev argued. The CPSU needed to "pull people to open clever debates about the questions that religion dealt with."[130] Gorbachev's view testified to Marxism-Leninism's enduring grip on the Soviet leaders. To them, religion could not coexist with communism and had to disappear. Strikingly, Gorbachev's call to reaffirm Marxism-Leninism dominance over Islam happened in parallel to his blessing Najibullah's Islamization of Afghanistan. Yet embracing Islam was the plan for a backward country; the USSR, by contrast, could not make any compromises on ideology.

Meanwhile, Uzbekistan witnessed a political and corruption scandal after years of falsifying its cotton production reports with the complicity of officials in Moscow. This so-called Cotton Affair received a nationwide echo when Andropov tried to curb corruption after the Brezhnev years.[131] It infamously implicated Sharof Rashidov, Uzbekistan's CPSU first secretary, who had died in 1983, many senior members of the Uzbek CPSU, and, importantly, Brezhnev-era elites in Moscow. The affair forced the politburo to look more closely at how the Soviet model worked in Central Asia, demonstrating again how it had remained blissfully unaware of the local accommodation between communism and Islam. The Russian elites meanwhile blamed the scandal on Central Asians that they described with the same stereotypes used for Karmal and other Afghans. As described by Chernyaev: "The 'Uzbek Affair' . . . showed not only the 'transformation' of the socialist order into an Eastern quasi-despotism but also the complete failure of the national policy of eliminating Islam with the help of domesticating it in the European-Russian way and imposing an internationalist atheistic ideology."[132]

After Andropov's death, the breadth of the scandal led Gorbachev to purge the entire Uzbek CPSU leadership in 1986. Coupled with strengthened anti-Islamic policies, this led to opposition in the Uzbek CPSU and among the Uzbek population. However, the Cotton Affair marked only the start of the turmoil in Uzbekistan. In an unrelated development that showed rising political volatility, interethnic clashes between Uzbeks and Meskhetian Turks erupted in 1989. *AFGHANews* rushed to express its solidarity with the Uzbeks' opposition to Moscow.[133]

The Cotton Affair came shortly before another political crisis in Central Asia. In Kazakhstan, Gorbachev dismissed Dinmukhamed Kunaev, the ethnic Kazakh who had headed the republic, for corruption and because of a conflict among local elites in 1986.[134] Kunaev's replacement by Gennady Kolbin, however, led to street protests in Alma-Ata. These were the first signs of national-ethnic strife in the USSR. The Kazakh crisis was a wake-up call for the Kremlin, which had been blind to Islam and nationalism's contestation potential. Gorbachev did not understand that the Kazakhs, although some had mobilized through Kunaev's patronage network, could not accept "being sent some [ethnic] Russian party secretary, like a commissar, from Ulyanovsk [in Central Russia]," one of Gorbachev's advisers noted.[135] Although disconnected from Afghanistan, turmoil in Uzbekistan and Kazakhstan had Islamic undertones in the view of Soviet policymakers. By some accounts, protesters, along with anti-Russian slogans, chanted "Glory to Islam's Banner!" and had green flags.[136] True or not, such reports testified to how nationalism and Islam increasingly came in resonance in the Kremlin's perceptions. These crises were the background to Gorbachev's comment to Najibullah as he grappled with this unexpected ideological challenge.

Like with the mujahideen's cross-border attacks, the KGB dealt with the protests in Central Asia and its interest in the Islamic factor grew as the political situation became more volatile. Yet, the KGB, as the Kremlin, saw the United States as having engineered these Islamic-colored protests. They "did not understand what was happening," Grachev argued. "These were traditional Cold War-era [perceptions]. They believed the United States had blown up the Islamic problem." In fact, for Grachev, the Soviet policymakers never thought of the Islamists as "independent forces, but only as US cronies."[137] This was also how Moscow saw Islamism at an international level and it was also exactly what Gorbachev told Najibullah about Uzbekistan.

Understandably, KGB's Kryuchkov was the Soviet policymaker most concerned with Islamism while explicitly making the connection between Afghanistan and Central Asia. Together with Shevardnadze, he was the one to engage with the United States on that. In 1987, he would argue at the politburo that the USSR "had to find a way to not lose Afghanistan as a friendly country, to not allow for anyone to create a place-of-arms there—Iran, Turkey, the fundamentalists."[138] The statement testified to his concern over the mujahideen eventually becoming a threat to Central Asia, either because they would come under the influence of another Muslim country or because they would establish their own Islamist state. In that latter case, they would probably come under US influence which was also unacceptable for the Soviets.

In Central Asia, the KGB increased its monitoring of homegrown Islamists. Davlat Khudonazarov, the future presidential candidate of the Tajik Islamist-democratic coalition, recalled how the KGB tried to force him into denouncing Sayid Abdulloh Nuri (Mullo Abdulloh), an apprentice to Hindustani and now the leader of an informal Islamist circle in Tajikistan and the future head of the Islamic Renaissance Party of Tajikistan (IRPT). Although Khudonazarov refused to participate in the KGB's provocation, the KGB still had Nuri sentenced for drug possession but what was really spreading Islamic propaganda. Khudonazarov argued that the KGB then had a tenuous grasp of Islam, knowing nothing of these local Islamist scholars. The intelligence services, he noted, believed that these scholars were all Iranian Islamists; all agents of Iran, not Afghanistan because the Afghans were seen as being in the midst of a civil war and under the control of the Soviets.[139] Yet there was no connection to Iran. Despite sympathies for Khomeini and the Islamic Revolution, Nuri and his circle were not Shia but Sunni Muslims. The KGB's misconception confirmed, however, how the Soviets always believed that puppet masters stood behind the Islamists at home and abroad. They had to be agents of Iran, the United States, or Pakistan. They were part of a conspiracy to undermine the USSR or, for that matter, the DRA. Because they were foreign agents, the KGB assessed the threat they represented in the USSR as limited.

This perception of Islamism endured. In 1988, Chebrikov's report on the KGB's work in curbing terrorism mentioned the "Islamists"—the term appeared for one of the first times in Soviet documents—among the groups conducting subversive activities in the USSR. "A moderate threat was represented," Chebrikov noted, "by the extremist tendencies of the followers of 'pure Islam' who were propagandizing" for a "holy war" against the Soviet regime.[140] For this reason, the Muslim Brotherhood and foreign intelligence services tried to recruit Arab students and Afghans in Soviet universities. Foreign forces were hence again to blame for Islamism. Chebrikov's report, however, said nothing more about the Islamist threat's potency while it was only one of the issues the KGB monitored. A year later, Kryuchkov's annual summary of the KGB's activities did not mention religion.[141]

Najibullah, the Soviets, and Islamism

The growing prominence of Islamism in Soviet policy on Afghanistan was the third factor that led the Kremlin to reassess its importance. Najibullah hence heightened the Soviet fears regarding Central Asia's security to keep Moscow involved in Afghanistan. In June 1988, he reiterated his idea of joint military action with India against Pakistan to hedge against an Islamist threat. The Soviets rebuffed him more decisively this time.[142] In September, Najibullah tried again to convince Gorbachev to delay the withdrawal by arguing that if the LCST left now, the forces riding "the waves of Islamic fanaticism" would come to power. Such people, Najibullah ominously said, "would not build relations with the Soviet Union on the foundation of friendship and cooperation."[143]

In his strategy, Najibullah found allies in Shevardnadze and Kryuchkov, who wanted the Kremlin to back the PDPA more energetically. After a mission to Afghanistan in 1989, both were outspoken about the Islamist threat. Islamic fundamentalists could take power in Kabul, they contended, if "Afghan friends" proved unable to consolidate. Such a scenario would "negatively influence the situation in Soviet Central Asia where already today fundamentalist-type Islamic attitudes were strengthening," they noted.[144] Pointing to Ittehadiya, Beg's armed group, the envoys then painted an especially dire picture: "The Pakistani special services are trying with the Afghan opposition groups' help to deploy anti-Soviet, pro-Islamic propaganda on the territory of the USSR. In this context, ideas are even put forward to recreate an Islamic State with its capital in Bukhara. The situation may be further complicated by the fact that Iran at least in the near perspective will remain a fundamentalist state. The fundamentalist attitudes are strong in Pakistan and we can observe their relative strengthening in Turkey."[145]

The statement echoed what Pakistan was telling the United States about an Islamic union among Muslim countries. This was hardly a coincidence. The Soviets were monitoring the Afghan debacle's impact across South Asia and the Middle East. There was no doubt that some Soviet policymakers now took the Islamist threat seriously. This showed how far they had come in their Afghan policies and their ideology. Shevardnadze, who had enthusiastically celebrated the internationalist help to Afghanistan, now argued that not only did Marxism-Leninism not work there, but that the ideology that had defeated the PDPA was so potent that it could confuse Soviet Muslims. These were the same atheist Muslims who were to serve as models to the Afghans.

Beyond this, it is striking how Shevardnadze and Kryuchkov's report conceptualized Islamism along three dimensions: (a) as a threat to Najibullah's regime; (b) as a threat that foreign powers could instrumentalize against the

Soviet Union; and (c) as an independent threat connected to nationalism in Central Asia. The geostrategic dimension (b) remained, however, dominant; it was, in addition to the United States, centered on Iran with whom relations were improving, and, to a lesser extent, on Pakistan. This was in line with the KGB's and Gorbachev's assessments.

In conclusion, Shevardnadze and Kryuchkov noted that, on their way back, they had met Islam Karimov, Uzbekistan's new head, and other Central Asian leaders who entirely confirmed their concerns. They feared that political instability might spread in Central Asia "if Islamic fundamentalism gained the upper hand in Afghanistan." While Karimov and the others may have been in part catering to the politburo hardliners' views, it was still remarkable that, after years of accommodation with Islam, they had suddenly decided that the Islamist threat was so potent. This pointed to the growing strains in Central Asia. The economic and political issues had taken center stage during glasnost and were leading to contestation amid an Islamic and national revival. After the Soviet collapse, the Islamists would indeed (briefly) challenge Karimov's rule. For now, Shevardnadze and Kryuchkov's recommendation was predictable: "keeping in some, even transformed, form the current [Afghan] regime responded to [Soviet] state interests." Moscow, they said, could not allow "Islamic fundamentalism's victory" in Afghanistan.[146] However, preventing it, they admitted, would be difficult.

Other Soviet policymakers challenged some of the hardliners' arguments. Georgy Shakhnazarov, one of Gorbachev's more liberal advisers, was astonished that Najibullah focused in his contacts on the "extremist" Hekmatyar. There was a risk of Hezb-e-Islami overtaking the PDPA if Najibullah's regime collapsed, Shakhnazarov argued. The USSR could then end up "with another reactionary fundamentalist regime under its belly," a reference to Iran that many Soviets evidently saw as a long-term problem.[147] Shakhnazarov then summed up the Afghan and Soviet thinking on Hezb-e-Islami, explaining why many considered it a viable partner: "Our comrades are showcasing as an advantage that Hekmatyar allegedly is taking anti-American positions, while Rabbani and A. Sh. Massoud are Tajiks and will be used to stir up trouble . . . in Central Asia. But this is obviously the 'American syndrome' from the previous era. One can ask, has nothing really changed for us in the relations with the USA? Could one think that fundamentalists if they were to come to power in Afghanistan would not conduct subversive activities in Central Asia?"[148]

Shakhnazarov thus emphasized Moscow's dilemma in Afghanistan. After the LCST's withdrawal, the Kremlin's priority had switched from propping Najibullah up at all costs to securing a regime that would not undermine the USSR. A shared understanding among Soviet hardliners and liberals that Islamism could destabilize Central Asia had meanwhile developed. The Soviet-Afghan War's dire end influenced that shift by showing Islamism's political mobilization potential. It was also the result of the Soviet model's failure in Central Asia.

Beyond this, Shakhnazarov's report testified to the enduring Soviet confusion as to the severity and nature of the Islamist threat. Some in the KGB, the Red Army, and the politburo argued that the United States, together with some Muslim countries, was trying to undermine the USSR using both Islamism and the national factor. This group, therefore, favored the mujahideen who both adopted anti-American positions and were Pashtuns. This automatically disqualified Jamiat-e-Islami's Tajiks while favoring Hezb-e-Islami. This was likewise the position of Najibullah and most of the PDPA which, having discarded Marxism-Leninism, increasingly operated based on ethnic solidarity. Shakhnazarov, by contrast, maintained that the Soviets needed to favor Massoud who was a more predictable and less radical leader than Hekmatyar.

The bottom line was that, as in the rest of the world, a paradigm shift was happening in the Kremlin. Gorbachev's thinking had challenged the long-standing Cold War framework. With the resurgence of religious and national factors, the Soviets increasingly struggled to frame the opposition they faced as part of their confrontation with the United States. The different mujahideen groups, like the Central Asian Islamists, had agency and their own ideology and goals. While some advisers argued the point, most Soviet policymakers had trouble changing their worldview. Although it had claimed to New Delhi and Washington that the radical Islamists were unacceptable partners, the Kremlin had negotiated with them in Afghanistan. As with Iran in 1979–81, it hoped to co-opt the mujahideen against the United States, hence fitting them into the old Cold War paradigm. This, in turn, showed the ambiguity of the Kremlin's reckoning with the Islamist threat: the Soviets were not against instrumentalizing the Islamists against the United States.

Despite being the CIA's man, Hekmatyar catered to Soviet views, aware of how many Soviet policymakers remained obsessed with the United States. After the LCST's withdrawal, he adopted neither the United States nor the USSR's position while Hezb-e-Islami's journal even published his interview with TASS in 1990.[149] Hekmatyar then claimed that the mujahideen "would never accept an American role in Afghanistan." If the Soviets cut all support to Najibullah, he hinted, the mujahideen could even "befriend Russia if it did not interfere in [Afghan] matters," honor some of the existing Soviet-Afghan agreements, and perhaps release the Soviet POWs as part of a "package deal."[150] These were indeed important incentives for Moscow to revise its Afghan policy.

FIGURE 6.3.   Front page of the Hezb-e-Islami journal following the Shahnawaz Tanai coup in Kabul (*The Mujahideen*, no. 2 [1990]). Gulbuddin Hekmatyar allied with the communist Tanai against Najibullah. Among the Soviets, some saw Hekmatyar as a potential ally due to his growing anti-Americanism.

There was tension in 1988–91 between the Soviets' growing perception that Islamism was a threat and their belief that they could mitigate or even instrumentalize it by negotiating with the Islamists or their sponsors. Most Soviets saw a foreign conspiracy behind radical Islamism's rise both in Afghanistan and in Central Asia. Some foreign countries may have "used the victory of Islam in Afghanistan to start a 'holy war' against the USSR," a KGB general argued.[151] This view dominated particularly in the KGB and the Red Army even before the end of the Soviet withdrawal.

Like India, Varennikov had pushed for—unrealistically at the time—the USSR to force Pakistan to dismantle the mujahideen's training camps on its territory as part of the Geneva Accords. Varennikov believed that foreign powers may use the mujahideen against the Soviet Union after the likely defeat of Najibullah. When the Kremlin failed to integrate this provision, Varennikov went as far as to argue that it testified to "an obvious conspiracy: on the one hand, Gorbachev and Shevardnadze, and, on the other, Reagan and Schultz." The Soviet military had been "betrayed by their 'leaders' to the Americans," he claimed.[152] Varennikov's logic was simple: the mujahideen were a proxy for Pakistan, which was a proxy for the United States, which was the USSR's enemy in the Cold War. If this simplistic analysis had been true to some extent in the mid-1980s, it had lost relevance by the war's end because Islamism had transformed. Varennikov, like many others in the military and the KGB, was a prisoner of old stereotypes.

Makhmut Gareev, the last chief Soviet military adviser in Kabul, likewise believed—and claimed that so did the Kremlin—that if the Islamists were to take power in Kabul, Pakistan and Iran's interests may coincide and lead to further destabilization in Central Asia where, he argued, "there was a strengthening of extremist Islamic attitudes." As Shevardnadze, Kryuchkov, and Varennikov, Gareev blamed the ISI and, between the lines, the United States for spreading anti-Islamic propaganda and destabilizing Central Asia through the mujahideen. In a transparent reference to Beg's Ittehadiya, he claimed that the Islamists wanted "the recreation of an Islamic state with its capital in Bukhara."[153] Gareev similarly saw the three dimensions of the Islamist threat but emphasized the Cold War geopolitical angle. However, like Shevardnadze and Kryuchkov, he had only a vague notion of the specifics of the Islamist threat. Gareev could not say if Islamism may be a threat to Central Asia without the United States guiding it from afar.

A KGB report on Afghanistan in 1989 took a similar perspective. The main Soviet objective, it argued, was to "have a political regime (or help create one such regime) that would have good neighborly relations with the USSR." Ideally, the Soviets would have preferred that the PDPA "remained an influential force" in such a regime. Beyond this, the report argued that Moscow must: oppose a union of the four Islamist parties; strengthen trade and economic cooperation with Kabul; have Afghanistan as an independent, nonaligned, and neutral state and preserve its territorial integrity; and think about measures to oppose the Islamists' ideological influence on Soviet Muslims and "take into account the possibility of a repetition of their armed actions in border regions of Soviet Central Asian republics."[154] The report confirmed how opposing Islamism's influence was a relatively low priority for the KGB, necessitating the least decisive actions in the short term. The issue's importance was dependent on Moscow's ability to secure a friendly regime in Kabul.

The Soviets perceived Islamism as a tool that the United States, Pakistan, Iran, or some mujahideen leaders could use against them. It was not an independent ideology, and the Islamists were not independent actors. As Egorychev summarized, it was about the "United States wagering on the rise to power in Afghanistan of anticommunist, anti-Soviet forces, and the creation with their help of a wide Islamic 'belt of enmity'" along the southern Soviet border. The United States wanted the "transfer of the ideological, nationalist and other infection to [Soviet] territory," he asserted.[155] Again, if this had been true earlier during the Soviet-Afghan War, it was no longer so by 1989. Washington had neither control over nor understanding of the Islamist forces it had supported in Afghanistan. Even if some in the United States had wanted to direct groups such as Hekmatyar's Hezb-e-Islami against the USSR, the Islamists had their own agenda.

Conversely, the USSR thought that Islamism worked in the same way as the various liberation movements in the Third World during the Cold War that it and the United States had cultivated through patronage networks. They thought they could defuse the threat they represented through negotiations and incentives to group leaders and sponsor countries, even potentially reorienting Islamism against the United States as the CPSU apparatchik, encountered in chapter 5, reporting on the Baku conference had hoped. Moscow had learned nothing from its failed attempt at co-opting Iran into an anti-US front.

In his report, Shakhnazarov concluded by recommending that the USSR and the PDPA deal with all the mujahideen leaders, not only Hekmatyar.[156] The Kremlin had to remember that, given the multitude of actors involved in Afghanistan, the long-term solution could only come from an inclusive agreement. Between the lines, Shakhnazarov's report demonstrated that an increasing number of people around Gorbachev outside the KGB and the MID saw support to the PDPA as a rear-guard battle and one that did not necessarily answer to Soviet interests anymore. The Soviets could deal with the Islamist threat without Najibullah.

Finally, Moscow saw Islamism's influence rise globally and it contributed to changing its assessment of the threat it represented to the USSR and its Muslim allies. Moscow had a growing awareness of Islamism's disrupting potential in Algeria, where the Soviets had an economic and military presence. Aleksandr Aksenenok, the Soviet ambassador to Algeria in 1991, noted that the crisis there saw Moscow support anti-Islamist forces. It was the first brush with radical Islam, but the Kremlin continued though to see it as a secondary issue.[157] This perception would only change in the following decade.

The Soviets also raised the topic of Islamism with Muslim countries as part of Gorbachev's New Thinking on foreign policy. After his mission to Syria, Egypt, the United Arab Emirates, Kuwait, and Saudi Arabia in 1987 and 1988, Brutents from the International Department argued that it was time for the Kremlin to think about how "to use Gulf countries, considering their presently relatively acceptable position regarding relations with [Soviet] Muslim republics . . . to neutralize the negative manifestations of the Islamic factor [in the USSR]." Assessing that Muslim countries' rapprochement with the USSR resulted from their fear of Iran and understanding of Soviet Muslims' relative political passivity, Brutents suggested creating an Islamic group in the Kremlin to deal with Islamism because "so far, unfortunately, the study of Islam did not go very productively in [Soviet] academia." It was time to change that, Brutents suggested, by focusing on (1) the Islamic factor's role in Soviet relations with other countries; (2) the foreign Islamic factor's influence on Soviet republics; and (3) the rivalry between "Islamic currents (and the states supporting them) to neutralize the negative manifestations of the 'Islamic factor' inside the [Soviet] Union." To this last point, Brutents added the term "Islamists."[158]

Several points were important in Brutents's note to Gorbachev. First, it confirmed how the International Department dismissed Soviet academic research on the Islamic factor. Second, it showed that some Soviets better understood Islam's diversity and the different dimensions of the Islamic factor in the USSR. Third, the Soviets did not see the Islamist threat as coming from the Gulf, as one would believe now, but from Iran and, indirectly, from the United States. Here, Brutents's thinking aligned with other Soviet policymakers' perceptions and, regarding Iran, with Reagan's claims to Gandhi. Fourth, the Soviets could deal with the Islamist threat by relying on the Sunni part of the Muslim world. In this last point, Brutents also acknowledged that there was a domestic contestation connected to Islamism, although he could not explain if it had endogenous origins. While the effect of Brutents report is unknown, it testified to both the evolving Soviet thinking about Islamism and its limitations.

Bidding Najibullah Farewell

When they met in Moscow in August 1990, Gorbachev and Najibullah were both in new positions. While the USSR crumbled and the Baltic States asserted their independence, Gorbachev faced a political challenge from Yeltsin. His economic reforms had been a disaster and the Soviet people's living conditions had plummeted. Maintaining the traditional Soviet allies abroad was no longer a priority for the Kremlin, which dissolved its Special Commission on Afghanistan in early 1990. The Soviet-Afghan War had become a reminder of the leadership's failings while the Congress of the People's Deputies of the Soviet Union, the new legislative body, adopted a resolution condemning the Soviet decision to intervene in 1989. The situation was different in Kabul. While still relying on the USSR for economic and military support, the ex-Afghan communists had become more assertive. Najibullah had consolidated his regime and fended off the mujahideen's assaults.

This last encounter between Gorbachev and Najibullah at the sunset of their political careers drew a line under the transformation of the PDPA and Soviet policy on Afghanistan. It rebooted the bilateral relationship, taking stock of the new situation. The meeting confirmed Soviet acknowledgment of Islam's importance as a mobilizing force in Afghanistan and, despite their misconceptions, the Soviet-Afghan assessment of radical Islamism, which had catalyzed during the Soviet-Afghan War, as a threat to the crumbling socialist system in Central Asia. The meeting, however, showed a lingering tension between Gorbachev arguing the relevance of the socialist model and the ongoing political transformations in Afghanistan and the USSR.

Gorbachev commended Najibullah for stabilizing Afghanistan, noting—maybe only half-jokingly—that now "in some ways the situation in Afghanistan was calmer" than in the USSR. He especially praised the decision to rename the PDPA, calling it a "timely move," and the constitutional reform. It showed Hezb-e Watan's "readiness to in politics and practice go for cooperation with all national forces." To Gorbachev, the apparent stabilization confirmed the correctness of the decision to start national reconciliation. In a key recommendation, he advised Najibullah to move forward "on the identified path, not losing reference points and not allowing defeatist moods." This, he noted, was advice he meant "for [Najibullah] and for himself."[159] Gorbachev showed no resentment over Najibullah finalizing an Islamic-nationalist platform with antisocialist and anti-Soviet elements. Pragmatism now dominated the Soviets' Afghan policy.

Gorbachev was, furthermore, surprisingly candid with Najibullah as to Soviet economic and political difficulties, likely because these were bound to affect Moscow's relationship with Kabul. "Today the question [in the USSR] was first about stopping the further expansion of crisis manifestations, [and] stabilizing the situation," he noted. While Gorbachev claimed that the USSR was only going through "growth problems," both he and Najibullah knew that the country was close to economic collapse. Still, Gorbachev maintained that he could salvage the Soviet system: "The gamble on left radicalism, on war communism has not passed the test of time and history. . . . This does not mean that consequently, the conclusion should inevitably be of socialism's crisis. Our own accumulated rich experience allows us to see the goals and convincingly continue the movement to a revolutionary renewal of the society under the framework of the socialist choice we made."[160]

This was certainly Gorbachev at his most contradictory: formulating far-reaching plans with no idea how to achieve them while being oblivious to reality. One may only wonder if he felt any sense of irony in explaining communism's ultimate victory to Najibullah, who embodied the Soviet ideological experiment's failure in Afghanistan and who was now working as hard as possible to distance himself from communism. Gorbachev could claim that the "fate of Afghanistan" was part of perestroika, but it still appeared that national reconciliation contradicted perestroika's core idea.[161] In Afghanistan, the Soviets had allowed the PDPA to do whatever it needed to retain power. There was no talk of rebooting a socialist project, even under an Islamic guise.

More practically, Najibullah had also come to Moscow to extract as much support as possible while his old allies were still in power. He pointed out to Gorbachev how Yeltsin had been forcefully calling for the USSR to cut its losses in Afghanistan. Obviously concerned, Najibullah insisted in return on the Soviets' sense of duty. It would be "treason to those who fought in Afghanistan," especially to "those soldiers who were still prisoners of the Afghan armed opposition" to now cut support to the ex-Afghan communists, he told Gorbachev. Therefore, after tactfully pointing out that the Soviets had recently delayed their grain and fuel shipments to Kabul, Najibullah asked to talk with the Soviet officials responsible for those supplies. Gorbachev's answer was noncommittal, showing that he, too, could not grant all Afghan requests. Although Moscow would continue supporting Kabul since their "interests coincided in the general strategic realm," he said, Najibullah had to understand that "Soviet help . . . could and should [now] have another nature, be done on a different scale."[162]

Finally, the two leaders' assessment of radical Islamism was particularly striking. Gorbachev clearly stated his fear of this new ideology. He now believed that the United States may be a partner in fighting it because they too were genuinely concerned over its rapid spread. This was a significant change of paradigm and a sign of how Gorbachev, unlike the Red Army and the KGB, was able to look past the Cold War to potential cooperation with the United States. Still, he feared that Washington may also try to instrumentalize Islamism against Soviet Muslims if the occasion presented itself. Gorbachev explained:

> There is the impression that Americans are truly concerned by the danger of Islamic fundamentalism's spread. They believe . . . that fundamentalism's consolidation today in Afghanistan, Pakistan, and Iran would mean that tomorrow this manifestation would overtake the entire Islamic World. There are already symptoms of that if one considers . . . Algeria. . . . It would be [though] naive, if someone allowed the thought that we see only this side of their policy but do not notice other aspects. It is clear the USA is not opposed to fundamentalism becoming the banner of 40 million Soviet Muslims, creating difficulties for the Soviet Union. They oppose it only when it touches their own interest.[163]

Like his advisers and the KGB and military leaders, Gorbachev, influenced by developments in Afghanistan, Central Asia, and the wider Muslim world, now believed that Islamism may spread to Soviet Muslims, a significant change from his earlier defense of socialism. Islamism's appeal in the USSR was a sign that Soviet Muslims had lost interest in communism. The only way for Gorbachev to solve that tension was to blame foreign countries for the Islamist threat. Like other Soviets, he saw Islamism as a state-based ideology that Iran, Pakistan, and sometimes the United States could channel against the USSR. The developments in Afghanistan and the contestation in parts of Central Asia, however, increasingly challenged that argument.

Beyond this, the meeting in Moscow demonstrated again how Najibullah cultivated Soviet fears. Returning to Islamism, he made the threat appear more ominous and doubled down on Gorbachev's suggestion that foreign powers were to blame: "Our opponents—the Afghan opposition and Pakistan and the USA—have not yet entirely opened their cards. I agree with you that they are interested in a strengthening of Islamic fundamentalism's positions not only among Soviet Central Asia's people but among all Soviet Muslims. To foil such plans, there is the need for adequate response actions and here, in our opinion, the interests of the Soviet Union and Afghanistan are closely interlinked."[164]

This statement served as a preamble for Najibullah's demand to discuss Soviet help to Afghanistan. Leaving aside Gorbachev's talk of socialism and solidarity with the Afghan brothers, it appeared that Najibullah did not doubt that his best chance to secure support was by insisting that Afghanistan may serve as a bulwark against Islamism's expansion into the USSR while also playing on Soviet Cold War fears. This was the agenda around which the Soviet-Afghan relationship could reconfigure.

Najibullah's strategy, however, suffered because the Kremlin did not believe that its sole option was to unequivocally back him to oppose the Peshwar-7. Various policymakers instead pushed to diversify the Soviet partners in Afghanistan. A remarkable report from the International Department to the Kremlin in 1991 nailed that point while summarizing Soviet thinking. The situation in Afghanistan had reached a "stalemate" in which Najibullah was only able to "defend his positions," it noted. Under these circumstances, the Soviets could not simply align with the Kabul regime since it "did not have the support of a large part of the population." This was not about, the report suggested, "letting go of old friends," but about taking into account Soviet interests in having a stable and friendly government in Kabul. Since the LC-ST's withdrawal, the Kremlin did not have a "comprehensive and far-seeing conception of its policy in Afghanistan" while Kabul squandered its help.[165] It was time to change that.

The report concluded by recommending the Kremlin show more pragmatism on Afghanistan, including by (1) removing ideology from its foreign policy; (2) supporting Najibullah but with fewer arm shipments and more humanitarian aid while working on a joint approach with the United States; and (3) reviewing its approach to the "irreconcilable armed opposition and the 'Peshawar Alliance.'" The Soviets had to "recognize [the mujahideen] as an actual political force" which had a "rather broad social base," the International Department claimed. At the end, one of the last recommendations was for Soviet policy on Afghanistan "to consider the processes happening in the Central Asian republics (especially the rebirth of Islamic fundamentalism)."[166] Unmistakably, the International Department report's golden thread was that it was time to let go of Najibullah whose regime was doomed. The Kremlin had to actively engage Hezb-e-Islami and Jamiat-e-Islami to gauge their plans after they took power.

Najibullah's attempt to scare the Soviets with Islamism had worked only to a certain extent. The threat, under his influence and of other factors, had registered but the Kremlin still believed that it could find an agreement with the mujahideen to not stir up trouble in Central Asia. As the International Department's analysis again showed, it continued to see the spread of Islamism from Afghanistan to Central Asia as a secondary threat.

The wish to retrieve the Soviet POWs and MIAs additionally explained the USSR and its successor republics' interest in talking to the mujahideen. During the Soviet-Afghan War, *AFGHANews* often used captured Soviets for propaganda purposes.[167] After 1989, the Soviets hoped to retrieve the approximately 100 POWs still held in Pakistan. The mujahideen leaders who came to Moscow in 1991 refused to disclose how many POWs each group had while telling the Soviets that their release would have a price. Moscow was to convince Najibullah to trade the captured mujahideen for the POWs. The problem for the Soviets was that Kabul could not share its prisoner lists without revealing that it had already executed most of the captured mujahideen and that Moscow was about to cut support to Najibullah.[168] Amid the collapse of Soviet institutions, the issue of POWs was instrumentalized in the struggles between Soviet and Russian elites. Ultimately, this led to Moscow stopping support to Najibullah before retrieving the Soviet POWs.[169]

The negotiations to retrieve the Soviet POWs resumed in Pakistan in February 1992, illustrating some of the chaos that followed the Soviet collapse. Leaving Moscow, the Russian delegation stopped in Tashkent to pick up the delegates from independent Uzbekistan. On arrival to Pakistan, however, it encountered a Kafkaesque situation. The head of the Uzbek delegation declared that the Uzbeks would act alone and changed his name to a more Islamic one. He afterward called Rabbani to brotherhood based on "common religion, [and] historical kinship." The Uzbeks, like the Russians, failed to recover any prisoners while Rabbani played one delegation off against the other. The mujahideen, as the Russians bitterly noted, were well aware that they had little to offer since they had already cut fuel and food supplies to Kabul. The only two things left were for Moscow to trade the Soviet POWs for the prisoners in Pul-e-Charkhi Prison and, as a mujahideen leader proposed, to break diplomatic relations with Kabul.[170] The return of Soviet POWs would be a protracted affair with some fighters returning only years later as new troubles overtook Afghanistan. This would long be the last issue keeping Russia involved with Kabul.

Afghanistan and Islam at the End of the Soviet Union

The late 1980s saw the Soviet Union enter a period of economic and political crisis. Suddenly, Moscow no longer had the resources to support Afghanistan and its other allies across the globe and pursue the ever more demanding arms race with the United States. Afghanistan and the military commitments abroad were, however, only one of the factors that strained the Soviet system. Generalized corruption and incompetence exemplified by the Chernobyl catastrophe and Gorbachev's ill-conceived reforms further destabilized the USSR. While Afghanistan was a symbolic problem, being the prime target for public criticism during glasnost, it did not by itself provoke the Soviet collapse. Still, aside from its human and economic cost, the Soviet-Afghan War was a glaring sign that Soviet ideology was bankrupt. The "backward" Afghans wanted nothing to do with Marxism-Leninism and had been able to thwart Soviet attempts to impose it by force. "The communist idea was in a large measure debunked in Afghanistan and the Soviet Union lost . . . its image as a defender and friend of the poor and oppressed countries," Slinkin perceptively concluded.[171] This blow to the Soviet ideal was difficult to hide at home and abroad. The conflict also created thousands of alienated veterans who returned home to participate in the new wars across the post-Soviet space.[172]

Beyond this, the Soviet-Afghan War showed how much the Soviet elites' reliance on Marxist-Leninism to understand the world was a problem. The politburo had wrongly believed in the "monolithic nature of the society, national unity, dependability of the army and [Soviet] inexhaustible economic resources" when it sent troops into Afghanistan, Vadim Kirpichenko, the First Deputy Head of the KGB's First Chief Directorate who had been involved with Amin's removal, reflected.[173] Ten years later, the Soviet-Afghan War had disproved all of that; yet the Soviet elites' perceptions had been slow to adjust. Gorbachev and his team still believed that they could reform the Soviet system from above, that they could keep agricultural collectivization, industrial socialism, centralized economy, and that non-Russian ethnic groups would want to remain part of a more egalitarian and democratic USSR.[174] Shevardnadze explained that "the problem of fundamentalism exists not only in religion but also in Marxism." What Moscow was doing was "socialism's rescue," he said.[175]

Between 1986 and 1988, financial, economic, and political crises grew worse as the Kremlin pushed new political forces to the fore while deconstructing the CPSU's role, undermining the centralized institutions, and delaying key economic reforms, including the reduction of state subsidies and price reforms. It also refused to give up support for its Third World allies despite the economic crises. According to the historian Vladislav Zubok, the Kremlin still articulated "its international behavior and security interests in both realist and ideological language."[176] Grachev notes that ideology also made Gorbachev's team overlook the rising nationalist contestation at home: "The Soviet leaders who came after Brezhnev and Andropov . . . had been Soviet party schools' students, they saw the world through ideological clichés, the opposition 'We' and the West, 'We' and imperialism. They believed that they had overcome such factors as religion, nationalism, and national identity. Even nonethnically Russian people such as Shakhnazarov did not believe that this was important. [Gorbachev's team] overlooked that the USSR represented itself this patchwork blanket, this multinational state that could effectively ignite."[177]

Gorbachev once similarly confessed that "at some point [he and his team] believed that the national question had been completely solved in [the USSR]."[178] Yet the democratic process and glasnost brought it back to the fore, including in Russified Ukraine and Byelorussia, where the Kremlin had least expected it. While Gorbachev still hoped to preserve the USSR, he could not stop its breakdown while new power structures mushroomed locally. This parade of sovereignties began with Estonia's declaration of sovereignty in November 1988. By the end of 1991, all the republics had left the Soviet Union. As described by the political scientist Mark Beissinger, one after the other they were able to "ride the tide of nationalism generated from the actions of others" during a period of "thickened history." The events acquired a momentum fostered by glasnost, leading to cross-case influences among republics and possibilities for the "expression of nationalist demands which, in normal times, were unthinkable."[179] The Soviet Union collapsed even though pro-Union opinions and attitudes were still strong in many places.

The drivers that thrust this dissolution caught the Kremlin by surprise as one fire ignited after another. "While [the Kremlin] had scared itself with the Baltic countries' 'departure,' Muslims [in Azerbaijan] started to break down the state," Chernyaev recalled.[180] Considerable credit should go to Gorbachev for refraining from the use of force at home and in Central Europe. However, for all his restraint, the Soviet leader did not get the much-needed economic support to stabilize the situation from the West at the G7 Summit in London in July 1991. Over time, some Western policymakers would come to regret not adopting a larger aid package for Russia at that point. Many Russians would, conversely, bitter that Gorbachev did not drive a hard enough bargain with the West for relinquishing Soviet strategic assets such as its hold over East Germany.

Beyond this, ruthless political competition between Gorbachev and Yeltsin for domestic leadership and for representing the country abroad accompanied the Soviet collapse. The MID's Adamishin recalled how Yeltsin just wanted to see Gorbachev fall while "all the rest was secondary." The larger Soviet republics then used this situation to get what they wanted. Few policymakers in Moscow cared much about Central Asia and even less so about Afghanistan; this was not where the stakes were. Ukraine was the big prize. Then, according to Adamishin, "because the Afghan syndrome was such a powerful thing, it was easy for Yeltsin to yield to US pressure and stop support to Najibullah."[181] For the emerging Russian elites, Islamism was secondary because of obvious geographical reasons but also because they wanted to limit the country's costly commitments abroad and break with the toxic Soviet legacy. Islamism had moreover surprisingly not come to the fore during the Soviet Union's breakup.

While modernization and urbanization amid rising nationalism and the enabling role of glasnost had favored successful mobilization across the USSR, the republics' Islamic backgrounds played no role.[182] This is not to say that Central Asia did not see rising nationalism come together with the Islamic revival that included homegrown Islamist groups. Islam personified aspects of Central Asia's history and "provided a framework for idealizing the past," and some Central Asians looked at Islam to meet their spiritual needs.[183] Yet, secularism and religion's cultural nature were ingrained in the region. Islam's importance was independent of Afghanistan and Iran, explaining why neither the Soviet-Afghan War nor the Iranian Revolution sparked an explosion.

It is striking the extent to which the idea that Soviet Muslims represented a challenge to the Soviet system—that they refuted the system's uniformity—proved to be wrong. With the possible exception of Azerbaijan, Soviet Muslims were more loyal to the Soviet Union than other groups. Afterward, while post-Soviet Muslim states saw an Islamic revival, it is remarkable that this was also the case for Christian ones and for Muslim regions in Russia and that none of them saw the establishment of an Islamic state on the models of Iran, Afghanistan, Saudi Arabia, or Pakistan. The elites and people of the newly independent countries continued to see Islamism mostly as a threat while the regimes that consolidated in Central Asia and Azerbaijan looked like the older Nasserite pre-Islamist authoritarian model.

The mujahideen's journals meanwhile took an increased interest in the Soviet Muslims' struggles but this contrasted with the limited solidarity that developed across the Amu Darya River. *AFGHANews* published an article in 1990 that mentioned the "jihad of Imam Shamil in the Caucasus and the struggle of Muslims in Central Asia, called the Basmachi." The article accused Gorbachev of crushing popular struggles in Tajikistan and Azerbaijan while criticizing "the indifference of Islamic countries in regard to the problems of [Soviet] Muslims." It was the mujahideen's role to "keep the world informed about [the] Soviet Muslim brothers," *AFGHANews* claimed.[184] The journal's tone was more assertive as compared to the 1980s, while Jamiat-e-Islami almost called Central Asians to insurrection.

In another article, *AFGHANews* noted that the KGB was blaming the mujahideen for destabilizing Central Asia. However, the protests against Tajikistan's head Qahhor Mahkamov in Dushanbe and the other troubles in Central Asia had nothing to do with Jamiat-e-Islami, *AFGHANews* argued, but testified to an Islamic awakening. "The Afghan struggle against a superpower had given the Muslims in the Soviet Union a sense of confidence. Muslims in Central Asia had started a campaign for greater national and religious freedoms," it noted.[185] In parallel, Hezb-e-Islami's journal ran articles on Azerbaijan.[186] While such publications continued afterward and heightened the fear of Islamism among the elites in Moscow and Central Asia, the only active manifestation of mujahideen support to Central Asian Islamists would come in the context of the Tajik Civil War after 1992. Even then, it would be of a limited nature.

While the mujahideen took an increased interest in Soviet Muslims, the place of Islam changed in the USSR. Having pushed for the PDPA to Islamize its platform after 1986, the CPSU eventually came to a similar policy at home. In 1990, the Ideology (formerly *Agitprop*) Department of the CC CPSU argued that although atheist propaganda had helped "create a scientific-materialistic world conception . . . fight religious stereotypes [and] stabilize the religious situation" in Muslim regions, perestroika had rendered it obsolete.[187] It was time to merge communism and Islam. Hence, concern with Islamism spreading from Afghanistan overlapped with the rehabilitation of religion in the USSR. In 1991, the Sekretariat of the CC CPSU maintained that religion was "a social and spiritual phenomenon, containing universal moral and cultural values." Fighting a rear-guard battle, it asserted that the problem was with the "extremist point of views that idealized religion" and presented "materialism and atheism as sources of immorality and impropriety."[188] The CPSU was starting to understand that it would be impossible to keep Marxism-Leninism while integrating religion; communism would need to give way. The PDPA had also learned this lesson. In many ways, the reports produced by the Soviet institutions were reminiscent of Karmal's awkward attempts to reconcile Marxism-Leninism and Islam. Reinforcing the parallel with the DRA, the Soviet official Islamic "clergy" came under fierce criticism from a new brand of Islamic leaders influenced from abroad.[189] Ironically, at the same time, the Afghan Islamic scholars who met with the Soviet diplomats in Kabul praised the "further democratization and spiritual renewal of the Soviet society."[190] They were glad that Soviet Muslims could now freely engage in Islamic rituals. Hence, even among pro-Najibullah Islamic scholars, no one seriously believed that the USSR was not repressing Islam. This was another demonstration of how the Soviets' initial approach of highlighting Central Asians as cultural Muslims had been problematic.

Against this background, Ruslan Khasbulatov, the ethnic Chechen who chaired the Supreme Soviet of the Russian Federation, visited Turkey and Saudi Arabia in 1992. His mission further demonstrated how perceptions of Islam had changed as it tried to rekindle Moscow's relations with the Muslim countries which had opposed it during the Cold War. The Russian delegation had also an Islamic diplomacy component incorporating Talgat Tadzhuddin, the Mufti of European Russia and Siberia, who, the trip's official account noted without evidence, commanded "considerable respect among the higher clergy of the Muslim countries." In Turkey, the talks paid "special attention" to the South Caucasus and Central Asia.[191] While Moscow and Ankara stressed their interest in these regions' stability, Russia feared that Turkey wanted to increase pressure on Armenia in its conflict with Azerbaijan and boost its influence among post-Soviet Muslims.[192]

The talks in Riyadh were more extensive and focused on Khasbulatov discussing Islam in Russia. "The [Saudis'] satisfaction was noticeable when they learned that 95 percent of Muslims in Russia were Sunnis (a peace-loving current in Islam, identical to the Islam [musul'manstvu] of Saudi Arabia that declared Christianism a parent [rodstvennoi] religion)," read the trip's official account.[193] If this was how the Russian delegation spoke about Islam in Saudi Arabia after years of Riyadh backing the Islamist mujahideen, there is no wonder their interlocutors were pleased. There is also no doubt that Riyadh was already aware of Russian Muslims' alignment after years of Soviet Hajj delegations and of SADUM being in the MWL. According to the Russians, the Saudis also offered them "to teach clergymen (svyashennosluzhitelei) that would be advocating peace, concord and lawfulness (by contrast to the 'wild mullahs' of the Shia current)."[194] The comment again appears surreal but at least it showed the extent to which Russia still saw Islamist contagion from Iran as a threat despite the improvement in relations. Overall, the report revealed that Islam was unfamiliar territory for the policymakers in Moscow, including those coming from Muslim republics. They had no clue about Islamism or that the KGB monitored the rising influence of foreign Sunni charities, including ones linked to the Gulf, in the Caucasus.[195] At the end of the talks, Khasbulatov thanked Riyadh for helping negotiate with the "Afghan mujahideen" (modzhakhedami), a term highly unusual in a Russian report, and release the Soviet POWs. In either, the Saudis had only a limited role.

Khasbulatov's encounter with the Saudis was a sign of how independent Russia's elites discounted the Islamist threat early on. This stemmed from their contradictory impulse to distance themselves from the Soviet legacy of opposition to Islamism in Afghanistan and, conversely, was part of the Soviet legacy of not taking religion too seriously. Soon, the Russian tone would change dramatically as the Tajik Civil War picked up traction and the Saudis backed the IRPT. Back in Riyadh in 1993, Khasbulatov came to warn the Saudis that: "Moscow would consider [support to the Tajik Islamists] as inimical not only toward Tajikistan but also to Russia given the 'transparency' of the borders of the [Commonwealth of Independent States] and Russia's national-state interests. [Saudi Arabia ought to] reconsider with all seriousness the negative consequences of the escalation of the tension around Tajikistan and use all its capacities domestically and through the OIC and League of Arab States [to prevent further conflict]."[196] By that point, the Kremlin would increasingly see the rise of Islamism in Central Asia as a problem for Russia's security.

The Kremlin had understood that radical Islamism had crystallized in Afghanistan by the end of the Soviet-Afghan War. Because of the mujahideen's incursions into the USSR with Pakistani and US support, the Islamic revival and nationalist protests in Central Asia, and rising Islamist trends across the Muslim world, hardliners and liberals in the Kremlin agreed that there was now a risk of Islamist contagion from Afghanistan to Central Asia. Pursuing their own interests, India and the Kabul regime also contributed to shaping the Soviet perception of the Islamist threat. While India feared that Pakistan would redirect radical Islamism against it, Najibullah hoped to use Islamism to maintain Soviet support to his regime despite having publicly adopted an anti-Soviet Islamic-nationalist platform. This completed the evolution of the Kabul regime's relationship to Islam: from opposition under Khalq (1978–79), to instrumentalization under Karmal (1980–85); integration under Najibullah (1986–88), and substitution after the Soviet withdrawal (1989–92). After the LCST left, Najibullah long coped with the mujahideen's attacks but was never able to entirely convince the Kremlin that he was the Soviets' only hope as a bulwark against Islamism.

While aware of the Islamist threat, the Kremlin was never able to articulate its dimensions. The Soviets looked at Islamism at three interconnected levels: (1) as the mujahideen's ideology; (2) as an ideology that foreign powers could use to destabilize the USSR; and (3) as an ideology that the Soviet Muslims may freely embrace. Among these, and while the KGB monitored the homegrown Islamist groups, the Kremlin conceptualized Islamism as primarily a disruptive tool that its Cold War enemies could use against it in Afghanistan or at home. It could therefore defuse the threat by negotiating with the states controlling the Islamists or by incentivizing some Islamist leaders who could be bought. Few Soviet policymakers believed that Islamism could appeal to Soviet Muslims freely and independently of any foreign conspiracy. There was in the Kremlin, as in US policy circles, little awareness of Islamism's protean form and genuine ideological appeal among Muslims, of its growing nonstate nature and transnational mobilizing force, or of the ideological differences between the Pashtun-dominated Hezb-e-Islami, the Tajik-dominated Jamiat-e-Islami, and the Afghan Arabs whom the Soviets always dismissed as mercenaries recruited by the CIA and the ISI.

The Kremlin's reckoning with the Islamist threat was reluctant; awareness did not mean massive concern. The Soviets never looked at Islamism holistically by dissociating it from a sponsor country. The United States because it was the Cold War enemy and Iran because Islamism was its state ideology loomed large in the Kremlin's imagination. This thinking explained why, during and after the withdrawal, the objective in Afghanistan never became to block the Islamists from taking power but to either find a way for one of the Islamist mujahideen groups to agree with Najibullah and consolidate on that basis or to strike a deal with the Islamists behind Najibullah's back. The domestic considerations during perestroika and the assessment that the seemingly eternal geopolitical Great Game in Central Asia was ongoing further dwarfed concern over Islamism. Of course, the Soviets were not the only ones to believe that either the Islamist appeal was restricted to Afghanistan or that they could be dealt with pragmatically through financial and political incentives. At the same time, as Islamism generally failed to consolidate in the post-Soviet space, their minimizing of Islamism as a domestic threat proved on point.

Although the USSR backed Najibullah until the end, the Russians had little interest in taking on board what they saw as a disastrous legacy. Because the Soviet-Afghan War had had little impact in stirring discord among Russia's Muslims, because the regimes that appeared in post-Soviet Muslim states were not keen on Islamism, because the Russians assessed religion positively, because the Kremlin now saw Islamism as entirely a foreign policy matter, and because more pressing domestic issues monopolized Yeltsin's attention, Islamism moved further to the sidelines of Russia's agenda. Concerns lingered in the KGB and the military, but the Kremlin ignored them until the Tajik Civil War and, especially, until the First Chechen War in 1994. The transition from the USSR to Russia erased the Islamist threat from the agenda almost as soon as it finally registered.

Conclusion

The Kremlin went through a double reckoning process during the Soviet-Afghan War. It realized Islam's paramount importance in garnering support for the Kabul regime and that Islamism—the conception of Islam as a political and social system—could challenge the Soviet state if it was to spread to Soviet Muslims from Afghanistan. One common thread between these processes was the Afghan communists' dominant role as they led their regime's Islamization and cautioned the Soviets about Islamism. Another was that both awakenings came belatedly, crystallizing as the Soviets were leaving Afghanistan.

Regarding the first reckoning process, by 1986, Moscow came to appreciate that the Marxism-Leninism which had infused its original approach did not work. This realization took the Soviets considerable time despite Moscow and Parcham having witnessed first-hand how Khalq's heavy-handed ideological approach had proved catastrophic. Still, it was only after Gorbachev came to power that the Soviets accepted that it was essential to not simply put an Islamic veneer on the Afghan regime but to integrate Islam in an attempt at "Islamic socialism" that they had dismissed decades previously at home. After Karmal's removal, Najibullah proved especially astute at the enterprise as he reframed the PDPA's platform before discarding Marxism-Leninism altogether for Islam and Pashtun nationalism. The relationship to Islam became a litmus test of the communists' political legitimacy in Afghanistan, and the delay in accepting it as such undermined their rule. If only Moscow and Kabul had gone for their national reconciliation policy right from the start, the Soviet-Afghan War might have ended differently. Instead, they shared responsibility for the failure of the communist experiment.

The transformation of the PDPA's platform owed much to Najibullah. Despite his grim record in KhAD, Najibullah was so successful at this endeavor that, unlike Karmal's, many Afghans have not stopped revering his memory.[1] In 2020, Hamdullah Mohib, the young Afghan national security adviser and aspiring president, went to visit Najibullah's grave in Paktia Province on the second day of Eid al-Fitr. At odds with the image of the Soviet puppet often attached to him, claiming Najibullah's legacy meant co-opting Pashtun nationalist and political legitimacy for Mohib. The other grave Mohib visited was Massoud's.[2] Najibullah and Massoud hence remain the two towering figures from the Soviet-Afghan War, overshadowing the likes of Karmal, Tanai, Mujaddidi, Rabbani, and Hekmatyar.

For many Afghans, Najibullah's message of opposition to radical Islamism, the ideology of Hekmatyar but also of the Taliban, continues to echo in the present. The former Afghan president Ashraf Ghani, who supported the mujahideen from the United States during the Soviet-Afghan War, said as much in 2020. "Dr Najibullah made the mistake of his life by announcing that he was going to resign," he noted. While his government was negotiating with the Taliban during the US withdrawal, Ghani further cautioned the West: "Please don't ask us to replay a film that we know well."[3] This was an amazing posthumous recognition of Najibullah's national reconciliation anchored in traditional Islam and of his credentials as a legitimate Afghan ruler. As Kabul fell to the Taliban in 2021, vindicating the ending Ghani had anticipated, more Afghans may have reassessed their relationship with their country's last communist ruler.

In foreign policy, the PDPA, with Soviet support, unremittingly tried to reestablish ties with the Muslim countries which rejected it after the Soviet intervention. This contributed to Kabul's strategy of boosting its domestic legitimacy and defusing support from Saudi Arabia, Iran, Pakistan, and Egypt to the mujahideen. Rejoining the Muslim world, however, proved an impossible challenge for the DRA in a context where the meta-narrative about the Soviet-Afghan War as one between Islam and atheism and between Afghans and invaders was too much of a stigma. Afghanistan's diplomacy remained limited to Soviet Cold War allies; and even Libya, Algeria, and, initially, Iraq and the PLO were reluctant to treat it as a fully fledged partner. Kabul recorded more diplomatic success after 1987. These successes were, however, less due to national reconciliation picking up traction than to the Soviet withdrawal and to improved Soviet relations with the Muslim world. It is striking that Kabul and Moscow put so much effort into arguing that Afghanistan was an Islamic country and into reaching out to fellow Muslim countries for so little return. The DRA's foreign policy, which had the potential to boost the standing of the regime at home, failed to play that role. It also did not help in limiting foreign support for the mujahideen. Here, too, things might have been different if Soviet allies in the PLO, Libya, and Iraq had more resolutely supported the PDPA in 1980.

The Soviet-Afghan War has been a crucial issue within the Muslim world and this, too, is an important part of its complex legacy. It helped the emergence of Islamic solidarity by providing a consensus on Afghanistan, although this remained long modest with some Muslim countries downplaying the Soviet-Afghan War against the backdrop of the troubles in the Middle East or in deference to the Soviets. Saudi Arabia meanwhile instrumentalized the conflict for the promotion of its brand of Islamism and to curtail Iranian influence. Few understood then that the opposition between Islam and atheism was multilayered as Islam itself was changing in Afghanistan and around the world. Inside Afghanistan, the rejection of Islam's transformation—exemplified by the Afghan Arabs—was one reason national reconciliation was close to succeeding and why many Afghans now recall Najibullah's regime with, if not nostalgia, at least an appreciation that it was no worse than the ones that followed.

On the Soviet side, although discussions about Islam, the Islamic clergy, and the Islamic factor abounded during the Soviet-Afghan War, they remained superficial and overshadowed by Marxist-Leninism. The Soviets' disregard for Islam and refusal to involve Afghanists in designing policy shed a crude light on the extent to which ideology blinded them. The wish for the DRA to be a testing ground for social-economic transformation on the Soviet model remained preponderant in Moscow's approach until Gorbachev. The USSR of the early 1980s was not a power in decline thinking of diluting its Marxism-Leninism and adapting its policies to the situation. Through Afghanistan, it was trying to recapture the October Revolution's zeal. It wished to prove that its modernization model could work in a backward Muslim country given close supervision by Soviet advisers and enough economic support. This was the Soviet intervention's irony and original sin: while the Soviets came to curtail Khalq's radicalism and claimed to have limited objectives, they at the same time reproduced many of Khalq's mistakes by sending a flurry of advisers to remodel Afghan society and its economy, industry, and culture. The Soviets' objectives were incompatible from the start.

The assessment of Soviet policy in Afghanistan begs parallels with the Soviet domestic realm. While accommodation between communism and Islam may have predominated in Soviet Muslim regions, it remained hidden from view to the Soviet people and the Kremlin, who believed the official line of Islam's decline. This dichotomy came to the fore as advisers and military from across the USSR went to Afghanistan and as Soviet policymakers had to look more closely at the Central Asian model. This was part of the explanation of their initial ideological blindness: the Soviet policymakers operated under the assumption that the Soviet model had worked as planned in Central Asia and that Islam had been on a steady decline since the Basmachi revolt. Accordingly, what they tried to implement in Afghanistan was not the model of the Central Asia of the 1920s that they only vaguely remembered and not even that of the Central Asia of the 1970s; it was an imagined model that existed only in the Soviet policymakers' heads.

As the attempt to build socialism monumentally failed in the DRA, and the PDPA replaced its Marxist-Leninist platform with a national-Islamic platform, the Kremlin questioned the situation in the USSR, but only to a limited extent. Gorbachev's team never foresaw the consequences of the failed Afghan adventure and remained blind to the importance of national and religious factors in the USSR. It also failed to note the similarities between the CPSU and the PDPA. This paradox was pregnant in Gorbachev's last meeting with Najibullah in 1990. Acknowledging how the PDPA had forsaken the Soviet connection and April Revolution and arguing for it to share power with the mujahideen, Gorbachev claimed that he could salvage communism in the USSR with a dominant role for the CPSU. Less than two years later, the USSR would collapse.

Regarding the second reckoning process, the Kremlin saw the Islamists by the end of the Soviet-Afghan War as linked to hostile foreign powers—Iran, Pakistan, and the United States—or, at best, a few pragmatic leaders, but not as autonomous actors with a potent ideology. Given the improved relations with the United States and Iran and the geostrategic situation in South Asia, the Kremlin believed that the Islamists and their ideology would be more of a threat to the Kabul regime and India than Central Asia. In this context, losing its allies in Kabul would be a lesser evil for the Kremlin if the mujahideen successor regime committed to staying away from the USSR, where nationalism was rising. This led the Soviets to support Najibullah until 1991, though downscaling the amount of Soviet aid, while simultaneously negotiating with the mujahideen to hedge against his removal.

The perspective was different in the KGB and among parts of the military who, since the 1970s at least, were more concerned about the disruptive potential of Islamism. Among the likes of Kryuchkov, there was the concern early on that Islamism may lead to unrest in Central Asia and this was one of the reasons for moving into Afghanistan in 1979. During the Soviet-Afghan War, and especially after 1987, the mujahideen's cross-border attacks into the USSR reinforced this fear and explained why the KGB, Shevardnadze, and some military commanders pushed the Kremlin to keep a stronger commitment to Najibullah after the LCST's withdrawal. Gorbachev and his team nevertheless assessed Islamism to be more of a nuisance than a real threat. By 1992, the Russian elites who replaced the Soviet apparatchiks were even less mindful of Islamism, while a glacis of independent Central Asian states now separated them from Afghanistan. They believed they could simply find an accommodation with Saudi Arabia, Turkey, and Iran to defuse attempts on their side to stir up trouble among Russian Muslims. They also initially did not believe that the religious factor was important in the conflicts that erupted in the post-Soviet space. As in the 1980s, the KGB and military—many of them Afgantsy—would have a different opinion.

The Soviet-Afghan War is frequently remembered as a midwife to the radical Islamism of the twenty-first century. Scholars trace direct continuities between Hekmatyar, the Afghan Arabs, and bin Laden's arrival to Afghanistan on one side and the Taliban, the 9/11 attacks, al-Qaeda's globalization, and the rise of the Islamic State in Iraq and Syria on the other. They often forget the intermediary period of the early to mid-1990s. That period, however, saw what many scholars in the West and Russia assessed to be Islamism's failure. The ideology that managed to defeat the Soviets in Afghanistan had trouble maturing into political regimes anywhere in the world save for Afghanistan, where the Taliban established an Islamist regime—although with Pashtun nationalist undercurrents—while continuing to battle Massoud's forces in the Panjshir. By contrast, the regimes that arose amid civil wars involving Islamist forces and Afghan veterans in the Balkans and Algeria did not have the religious radicalism preached by the likes of Hekmatyar and bin Laden.

In the post-Soviet space, the picture was even more striking. Contrary to what Western experts had forecast during the Cold War, Soviet Muslim republics, which quickly moved to join the Muslim world through the OIC and diplomatic ties with Muslim countries, far from seeing a rise of Islamism, saw instead former communists cloak themselves in nationalism and Islam and operate a soft transition from the Soviet Union to independence. Such a transition was not unusual in the post-Soviet space but went especially smoothly in Muslim republics. Uzbekistan under Karimov, Kazakhstan under Nursultan Nazarbayev, and Turkmenistan under Saparmurat Niyazov had the CPSU first secretary of the republic stay in power after independence. Azerbaijan, after infighting among local elites against the backdrop of the Nagorno-Karabakh conflict, saw the triumphal return to power of Heydar Aliyev, former first secretary of the local

CPSU. Kyrgyzstan, with the rise of Askar Akayev, an academic who became an alternative after the leaders of the local CPSU were discredited, was one exception. Another was Tajikistan, where the post-Soviet period witnessed a prolonged civil war involving Islamists and regional elites that still ended up seeing the victory of the ancien régime. Emomali Rakhmon (Rakhmonov), a former head of a state-owned farm, became president in 1994 and was still in power as of 2023.

In Russia, the new political elites were not from the highest echelon of the CPSU and had not been part of the Kremlin's belated and partial reassessment of Islamism. Many of these young and liberal reformers centered on Egor Gaidar and had no ties with former CPSU influence groups, especially among the security services. Even Yeltsin, while a politburo member in 1986–87, had not thereafter been part of the USSR's top leadership. He relied on grassroots support born after his speech criticizing Gorbachev and the pace of perestroika at the CPSU Plenum in 1987.[4] The highest Soviet leadership, including Gorbachev and Shevardnadze, was by 1992 either marginalized or had moved to other post-Soviet republics. By contrast, the elites' continuity was considerably stronger in military and intelligence bureaucracies. Red Army commanders and intelligence chiefs, save for the hardliners sidelined after the August 1991 coup, remained in decision-making positions. Meanwhile, many Afgantsy, including Pavel Grachev, Gromov, and Alexander Rutskoy, gained prominent roles in Russian politics. Apparently untouched by the Afghan stigma, they were folk heroes whose popularity political elites tried to co-opt. Rutskoy was at the last minute selected as Yeltsin's vice president for purely electoral reasons in the 1991 presidential election, while Gromov was the vice-presidential candidate on the losing communist ticket.[5]

Despite the heated political battles in Russia in 1991–93, the country saw limited violence and most internal republics stayed subordinate to Moscow. The exceptions were Tatarstan, where Muslim elites obtained an extensive level of autonomy after intense negotiations with the Kremlin and parts of the North Caucasus. There, conflicts surged as borderlines were contested, the socio-economic situation deteriorated, and ethnic and national enmities resurfaced.[6] Chechnya-Ingushetia was the autonomous republic that pushed for independence most forcefully amid struggles for power between local clans and elites, supporters and opponents of Russia.

These, too, involved former Soviet elites, including those on the separatists' side. Dzhokhar Dudayev, the Chechen leader who opposed the republic's Soviet-era rulers, had himself been part of the Soviet system. A well-regarded air force general and member of the CPSU, Dudayev was also an Afganets who had bombed Afghanistan. Dudayev, like many Central Asian rulers and the

PDPA, used Islam to consolidate his position but gravitated toward a secular regime. Between 1992 and 1994, the growing tensions between him and the Kremlin led to Russia's brutal war in Chechnya. Following Russia's defeat, the now de facto independent Chechnya saw the growing influence of radical Islamists looking to build ties with global radical Islamist networks and marginalize national and national-Islamist elites in a process reminiscent of what had happened among the mujahideen.[7] Meanwhile, Russia saw the return to power of statist and security elites in the wake of former Soviet-era Institute of Oriental Studies chief and KGB operative Primakov's nomination as minister of foreign affairs in 1996 and prime minister in 1998. Less inclined toward the West, these new-old elites were more preoccupied with Russia's international status and influence in the former USSR. They also remembered the Soviet-era threat assessments.

This review of post-Soviet transitions in Muslim republics highlighted two important aspects. First, many senior political and military elites managed to stay in power after the Soviet Union's breakup, either in the newly independent countries or in Russia's internal republics. While in Central Asia and most Russian republics this meant a soft transition and overall loyalty to Moscow, Chechnya was different. Second, the Islamist threat to the Russian state did not consolidate outright. Islamism as an ideology of contestation against the Russian center in the North Caucasus or against former communist rulers in Central Asia stayed weak, save for Tajikistan, the Fergana Valley in Uzbekistan, and to a lesser extent Chechnya. Despite the Soviet Union being most responsible for destabilizing Afghanistan, the Afghan fallout largely bypassed the CIS. Ironically, in underplaying the Islamist threat for the USSR, Gorbachev's politburo had been right.

Ultimately, continuities from the Soviet-Afghan War to the post-Soviet conflicts seem clearer if one constructs deterministic narratives in retrospect or holds an ideological bias. However, such continuities were not obvious when the events unfolded. As this book has shown, there were serious concerns about Islamism in the KGB and the Red Army and ultimately among some policymakers in the Kremlin in Soviet times. Yet, these concerns took considerable time to be registered among post-Soviet Russian political elites. In fact, security services, including Afgantsy and regional elites such as Karimov, played a key role in highlighting the Islamist threat's importance to Yeltsin in the Tajik Civil War in 1992 and, to a lesser extent, the First Chechen War in 1994.[8]

Still, the Kremlin was long unconvinced. The Russian elites initially supported the Islamists in Tajikistan and dismissed, much as the Soviets had done, Islam's importance there and in the North Caucasus. As in Afghanistan, it was only as the Tajik Civil War and the First Chechen War progressed that the

Kremlin decided that radical transnational Islamism represented a threat to Russia. The Islamist threat which Gorbachev had noted and Yeltsin initially discarded was rediscovered as radical Islamist movements took an increasing interest in the North Caucasus and the Taliban consolidated in Afghanistan in the late 1990s. This vividly underlines how the definition of Islamism as a threat to the state—Russia's Islamist moment—did not stream directly from the Soviet-Afghan War but emerged only belatedly, just before the Second Chechen War. With the rise to power of Primakov and then Vladimir Putin—two KGB veterans influenced by Soviet threat assessments—the Islamist threat would become central in defining Russia's national security.

Notes

Introduction

1. Shiraz Maher, *Salafi-Jihadism: The History of an Idea* (London: Oxford University Press, 2016), 31–32.

2. Rodric Braithwaite, *Afgantsy: The Russians in Afghanistan 1979–89* (London: Oxford University Press, 2013), 331. The number of Soviets killed in the war remains contested.

3. The PDPA avoided calling itself "communist" to not appear aligned with the USSR. Yet Afghans and Soviets referred to the regime in Kabul as communist.

4. Alexander Lyakhovsky, *Tragediya i doblest' Afgana* (Moscow: GPI Iskona, 1995), 616.

5. Boris Gromov, *Ogranichennyi kontingent* (Moscow: Progress-Kul'tura, 1994), 332.

6. Olivier Roy, *The Failure of Political Islam* (Cambridge, MA: Harvard University Press, 1994), ix.

7. Cemil Aydin, *The Idea of the Muslim World* (Cambridge, MA: Harvard University Press, 2017); Hamadi Redissi, *Une histoire du wahhabisme. Comment l'Islam sectaire est devenu l'Islam* (Paris: Seuil, 2007).

8. Gabriel Martinez-Gros and Lucette Valensi, *L'Islam, l'Islamisme et l'Occident* (Paris: Seuil, 2004).

9. Gilles Kepel, *Jihad* (Paris: Gallimard, 2017).

10. Steve Coll, *The Bin Ladens: An Arabian Family in the American Century* (New York: Penguin Press, 2008); Thomas Hegghammer, *The Caravan: Abdallah Azzam and the Rise of Global Jihad* (Cambridge: Cambridge University Press, 2020); Maher, *Salafi-Jihadism*, 7–11; Olivier Roy, *Globalized Islam* (London: Hurst, 2004).

11. Craig Whitlock, *The Afghanistan Papers: A Secret History of the War* (New York: Simon & Schuster, 2021).

12. Micheline Centlivres-Démont et al., *Afghanistan. La colonisation impossible* (Paris: Éditions du Cerf, 1984); Anthony Hyman, *Afghanistan under Soviet Domination, 1964–83* (London: Macmillan, 1984); Olivier Roy, *Islam and Resistance in Afghanistan* (Cambridge: Cambridge University Press, 1990).

13. David A. Welch and Odd Arne Westad, eds., *The Intervention in Afghanistan and the Fall of Détente*, Nobel Symposium 95, Lysebu, 17–20 September 1995 (Oslo: Norwegian Nobel Institute, 1996).

14. Diego Cordovez and Selig S. Harrison, *Out of Afghanistan: The Inside Story of the Soviet Withdrawal* (London: Oxford University Press, 1995); David B. Edwards, *Before Taliban: Genealogies of the Afghan Jihad* (Oakland: University of California Press,

2002); Raymond Garthoff, *Detente and Confrontation: American-Soviet Relations from Nixon to Reagan*, revised edition (Washington, DC: Brookings Institution Press, 1994); David N. Gibbs, "Reassessing Soviet Motives for Invading Afghanistan: A Declassified History," *Critical Asian Studies* 38, no. 2 (2006): 239–63; Lester W. Grau, Michael A. Gress, and the Russian General Staff, *The Soviet-Afghan War: How a Superpower Fought and Lost* (Lawrence: University Press of Kansas, 2002); Fred Halliday and Zahir Tanin, "The Communist Regime in Afghanistan 1978–1992: Institutions and Conflicts," *Europe-Asia Studies* 50, no. 8 (1998): 1357–80; Valentin Runov, *Afganskaya Voina* (Moscow: Yauza, 2016); Mohammad Yousaf and Mark Adkin, *Afghanistan—The Bear Trap, The Defeat of a Superpower* (Barnsley, UK: Leo Cooper, 2001); Odd Arne Westad, "Prelude to Invasion: The Soviet Union and the Afghan Communists, 1978–1979," *International History Review* 16, no. 1 (1994): 49–69.

15. Svetlana Alexievich, *Zinky Boys: Soviet Voices from the Afghanistan War* (New York: W. W. Norton, 1992); Artyom Borovik, *The Hidden War* (New York: Grove Press, 1990); Marc Galeotti, *Afghanistan: The Soviet Union's Last War* (London: Routledge, 1995). See also Gregory Feifer, *The Great Gamble, The Soviet War in Afghanistan* (New York: HarperCollins, 2009) and Yaacov Ro'i, *The Bleeding Wound, The Soviet War in Afghanistan and the Collapse of the Soviet System* (Redwood City, CA: Stanford University Press, 2022) for interviews with Soviet soldiers.

16. M. Hassan Kakar, *Afghanistan, The Soviet Invasion, and the Afghan Response, 1979–1982* (Berkeley: California University Press, 1995); Aleksandr Maiorov, *Pravda ob Afganskoi voine* (Moscow: Prava cheloveka, 1996); Vladimir Plastun and Vladimir Andrianov, *Nadzhibulla, Afganistan v tiskakh geopolitiki* (Moscow: Russkii biograficheskii institut / "Sokrat," 1998).

17. Thomas Barfield, *Afghanistan, A Cultural and Political History* (Princeton, NJ: Princeton University Press, 2010); Gilles Dorronsoro, *Revolution Unending* (London: Hurst, 2005); Antonio Giustozzi, *War, Politics, and Society in Afghanistan, 1978–1992* (London: Hurst, 2000); Barnett R. Rubin, *The Fragmentation of Afghanistan, State Formation and Collapse in the International System* (New Haven, CT: Yale University Press, 2002).

18. Chantal Lobato, "Islam in Kabul: The Religious Politics of Babrak Karmal," *Central Asian Survey* 4, no. 4 (1985): 111–20; Eren Tasar, "The Central Asian Muftiate in Occupied Afghanistan, 1979–87," *Central Asian Survey* 30, no. 2 (2011): 213–26. One book focusing on the longue durée of Islam in Afghanistan says nothing of the Soviet period: Nile Green, ed., *Afghanistan's Islam: From Conversion to the Taliban* (Berkeley: University of California Press, 2016).

19. Ro'i, *Bleeding Wound*, 258–78.

20. Jeremy Friedman, *Ripe for Revolution: Building Socialism in the Third World* (Cambridge, MA: Harvard University Press, 2022); Samuel Helfont, *Compulsion in Religion: Saddam Hussein, Islam, and the Roots of Insurgencies in Iraq* (London: Oxford University Press, 2018).

21. Steve Coll, *Ghost Wars: The Secret History of the CIA, Afghanistan, and Bin Laden* (New York: Penguin, 2005).

22. Braithwaite, *Afgantsy*; David B. Edwards, *Caravan of Martyrs: Sacrifice and Suicide Bombing in Afghanistan* (Oakland: University of California Press, 2017); Artemy M. Kalinovsky, *A Long Goodbye, The Soviet Withdrawal from Afghanistan* (Cambridge, MA: Harvard University Press, 2011); Elisabeth Leake, *Afghan Crucible: The Soviet Inva-*

sion and the Making of Modern Afghanistan (London: Oxford University Press, 2022); Ro'i, *Bleeding Wound*; Paul Robinson and Jay Dixon, *Aiding Afghanistan, A History of Soviet Assistance to a Developing Country* (London: Hurst, 2013).

23. Robert D. Crews, *Afghan Modern: The History of a Global Nation* (Cambridge, MA: Harvard University Press, 2015); Timothy Nunan, *Humanitarian Invasion, Global Development in Cold War Afghanistan* (London: Cambridge University Press, 2016).

24. David Gai and Vladimir Snegirev, *Vtorzhenie, neizvestnye stranitsy neob"yavlennoi voiny* (Moscow: SP IKPA, 1991); Vasili Khristoforov, *Afganistan, pravyashchaya partiya i armiya* (Moscow: Granitsa, 2009); Nikolai Kozyrev, *Zhenevskie soglasheniya 1988 goda i Afganskoe uregulirovanie* (Moscow: DAMIDRF, 2000); Vladimir Plastun, *Iznanka Afganskoi voiny* (Moscow: IV RAN, 2016); Vladimir Snegirev and Valerii Samunin, *Virus "A," Kak my zaboleli vtorzheniem v Afganistan* (Moscow: Rossiiskaya Gazeta, 2011). The conflict has also gained interest in Central Asia: Sultan Akimbekov, *Istoriya Afganistana* (Almaty: IMPE pri FPR, 2015).

25. Boris Gromov and Dmitry Rogozin, "Russian Advice on Afghanistan," *New York Times*, 11 January 2010; Alexander Knyazev, *Istoriya afganskoi voiny 1990-kh gg. i prevrashchenie Afganistana v istochnik ugroz Tsentral'noi Azii* (Bishkek: KRSU, 2001); Valerii Marchenko, *Afganskii Razlom. Istoki Mirovogo Terrorizma* (Moscow: Piter, 2018); I. Zhuravlev, S. Mel'kov, and L. Shershnev, *Put' Voinov Allakha* (Moscow: Veche, 2004).

26. Rossiiskii Gosudarstvennyi Arkhiv Sotsial'no-Politicheskoi Istorii (RGASPI), November 1988, fond (f.) 797, opis' (o.) 1, delo (d.) 33, list (l.) 1.

27. Melvyn J. Leffler, *For the Soul of Mankind, The United States, the Soviet Union and the Cold War* (New York: Hill and Wang, 2007), 338–450; Vladislav M. Zubok, *A Failed Empire, The Soviet Union in the Cold War from Stalin to Gorbachev* (Chapel Hill: University of North Carolina Press, 2007); Vladislav M. Zubok, *Collapse: The Fall of the Soviet Union* (New Haven, CT: Yale University Press, 2021).

28. Jeremy Friedman, *Shadow Cold War: The Sino-Soviet Competition for the Third World* (Chapel Hill: University of North Carolina Press, 2015).

29. Odd Arne Westad, *The Global Cold War: Third World Interventions and the Making of Our Times* (London: Cambridge University Press, 2011), 5. See also Odd Arne Westad, *The Cold War, A World History* (New York: Basic Books, 2017).

30. Michael M. Hunt, "Ideology," *Journal of American History* 77, no. 1 (1990): 110. See also Michael M. Hunt, *Ideology and U.S. Foreign Policy* (New Haven, CT: Yale University Press, 1987).

31. Lorenz M. Lüthi, *The Sino-Soviet Split, Cold War in the Communist World* (Princeton, NJ: Princeton University Press, 2008), 8.

32. Friedman, *Ripe for Revolution*, 263–65.

33. Hunt, "Ideology," 108; Lüthi, *The Sino-Soviet Split*, 8.

34. Michael David-Fox, *Revolution of the Mind: Higher Learning among the Bolsheviks, 1918–1929* (Ithaca, NY: Cornell University Press, 1997); Zubok, *Failed Empire*.

35. Jochen Hellbeck, *Revolution on My Mind, Writing a Diary under Stalin* (Cambridge, MA: Harvard University Press, 2009); Stephen Kotkin, *Magnetic Mountain, Stalinism as a Civilization* (Berkeley: University of California Press, 1997); Timothy Snyder, *Bloodlands: Europe Between Hitler and Stalin* (New York: Basic Books, 2012).

36. William Taubman, *Khrushchev: The Man and His Era* (New York: W. W. Norton, 2003).

37. Friedman, *Shadow Cold War*, 16.

38. Alexei Yurchak, *Everything Was Forever, until It Was No More: The Last Soviet Generation* (Princeton, NJ: Princeton University Press, 2006).

39. Christopher Andrew and Vasili Mitrokhin, *The World Was Going Our Way: The KGB and the Battle for the Third World: Newly Revealed Secrets from the Mitrokhin Archive* (New York: Basic Books, 2006).

40. Georgiy Mirsky, "The Soviet Perception of the US Threat," in *The Middle East and the United States, A Historical and Political Reassessment,* edited by David W. Lesch (Boulder, CO: Westview Press, 2007), 440–43; Mikhail Voslensky, *Nomenklatura* (Moscow: Zakharov, [1990] 2016).

41. Artemy M. Kalinovsky, *Laboratory of Socialist Development: Cold War Politics and Decolonization in Soviet Tajikistan* (Ithaca, NY: Cornell University Press, 2018). As an example of that process in another context: Nathan J. Citino, *Envisioning the Arab Future: Modernization in the Middle East* (Cambridge: Cambridge University Press, 2017).

42. Robert D. Crews, *For Prophet and Tsar* (Cambridge, MA: Harvard University Press, 2006), 367.

1. The Basmachi and Soviet Islam

1. Dominic Rubin, *Russia's Muslim Heartlands, Islam in the Putin Era* (London: Hurst, 2018).

2. Vladimir Bobrovnikov et al., eds. *Musul'mane v novoi imperskoi istorii* (Moscow: Sadra, 2017).

3. Crews, *Prophet and Tsar*, 7–13, 287–92.

4. Alexandre Bennigsen and Chantal Lemercier-Quelquejay, *Le Soufi et le commissaire: Les confréries musulmanes en URSS* (Paris: Seuil, 1986); Marie Broxup and Alexandre Bennigsen, *The Islamic Threat to the Soviet State* (London: Routledge, 2010). For a critical review: Artemy M. Kalinovsky, "Encouraging Resistance: Paul Henze, the Bennigsen School, and the Crisis of Détente," in *Reassessing Orientalism, Interlocking Orientologies during the Cold War,* ed. Michael Kemper and Artemy M. Kalinovsky (London: Routledge, 2015), 211–32.

5. Fred Halliday, "'Islam' and Soviet Foreign Policy," *Journal of Communist Studies* 3, no. 1 (1987): 217–18.

6. Bobrovnikov, *Musul'mane*, 11 and Devin Deweese, "Islam and the Legacy of Sovietology: A Review Essay on Yaacov Roy's Islam in the Soviet Union," *Journal of Islamic Studies* 13, no. 3 (2002), 313 for discussions of Yaacov Ro'i, *Islam in the Soviet Union: From the Second World War to Gorbachev* (London: Hurst, 2000); Olivier Roy, *La Nouvelle Asie centrale ou la fabrication des nations* (Paris: Seuil, 1997). Soviet sources on Afghanistan also abuse the ill-defined term "clergy." This book uses the term clergy to mean Islamic scholars when discussing Soviet and Afghan communist policies.

7. Sergei Abashin, *Sovetskii Kishlak: Mezhdu kolonializmom i modernizatsiei* (Moscow: Novoe Literaturnoe Obozrenie, 2015); Muriel Atkin, *The Subtlest Battle: Islam in Soviet Tajikistan* (Lanham, MD: University Press of America, 1989); Eren Tasar, *Soviet and Muslim, The Institutionalization of Islam in Central Asia* (London: Oxford University Press, 2017).

8. D. Arapov, ed., *Islam i sovetskoe gosudarstvo (1917–1936). Vypusk 2* (Moscow: Mardzhani, 2010).

9. Quoted in Halliday, "Islam and Soviet Foreign Policy," 220; Friedman, *Shadow Cold War*, 8.

10. Tasar, *Soviet and Muslim*, 45.

11. Martha B. Olcott, "The Basmachi or Freemen's Revolt in Turkestan 1918–24," *Soviet Studies* 33, no. 3 (1981): 352.

12. D. Arapov and G. Kosach, eds., *Islam i sovetskoe gosudarstvo. Vypusk 1* (Moscow: Mardzhani, 2010), 14.

13. Glenda Fraser, "Basmachi—I," *Central Asian Survey* 6, no. 1 (1987): 53–65; Glenda Fraser, "Basmachi—II," *Central Asian Survey* 6, no. 2 (1987): 7–42.

14. Adeeb Khalid, *The Politics of Muslim Cultural Reform: Jadidism in Central Asia* (Berkeley: University of California Press, 1999).

15. Yu. Tikhonov, ed., *Sovetskaya Rossiya v bor'be za "afganskii koridor" (1919–1925)* (Moscow: Kvadriga, 2017); Akimbekov, *Istoriya Afganistana*, 160–76.

16. Rossiiskii Gosudarstvennyi Arkhiv Noveishei Istorii (RGANI), 20 October 1937, f. 89, o. 73, d. 104, ll. 1–2; RGANI, 25 July 1937, f. 89, o. 48, d. 07, l. 1.

17. Vasiliy Mitrokhin, *The KGB in Afghanistan* (Washington, DC: Cold War International History Project Digital Collection [CWIHPDC], 2002), 17. Mitrokhin claims there were 750,000 Soviet Central Asia descendants in Afghanistan in 1979.

18. Olcott, "Basmachi," 364.

19. Adeeb Khalid, *Central Asia, A New History from the Imperial Conquests to the Present* (Princeton, NJ: Princeton University Press, 2021); Beatrice Penati, "The Reconquest of East Bukhara: The Struggle against the Basmachi as a Prelude to Sovietization," *Central Asian Survey* 26, no. 4 (2007): 521–38.

20. Stephane Cronin, "Introduction: Edward Said, Russian Orientalism, and Soviet Iranology," *Iranian Studies* 48, no. 5 (2015): 647–62; Lorraine de Meaux, *La Russie et la tentation de l'Orient* (Paris: Fayard, 2010).

21. Braithwaite, *Afgantsy*, 167.

22. Pierre Centlivres and Micheline Centlivres-Démont, "Et si on parlait de l'-Afghanistan?," *Actes de la recherche en sciences sociales* 34, no. 1 (1980): 3–16.

23. Alexander Lyakhovsky, *Inside the Soviet Invasion of Afghanistan and the Seizure of Kabul, December 1979* (Washington, DC: CWIHPDC, 2007), 3; Mitrokhin, *KGB in Afghanistan*, 143.

24. Ro'i, *Islam in the Soviet Union*, 572–84; National Archives Digital Collection, Washington, DC (NARADC), US Department of State (USDoS), Abu Dhabi, 3 April 1974.

25. NARADC, USDoS, Ankara, 4 October 1978.

26. Tasar, *Soviet and Muslim*, 372.

27. Alexandre Bennigsen, "Soviet Islam since the Invasion of Afghanistan," *Central Asian Survey* 1, no. 1 (1982): 65–78; RGANI, 1972–73, f. 4, o. 22, d. 1836, ll. 3–5; Ro'i, *Islam in the Soviet Union*, 615.

28. Quoted in Kalinovsky, *Laboratory of Socialist Development*, Loc. 658.

29. Yaacov Ro'i, "The Task of Creating the New Soviet Man: 'Atheistic Propaganda' in the Soviet Muslim Areas," *Soviet Studies* 36, no. 1 (1984): 26, 30. In the first half of 1980, 4,000 lectures on atheism were conducted in Dagestan.

30. Ro'i, *Islam in the Soviet Union*, 250–53, 262, 427, 285, 334. Davlat Khudonazarov, Interview, Moscow, February 2019; Khudonazarov is a Soviet Tajik film director. He participated in cultural missions to Afghanistan before and after the Soviet-Afghan War. In

1992, he was the candidate for the Islamist-democratic block at the Tajik presidential election. Djamboulat Souleimanov, Phone Interview, January and July 2019; Souleimanov was a Chechen commander during the wars with Russia. He was one of the first Chechens to travel for Islamic education to Pakistan in the early 1990s. Mairbek Vatchagaev, Phone Interview, December 2018. Vatchagaev is a Chechen politician and historian who was an adviser to Chechen leaders in the 1990s.

31. Deweese, "Islam and the Legacy of Sovietology," 310.

32. Gosudarstvennyi Arkhiv Rossiiskoi Federatsii (GARF), 17 October 1981, f. R6991, o. 6, d. 2206.

33. Ro'i, *Islam in the Soviet Union*, 90, 49–64, 323, 326, 383, 572–84.

34. Anatoly Chernyaev, *The Diary of Anatoly Chernyaev* (Washington, DC: National Security Archive Digital Collection [NSADC], 2003, October 1984).

35. Michael Kemper and Stephan Conermann, eds., *The Heritage of Soviet Oriental Studies* (London: Routledge, 2011); NARADC, USDoS, Leningrad, 28 March 1979; NARADC, USDoS, Moscow, 26 September 1979.

36. GARF, 26 October–24 December 1981, f. R6991, o. 6, d. 2206, l. 11; Vasilii Kravtsov, Interview, Moscow, February 2019. Kravtsov is a KGB Senior Lieutenant who trained Afghans in the USSR during the Soviet-Afghan War and was an adviser to KhAD in 1988–91. He worked afterward for the Russian Ministry of Foreign Affairs in Afghanistan.

37. Yaacov Ro'i, "The Impact of the Islamic Fundamentalist Revival of the late 1970s on the Soviet View of Islam," in *The USSR and the Muslim World: Issues in Domestic and Foreign Policy*, ed. Yaacov Ro'i, 167–68 (London: Routledge, 2016 [1984]).

38. Ro'i, *Islam in the Soviet Union*, 684.

39. Quoted in Ro'i, "Impact of the Islamic Fundamentalist Revival," 166.

40. Quoted in Ro'i, "Impact of the Islamic Fundamentalist Revival," 158–59.

2. Khalq's Islam and the Decision to Intervene

Epigraph 1: Valerii Pulyarkin, *Afganistan* (Moscow: Mysl', 1964), 53.

Epigraph 2: Lyakhovsky, *Tragediya*, 101.

1. Cordovez and Harrison, *Out of Afghanistan*, 27; Vladimir Toporkov, *Afganistan: Sovetskii faktor v istokakh krizisa* (Cheboksary: TSNS Interaktiv Plyus, 2014), 61; Ro'i, *Bleeding Wound*, 9–17. For an Afghan account of the coup, see Saburulla Siasang, *Aprel' 1978: Nachalo tragedii Afganistana* (Moscow: "U nikitskikh vorot," 2009).

2. Garthoff, *Détente and Confrontation*, 985–1046; Vladimir Basov, "Interv'yu: K 15-i godovshchine vyvoda voisk iz Afganistana" (Moscow, 2004), https://www.youtube.com/watch?v=ab6bpIsUg_g.

3. Andrey Grachev, Interview, Moscow, September 2019. Grachev worked in the CC CPSU International Department (1973–78) and the CC CPSU Department of Foreign Political Propaganda (1978–89). From 1989 to 1991, he was the deputy chief of the CC CPSU International Department. In 1991, he was Gorbachev's press secretary.

4. Toporkov, *Afganistan*, 75.

5. Abdul Darmanger, Interview, Bole (Switzerland), January 2020. Darmanger was a Khalqi deputy minister of health and of foreign affairs in 1978–79. He knew Taraki, Amin, Karmal, and Najibullah, being a member of the PDPA since its early days. He was Taraki's confidant and had Amin as a teacher in school. After Karmal came to

power, Darmanger was imprisoned until 1986. On Khalq and Parcham: Mikhail Slinkin, "Khal'k i Parcham," *Kul'tura narodov Prichernomor'ya* 9 (1999): 98–107.

6. Halliday and Tanin, "Communist Regime," 1360–63.

7. Edwards, *Before Taliban*, 54.

8. GARF, 9 May 1978, Telegrafnoe Agentstvo Sovetskogo Soyuza (TASS), f. R4459, o. 43, d. 19648, ll. 237–46.

9. NSADC, RGANI, 31 May 1978, f. 5, o. 75, d. 1179, ll. 2–17.

10. "Document 10," 30 April 1978, *Foreign Relations of the United States (FRUS), 1977–1980, Volume XII, Afghanistan*, eds. David Zierler and Adam M. Howard. Washington, DC: Government Printing Office, 2018, 19–21.

11. Darmanger, Interview.

12. RGANI, 1981–84, f. 117, o. 1, d. 10, ll. 9–158; NSADC, Yevgeni Primakov, ed., *Polozhenie v polose Pushtunskikh plemen Afganistana i Pakistana i ego vliyanie na obstanovku v DRA* (Moscow: Oriental Studies Institute, May 1981).

13. KhAD head of department, Interview, Moscow, February 2019. The person worked in KhAD until 1990 before emigrating to the USSR. He worked afterward with the Afghan Ministry of Foreign Affairs.

14. Barfield, *Afghanistan*, 230–31; Fred Halliday, "War and Revolution in Afghanistan," *New Left Review* 119 (1980): 20–41; Rubin, *Fragmentation of Afghanistan*, 115–21; Snegirev and Samunin, *Virus "A,"* ch. 5.

15. RGANI, June 1978–Jan 1979, f. 5, o. 75, d. 1181, l. 29.

16. Hyman, *Afghanistan*, 96–114; RGANI, 1988, f. 117, o. 1, d. 22, ll. 69–72.

17. Edwards, *Before Taliban*, 71, 135–36; Gai and Snegirev, *Vtorzhenie*, 197.

18. Sultan Ali Keshtmand, *Political Notes and Historical Events: Memories from Moments in the Contemporary History of Afghanistan*, trans. Hafizullah Nadiri (Kabul: Najib Kabir Publications, 2002), 518.

19. Barfield, *Afghanistan*, 40.

20. KGB Officer, Email, February 2020. The person trained KhAD recruits at the training center in Tashkent. He was an adviser in KhAD in Afghanistan after 1985.

21. Viktor Merimsky, *Zagadki Afganskoi voiny* (Moscow: Veche, 2015), 22–26.

22. Hafizullah Ehmadi, *State, Revolution, and Superpowers in Afghanistan* (New York: Praeger, 1990), 82; Amin Saikal, with Ravan Farhadi and Kirill Nourzhanov, *Modern Afghanistan: A History of Struggle and Survival* (London: I.B. Tauris, 2004), 188–89.

23. Georgy Kornienko, *Kholodnaya voina, Svidetel'stvo ee uchastnika* (Moscow: Olma-Press, 2001), 239.

24. Khristoforov, *Afganistan*, 144. If combined with the World Bank population estimate (13.4 million) for 1979, this would mean one religious figure per forty-five Afghans. The World Bank, "Afghanistan, Data" (2019). The estimate provided by Khristoforov is one per sixty.

25. Abdul Darmanger, *L'Afghanistan, terrain du "Grand Jeu"* (Neuchâtel: Attinger SA, 2015), 61.

26. Roy, *Islam and Resistance*, 33.

27. NARADC, USDoS, Kabul, 16 August 1979.

28. RGANI, 1978–79, f. 5, o. 76, d. 1043, ll. 112–16; RGANI, April–October 1979, f. 5, o. 76, d. 1042, ll. 16–26; RGANI, May 1978–April 1979, f. 5, o. 75, d. 1180, ll. 50, 81; RGANI, January 1979–February 1980, f. 5, o. 76, d. 1045, ll. 51–59.

29. NSADC, "Zapis' besedy s poslami sotsstran," 16 May 1978, RGANI (?).

30. NSADC, "Further Comments by East German Ambassador," USDoS, Afghanistan, 19 July 1979.

31. Vladimir Kryuchkov, *Lichnoe delo, Chast' pervaya* (Moscow: Olimp, 1996), 191–92.

32. Snegirev and Samunin, *Virus "A,"* ch. 6.

33. GARF, 7 July 1979, TASS, f. R4459, o. 43, d. 20977, l. 140. DOMA senior official, Interview, Moscow, January / April 2020–August 2021. The person was a senior member of DOMA (the Afghan Komsomol) in the 1980s. He worked afterward as a political scientist in Moscow and senior staff at the Afghan embassy. See also Saikal, *Modern Afghanistan*, 190.

34. Lyakhovsky, *Inside Soviet Invasion*, 3.

35. "Document 39," 23 March 1979, *FRUS, 1977–1980*, 111–14.

36. Quoted in Halliday and Tanin, "Communist Regime," 1360; Valentin Varennikov. *Nepovtorimoe, Kniga 5* (Moscow: Sovetskii pisatel', 2001), ch. 1.

37. Khristoforov, *Afganistan*, 145–46.

38. Rubin, *Fragmentation of Afghanistan*, 186.

39. Dorronsoro, *Revolution Unending*, 97–98, 106–11; Roy, *Islam and Resistance*, 98–109; Rubin, *Fragmentation of Afghanistan*, 177–219.

40. Braithwaite, *Afgantsy*, 45; Cordovez and Harrison, *Out of Afghanistan*, 36; Keshtmand, *Political Notes*, 536 sees the revolt as a response to Khalq's attacks against Hazaras.

41. NARADC, USDoS, Kabul, 5 April 1979.

42. Gromov, *Ogranichennyi kontingent*, 34–40.

43. RGANI, 17 March 1979, f. 89, o. 25 d. 1, ll. 1–25. Karen Brutents, *Tridtsat' let na staroi ploshchadi* (Moscow: Mezhdunarodnye Otnosheniya, 1998), part 4, ch. 5.

44. CWIHPDC, RGANI, 20 March 1979, f. 89, o. 14, d. 25, l. 8.

45. Grachev, Interview.

46. RGANI, January 1979–February 1980, f. 5, o. 76, d. 1045, ll. 38, 42.

47. Grachev, Interview.

48. RGANI, 12 April 1979, f. 89, o. 42, d. 4, ll. 1–12; RGANI, 1979, f. 89, o. 14, d. 27, ll. 1–12.

49. RGANI, January 1979–February 1980, f. 5, o. 76, d. 1045, ll. 38, 42.

50. Grachev, Interview.

51. Brutents, *Tridtsat' let*, part 4, ch. 5.

52. Lyakhovsky, *Tragediya*, 125–26.

53. NSADC, "Vypiska iz protokola No. 156 zasedaniya politburo TSK KPSS," 28 June 1979, Archive of the President of the Russian Federation (APRF).

54. RGANI, 1979, f. 5, o. 76, d. 1043, ll. 16–22, 51–58; RGANI, January 1979–February 1980, f. 5, o. 76, d. 1045, l. 95.

55. NSADC, 28 June 1979.

56. NARADC, USDoS, Kabul, 18 September 1979.

57. Snegirev and Samunin, *Virus "A,"* ch. 5. The KGB's understanding of Islam in Afghanistan had limitations as is clear from the longer text.

58. Anatoly Adamishin, Interview, Moscow, August 2019. Adamishin served as the Soviet deputy minister of foreign affairs (1986–90), Soviet and Russian first deputy minister of foreign affairs (1992–94), and Russian minister for the Commonwealth of

Independent States (1997–98). He was part of Shevardnadze's team that negotiated the Geneva Accords on Afghanistan.

59. Georgy Arbatov, *Svidetel'stvo sovremennika, zatyanuvsheesya vyzdorovlenie (1953–1985 gg.)* (Moscow: Mezhdunarodnye Otnosheniya, 1991), 230.

60. RGANI, January 1979–February 1980, f. 5, o. 76, d. 1041, l. 44.

61. Andrei Gromyko, *Pamyatnoe, Kniga vtoraya* (Moscow: Politizdat, 1990), 177–78; Kalinovsky, *Long Goodbye*, 23; Kryuchkov, *Lichnoe delo*, 201. The Soviets had likely mismanaged the situation, making it seem as if they had told Taraki, who had just been to Moscow, to eliminate Amin. Taraki may have met Karmal there. Brezhnev resented Amin for Taraki's death and became more open to intervention.

62. Chernyaev, *Diary, 1980*; Lyakhovsky, *Tragediya*, 104–19.

63. Cordovez and Harrison, *Out of Afghanistan*, 28–43; Mitrokhin, *KGB in Afghanistan*, 47–50, 83–85; Snegirev and Samunin, *Virus "A,"* ch. 8.

64. Adamishin, Interview; Basov, "Interv'yu."

65. Leonid Shebarshin, *Ruka Moskvy, Zapiski nachal'nika vneshnei razvedki* (Moscow: Algoritm, 2017), 222.

66. Brutents, *Tridtsat' pet*, part 4, ch. 5.

67. NSADC, "Meeting with President Amin," USDoS, Afghanistan, 28 October 1979.

68. RGANI, March 1979–February 1980, f. 5, o. 75, d. 1046, ll. 67–70.

69. RGANI, June 1978–January 1979, f. 5, o. 75, d. 1181, ll. 5–16, 63; RGANI, January 1979–August 1979, f. 5, o. 76, d. 1044, ll. 3–9, 52–69; RGANI, March 1979–February 1980, f. 5, o. 76, d. 1046, ll. 1, 55.

70. Vadim Kirpichenko, *Razvedka: Litsa i lichnosti* (Moscow: Mezhdunarodnye Otnosheniya, 2017), 347–64; Larisa Kucherova, *KGB v Afganistane* (Moscow: Yauza-Press, 2017), 192, 273; LCST infantry general, Interview, Moscow, December 2017. The general, an ethnic Russian from Uzbekistan, has participated in the Soviet-Afghan War and the First Chechen War.

71. Gai and Snegirev, *Vtorzhenie*, 107. Adamishin, Interview, says that a KGB telegram shortly before the intervention claimed that "the Americans were coming, that they were about to land in Afghanistan."

72. Robert M. Gates, *From the Shadows: The Ultimate Insider's Story of Five Presidents and How They Won the Cold War* (New York: Simon & Schuster, 2011 [1996]), 144; "Les Révélations d'un Ancien Conseiller de Carter," *Le Nouvel Observateur*, 15 January 1998.

73. RGANI, 17 March 1979.

74. Welch and Westad, *Intervention in Afghanistan*, 15.

75. Grachev, Interview.

76. NSADC, "Stasi Note on Meeting," 11 July 1981, Office of the Federal Commissioner for the Stasi Records (BStU), ZAIG 5382, 1–19.

77. Adamishin, Interview.

78. RGANI, 1991, f. 117, o. 1, d. 6, ll. 4–5; Shebarshin, *Ruka Moskvy*, 222. Some Soviets attribute a role in pushing for the intervention to Mikhail Suslov, the chief Soviet ideologue.

79. Anatoly Adamishin, *V raznye gody, Vneshnepoliticheskie ocherki* (Moscow: Ves' Mir, 2016), 143; Sergey Akhromeyev and Georgy Kornienko, *Glazami marshala i diplomata, Kriticheskii vzglyad na vneshnyuyu politiku SSSR do i posle 1985 goda* (Moscow: Mezhdunarodnye Otnosheniya, 1992), 170–75; Andrei Alexandrov-Agentov, *Ot Kollontai*

do Gorbacheva, vospominaniya diplomata, sovetnika A.A. Gromyko, pomoshchnika L.I. Brezhneva, Yu. V. Andropova, K.U. Chernenko i M.S. Gorbacheva (Moscow: Mezhdunarodnye Otnosheniya, 1994), 244; Chernyaev, Diary, 1979, 30 December 1979. Some Soviets assign a role to Alexandrov-Agentov in pushing Brezhnev toward intervention.

80. Brutents, Tridtsat' Let, part 4, ch. 5.

81. Jonathan Power, "From Stalin to Putin, An Insider's View: Talking with Georgi Arbatov," World Policy Journal 24, no. 3 (2007): 83–88.

82. Borovik, Hidden War, 14; Lyakhovsky, Tragediya, 121.

83. Maiorov, Pravda, ch. 14.

84. Varennikov and Samarina, "Afganskii vopros ostanetsya v istorii," Voenno-promyshlennyi kur'er 5 (2004): 11–17, Gorbachev Foundation (GFA); Mitrokhin, KGB in Afghanistan, 109.

85. NSADC, "Archer K. Blood," 27 June 1989, Interview by Henry Precht.

86. Gai and Snegirev, Vtorzhenie, 79.

87. Kakar, Afghanistan, 270; Keshtmand, Political Notes, 579. Amin may have reached out to Hezb-e-Islami to make an alliance. If so, this would have also meant the loss of the progressive revolution.

88. "Document 275," 24 May 1980, FRUS, 1977–1980, 736–37; Lyakhovsky, Inside Soviet Invasion, 27–29.

89. Kryuchkov, Lichnoe delo, 199–201, 242.

90. Snegirev and Samunin, write in Virus "A," ch. 8 of "radical Islamists," a term that would have been an anachronism for the Soviets.

91. Borovik, Hidden War, 9; "Document 275," 24 May 1980; Makhmut Gareev, Moya poslednyaya voina (Moscow: INSAN, 1996), 188–89; Garthoff, Détente and Confrontation, 1033; Gromov, Ogranichennyi kontingent, 21; Toporkov, Afganistan, 22. Garthoff quotes the deputy prime minister of Kyrgyzstan as stating that the intervention was needed to combat a local plague in Afghanistan "that could have spread to [Kyrgyzstan]."

92. BStU, 11 July 1981. See also Ro'i, Bleeding Wound, 252.

93. Brutents, Tridtsat' let, part 4, ch. 5.

94. Snegirev and Samunin, Virus "A," chs. 5, 8.

95. Brutents, Tridtsat' let, part 4, ch. 5; Mitrokhin, KGB in Afghanistan, 111.

96. Adamishin, Interview. See also Basov, "Interv'yu."

97. Alexandrov-Agentov, Kollontai do Gorbacheva, 246; Nikolai Egorychev, Soldat, politik, diplomat (Moscow: Tsentrpoligraf, 2017), 300.

98. RGANI, January 1979–February 1980, f. 5, o. 76, d. 1045, l. 152.

99. Marie Broxup, "Recent Developments in Soviet Islam," Religion in Communist Lands 11, no. 1 (March 1983): 35, claims that Moscow sent "antireligious specialists" after the April Revolution. There are no sources corroborating that.

100. RGANI, 1986, f. 117, o. 1, d. 15, l. 11; "Suleiman Laik: Vlkad Sovetskogo Soyuza," Afghanistan.ru, 11 May 2016.

101. Keshtmand, Political Notes, 159–63. Edwards, Before Taliban and Leake, Afghan Crucible discuss the similarities between the PDPA and the Muslim Youth/Jamiat-e-Islami and Hezb-e-Islami parties.

102. PDPA Ministry of Foreign Affairs official, Interview, Moscow, August 2021. The person worked in the PDPA's Ministry of Foreign Affairs in the 1980s. He went to the USSR in the mid-1980s to oversee the activities of the Afghans dispatched there by the PDPA.

103. Arkhiv Vneshnei Politiki Rossiiskoi Federatsii (AVPRF), 24 July 1978, f. 159, o. 90, papka (p.) 150, d. 8, l. 117 and 2 September 1978, ll. 171–72.

104. Edwards, *Before Taliban*, 80–81. As noted above, S. Mujaddidi also called for jihad against the regime in March 1989. His call carried weight since he was a recognized Islamic authority.

105. NARADC, USDoS, Kabul, 16 October 1978.

106. AVPRF, 9 September 1978, f. 159, o. 90, p. 150, d. 8, l. 174.

107. AVPRF, 5 July 1978, f. 159, o. 90, p. 150, d. 8, l. 35.

108. GARF, 21 March 1979, TASS, f. R4459, o. 43, d. 20974, ll. 258–64; Edwards, *Before Taliban*, 78–86.

109. GARF, April 1979, TASS, f. R4459, o. 43, d. 20975, ll. 167–68.

110. Darmanger, Interview.

111. RGANI, June 1978–January 1979, f. 5, o. 75, d. 1181, l. 63; RGANI, March 1979–February 1980, f. 5, o. 76, d. 1046, ll. 83–85.

112. GARF, 9 April 1979, TASS, f. R4459, o. 43, d. 20975, ll. 167–68.

113. NARADC, USDoS, Kabul, 4 June 1979.

114. Darmanger, Interview.

115. NARADC, 4 June 1979.

116. Edwards, *Before Taliban*, 144.

117. RGANI, April–October 1979, f. 5, o. 76, d. 1042, ll. 4–11; RGANI, January–August 1979, f. 5, o. 76, d. 1044, ll. 1–69.

118. GARF, 10 August 1979, TASS, f. R4459, o. 43, d. 20978, l. 1.

119. GARF, 20 September 1979, TASS, f. R4459, o. 43, d. 20978, l. 189.

120. RGANI, March 1979–February 1980, f. 5, o. 76, d. 1046, ll. 1–39.

121. GARF, 21 September 1979, TASS, f. R4459, o. 43, d. 20978, l. 198.

122. AVPRF, 1 October 1979, f. 159, o. 91, p. 156, d. 11, l. 85.

123. GARF, 22 October 1979, TASS, f. R4459, o. 43, d. 20979, l. 33.

124. Ehmadi, *State, Revolution*, 87.

125. RGANI, 1979, f. 5, o. 76, d. 1043, ll. 16–22, 51–58; RGANI, March 1979–February 1980, f. 5, o. 76, d. 1046, l. 40.

126. NARADC, USDoS, Kabul, 6 November 1979.

127. Snegirev and Samunin, *Virus "A,"* ch. 2 quotes a Sufi sheikh speaking to a KGB operative.

128. KhAD head of department, Interview.

129. NARADC, USDoS, Kabul, 1 August 1979.

130. NARADC, USDoS, Kabul, 21 May 1978.

131. Khalq would much later send a letter to Gorbachev arguing that Pakistan and Parcham had made Taraki look like "Islam's mortal enemy." RGANI, 28 August 1989, f. 84, o. 1, d. 348, ll. 23–32.

132. Plastun and Andrianov, *Nadzhibulla*, 182. A PDPA official used the expression.

133. Brutents, *Tridtsat' let*, part 4, ch. 3; Primakov, *Konfidentsial'no, Blizhny Vostok na stsene i za kulisami* (Moscow: Tsentrpoligraf, 2016), 51.

3. Ideology in the Karmal Era

Epigraph 1: *Kucherova*, KGB, 171.
Epigraph 2: Borovik, *Hidden War*, 12.

1. Gai and Snegirev, *Vtorzhenie*, 115; Lyakhovsky, *Tragediya*, 176–77.

2. RGANI, 23 June 1980, f. 2, o. 3, d. 279, ll. 46–48.

3. RGANI, 23 June 1980, f. 2, o. 3, d. 279, ll. 13–39.

4. Adamishin, Interview.

5. Shebarshin, *Ruka Moskvy*, 200. See also RGANI, 1981–84, f. 117, o. 1, d. 10, l. 198.

6. Vladimir Snegirev, Phone/Email Interview, January 2019. Snegirev was a journalist in Afghanistan for the journals *Komsomolskaya Pravda*, *Pravda*, and *Trud* in the 1980s. He was the first Soviet journalist to interview Ahmad Shah Massoud. After 1992, he worked in Afghanistan as a Russian journalist and has been involved in programs to find remaining Soviet prisoners of war.

7. Maiorov, *Pravda*, ch. 15.

8. RGANI, 1988, f. 117, o. 1, d. 17, l. 36.

9. Grachev, Interview.

10. Grachev, Interview.

11. RGANI, 1988, f. 117, o. 1, d. 17, ll. 2–13.

12. Artemy M. Kalinovsky, *The Blind Leading the Blind: Soviet Advisors, Counter-Insurgency and Nation-Building in Afghanistan* (Washington, DC: CWIHPDC, 2010), 20–21.

13. Mikhail Slinkin, "Afganskie vstrechi i besedy," *Kul'tura narodov Prichernomor'ya* 113 (2007), 38.

14. Ramazan Daurov, ed., *Dnevnikovye zapisi M.F. Slinkina* (Moscow: IV RAN, 2016), 37.

15. "Afganskaya vakhta Tabeeva," *Business-Gazeta.ru*, 3 March 2013.

16. Plastun and Andrianov, *Nadzhibulla*, 171; RGANI, 1988, f. 117, o. 1, d. 17, ll. 2–13. The number of CPSU advisers was at its maximum (240) in the mid-1980s.

17. KGB Officer, Email. Nabi Azimi, *The Army and Politics: Afghanistan, 1963–1993*, Kindle (Bloomington, IN: AuthorHouse, 2019), Loc. 7827; Victor Korgun, *Istoriya Afganistana, XX vek* (Moscow: IV RAN/Izdatel'stvo "Kraft," 2004), ch. VII. Azimi writes: "being sycophantic towards the Russian authorities during the night parties and Russian Embassy invitations could make one's life easier. At these invitations guests behaved as if they were servants shouting slogans and giving speeches in favor of the USSR."

18. Kucherova, *KGB*, 371–72.

19. GFA, 20 February 1989, f. 3, o. 1, d. 0.

20. RGANI, 15 January 1980, f. 4, o. 44, d. 25, ll. 14–17.

21. Brutents, *Tridtsat' let*, part 4, ch. 5.

22. NSADC, APRF, 7 February 1980, f. 3, o. 120, d. 44, ll. 73, 77–80.

23. Basov, "Interv'yu"; Grachev, Interview; Shebarshin, *Ruka Moskvy*, 221–22; Snegirev, Interview.

24. Plastun, *Iznanka*, 638, 189.

25. Kucherova, *KGB*, 193, 262, 317, 324, 364; Plastun and Andrianov, *Nadzhibulla*, 68; Welch and Westad, *Intervention in Afghanistan*, 153–56.

26. Toporkov, *Afganistan*, 81–83. Azimi, *Army*, Loc. 5833, 5847 notes that the KGB underutilized Afghans' knowledge, fearing "Afghan Army intelligence" was "unreliable."

27. RGANI, 18 February 1980, f. 4, o. 44, d. 25, ll. 46–49.

28. RGANI, 18 February 1980, f. 4, o. 44, d. 25, l. 127. This was a constant of Soviet cultural diplomacy. Khudonazarov, Interview. Khudonazarov recalled being part of a mission to the Republic of Afghanistan in the 1970s where the Soviet delegation had

the idea of showing a screening of the Moscow ballet. Before the end of the show, all Afghans had left the screening.

29. RGANI, 16 December 1980, f. 89, o. 46, d. 74, ll. 1–24.

30. Merimsky, *Zagadki*, 88, 122–23; RGANI, 1988, f. 117, o. 1, d. 21, l. 56; Mikhaïl Slinkin, "Afganistan: Uroki informatsionnoi voiny," *Kul'tura narodov Prichernomor'ya* 15 (2000), 89, 94. There was no system in place to bring newspapers from Kabul to Kandahar. The main newspaper, *Khakikat-e Inquilab-e Saur*, sold only one copy in Kandahar between July 1981 and July 1982.

31. Oleg Cherneta, ed., *Afganistan: Bor'ba i sozidanie* (Moscow: Voenizdat, 1984), 123; Kucherova, KGB, 76, 155, 200. Centlivres, Pierre et Micheline Centlivres-Démont, Interview, Neuchâtel (Switzerland), October 2019. Centlivres and Centlivres-Démont are Swiss ethnographers who conducted field research in Afghanistan before and after the Soviet-Afghan War and in refugee camps in Pakistan during the conflict.

32. Snegirev, Interview.

33. NSADC, "Dokladnaya zapiska ob Afganistane," 12 November 1981, 43; Maiorov notes that 60–65 percent of the territory was controlled by the opposition in mid-1981. Maiorov, *Pravda*, ch. 13.

34. Graduate Institute of International and Development Studies (IHEID), Fonds Micheline Centlivres-Démont (FCFA) 133/1, January 1981, Jean-José Puig, "Rapport Afghanistan," 34–55.

35. Gai and Snegirev, *Vtorzhenie*, 109.

36. LCST general, Interview; RGANI, 1979–85, f. 117, o. 1, d. 36, l. 22; Shebarshin, *Ruka Moskvy*, 199.

37. Maiorov, *Pravda*, ch. 7; Plastun and Andrianov, *Nadzhibulla*, 85.

38. NSADC, 12 November 1981, 51–53.

39. Borovik, *Hidden War*, 286–87; Plastun and Andrianov, *Nadzhibulla*, 182.

40. Maiorov, *Pravda*, chs. 8–10; Varennikov, *Nepovtorimoe*, chs. 2–3.

41. NSADC, 12 November 1981, 51–53.

42. KGB Officer, Email.

43. Anton Minkov and Gregory Smolynec, "4-D Soviet Style: Defense, Development, Diplomacy and Disengagement in Afghanistan during the Soviet Period, Part I: State Building," *Journal of Slavic Military Studies* 23, no. 2 (2010): 306–27; Anton Minkov and Gregory Smolynec, "4-D Soviet Style: Defense, Development, Diplomacy, and Disengagement during the Soviet Period, Part II: Social Development," *Journal of Slavic Military Studies* 23, no. 3 (2010): 391–411; Anton Minkov and Gregory Smolynec, "4-D Soviet Style: Defense, Development, Diplomacy, and Disengagement during the Soviet Period, Part III: Economic Development," *Journal of Slavic Military Studies* 23, no. 4 (2010): 597–611.

44. Kalinovsky, *Long Goodbye*, 42; Anthony Arnold, *The Fateful Pebble: Afghanistan's Role in the Fall of the Soviet Empire* (New York: Presidio Press, 1993), 185, puts the war's cost at $4–8 billion/year.

45. Lyakhovsky, *Tragediya*, Annex 8 gives the estimate of 5 billion rubles/year circulated in the CC CPSU as of 1988, so approximately 3.25 billion dollars/year. The Soviets also transferred 830 million rubles of infrastructure used by the LCST to Kabul after the withdrawal; N. Egorychev argues the war cost $15 billion/year in 1988. Yevgeny Zhirnov, "Afganistan stoil nam 15 milliardov dollarov v god," *Kommersant Vlast'*, no. 46, 25 November 2002.

46. Mikhail Gorbachev, ed., *Otvechaya na vyzov vremeni. Vneshnyaya politika pere-stroiki: Dokumental'nye svidetel'stva* (Moscow: The Gorbachev Foundation/Ves' Mir, 2010), 610, 636. In 1987, some say it was $1 billion/year and some say 2–3; by 1988, the estimate was at 6 billion rubles/year, roughly $3.9 billion/year.

47. Maria Nabat, "The USSR's Economic Assistance Strategy to Afghanistan on the Threshold of the Soviet Troops' Withdrawal," *Vestnik of Saint Petersburg University* 10, no. 1 (2018): 118–32; Nunan, *Humanitarian Invasion*; Robinson and Dixon, *Afghanistan*.

48. RGANI, 1981, f. 117, o. 1, d. 33, ll. 10–16.

49. LCST general, Interview.

50. Centlivres and Centlivres-Démont, "On parlait de l'Afghanistan," 10.

51. RGANI, 28 January 1980, f. 89, o. 34, d. 3, ll. 1–8.

52. NSADC, 7 February 1980.

53. RGANI, 10 January 1983, f. 89, o. 42, d. 51, ll. 1–4.

54. Azimi, *Army*, Loc. 7133. The communists sent 1,400 Afghan students to Soviet institutes in 1983.

55. *AFGHANews*, 11 November 1985, 4. *AFGHANews* journals are available in IHEID FCFA.

56. CWIHPDC, BStU, 7 November 1983, Abt. X, Nr. 2020, S. 1–7.

57. AIC, *Monthly Bulletin*, no. 57, Dec 1985, 7–8. Kakar, *Afghanistan*, 155. AIC bulletins are available in IHEID FCFA.

58. RGANI, 6 May 1980, f. 4, o. 44, d. 25, ll. 163–65.

59. *AFGHANews*, 11 November 1985, 4.

60. Halliday and Tanin, "Communist Regime," 1373.

61. Halliday and Tanin, "Communist Regime," 1373. For examples of Afghans getting Soviets recalled: Azimi, *Army*, Loc. 5760.

62. Mitrokhin, *KGB in Afghanistan*, 124.

63. Plastun, *Iznanka*, 269, 307; Slinkin, "Afganskie vstrechi," 9. A parallel issue was that lower-level advisers, translators, and social scientists from Central Asia had a better understanding of the context than higher-ups.

64. Basov, "Interv'yu." In the words of a PDPA official: "Everybody advised everybody amid talks about what did Lenin write." DOMA senior official, Interview.

65. Toporkov, *Afganistan*, 82.

66. Borovik, *Hidden War*, 13; Brutents, *Tridtsat' let*, part 4, ch. 1; Shebarshin, *Ruka Moskvy*, 223–24.

67. Maiorov, *Pravda*, chs. 10, 8.

68. Maiorov, *Pravda*, chs. 10, 8. See also RGANI, 1992, f. 117, o. 1, d. 4, l. 3.

69. LCST general, Interview. This chapter is derived in part from an article published in the *Journal of Cold War Studies* on 5 January 2022, copyright by MIT Press, available at https://doi.org/10.1162/jcws_a_01055. See Vassily Klimentov, "'Communist Muslims': The USSR and the People's Democratic Party of Afghanistan's Conversion to Islam, 1978–1988," *Journal of Cold War Studies* 24, no. 1 (2022): 4–38.

70. Rahmatullo Abdulloev, Phone Interview, March 2020.

71. Nunan, *Humanitarian Invasion*, 172–73. Nunan provides the story of a Tajik translator stopped at a checkpoint and quizzed about basic concepts in Islam. The translator managed to impress the mujahideen and got free passage by asking them in return a "riddle" about the proper "Islamic" conduct to have in a specific situation.

72. RGANI, 1988–89, f. 117, o. 1, d. 27, l. 26; RGANI, 1988, f. 117, o. 1, d. 20, l. 4.

73. Kucherova, *KGB*, 193, 262, 317, 324.

74. GARF, February–June 1980, f. P9576, o. 20, d. 2800, ll. 32–51.

75. Gai and Snegirev, *Vtorzhenie*, 330.

76. Braithwaite, *Afgantsy*, 167.

77. RGANI, April–October 1979, f. 5, o. 76, d. 1042, ll. 4–11; Tasar, "Central Asian Muftiate," 215–16.

78. RGANI, 1980, f. 5, o. 76, d. 1043, ll. 16–22, 51; GARF, 6 July 1980, TASS, f. R4459, o. 43, d. 22325, l. 44.

79. GARF, 1985, f. R9576, o. 21, d. 46, l. 7; GARF, January–December 1984, f. R9587, o. 4, d. 90; GARF, January–June 1985, f. R9587, o. 4, d. 242; GARF, July–December 1985, f. R9587, o. 4, d. 243; GARF, January–December 1986, f. R9587, o. 4, d. 417; GARF, January–June 1987, f. R9587, o. 4, d. 603; GARF, July–December 1987, f. R9587, o. 4, d. 604.

80. GARF, 22 January 1980, TASS, f. R4459, o. 43, d. 22313, l. 235.

81. GARF, 1 July 1981, TASS, f. R4459, o. 44, d. 84, ll. 41–3, 52–53.

82. No eyewitness account mentioned that such a representative was present. Hence, even if such a person existed, it had little influence. The Soviets embassy discussed sending a religious specialist for a short period in 1980. GARF, February–June 1980, f. P9576, o. 20, d. 2800, ll. 32–51.

83. GARF, January–November 1984, f. P9576, o. 20, d. 4387; RGASPI, 1987, f. 17, o. 156, d. 2069, ll. 43–44; Tasar, "Central Asian Muftiate," 217–18; Lobato, "Islam in Kabul," 115.

84. GARF, January–August 1991, f. P9576, o. 20, d. 6485, l. 123; Eren Tasar, "The Official Madrasas of Soviet Uzbekistan," *Journal of Economic and Social History of the Orient* 59, no. 1–2 (2016): 265–302.

85. Vladimir Plastun, Interview, May 2019/April 2020.

86. GARF, 1982–84, f. P9606, o. 11, d. 323; GARF, 1984–87, f. P9606, o. 11, d. 324.

87. Snegirev, Interview.

88. RGANI, 1988, f. 117, o. 1, d. 17, ll. 2–13.

89. Maiorov, *Pravda*, ch. 3.

90. Kravtsov, Interview.

91. Tasar, *Soviet and Muslim*, 277–95; Plastun, Interview.

92. RGASPI, September–November 1988, f. 797, o. 1, d. 33, l. 1; RGANI, 1988, f. 117, o. 1, d. 17, ll. 13–15; RGANI, 1981, f. 117, o. 1, d. 33, l. 33.

93. GARF, 24 February 1980, TASS, f. R4459, o. 43, d. 22317, l. 49. One article notes that Soviets "not only wholly respected the holy religion of Islam but also protected it."

94. Maiorov, *Pravda*, ch. 8.

95. DOMA senior official, Interview; PDPA foreign affairs official, Interview.

96. GARF, February–June 1980, f. P9576, o. 20, d. 2800, ll. 32–51.

97. GARF, 5 October 1983, f. R9576, o. 20, d. 3986, ll. 25–46.

98. GARF, 14 March 1984, f. R9576, o. 20, d. 4388, ll. 38–42.

99. GARF, 13 April 1984, f. R9576, o. 20, d. 4388, l. 56.

100. GARF, 29 April 1984, f. R9576, o. 20, d. 4388, l. 62.

101. GARF, 11 April 1984, f. R9576, o. 20, d. 4388, 49.

102. GARF, 1985, f. R9576, o. 21, d. 46, l. 7. The new policy also supported Najibullah's national reconciliation program. GFA, 3 March 1987, f. 2, o. 1, d. 2; Robinson and Dixon, *Afghanistan*, 142–47.

103. *AFGHANews* 3, no. 13, 1 July 1987, 1. AFGHANews is published by Jamiat-e Islami.

104. Igor Biryukov, Phone Interview, January 2020. Biryukov, a Russian from Uzbekistan, was deployed to Afghanistan in 1988. He was a senior lieutenant in the LCST's Propaganda Department, handling an army journal and counterpropaganda in Afghanistan. He was based in Tajikistan after the war.

105. Nikolai Pikov, *Spetspropagandist o Dubynine V.P.* (Moscow: Soyuz Veteranov Voennogo Instituta Inostrannykh Yazykov, 2018), 3. Also, Andrei Musalov, *Zelenye pogony Afganistana* (Moscow: Yauza-Katalog, 2019), 69–70.

106. Gai and Snegirev, *Vtorzhenie*, 195–206; Pikov, *Spetspropagandist*, 9–10.

107. Pikov, *Spetspropagandist*, 4; Plastun, *Iznanka*, 334–35. See also Azimi, *Army*, Loc. 5305 provides an Afghan view on *agitprop* that highlights how the units became more efficient after they included Afghans.

108. Musalov, *Pogony*, 70, 136; Pikov, *Spetspropagandist*, 5.

109. AIC, *Monthly Bulletin*, no. 60, March 1986, 8; Plastun, *Iznanka*, 334–35; Pikov, *Spetspropagandist*, 37–40.

110. Pikov, *Spetspropagandist*, 37.

111. Tatiana Polukazakova, "Ubit' mogli," 4 March 2019, TVzvezda.ru.

112. AIC, *Monthly Bulletin*, no. 85, April 1988, 29. The AIC notes that in some areas the population thought that the aid provided was "a *jazya*, a poll-tax in lieu of conversion to Islam." Valerii Marchenko, *Afganskii Razlom*, 156–58.

113. Pikov, *Spetspropagandist*, 33; Aleksandr Knyazev, Phone Interview, Nov 2019.

114. NSADC, "Otdel organizatsionno-partiinoi raboty TSK KPSS," 15 January 1980; NSADC, Primakov, 16–18 formulated the same advice about the institutionalization of Islam-state relations.

115. NSADC, "Situation in Afghanistan, October 26–November 1, 1982," US Embassy (USE), Afghanistan. Some Afghans differentiated between the Soviets and Karmal, supporting the latter but denouncing the occupation.

116. Edwards, *Before Taliban*, 35–39; Elisabeth Leake, "Afghan Internationalism and the Question of Afghanistan's Political Legitimacy," *Afghanistan* 1, no. 1 (2018): 68–94. On PDPA's media: M. Halim Tanwir, *Afghanistan: History, Diplomacy and Journalism* (Bloomington, IN: Xlibris Corporation, 2013), 365–77.

117. GARF, 19 January 1980, TASS, f. R4459, o. 43, d. 22313, ll. 107–15.

118. GARF, 26 January 1980, TASS, f. R4459, o. 43, d. 22314, l. 138.

119. GARF, 28 April 1980, TASS, f. R4459, o. 43, d. 22321, ll. 128–29.

120. GARF, 26 January 1980.

121. CWIHPDC, APRF, 17 January 1980, f. 3, o. 120, d. 44, ll. 3, 31, 42–44.

122. GARF, 21 October 1982, TASS, f. R4459, o. 44, d. 1618, l. 61; GARF, 19 June 1985, TASS, f. R4459, o. 44, d. 6178, ll. 8–9; KhAD head of department, Interview.

123. Maiorov, *Pravda*, ch. 7.

124. NSADC, "Situation in Afghanistan, June 30–July 7, 1981," USE, Afghanistan.

125. GARF, 10 August 1985, TASS, f. R4459, o. 44, d. 6178, ll. 213–14. The same was true in provincial centers such as Mazar-i-Sharif. Keshtmand, *Political Notes*, 901–15.

126. GARF, 27 September 1984, TASS, f. R4459, o. 44, d. 4573, l. 182.

127. GARF, 15 June 1981, TASS, f. R4459, o. 44, d. 83, ll. 167–78.

128. GARF, 21 July 1980, TASS, f. R4459, o. 43, d. 22324, l. 210.

129. GARF, 11 April 1985, TASS, f. R4459, o. 44, d. 6176, ll. 191–92.

130. AIC, *Monthly Bulletin*, no. 49, April 1985, 2–4.

131. Lobato, "Islam in Kabul," 112.

132. Adkin and Yousaf, *Bear Trap*, 146; Dorronsoro, *Revolution Unending*, 179; Keshtmand, *Political Notes*, 901-15; Lyakhovsky, *Tragediya*, 165, 248-50.

133. GARF, 16 March 1984, TASS, f. R4459, o. 44, d. 4570, l. 227.

134. IHEID, FCFA127/1-6, François Houtart, February 1982, "L'Afghanistan entre deux mondes." One limitation was that Houtart limited his investigation to regime areas.

135. Slinkin, "Afganskie vstrechi," 44. See also: Giustozzi, *War*, 134; Rubin, *Fragmentation of Afghanistan*, 134-35.

136. GARF, 15 June 1980, TASS, f. R4459, o. 43, d. 22323, l. 202.

137. GARF, 2 April 1981, TASS, f. R4459, o. 44, d. 82, ll. 61-62.

138. GARF, 25 June 1984, TASS, f. R4459, o. 44, d. 4572, l. 75.

139. Marlene Laruelle, Botagoz Rakisheva, and Gulden Ashkenova, eds., *Pamyat' iz plameni Afganistana, Kniga 2, Uzbekistan* (Astana: KISI pri Prezidente RK, 2016), 84.

140. Khristoforov, *Afganistan*, 148-49.

141. Plastun, *Iznanka*, 362, 424-25.

142. GARF, 22 April 1980, TASS, f. R4459, o. 43, d. 22321, l. 7; Keshtmand, *Political Notes*, 650-51.

143. "Document 282," 2 June 1980, *FRUS, 1977-1980*, 753-56.

144. NSADC, "Uroki zemel'noi reformy v Afganistane," 25 January 1980, 2-4; Tabeev once even took it upon himself to correct some mistakes by reallocating land to a peasant family. "Vakhta Tabeeva," 2013.

145. GARF, 11 August 1981, TASS, f. R4459, o. 44, d. 84, ll. 241-43.

146. GARF, 7 June 1986, TASS, f. R4459, o. 44, d. 7569, l. 204; Merimsky, *Zagadki*, 24-25.

147. NSADC, "Otchet o prodolzhenii zemel'noi reformy," 28 October 1981. One interesting aspect was that, according to the embassy, the original reform did not include *waqfs*. This may suggest that abuses were so prevalent that the revisions had to clarify the status of *waqfs* anyway.

148. NSADC, 12 November 1981, 47-49.

149. RGANI, 1979-85, f. 117, o. 1, d. 36, ll. 10-24, 40.

150. Centlivres-Démont, *Colonisation Impossible*, 57-80; Rubin, *Fragmentation*, 118, 142-43, 172-73. Korgun, *Istoriya*, ch. VII.

151. Dorronsoro, *Revolution Unending*, 180 claims that proregime Islamic scholars were "illiterate mullahs, educated in private *madrasas*." This characterization may be too strong but emphasizes the same points.

152. Mitrokhin, *KGB in Afghanistan*, 142 claims the KGB allocated 25 million hard-currency rubles to that end.

153. DOMA senior official, Interview. The interviewee reached out to a former KhAD 7th Department collaborator for this information.

154. KhAD head of department, Interview.

155. Lyakhovsky, *Tragediya*, 253, Annex 8.

156. AIC, *Monthly Bulletin*, no. 32-33, November-December 1983, 5-6.

157. *AFGHANews* 2, no. 10, 15 May 1986, 1.

158. AIC, *Monthly Bulletin*, November-December 1983.

159. Giustozzi, *War*, 63.

160. *AFGHANews* 2, no. 10, 15 May 1986, 1.

161. AIC, *Monthly Bulletin*, no. 56, Nov 1985, 3; Korgun, *Istoriya*, ch. VII. The Soviets supported these changes.

162. GARF, 14 March 1982, TASS, f. R4459, o. 44, d. 1615, ll. 14–53.

163. Daurov, *Zapisi*, 61; DOMA senior official, Interview.

164. For an overview: Braithwaite, *Afgantsy*, 226; Plastun, *Iznanka*, 207, 434. This section looks at a selection of handbooks provided by Kravtsov following the interview.

165. G. Arzumanov and L. Shershnev, eds., *Sovetskomu voinu ob Afganistane* (Tashkent: Politicheskoe Upravlenie Krasnoznamennogo Turkestanskogo Voennogo Okruga [PUKTVO], 1981), 6, 11.

166. Arzumanov and Shershnev, *Sovetskomu voinu*, 3.

167. Arzumanov and Shershnev, *Sovetskomu voinu*, 12, 17, 32, 18.

168. Arzumanov and Shershnev, *Sovetskomu voinu*, 29, 20.

169. Maiorov, *Pravda*, ch. 7.

170. Arzumanov and Shershnev, *Voinu*, 41–43; Musalov, *Pogony*, 150–51.

171. G. Arzumanov et al., *Byt, nravy i obychai narodov Afganistana* (Tashkent: PUKTVO, 1984).

172. Marlene Laruelle, Botagoz Rakisheva, and Gulden Ashkenova, eds., *Pamyat' iz plameni Afganistana, Kniga 1, Kazakhstan* (Astana: KISI pri Prezidente RK, 2016), 78. It is unclear to which extent Soviets followed the recommendations in the handbooks. Stories tell of enterprising soldiers who grasped that the best time to steal at markets was during *namaz*. Kucherova, *KGB*, 131.

173. G. Arzumanov, V. Gubrii, and V. Sokol, *Sovetskomu voinu ob Afganistane* (Tashkent: PUKTVO, 1987), 13. There have been other editions of the general handbook aside from the two analyzed here.

174. Cherneta, *Afganistan*, 18.

175. Musalov, *Pogony*, 301–4.

176. Malik Tynystanov, Phone Interview, November 2019. Tynystanov was a conscript from Kyrgyzstan who served in a motorized rifle battalion in the LCST from October 1981 to July 1983. He participated in the Panjshir offensive.

177. *Tema: "'Znat' i uvazhat' traditsii, nravy i obychai Afganskogo Naroda"* (Tashkent: PUKTVO, 1985).

178. V. Zakharov et al., *I. Znat' i uvazhat' traditsii, nravy i obychai Afganskogo naroda* (Tashkent: PUKTVO, 1987).

179. A. Bondarenko, *Aktual'nye problemy formirovaniya u lichnogo sostava ponimaniya tselei i zadach prebyvaniya sovetskikh voisk v DRA* (Tashkent: PUKTVO, 1985), 11, 15.

180. Bondarenko, *Aktual'nye problemy formirovaniya*.

181. L. Shershnev and V. Granitov, eds., *Islam v sovremennom Afganistane* (Tashkent: PUKTVO, 1982), 4–6.

182. Shershnev and V. Granitov, *Islam* 14.

183. Shershnev and V. Granitov, *Islam*, 16.

184. Biryukov, Interview suggests that this is how the Soviets understood that discourse.

185. Shershnev and Granitov, *Islam*, 17–19, 21–22.

186. Shershnev and Granitov, *Islam*, 23, 33.

187. Shershnev and Granitov, *Islam*, 40–44.

188. Shershnev and Granitov, *Islam*, 45.

189. V. Shur, *Real'naya sushchnost' islamskoi "svyashchennoi bor'by za veru"* (Tashkent: PUKTVO, 1987), 13. The criticism was difficult to articulate because the author had to explain that sometimes jihad served "liberation struggles."

190. Five LCST Veteran Officers, Interview, Moscow, December 2017.

191. Biryukov, Interview has provided the estimate. It remains contested. Markus Balázs Göransson, "At the Service of the State, Soviet-Afghan War Veterans in Tajikistan, 1979–1992" (PhD diss., Aberystwyth University, 2015), 36–37. Göransson suggests that 130,000 Central Asians took part in the conflict.

192. Braithwaite, *Afgantsy*, 329; Kryuchkov, *Lichnoe delo*, 209 gives the higher number of 900,000 soldiers. Gorbachev, *Otvechaya na vyzov*, 663 notes that more than 1 million soldiers went through Afghanistan. The discrepancies may be due to some estimates, including the Soviet advisers in Afghanistan.

193. Braithwaite, *Afgantsy*, 121, Göransson, *Service of the State*, 18.

194. Kalinovsky, *Laboratory of Socialist Development*, Loc. 4911.

195. Abdulloev, Interview; Gai and Snegirev, *Vtorzhenie*, 91; Kucherova, *KGB*, 325; Laruelle, *Uzbekistan*, 54.

196. *AFGHANews* 3, no. 8, 15 April 1987, 4; *AFGHANews* 3, no. 19, 15 September 1987, 4; NSADC, "Open Hearing of the Congressional Task Force on Afghanistan," 17 February 1987, US Congress (USC); Kucherova, *KGB*, 112. Central Asians were fewer in KGB border guard units where there was some concern about their loyalty.

197. AIC, *Monthly Bulletin*, no. 32–33, November–December 1983, 18–19; Mitrokhin, *KGB in Afghanistan*, 112. See also Ro'i, *Bleeding Wound*, 254–69.

198. Kucherova, *KGB*, 128–29.

199. Plastun, *Iznanka*, 205.

200. NSADC, RAND Corporation, *Soviet Central Asian Soldiers in Afghanistan* (Washington, DC, January 1981); Tynystanov, Interview, notes that Central Asians suffered significant casualties early on because of their unpreparedness and lack of proficiency in the Russian language used for commands.

201. Roy, *Islam and Resistance*, 195.

202. Gai and Snegirev, *Vtorzhenie*, 241–49. Snegirev, Interview, provided the numbers. Peter Tomsen, *The Wars of Afghanistan: Messianic Terrorism, Tribal Conflicts, and the Failures of Great Powers* (New York: PublicAffairs, 2011), 463–69, 498–503 provides similar numbers. Laruelle, *Kazakhstan*; Marlene Laruelle, Botagoz Rakisheva, and Gulden Ashkenova, eds., *Pamyat' iz plameni Afganistana, Kniga 3, Tadzhikistan* (Astana: KISI pri Prezidente RK, 2016); Laruelle, *Uzbekistan* confirms Central Asians' lack of interest in defecting.

203. Laruelle, *Kazakhstan*, 27, 130; Laruelle, *Tadzhikistan*, 176, 188, 226; Laruelle, *Uzbekistan*. See also Abdulloev, Interview; Biryukov, Interview; Tynystanov, Interview.

204. Tynystanov, Interview.

205. Centlivres and Centlivres-Démont, Interview.

206. NSADC, "Vozvrashchenie na rodinu," 8 September 1981.

207. Göransson, *Service of the State*, 170–71, 187–88.

208. LCST veterans, Interview.

209. Pikov, *Spetspropagandist*, 9.

210. A limit of Laruelle et al.'s interviews is that they were obtained through veterans' organizations and hence tended to have people who retained "pride in their

service." Artemy M. Kalinovsky, "Central Asian Soldiers and the Soviet War in Afghanistan, An Introduction," in *The Central Asia–Afghanistan Relationship: From Soviet Intervention to the Silk Road Initiatives*, ed. Marlene Laruelle (Lanham, MD: Lexington Books, 2017), 16.

211. Laruelle, *Kazakhstan*, 42.

212. Laruelle, *Kazakhstan*, 126.

213. Laruelle, *Uzbekistan*, 61.

214. Laruelle, *Tadzhikistan*, 109.

215. Laruelle, *Tadzhikistan*, 176.

216. Laruelle, *Tadzhikistan*, 140.

217. Laruelle, *Kazakhstan*, 160.

218. Ro'i, *Islam in the Soviet Union*, 225; Ro'i, "Impact of Islamic Fundamentalist Revival," 39

219. Tynystanov, Interview.

220. Snegirev, Interview.

221. Chernyaev, *Diary*, August 1985 notes that there had been incidents on religious grounds with Caucasian Muslims sent to Afghanistan.

222. Nunan, *Humanitarian Invasion*, 99–100. Göransson, *Service of the State*, 26–27, 190 writes that "veterans, in many ways, became more closely involved with Soviet power as a result of their service."

223. Darmanger, *L'Afghanistan*, 253–54; *AFGHANews* 7, no. 15, 1 August 1991, 4; Varennikov, *Nepovtorimoe*, chs. 3–4.

224. Maiorov, *Pravda*, ch. 7.

225. KhAD head of department, Interview; Tabeev made clear to S. Harrison that the Soviets thought Karmal's ethnicity was an issue. Cordovez and Harrison, *Out of Afghanistan*, 154.

226. Roy, *Islam and Resistance*, 47.

227. Edwards, *Before Taliban*, 39–40.

228. GARF, 31 March 1980, TASS, f. R4459, o. 43, d. 22320, l. 57.

229. GARF, 4 June 1984, TASS, f. R4459, o. 44, d. 4572, ll. 18–21

230. GARF, 4 November 1985, TASS, f. R4459, o. 44, d. 6180, ll. 114–17.

231. For the AIC, he represented a liability for Moscow since 1984. AIC, *Monthly Bulletin*, no. 62, May 1986, 3–8; IHEID, FCFA133/1, January 1981, Jean-José Puig, "Rapport Afghanistan," 34–55, notes that speculations were ongoing about the Soviets changing for another ruler since 1981. RGANI, 1988–89, f. 117, o. 1, d. 27, l. 32. Polyanichko wondered if the decision to remove Karmal did not come too late.

232. Chernyaev, *Diary*, August 1984. Chernyaev notes that the comment made the Soviet Muslim and Caucasian *apparatchiks* present clearly uneasy.

233. Kirpichenko, *Razvedka*, 359.

234. Kucherova, *KGB*, 314; Vitaly Vorotnikov, *A bylo eto tak . . .* (Moscow: Sovet Veteranov Knigoizdaniya SI-MAR, 1995), 46–48.

235. Chernyaev, *Diary*, August 1984; Gromyko, *Pamyatnoe*, 179–80; Kirpichenko, *Razvedka*, 359.

236. Varennikov, *Nepovtorimoe*, chs. 3–4.

237. Cordovez and Harrison, *Out of Afghanistan*, 44–46.

238. Gai and Snegirev, *Vtorzhenie*, 101–3.

239. Maiorov, *Pravda*, chs. 8–9; Shebarshin, *Ruka Moskvy*, 233–34; Slinkin, "Afganskie vstrechi," 9. "Eto byla oshibka," *Kommersant*, no. 20, 12 February 1999. Kakar, *Afghanistan*, 64–69, 74 notes that Karmal was the only one in Parcham who had national legitimacy; Azimi, *Army*, Loc. 6090, 6162, 6055, 7414 provides positive assessments of Karmal.

240. Andrei Grachev, *Gorbatchev, Le pari perdu? De la perestroïka a l'implosion de l'URSS* (Paris: Armand Colin, 2008). Valery Boldin claims that Gorbachev was ideological and "the ultimate 'man of [Lenin's] quotes." "Gorbachev sorvalsya s rez'by," *Kommersant Vlast'* 19, no. 15, May 2001.

241. Chernyaev, *Diary*, April 1985; Kalinovsky, *Long Goodbye*, 87. Eduard Shevardnadze, *Kogda rukhnul zheleznyi zanaves* (Moscow: Evropa, 2009), 91–93. The Soviets intensified military operations and tried to seal the border with Pakistan after 1986, but this was more a continuation of ongoing policies than a surge.

242. RGANI, 1988, f. 117, o. 1, d. 21, ll. 32–34; RGANI, 1991, f. 117, o. 1, d. 6, ll. 4–5.

243. RGANI, 1988, f. 117, o. 1, d. 21, ll. 75–85.

244. Chernyaev, *Diary*, October 1985.

245. KhAD head of department, Interview.

246. Chernyaev, *Diary*, October 1985; RGANI, 1988, f. 117, o. 1, d. 21, ll. 75–85.

247. Chernyaev, *Diary*, October 1985.

248. RGANI, 1985, f. 117, o. 1, d. 12, ll. 2–3.

4. Najibullah's Islamization

Epigraph: GARF, 5 February 1987, TASS, f. R4459, o. 44, d. 8838, ll. 225–29.

1. Shebarshin, *Ruka Moskvy*, 230.

2. Slinkin, "Afganskie Vstrechi," 9–11, 21, 38.

3. Ala Smolina, "Dai svoi adres," *Art of War*, 21 November 2011; Kryuchkov, *Lichnoe Delo*, 227–29 downplays the problems associated with Karmal's removal.

4. RGANI, 1986, f. 117, o. 1, d. 14, ll. 22–29; RGANI, 1988, f. 117, o. 1, d. 21, ll. 64–73.

5. The military supported Asadullah Sarwari, a Khalqi and Najibullah's predecessor in KhAD's equivalent under Taraki. The Soviets also considered other PDPA candidates. It is unlikely they considered nonaligned leaders. Fred Halliday, "Soviet Foreign Policymaking and the Afghanistan War: From 'Second Mongolia' to 'Bleeding Wound,'" *Review of International Studies* 25, no. 4 (1999): 683; Lyakhovsky, *Tragediya*, 314–23; Plastun and Andrianov, *Nadzhibulla*, 60; Varennikov, *Nepovtorimoe*, ch. 6.

6. AIC, *Monthly Bulletin*, no. 62, May 1986, 3–8; Kakar, Afghanistan, 153–68, 179–86, 206.

7. Darmanger, Interview.

8. Kalinovsky, *Long Goodbye*, 99; Kirpichenko, *Razvedka*, 359–60.

9. RGANI, 1991, f. 117, o. 1, d. 6, ll. 4–5.

10. Plastun and Andrianov, *Nadzhibulla*, 46.

11. GFA, ND (1989?), f. 2, o. 1, d. 0.

12. Gorbachev, *Otvechaya na vyzov*, 600.

13. RGASPI, 1988, f. 797, o. 1, d 33, l. 1.

14. RGANI, 1988, f. 117, o. 1, d. 17, ll. 2–13.

15. Anatoly Chernyaev, ed., *V Politburo TSK KPSS . . .* (Moscow: Gorbachev Foundation, 2008), 64.

16. Chernyaev, *Diary*, 10 December 1986.

17. GFA, 3 March 1987. According to Shevardnadze, advisers, the MID, and the military had trouble adjusting to the fact that Najibullah was now fully in charge. Gorbachev, *Otvechaya na vyzov*, 606.

18. NSADC, "Zapis' besedy M.S. Gorbacheva s Prezidentom Afganistana," 13 June 1988, GFA.

19. NSADC, "Stenogramma soveshchaniya provedennogo t. Yakovlevym A.N.," 22 February 1988, GARF.

20. GFA, 18 June 1986, f. 2, o. 1, d. 1.

21. RGANI, 17–18 February 1988, f. 2, o. 6, d 302, l. 82.

22. GFA, 13 June 1988.

23. Grachev, Interview.

24. Gromov, *Kontingent*, 234–39; Vorotnikov, *Bylo eto tak*, 102, 111.

25. RGANI, 13 November 1986, f. 89, o. 42, d. 16, ll. 7–8.

26. RGANI, 1988–89, f. 117, o. 1, d. 27, l. 1

27. RGANI, 1988–89, f. 117, o. 1, d. 27, ll. 2–20; GARF, 11 May 1986, TASS, f. R4459, o. 44, d. 7569, ll. 1–3.

28. GARF, 14 January 1986, TASS, f. R4459, o. 44, d. 7565, ll. 137–39.

29. RGANI, 1988–89, f. 117, o. 1, d. 27, ll. 2–20; GARF, 14 January 1987, TASS, f. R4459, o. 44, d. 8837, ll. 214–21.

30. Lyakhovsky, *Tragediya*, 323–24.

31. GARF, 12 May 1987, TASS, f. R4459, o. 44, d. 8841, ll. 22–45.

32. GARF, 14 January 1987.

33. NSADC, "Zapis' besedy M.S. Gorbacheva s General'nym sekretariem TSK NDPA," GFA, 20 July 1987.

34. IHEID, FCFA132/1–5, NA, *The Role of Ulemas in the Invitation to Peace*, trans. Sher Alam Abasi (Kabul, 1988).

35. AIC, *Monthly Bulletin*, no. 70, January 1987, 4.

36. AIC, *Dossier Trimestriel*, no. 1, October–December 1986, 7. The AIC called it Najibullah's "double language."

37. GARF, 4 October 1987, TASS, f. R4459, o. 44, d. 8843, l. 236. Plastun and Andrianov, *Nadzhibulla*, 18.

38. Cordovez and Harrison, *Out of Afghanistan*, 252; Kakar, *Afghanistan*, 153–68; Mitrokhin, *KGB in Afghanistan*, 135–42.

39. GARF, 3 January 1987, TASS, f. R4459, o. 44, d. 8837, ll. 37–45.

40. GARF, 22 November 1986, TASS, f. R4459, o. 44, d. 7573, ll. 7–14.

41. GARF, 12 May 1987.

42. AIC, *Monthly Bulletin*, no. 71–72, February–March 1987, 3; RGANI, 1988, f. 117, o. 1, d. 22, ll. 14–18, 69–72, 107–8, 113.

43. AIC, *Monthly Bulletin*, no. 78, September 1987, 5.

44. GARF, 12 May 1987.

45. Khristoforov, *Afganistan*, 147; Rubin, *Fragmentation of Afghanistan*, 165–66.

46. AIC, *Monthly Bulletin*, no. 85, April 1988, 14–20; Plastun, Interview.

47. Khristoforov, *Afganistan*, 147; Lobato, "Islam in Kabul," 119.

48. GARF, 14 May 1987, TASS, f. R4459, o. 44, d. 8841, l. 75.

49. GARF, 9 April 1987, TASS, f. R4459, o. 44, d. 8840, l. 18. The latter expanded to include a Shia department. Keshtmand, *Political Notes*, 901–15. GARF, 1 January 1987, TASS,

f. R4459, o. 44, d. 8837, ll. 1–10. Giustozzi, *War*, 60; Khristoforov, *Afganistan*, 147. GARF, 30 December 1986, TASS, f. R4459, o. 44, d. 7573, l. 208. NSADC, "Afghanistan Situation Report April 13–April 19, 1987," USE, Afghanistan; RGANI, 1987, f. 117, o. 1, d. 16, l. 10.

50. RGANI, 1988, f. 117, o. 1, d. 22, ll. 14–18, 69–72, 107–8, 113; RGANI, 1988–89, f. 117, o. 1, d. 27, l. 47; GARF, 12 June 1986, TASS, f. R4459, o. 44, d. 7569, l. 220.

51. Pierre Centlivres, "Violence légitime et violence illégitime: À propos des pratiques et des représentations dans la crise afghane," *L'Homme, 37e Année* 144 (1997), 61.

52. AIC, *Monthly Bulletin*, no. 84, March 1988, 5.

53. AIC, *Monthly Bulletin*, no. 85, 14–20.

54. Cherneta, *Afghanistan*, 47; Gai and Snegirev, *Vtorzhenie*, 103.

55. AIC, *Monthly Bulletin*, no. 97, April 1989, 4–15.

56. GARF, 5 February 1987.

57. GARF, 5 February 1987.

58. GARF, 14 January 1987.

59. Plastun, Interview.

60. RGANI, 1988–89, f. 117, o. 1, d. 27, ll. 2–20. See also Kalinovsky, "Blind Leading the Blind," 23. Soviet advisers on a Moscow-Kabul flight chose the policy's name after the processes happening in post-Franco Spain.

61. GARF, 7 June 1986.

62. RGASPI, 25–27 July 1988, f. 797, o. 1, d 32, ll. 1–34.

63. KhAD head of department, Interview.

64. Pikov, *Spetspropagandist*, 38–39.

65. RGANI, 1985–86, f. 117, o. 1, d. 11, l. 45; RGANI, 1985, f. 117, o. 1, d. 13, ll. 1–4; RGANI, 1991, f. 117, o. 1, d. 6, ll. 4–5.

66. Shur, *Real'naya sushchnost'*, 17.

67. Arzumanov, Gubrii, Sokol, *Sovetskomu Voinu*, 4.

68. Chernyaev, *V Politburo*, 186; CWIHPDC, "Notes from Politburo Meeting," GFA, 22 May 1987.

69. GARF, 18 October 1987, TASS, f. R4459, o. 44, d. 8844, ll. 1–9.

70. GFA, 22 May 1987, f. 2, o. 1, d. 2; GFA, 3 December 1987, f. 2, o. 1, d. 2.

71. Chernyaev, *V Politburo*, 145.

72. Plastun, *Iznanka*, 309–10.

73. Gai and Snegirev, *Vtorzhenie*, 195–98.

74. Plastun, *Iznanka*, 208–9.

75. Lyakhovsky, *Tragediya*, 320–21, 336–37, 385; Slinkin, "Afganskie vstrechi"; Varennikov, *Nepovtorimoe*, ch. 7.

76. Quoted in Tasar, "Central Asian Muftiate," 219.

77. Plastun and Andrianov, *Nadzhibulla*, 214–15.

78. Maiorov, *Pravda*, ch. 12.

79. Dzhamshid Amiri, "Farid Akhmad Mazdak," Afghanistan.ru, 9 August 2016.

80. Plastun, *Iznanka*, 186.

81. Azimi, *Army*, Loc. 5714, 7452. Azimi attributes some of national reconciliation's success to Karmal.

82. Shevardnadze, *Kogda rukhnul*, 91–98.

83. Varennikov, *Nepovtorimoe*, chs. 1, 7. Chief military advisers represented the Ministry of Defense. Until Varennikov, they reported to the head of the Operational

Group of the Ministry of Defense, Marshal Sergei Sokolov until 1985. In 1985, Varennikov took Sokolov's position but was now based in Kabul.

84. Slinkin, "Afganskie vstrechi," 21. See also Maiorov, *Pravda*, ch. 10.

85. Plastun, *Iznanka*, 322, 354–56.

86. Vorotnikov, *Bylo eto tak*, 124.

87. KhAD head of department, Interview.

88. Slinkin, "Afganskie vstrechi," 21. Some Western accounts downplayed Najibullah's role. Tomsen, *Afghanistan*, 226.

89. Egorychev, *Soldat*, 322; Gromov, *Kontingent*, 238–39; Plastun, *Iznanka*, 682; RGANI, 1988, f. 117, o. 1, d. 22, ll. 14–18, 69–72, 107–8, 113; RGANI, 1988–89, f. 117, o. 1, d. 27, l. 47.

90. Adamishin, Interview.

91. GFA, 20 July 1987, 9.

92. Rubin, *Fragmentation of Afghanistan*, 171–74. Plastun, *Iznanka*, 375–83, 410–13 has an analysis of the regime's tribal policy. Kakar, *Afghanistan*, 169–85, 253–77 notes its relative success under Najibullah. RGANI, 1988–89, f. 117, o. 1, d. 27, ll. 2–20. Polyanichko stresses the importance of the policies on minorities.

93. GFA, 20 July 1987.

94. NSADC, "Zapis' besedy M.S. Gorbacheva s prezidentom Afganistana," 7 April 1988, GFA.

95. NSADC, "Zapis' besedy M.S. Gorbacheva s chlenom politbyuro TSK NDPA," GFA, 9 September 1988; Khalqis told Gorbachev that Najibullah had to resign in favor of a nonparty figure and that no negotiation with the mujahideen would be possible until that happened. Azimi, *Army*, Loc. 8167.

96. RGANI, 1988–89, f. 117, o. 1, d. 27, ll. 2–20.

97. RGASPI, 1988, f. 797, o. 1, d 34, ll. 14–19.

98. Egorychev, *Soldat*, 309–11.

99. Plastun, *Iznanka*, 209, 223, 283.

100. Plastun, *Iznanka*, 35.

101. Plastun and Andrianov, *Nadzhibulla*, 83. Polyanichko mentions the military's limited interest in national reconciliation. RGANI, 1988–89, f. 117, o. 1, d. 27, ll. 2–26.

102. Plastun and Andrianov, *Nadzhibulla*, 228. Azimi, *Army*, Loc. 5847.

103. Plastun, *Iznanka*, 342, 414.

104. RGANI, 16 November 1987, f. 84, o. 1, d 348, ll. 1–8.

105. Plastun, Interview notes that such opinions existed.

106. Slinkin, "Afganskie besedy," 10.

107. RGANI, 16 March 1988, f. 84, o. 1, d 348, ll. 9–20.

108. RGANI, 16 March 1988, f. 84, o. 1, d 348, ll. 9–20.

109. NSADC, "Postanovlenie Sekretarya TSK Kommunisticheskoi partii Sovetskogo Soyuza," 13 February 1988, 20.

110. Knyazev, Interview.

111. RGASPI, 5 October 1988, f. 797, o. 1, d 33, l. 148.

112. GARF, 6 July 1987, TASS, f. R4459, o. 44, d. 8842, l. 105.

113. GARF, 11 September 1987, TASS, f. R4459, o. 44, d. 8843, l. 158.

114. Lyakhovsky, *Tragediya*, 348–49.

115. GARF, 8 September 1987, TASS, f. R4459, o. 44, d. 8843, ll. 140–41.

116. Egorychev, *Soldat*, 311; Rubin, *Fragmentation of Afghanistan*, 147. Polyanichko notes that one should not take such claims at face value. Many Afghans by then copied the Soviets' dry writing style for official documents. RGANI, 1988, f. 117, o. 1, d. 22, ll. 14–18, 69–72, 107–08, 113; RGANI, 1988–89, f. 117, o. 1, d. 27, l. 47.

117. Basov, "Interv'yu."

118. RGANI, 1988, f. 117, o. 1, d. 22, ll. 14–18, 69–72, 107–8, 113.

119. GARF, 8 September 1987.

120. GARF, 30 November 1987, TASS, f. R4459, o. 44, d. 8844, l. 191.

121. GARF, 1 December 1987, TASS, f. R4459, o. 44, d. 8844, l. 200.

122. AIC, *Monthly Bulletin*, no. 85, 14–20.

123. Giustozzi, *War*, 59–64.

124. Centlivres and Centlivres-Démont, Interview.

125. Shebarshin, *Ruka Moskvy*, 205–96.

126. AIC, *Monthly Bulletin*, no. 85, 14–20.

127. AIC, *Monthly Bulletin*, no. 111, June 1990, 24; Giustozzi, *War*, 156–57.

128. Plastun, *Iznanka*, 216.

129. Edwards, *Before Taliban*, 25–56.

130. Toporkov, *Afganistan*, 160.

131. Chernyaev, *V Politburo*, 187.

132. Biryukov, Interview.

133. Lyakhovsky, *Tragediya*, 369–71, 433, 465.

134. Gromyko, *Pamyatnoe*, 179–80.

135. Lyakhovsky, *Tragediya*, 344–49. See also Gareev, *Voina*, 67–68.

136. RGANI, 1988, f. 117, o. 1, d. 17, ll. 36–47.

137. IHEID, FCFA46, July 1987, AIC, "What o Afghan Refugees Think?"; IHEID, FCFA122, Centre de Recherches et d'études documentaires sur l'Afghanistan (CERE-DAF), no. 31, May 1987.

138. IHEID, FCFA122, CEREDAF, no. 32, June 1987; Kravtsov, Interview.

139. RGANI, 1988–89, f. 117, o. 1, d. 27, ll. 2–26.

140. Plastun, *Iznanka*, 619.

141. RGANI, 1988, f. 117, o. 1, d. 28, ll. 6–7.

142. Gromov, *Kontingent*, 241; Lyakhovsky, *Tragediya*, 385; Plastun and Andrianov, *Nadzhibulla*, 76–78, 211.

143. NSADC, 7 April 1988.

144. Saikal, *Modern Afghanistan*, 205.

145. IHEID, FCFA133/1, June 1988, Jean-José Puig, Lettre.

146. "Report," 26 February 1988, E/CN.4/1988/25, UN. digitallibrary.un.org; GARF, 19 August 1987, TASS, f. R4459, o. 44, d. 8843, l. 60. This report was criticized by the *mujahideen*. *AFGHANews* 3, no. 24, 15 December 1987, 8.

147. IHEID, July 1987.

148. GARF, 1 December 1987, TASS, f. R4459, o. 44, d. 8844, l. 212.

149. AIC, *Monthly Bulletin*, no. 85, 14–20.

150. Coll, *Ghost Wars*; Plastun, *Iznanka*, 21–188; Andrew Hartman, "The 'Red Template': US Policy in Soviet-Occupied Afghanistan," *Third World Quarterly* 23, no. 3, (2002): 467–89; Mahmood Mamdani, *Good Muslim, Bad Muslim: America, the Cold War, and the Roots of Terror* (New York: Pantheon Books, 2004), 156–58; John Prados, "Notes on the

CIA's Secret War in Afghanistan," *Journal of American History* 89, no. 2, (2002): 466–71. NSADC, "Oral History Interview with Ambassador Dean," 6 September 2000, Carter Presidential Library (CPL). Dean, the American ambassador in India from 1985 to 1988, recalled: "Covertly, we supported the Islamic fundamentalist Gulbuddin Hekmatyar who received the lion share of the arms and funds provided to the Afghan resistance. He was at the time 'America's man.'"

151. GARF, 1992–93, f. 10026, o. 4, d 3387, ll. 1–26. Victor Spolnikov, *Afganistan, Islamskaya oppositsiya* (Moscow: Nauka, 1990), 42, 66, 109.

152. Coll, *Ghost Wars*, 181; Edwards, *Before Taliban*, 177–279.

153. *AFGHANews*, 22 October 1985, 1.

154. Edwards, *Caravan of Martyrs*, 56, 68–69.

155. Centlivres, "Violence Légitime," 59.

156. Barfield, *Afghanistan*, 174–224.

157. Jolanta Sierakowska-Dyndo, "Peculiarity of the Afghan Clergy," *Afghanica* 4, no. 6–7 (March–September 1990): 14–17.

158. RGASPI, 3 September 1988, f. 797, o. 1, d 33, ll. 8–9.

159. NSADC, Barnett R. Rubin, "The Situation in Afghanistan," 3 May 1990, USC, 8.

160. Spolnikov, *Afganistan*, 120–21, 165–66. Varennikov, *Nepovtorimoe*, ch. 6 notes a similar idea. See also Edwards, *Before Taliban*, 178.

161. Lyakhovsky, *Tragediya*, 508.

162. Alexander Lyakhovsky and Vyacheslav Nekrasov, *Grazhdanin, politik, voin* (Moscow: Grif i K, 2007); Varennikov, *Nepovtorimoe*, chs. 6–7.

163. Knyazev, Interview.

164. Varennikov, *Nepovtorimoe*, chs. 4, 7. Basov, "Interv'yu" suggests that the concessions floated to Massoud were extensive. The GRU was criticized for that in the Kremlin in 1988. Gorbachev, *Otvechaya na vyzov*, 652.

165. RGASPI, 25–27 July 1988, f. 797, o. 1, d 32, ll. 1–34; RGANI, 1988–89, f. 117, o. 1, d. 27, ll. 2–26.

166. *AFGHANews*, 11 November 1985, 1; *AFGHANews* 3, no. 10, 15 May 1987, 4; *AFGHANews* 3, no. 13, 1 July 1987, 9.

167. *AFGHANews*, 4 December 1985, 3.

168. Edwards, *Caravan of Martyrs*, 64–66.

169. *AFGHANews* 3, no. 4, 1 January 1987, 6.

170. *AFGHANews* 3, no. 11, 1 June 1987, 6.

171. Bennigsen and Marie Broxup wrote in AFGHANews: *AFGHANews* 3, no. 8, 15 April 1987, 4; *AFGHANews* 3, no. 19, 15 September 1987, 4, 9.

172. *AFGHANews* 3, no. 14, 15 July 1987, 1–3.

173. *AFGHANews* 4, no. 10, 15 May 1988, 8.

174. *News of Jihad* 13, 26 August 1987, 2–3.

175. Lyakhovsky, *Tragediya*, 459–60. Kakar, *Afghanistan*, 263 argues that the mujahideen could not ignore national reconciliation.

176. *AFGHANews* 3, no. 20, 15 October 1987, 6.

177. *AFGHANews* 3, no. 21, 1 November 1987, 4–6.

178. Halliday, "Soviet Foreign Policymaking," 689.

179. Cordovez and Harrison, *Out of Afghanistan*, 245.

5. The USSR, Afghanistan, and the Muslim World

Epigraph: CWIHPDC, "Record of a conversation of M.S. Gorbachev with Italian Minister of Foreign Affairs," 27 February 1987, GFA.

1. NARADC, USDoS, Kabul, 3 August 197.

2. Azimi, *Army*, Loc. 5353; Chernyaev, *Diary*, 9 March 1981. This chapter is derived in part from an article published in the *Cold War History* journal on 2 October 2022, copyright to Taylor & Francis, available at https://www.tandfonline.com/doi/full/10.1080/14682745.2022.2103114. See Vassily A. Klimentov, "In Search of Islamic Legitimacy: The USSR, the Afghan Communists and the Muslim World," *Cold War History* 23, no. 2 (2022): 283–305.

3. UN, Resolution *35/37. Afghanistan*, 20 November 1980, digitallibrary.un.org.

4. Robert O. Freedman, *Moscow and the Middle East, Soviet Policy since the Invasion of Afghanistan* (London: Cambridge University Press, 1991), 318–20.

5. UN, Resolution *36/34. Afghanistan*, 18 November 1981, digitallibrary.un.org.

6. Grachev, Interview. See also Brutents, *Tridtsat' let*, part 4, ch. 5; Kirpichenko, *Razvedka*, 363.

7. NARADC, USDoS, Cairo, 26 November 1979; Gates, *From the Shadows*, 250.

8. NARADC, USDoS, Abu Dhabi, 31 December 1979; NARADC, USDoS, Cairo, 30 December 1979.

9. NSADC, "Zapis' osnovnogo soderzhaniya besedy A.A. Gromyko," RGANI, 4 January 1980, f. 89, o. 14, d. 36.

10. KhAD head of department, Interview.

11. GARF, 24 January 1980, TASS, f. R4459, o. 43, d. 22314, l. 2.

12. Aydin, *Idea of the Muslim World*, 214; Gates, *From the Shadows*, 82.

13. Lyakhovsky, *Tragediya*, 171–74.

14. GARF, 27 December 1980, TASS, f. R4459, o. 43, d. 22936, l. 290; GARF, 6 June 1981, TASS, f. R4459, o. 44, d. 689, l. 11.

15. NARADC, USDoS, Cairo, 31 December 1979.

16. NSADC, "Al Azhar Attacks Soviets," USDoS, Egypt, 20 January 1980.

17. NSADC, "Sadat Address to Joint Session," USDoS, Egypt, 3 November 1980. By 1982, after Sadat, the Arab League would start rethinking its position on the Arab-Israel conflict and improving its relations with Egypt. Abdel Monem Said Aly, Shai Feldman, and Khalil Shikaki, *Arabs and Israelis: Conflict and Peacemaking in the Middle East* (London: Red Globe Press, 2013), 225.

18. Adkin and Yousaf, *Bear Trap*, 26. See also Leake, *Afghan Crucible*, 107–31.

19. NSADC, Primakov, 11–12.

20. Gates, *From the Shadows*, 92; Coll, *Ghost Wars*, 103.

21. NSADC, "The U.S. and the Islamic World," 27 November 1979, US National Security Council (NSC).

22. NSADC, "Soviet Intervention in Afghanistan," 31 December 1979, USNSC.

23. NSADC, "Radio Liberty Broadcasts," USDoS, 11 January 1980.

24. NSADC, "Current Foreign Relations, Issue No. 8, February 20, 1980," USDoS.

25. RGANI, 28 January 1980.

26. RGANI, 28 January 1980.

27. RGANI, 1980, f. 4, o. 44, d. 26, ll. 24–30, 119–20, 157–59.

28. GARF, 1984, f. R9587, o. 4, d. 90; GARF, 1985, f. R9587, o. 4, d. 242; GARF, July–December 1985, f. R9587, o. 4, d. 243; GARF, 1986, f. R9587, o. 4, d. 417; GARF, 1987, f. R9587, o. 4, d. 603; GARF, 1987, f. R9587, o. 4, d. 604.

29. Grachev, Interview.

30. Y. Volkov et al., *The Truth about Afghanistan* (Moscow: Novosti Press Agency Publishing House, 1980).

31. Volkov, *Truth,* 57–58.

32. Kalinovsky, *Long Goodbye,* 56–57.

33. Volkov, *Truth,* 59–62.

34. All newspaper names are transliterated based on the Russian sources for consistency.

35. GARF, 16 March 1980, TASS, f. R4459, o. 43, d. 22933, l. 56.

36. CWIHPDC, "KGB Active Measures," Mitrokhin Archives, April 2004; Mitrokhin, *KGB in Afghanistan,* 140, 150. Mitrokhin claims that in this instance the aim was to influence the PDPA by showing how the United States instrumentalized disagreements between Khalq and Parcham.

37. RGANI, April–June 1982, f. 5, o. 88, d. 121, l. 1.

38. GARF, 21 January 1986, TASS, f. R4459, o. 44, d. 7565, l. 239.

39. GARF, 31 January 1986, TASS, f. R4459, o. 44, d. 7566, l. 45.

40. GARF, 4 November 1985, TASS, f. R4459, o. 44, d. 1615, ll. 114–17.

41. On the DRA media: GARF, January–June 1987, f. R9587, o. 4, d. 603, ll. 89–94, 116; GARF, August 1987, f. 9587, o. 4, d. 604, l. 16.

42. *AFGHANews 5,* no. 21, 1 November 1989, 8.

43. KhAD head of department, Interview.

44. Halliday, "Islam and Soviet Foreign Policy," 218.

45. Ro'i, *Islam in the Soviet Union,* 589. See also Tasar, *Soviet and Muslim,* 242–98.

46. NARADC, USDoS, 11 May 1979.

47. RGANI, March–July 1979, f. 5, o. 76, d. 186, ll. 1–3.

48. Garthoff, *Détente and Confrontation,* 1033; Kalinovsky, *Long Goodbye,* 57.

49. Roman Silantyev, "Mezhdunarodnaya deyatel'nost' dukhovnykh upravlenii musul'man SSSR v gody perestroiki (1985–1991 gg.)," *Vlast'* 22, no. 3 (2014): 154–56.

50. GARF, 22 May 1986, f. R6991, o. 6, d. 3377.

51. GARF, 22 May 1986, f. R6991, o. 6, d. 3378.

52. GARF, 28 August 1986, f. R6991, o. 6, d. 3376, ll. 137–38.

53. GARF, 28 August 1986, f. R6991, o. 6, d. 3376, ll. 137–38.

54. GARF, August 1990, f. P9578, o. 21, d. 83, l. 6.

55. GARF, January–August 1991, f. P9576, o. 20, d. 6485, ll. 103–23.

56. GARF, 14 January 1987, f. R6991, o. 6, d. 3376, ll. 182–95.

57. GARF, 14 January 1987, f. R6991, o. 6, d. 3376, ll. 182–95.

58. NARADC, USDoS, Kabul, 30 May 1978; NARADC, USDoS, Kabul, 31 May 1978.

59. RGANI, June 1978–January 1979, f. 5, o. 75, d. 1181, l. 16.

60. NSADC, "Puzzlement of the East German Ambassador," 11 July 1979, USE, Afghanistan; NSADC, RGANI, 6 June 1979, f. 5, o. 76, d. 1044, ll. 47–51.

61. RGANI, January 1979–September 1979, f. 5, o. 76, d. 1043, ll. 51–58.

62. Snegirev and Samunin, *Virus "A,"* ch. 5; Welch and Westad, *Intervention in Afghanistan,* 153–56.

63. Adamishin, *Raznye Gody,* 48.

64. NSADC, "O zayavlenie vsemirnogo Soveta mira," 14 June 1979; NSADC, "Ob opublikovanii dokumenta Organizatsii Solidarnosti narodov Azii i Afriki," 20 June 1979.

65. Mitrokhin, *KGB in Afghanistan*, 105–6.

66. RGANI, 4 January 1980.

67. Mitrokhin, *KGB in Afghanistan*, 105–6.

68. Mitrokhin, *KGB in Afghanistan*. Mitrokhin mentions this about the Soviets meeting representatives of Muslim countries in Beijing. One can assume that Moscow sent similar instructions to other Soviet embassies.

69. "Situation, June 30–July 7, 1981." Algeria called on Syria not to open an embassy in Afghanistan.

70. GARF, 27 October 1981, TASS, f. R4459, o. 44, d. 86, l. 71; GARF, 15 April 1986, TASS, f. R4459, o. 44, d. 7568, ll. 127–28.

71. GARF, 26 September 1982, TASS, f. R4459, o. 44, d. 1617, l. 278; Brutents, *Tridtsat' let*, part 4, ch. 3; GARF, 28 April 1983, TASS, f. R4459, o. 44, d. 3112, l. 164.

72. GARF, 13 May 1985, TASS, f. R4459, o. 44, d. 6177, l. 93; GARF, 7 January 1987, TASS, f. R4459, o. 44, d. 8837, l. 145; GARF, 11 November 1985, TASS, f. R4459, o. 44, d. 6180, l. 170; GARF, 24 February 1986, TASS, f. R4459, o. 44, d. 7566, l. 268; GARF, 6 June 1987, TASS, f. R4459, o. 44, d. 8841, l. 219.

73. *AFGHANews* 3, no. 12, 1 June 1987, 5.

74. James Clay Moltz and Dennis B. Ross, "The Soviet Union and the Iran-Iraq War, 1980–88," in *Soviet Strategy in the Middle East*, ed. George W. Breslauer (Boston: Unwin Hyman, 1990), 123–49; GARF, 26 May 1985, TASS, f. R4459, o. 44, d. 6177, l. 162.

75. GARF, 10 December 1987, TASS, f. R4459, o. 44, d. 8845, l. 32.

76. GARF, 12 November 1985, TASS, f. R4459, o. 44, d. 6180, l. 181.

77. Galia Golan, *Soviet Policies in the Middle East from World War Two to Gorbachev* (London: Cambridge University Press, 1990), 155; Fred Halliday, "Gorbachev and the 'Arab syndrome': Soviet Policy in the Middle East," *World Policy Journal* 4, no. 3 (1987): 418. Brutents, *Tridtsat' let*, part 4, ch. 3.

78. GFA, 20 July 1987.

79. Khristoforov, *Afganistan*, 120–21.

80. IHEID, FCFA133/1, August 1990, Puig, Jean-José, "Afghanistan," 12–15; RGANI, 13 May 1989, f. 89, o. 10, d. 35, ll. 1–4; Plastun, *Iznanka*, 539, 595.

81. Daurov, *Zapisi*, 14–15, 25.

82. RGANI, 1979–85, f. 117, o. 1, d. 39, l. 29.

83. Brutents, *Tridtsat' let*, part 4, ch 3.

84. Melvin A Goodman and Carolyn McGiffert Ekedahl, "Gorbachev's 'New Directions' in the Middle East," *Middle East Journal* 42, no. 4 (1988): 579.

85. Samuel Helfont, "Islam in Saudi Foreign Policy: The Case of Ma'ruf al-Dawalibi," *International History Review* 42, no. 3 (2020): 449–64.

86. RGANI, 1987, f. 117, o. 1, d. 16, l. 11; Vorotnikov, *Bylo eto tak*, 207. See also Saikal, *Modern Afghanistan*, 199.

87. GARF, 11 August 1981, TASS, f. R4459, o. 44, d. 84, l. 237.

88. GARF, 20 April 1984, TASS, f. R4459, o. 44, d. 4571, l. 92.

89. GARF, 20 November 1984, TASS, f. R4459, o. 44, d. 4574, ll. 169–70.

90. NSADC, Primakov, 16–18.

91. GARF, 14 April 1982, TASS, f. R4459, o. 44, d. 1615, l. 308.

92. GARF, 11 January 1986, TASS, f. R4459, o. 44, d. 7565, ll. 41, 110–11. Leftist Pakistani exiles, including Pashtun and Baluch leaders with tribal links in Afghanistan, also lived in Kabul. Cordovez and Harrison, *Out of Afghanistan*, 152.

93. AIC, *Monthly Bulletin*, no. 38, May 1984; AIC, *Monthly Bulletin*, no. 61, April 1986.

94. GARF, 19 December 1987, TASS, f. R4459, o. 44, d. 8845, l. 57.

95. GARF, 5 December 1985, TASS, f. R4459, o. 44, d. 6181, l. 40.

96. Gates, *From the Shadows*, 130; Kravtsov, Interview downplays these concerns; Lyakhovsky, *Tragediya*, 121.

97. NARADC, USDoS, Moscow, 30 March 1979; Chernyaev, *Diary 1986*, 27 November 1986.

98. NARADC, USDoS, Moscow, 13 March 1979.

99. Halliday, "Islam and Soviet Foreign Policy," 221–22. On USSR-Iran relations: Friedman, *Ripe for Revolution*, 211–65; Timothy Nunan, "'Doomed to Good Relations': The USSR, the Islamic Republic of Iran, and Anti-Imperialism in the 1980s," *Journal of Cold War Studies* 24, no 1 (2022): 39–77.

100. RGANI, March 1979–April 1980, f. 5, o. 76, d. 1055, ll. 1–54.

101. Grachev, Interview.

102. RGANI, 23 June 1980.

103. Grachev, Interview; Dmitry Asinovskiy, "'A Priest Does Not Consider the Toppling of the Shah as an Option': The KGB and the Revolution in Iran," *Iranian Studies* (2022): 11–13.

104. Shebarshin, *Ruka Moskvy*, 144–47.

105. KhAD head of department, Interview.

106. NARADC, USDoS, Moscow, 22 November 1979.

107. RGANI, 9 June 1980, f. 89, o. 32, d. 33, ll. 1–4; RGANI, 11 July 1980, f. 89, o. 39, d. 22, ll. 1–3.

108. GARF, 22 July 1980, TASS, f. R4459, o. 43, d. 22935, l. 224.

109. Friedman, *Ripe for Revolution*, Loc. 5239; Grachev, Interview, notes: "Tudeh's communists played a very prominent role; they were almost the first victims of the shah's regime. . . . Even the arrival of Khomeini, at the beginning, it did not look like the announcement of some green flag of Islam coming"; NSADC, "Soviet Policy toward Iran and the Strategic Balance," USC, 7 October 1986, 24–28.

110. NSADC, RGANI, 10 October 1979, f. 5, o. 76, d. 1355, ll. 17–20.

111. RGANI, 28 January 1980.

112. RGANI, 8 July 1980, f. 89, o. 39, d. 6, ll. 1–13.

113. Abdul Wakil, "Iran's Relations with Afghanistan after the Islamic Revolution," *Orient* 32, no. 1 (1991): 99–100.

114. GARF, 25 April 1979, TASS, f. R4459, o. 43, d. 20976, l. 34.

115. NARADC, USDoS, Kabul, 21 August 1979.

116. RGANI, April–October 1979, f. 5, o. 76, d. 1042, ll. 3–7; RGANI, March 1979–February 1980, f. 5, o. 76, d. 1046, ll. 80–90.

117. RGANI, March 1979–February 1980, f. 5, o. 76, d. 1046, ll. 80–90; NARADC, USDoS, Cairo, 31 December 1979.

118. GARF, 13 January 1980, TASS, f. R4459, o. 43, d. 22311, ll. 271–76.

119. Rubin, *Fragmentation of Afghanistan*, 115.

120. GARF, 21 January 1980, TASS, f. R4459, o. 43, d. 22313, l. 159.

121. "Suleiman Laik," Afghanistan.ru; Keshtmand, *Political Notes*, 650–51; Wakil, "Iran's Relations," 101.

122. GARF, 28 January 1980, TASS, f. R4459, o. 43, d. 22314, l. 245; GARF, 7 March 1980, TASS, f. R4459, o. 43, d. 22318, l. 171.

123. GARF, 6 February 1980, TASS, f. R4459, o. 43, d. 22315, l. 209.

124. M. Danesch and D. Wild, "Ist das die europäische Kultur?" *Spiegel*, 30 June 1980.

125. Mikhail Slinkin, *Afganskie stranitsy istorii* (Simferopol: TGU, 2003), 19.

126. GARF, 24 March 1980, TASS, f. R4459, o. 43, d. 22319, l. 168.

127. GARF, 29 April 1980, TASS, f. R4459, o. 43, d. 22934, l. 90.

128. GARF, 28 August 1980, TASS, f. R4459, o. 43, d. 22326, l. 220.

129. Freedman, *Moscow and the Middle East*, 126–28; Golan, *Soviet Policies*, 171; NARADC, USDoS, Baghdad, 18 January 1979.

130. Shebarshin, *Ruka Moskvy*, 166.

131. GARF, 14 April 1981, TASS, f. R4459, o. 44, d. 688, l. 242; Wakil, "Iran's Relations," 102.

132. Asinovskiy, "Priest Does Not Consider," 16–17; Moltz and Ross, "The Soviet Union," 126.

133. GARF, 22 June 1980, TASS, f. R4459, o. 43, d. 22934, l. 336.

134. Freedman, *Moscow and the Middle East*, 99; Friedman, *Ripe for Revolution*, Loc. 5576; RGANI, 20 February 1981, f. 2, o. 6, d. 281, l. 11.

135. GARF, 24 August 1981, TASS, f. R4459, o. 44, d. 689, ll. 94–98.

136. GARF, 26 January 1982, TASS, f. R4459, o. 44, d. 1614, l. 110.

137. Wakil, "Iran's Relations," 102, 112.

138. Shebarshin, *Ruka Moskvy*, 183.

139. Halliday, "Islam and Soviet Foreign Policy," 221; RGANI, 23 January 1991, f. 89, o. 4, d. 27, l. 1. The USSR provided asylum to Iranian communists in the 1980s.

140. Moltz and Ross, "The Soviet Union," 133–37; Wakil, "Iran's Relations," 102, 108.

141. "Soviet Policy toward Iran," 40.

142. GARF, 25 July 1983, TASS, f. R4459, o. 44, d. 3113, l. 192.

143. GARF, 13 March 1984, TASS, f. R4459, o. 44, d. 4570, l. 195; GARF, 9 February 1985, TASS, f. R4459, o. 44, d. 6175, l. 263.

144. GARF, 22 October 1986, TASS, f. R4459, o. 44, d. 7572, l. 120.

145. GARF, 12 July–25 August 1984, TASS, f. R4459, o. 44, d. 4573, ll. 105, 136.

146. GARF, 25 December 1984, TASS, f. R4459, o. 44, d. 4575, ll. 71–72.

147. GARF, 10 April 1985, TASS, f. R4459, o. 44, d. 6176, l. 189.

148. GARF, 11 January 1987, TASS, f. R4459, o. 44, d. 8837, l. 181.

149. RGANI, 4 July 1986, f. 89, o. 13, d. 2, ll. 1–7.

150. NSADC, "Ambassador Dean's Cable," 27 November 1987, USE, New Delhi.

151. NSADC, "Excerpt from Record of Conversation between Mikhail Gorbachev and George Shultz," 22 February 1988, GFA, f. 1, o. 1. NSADC, "Excerpt from Record of Conversation between Mikhail Gorbachev and George Shultz," 22 April 1988, GFA, f. 1, o. 1.

152. NSADC, "Stenogramma soveshchaniya provedennogo t. Yakovlevym A.N.," 22 February 1988, GARF, f. 10003, o. 1, d. 248 (?).

153. *AFGHANews* 4, no. 4, 15 February 1988, 8.

154. Sergey Radchenko, *Unwanted Visionaries: The Soviet Failure in Asia at the End of the Cold War* (London: Oxford University Press, 2014), 108. Grachev handled the response, noting the Soviets "would not change their red flag for the green flag." Grachev, Interview.

155. *AFGHANews 5*, no. 13, 1 July 1989, 1–3.

156. Wakil, "Iran's Relations," 115; Azimi, *Army*, Loc. 10167.

157. RGANI, 16 August 1989, f. 89, o. 10, d. 46, ll. 1–13.

158. Kalinovsky, *Long Goodbye*, 193.

159. Quoted in Wakil, "Iran's Relations," 108, 115.

160. KhAD head of department, Interview.

161. KhAD head of department, Interview.

162. GARF, 15 March 1979, TASS, f. R4459, o. 43, d. 20974, l. 206.

163. RGANI, March 1979–February 1980, f. 5, o. 76, d. 1046, ll. 69–81.

164. RGANI, April–October 1979, f. 5, o. 76, d. 1042, ll. 70–76.

165. GARF, 20 February 1980, TASS, f. R4459, o. 43, d. 22316, l. 229; GARF, 16 February 1980, TASS, f. R4459, o. 43, d. 22931, ll. 214–15.

166. GARF, 26 October 1982, TASS, f. R4459, o. 44, d. 1618, l. 88.

167. GARF, 30 November 1983, TASS, f. R4459, o. 44, d. 3114, l. 177. On the situation in Lebanon: Said Aly, Feldman and Shikaki, *Arabs*, 204.

168. GARF, 18 September 1984, TASS, f. R4459, o. 44, d. 4573, l. 142.

169. Quoted in Roland Dannreuther, *The Soviet Union and the PLO* (London: Macmillan, 1998), 105–7.

170. Gates, *From the Shadows*, 274.

171. Primakov, *Konfidentsial'no*, 36; Goodman and McGiffert Ekedahl, "Gorbachev's 'New Directions,'" 584.

172. RGANI, 7 July 1983, f. 89, o. 42, d. 64, ll. 1–8.

173. GFA, 9 February 1988, f. 2, o. 1, d. 3; Gorbachev did meet Arafat. Goodman and McGiffert Ekedahl, "Gorbachev's 'New Directions,'" 578.

174. Said Aly, Feldman and Shikaki, *Arabs*, 197; RGANI, March 1979–February 1980, f. 5, o. 76, d. 1046, ll. 69–81.

175. GARF, 22 January 1980, TASS, f. R4459, o. 43, d. 22313, ll. 180–82.

176. GARF, 10 April 1980, TASS, f. R4459, o. 43, d. 22320, l. 170; GARF, 20 August 1981, TASS, f. R4459, o. 44, d. 84, l. 347.

177. GARF, 29 March 1981, TASS, f. R4459, o. 44, d. 82, ll. 16–17.

178. GARF, 3 January 1981, TASS, f. R4459, o. 44, d. 79, ll. 17–25.

179. Dannreuther, *Soviet Union and the PLO*, 110.

180. GARF, 4 May 1983, TASS, f. R4459, o. 44, d. 3112, l. 189.

181. GARF, 27 June 1984, TASS, f. R4459, o. 44, d. 4572, l. 78.

182. GARF, 17 July 1986, TASS, f. R4459, o. 44, d. 7570, l. 140.

183. Slinkin, *Afganskie Stranitsy*, 46.

184. *AFGHANews 5*, No. 13, 1 July 1989, 1–3.

185. *AFGHANews 4*, no. 1, 1 January 1988, 7.

186. "Mujahideen Leader Meets PLO," *Southeast Asian & Afghanistan Review* 9, 15 (1989): 5.

187. IHEID, FCFA122, CEREDAF, no. 66, February 1991; *AFGHANews 6*, no. 9, 1 May 1990; Darmanger, *Afghanistan*, 203–05; Gareev, *Voina*, 73; Khristoforov, *Afganistan*, 118; Plastun, *Iznanka*, 593; Toporkov, *Afganistan*, 154.

188. *AFGHANews* 3, no. 18, 15 September 1987, 1–2.

189. *AFGHANews* 4, no. 21, 1 November 1987, 9.

190. *AFGHANews* 2, no. 22, 15 November 1986.

191. *AFGHANews* 4, no. 2, 15 January 1988, 7.

192. *AFGHANews* 4, no. 2, 15 January 1988, 7.

193. Aydin, *Idea of the Muslim World*, 191.

194. Tasar, *Soviet and Muslim*, 281–86. The Saudis refused to have Soviet students come study in their country. Tasar has a different interpretation of the MWL-SADUM contacts.

195. Turan Kayaoglu, *The Organization of Islamic Cooperation: Politics, Problems and Potential* (New York: Routledge, 2015), 6.

196. Aydin, *Idea of the Muslim World*, 211.

197. Syed Sharifuddin Pirzada, "Pakistan and the OIC," *Pakistan Horizon* 40, no. 2 (1987): 25.

198. GARF, 8 April 1980, TASS, f. R4459, o. 43, d. 22320, l. 88.

199. Khristoforov, *Afganistan*, 148.

200. GARF, 29 May 1980, TASS, f. R4459, o. 43, d. 22322, l. 88.

201. Organisation of the Islamic Conference (OIC), *R19/11-P*, 17–22 May 1980, www.oic-oci.org.

202. Freedman, *Moscow and the Middle East*, 75.

203. GARF, 25 May 1980, TASS, f. R4459, o. 43, d. 22322, l. 180.

204. GARF, 23 May 1980, TASS, f. R4459, o. 43, d. 22322, l. 158.

205. OIC, *R3/3-P (IS)*, 25–8 January 1981, www.oic-oci.org.

206. Cordovez and Harrison, *Out of Afghanistan*, 64.

207. GARF, 28 January 1981, TASS, f. R4459, o. 44, d. 79, l. 253.

208. GARF, 7 June 1981, TASS, f. R4459, o. 44, d. 83, l. 113.

209. NSADC, "Foreign Relations," 10 June 1981, USE, Afghanistan.

210. OIC, *R9/4-P (IS)*, 16–19 January 1984, www.oic-oci.org.

211. GARF, 23 January 1984, TASS, f. R4459, o. 44, d. 4570, l. 73.

212. GARF, 14 May 1984, TASS, f. R4459, o. 44, d. 4571, l. 184.

213. Pirzada, "Pakistan and the OIC," 35.

214. GARF, 11 December 1985, TASS, f. R4459, o. 44, d. 6181, l. 72.

215. OIC, *R19/16-P*, 6–10 January 1986, www.oic-oci.org.

216. Tasar, *Soviet and Muslim*, 284–85.

217. *AFGHANews* 2, No. 2, 19 January 1986, 3.

218. IHEID, FCFA127/ 1–6, April 1986, Olivier Roy, "La résistance," CEREDAF, no. 21.

219. Silantyev, "Mezhdunarodnaya deyatel'nost'," 154–56; GARF, 5 December 1986, TASS, f. R4459, o. 44, d. 7573, l. 85.

220. RGANI, 1988–89, f. 117, o. 1, d. 27, ll. 2–20; GARF, 18 January 1987, TASS, f. R4459, o. 44, d. 8838, l. 8.

221. Slinkin, *Afganskie Stranitsy*, 44–45.

222. Carol R. Saivetz, "Islam and Gorbachev's Foreign Policy in the Middle East," *Journal of International Affairs* 42, no. 2 (1989): 443–44.

223. OIC, *R11/5-P(IS)*, 26–29 January 1987, www.oic-oci.org.

224. GARF, 3 February 1987, TASS, f. R4459, o. 44, d. 8838, l. 191.

225. CWIHPDC, "Report on meeting between Minister Chnoupek," 6 May 1987, State Central Archive Prague, 02/1.

226. Slinkin, *Afganskie Stranitsy*, 48.

227. Spolnikov, *Afganistan*, 128.

228. Kalinovsky, *Long Goodbye*, 122–46.

229. *AFGHANews* 3, no. 6 7, 1 April 1987, 6.

230. *AFGHANews* 3, no. 12, 1 June 1987, 5.

231. *AFGHANews* 3, no. 14, 15 July 1987, 1–3.

232. *AFGHANews* 3, no. 14, 15 July 1987, 1–3.

233. Kalinovsky, *Long Goodbye*, 147–78.

234. GFA, 22 May 1987.

235. GARF, 7 October 1987, TASS, f. R4459, o. 44, d. 8843, l. 247.

236. Freedman, *Moscow and the Middle East*, 279; Grachev, Interview.

237. Khristoforov, *Afganistan*, 120–21.

238. On Soviet-Afghan tensions over the Geneva Accords: Kalinovsky, *Long Goodbye*, 138–64.

239. OIC, *R23/17-P*, 21–5 March 1988, www.oic-oci.org.

240. Spolnikov, *Afganistan*, 143–44, 149–50.

241. OIC, *R18/18-P*, 13–6 March 1989, www.oic-oci.org.

242. Keith Tribe, ed., *Max Weber, Economy and Society, A New Translation* (London: Harvard University Press, 2019), 338–43.

6. Moscow's Islamist Threat

Epigraph: NSADC, "Zapis' besedy M.S. Gorbacheva s chlenom politburo TSK NDPA," GFA, 23 August 1990, 60.

1. Edwards, *Caravan of Martyrs*, 82.

2. Gai and Snegirev, *Vtorzhenie*, 197; RGASPI, 19 May 1988, f. 9797, o. 1, d. 34, l. 29; RGASPI, 15 August 1988, f. 797, o. 1, d. 30, ll. 15–17.

3. RGASPI, 1988, f. 797, o. 1, d. 33, ll. 145–46.

4. RGASPI, 25–27 July 1988, f. 797, o. 1, d. 32, ll. 1–34.

5. GFA, 20 February 1989.

6. Chernyaev, *V Politburo*, 310, 337, 353.

7. Chernyaev, *Diary 1989*, 20 January 1989; Gai and Snegirev, *Vtorzhenie*, 372–78; Lyakhovsky, *Tragediya*, 423, 454, 484–89. The Soviets discussed the possibility of air-strikes for the last time in March 1990. Even Shevardnadze was against it by then. On the Soviet negotiating team's view of the Geneva Accords: Kozyrev, *Zhenevskie soglasheniya*, 21–22; Saikal, *Modern Afghanistan*, 200–203.

8. Gareev, *Voina*, 198–99; Kalinovsky, *Long Goodbye*, 155; Spolnikov, *Afganistan*, 173–74.

9. RGANI, 13 May 1989.

10. AIC, *Monthly Bulletin*, no. 101, August 1989, 7.

11. AIC, *Monthly Bulletin*, no. 105–6, December 1989–January 1990, 16–177.

12. Leake, "Afghan Internationalism," 25–28. With so many Afghan Pashtuns taking refuge in Pakistan, the regime defined "being Afghan" as "living in Afghanistan," reinforcing non-Pashtuns' influence.

13. Centlivres and Centlivres-Démont, Interview.

14. Lyakhovsky, *Tragediya*, 541.

15. Plastun and Andrianov, *Nadzhibulla*, 46–47.

16. KhAD head of department, Interview.

17. *AFGHANews* 6, no. 10, 15 May 1990, 4–5.

18. AIC, *Monthly Bulletin*, no. 96, March 1989, 23, 26–28.

19. Plastun, *Iznanka*, 581–82.

20. Khristoforov, *Afganistan*, 289; Kucherova, *KGB*, 83.

21. Gareev, *Voina*, 145–47, 166.

22. Coll, *Ghost Wars*, 155, 201; KhAD head of department, Interview; Mamdani, *Good Muslim*, 126–28, 132–38. The number of Arab fighters is difficult to gauge. Coll estimates them at 4,000–5,000 fighters in 1980; others such as Mamdani and a KhAD officer suggest their overall number was around 30,000.

23. AIC, *Monthly Bulletin*, no. 97, April 1989, 15; Edwards, *Caravan of Martyrs*, 108.

24. Coll, *Ghost Wars*, 134, 200–201; Edwards, *Caravan of Martyrs*, 24.

25. AIC, *Monthly Bulletin*, no. 96, March 1989, 32.

26. Kravtsov, Interview.

27. LCST Veterans, Interview.

28. RGANI, 16 August 1989.

29. GARF, August 1990, f. P9578, o. 21, d. 83, l. 6; GARF, January–August 1991, f. P9576, o. 20, d. 6485, ll. 6–123.

30. AIC, *Monthly Bulletin*, no. 96, March 1989, 26; Kakar, *Afghanistan*, 265.

31. Yousaf and Adkin, *Bear Trap*, 33.

32. Coll, *Ghost Wars*, 181.

33. Lyakhovsky, *Tragediya*, 611–13; Plastun and Andrianov, *Nadzhibulla*, 6; Mikhail Slinkin. "Myatezh Generala Sh. N. Tanaya." *Kul'tura narodov Prichernomor'ya* 8 (1999): 94–100.

34. *The mujahideen*, April–May 1990, 4; *AFGHANews* 6, no. 7, April 1990, 6. The Tanai Coup marked the climax of the Soviet mismanagement of the Khalq-Parcham split. See also Tanai's comment: "Shahnawaz Tanai: Doktor Nadzhib," Afghanistan. ru, 26 August 2016.

35. AIC, *Monthly Bulletin*, no. 108, March 1990, 2.

36. Plastun, *Iznanka*, 607.

37. AIC, *Monthly Bulletin*, no. 118, January 1991; Tomsen, *Afghanistan*, 364. On mujahideen's disunion: Shah M. Tarzi. "Politics of the Afghan Resistance Movement: Cleavages, Disunity, and Fragmentation," *Asian Survey* 31, no. 6 (1990): 479–95.

38. AIC, *Monthly Bulletin*, no. 119, February 1991, 12.

39. Halliday and Tanin, "Communist Regime," 1375; KhAD head of department, Interview; Lyakhovsky, *Tragediya*, 577–79, 592–696; Plastun and Andrianov, *Nadzhibulla*, 187–97.

40. Gareev, *Voina*, 198–99.

41. *Afghan Jehad, Quarterly Magazine* 5, no. 1, October–December 1991, 22; *AFGHANews* 7, no. 23, 1 December 1991, 4. Amazingly, Rabbani led a prayer in a mosque in Moscow; Lyakhovsky, *Tragediya*, 586–89; Khristoforov, *Afganistan*, 292.

42. Kalinovsky, *Long Goodbye*, 199. This support was by then already limited, only 10 percent of the support contracted during the year reached Kabul in 1991.

43. Lyakhovsky, *Tragediya*, 601, 610.

44. Mitrokhin, *KGB in Afghanistan*, 116–17.

45. Musalov, *Pogony*, 38, 50–51.

46. Maiorov, *Pravda*, ch. 10.

47. NSADC, "KGB Chairman Viktor Chebrikov," Ukrainian KGB Archive, 12 January 1983, f. 13 o. 678, 117–34.

48. Marie Broxup, "Afghanistan According to Soviet Sources, 1980–1985," *Central Asian Survey* 7, no. 2/3 (1988): 197–204; Broxup, "New Developments," 32; Bennigsen, "Soviet Islam," 69–70; Broxup and Bennigsen argue the opposite. The United States similarly speculated as to a Soviet fear over Soviet Muslims embracing Islamism. NSADC, "Soviets Employ Kazakhs," 23 June 1987, USE, Afghanistan. See also Ro'i, *Bleeding Wound*, 254–55.

49. Kalinovsky, "Encouraging Resistance," *Reassessing Orientalism*, 21; Ro'i, *Islam in the Soviet Union*, 551–52; Tasar, *Soviet and Muslim*, 312–21.

50. "USSR: Domestic Fallout," CIA Intelligence Assessment, February 1988, 12, cia.gov

51. B.M. Babadzhanov, A. K. Muminov, and Martha Brill Olcott, "Mukhammadzhan Khindustani (1892–1989) i religioznaya sreda ego epokhi," *Vostok (Oriens)* 5 (2004): 43–59; Vitaly Naumkin, *Radical Islam in Central Asia: Between Pen and Rifle* (Lanham, MD: Rowman & Littlefield, 2005); Martha Brill Olcott, *Roots of Radical Islam in Central Asia* (Washington, DC: Carnegie, 2007).

52. Quoted in Ro'i, *Islam in the Soviet Union*, 346.

53. Quoted in Ro'i, *Islam in the Soviet Union*, 426. In Ro'i's study, these are the only examples of opposition to the Soviet-Afghan War. More may be available in CRA sources but such opinions were clearly not widespread.

54. Ro'i, *Islam in the Soviet Union*, 583. See also Ro'i, *Bleeding Wound*, 254–55, 273.

55. Kravtsov, Interview; Saivetz, "Islam and Gorbachev," 441.

56. KhAD head of department, Interview; Lyakhovsky, *Tragediya*, 330, 637; Varennikov, *Nepovtorimoe*, ch. 7.

57. KGB officer, Email.

58. GARF, 1992–93; Knyazev, *Istoriya*, 83. Knyazev argues that Azad Beg descended from the last ruler of Kokand and was related to the Pakistani general, Mirza Aslam Beg.

59. Varennikov, *Nepovtorimoe*, ch. 7.

60. Coll, *Ghost Wars*, 89.

61. Coll, *Ghost Wars*, 104–5; Ro'i, *Bleeding Wound*, 274–75. CIA operatives denied that the CIA was the one to push for cross-border operations in the USSR; the Pakistani claimed otherwise.

62. Adkin and Yousaf, *Bear Trap*, 189–206.

63. Adkin and Yousaf, *Bear Trap*; Coll, *Ghost Wars*, 162.

64. NSADC, "Mujahidin Reportedly Target Factory," 31 March 1987, USE, Afghanistan; NSADC, "Afghanistan: Correspondent Reports," 29 April 1987, USE, Pakistan.

65. Adkin and Yousaf, *Bear Trap*, 205.

66. NSADC, "Mujahidin Cross Border Cow Raid," 14 June 1987, US Consulate (USCO), Peshawar; NSADC, "Afghan Resistance Claims," 26 September 1987, USCO, Peshawar.

67. Adkin and Yousaf, *Bear Trap*, 205.

68. NSADC, "Iran: Afghans Infiltrate," 15 May 1987, US Foreign Broadcast Information Service (USFBIS), Cyprus; NSADC, "Iran: Soviet Muslims," 15 May 1987, US-FBIS, Cyprus.

69. Varennikov, *Nepovtorimoe*, ch 7.

70. NSADC, "Pravda Denies Dushman," 1 May 1987, USFBIS, London.

71. NSADC, "Belyayev Views," 21 May 1987, USFBIS, London.

72. Borovik, *Hidden War*, 10. Hekmatyar was more assertive about the need to bring the war to the USSR.

73. NSADC, "Jamiat-i-Islami Comment," 29 April 1987, USCO, Peshawar; NSADC, "A Mujahidin Cross-Border," 18 May 1987, USCO, Peshawar.

74. *AFGHANews* 3, no. 9, 1 May 1987, 9–10.

75. NSADC, 29 April 1987.

76. *AFGHANews*, 1 May 1987, 9–10; *AFGHANews* 3, no. 17, 1 September 1987, 9.

77. *AFGHANews* 3, no. 14, 15 July 1987, 9.

78. Davlat Khudonazarov, notes from meetings with Massoud, 1990–97. Khudonazarov writes: "Somewhere in the Panjshir Valley lives the one who had become an undisputed authority for all Tajiks on both sides of the Panj [Amu Darya River's tributary]."

79. Ro'i, *Islam in the Soviet Union*, 717. The number is claimed to be correct by Broxup, "New Developments," 34.

80. *AFGHANews* 3, no. 17, 1 September 1987, 1

81. *AFGHANews* 3, no. 13, 1 July 1987, 1.

82. NSADC, Primakov, May 1981, 16–18.

83. Radchenko, *Unwanted Visionaries*, 92.

84. Bhabani Sen Gupta. *The Afghan Syndrome: How to Live with Soviet Power* (London: Croom Helm, 1982), 12–18, 106–40.

85. Gates, *From the Shadows*, 252.

86. Cordovez and Harrison, *Out of Afghanistan*, 92, 162. US senator Charles Wilson contended that Zia "saw the world as a conflict between Muslims and Hindus." It is remarkable it was not between Muslims and non-Muslims or Islam and Communism.

87. NSADC, "Reagan Letter to Gandhi," 25 March 1987, CPL.

88. NSADC, "Memorandum of Conversation between Mikhail Gorbachev and Rajiv Gandhi," GFA, 2 July 1987, f. 1, o. 1.

89. Chernyaev, *V Politburo*, December 1986, 110–11.

90. Kryuchkov, *Lichnoe delo*, 231; Vorotnikov, *Bylo eto tak*, 136.

91. NSADC, "Cable from Ambassador Dean to Secretary of State," 11 July 1987, CPL.

92. GFA, 20 July 1987. Gorbachev said the same thing at the politburo in January 1987. Gorbachev, *Otvechaya na vyzov*, 610.

93. About the term's origins: Gerald Morgan, "Myth and Reality in the Great Game," *Asian Affairs* 4, no. 1 (1973): 55–65.

94. GFA, 20 July 1987.

95. "Ambassador Dean's Cable," 27 November 1987.

96. "Ambassador Dean's Cable," 27 November 1987. The PDPA also engaged in such negotiations: NSADC, 7 April 1988.

97. NSADC, "Zapis' besedy M.S. Gorbacheva s Nadzhibulloi," 23 August 1990.

98. NSADC, "Ambassador Dean Cable," 4 December 1987, CPL.

99. NSADC, "Reagan Letter to Gandhi," 18 December 1987, CPL.

100. NSADC, "Gandhi Letter to Reagan," 24 December 1987, CPL.

101. NSADC, "Reagan Message to Rajiv Gandhi," February 1988, CPL.

102. NSADC, "Reagan Message to Rajiv Gandhi," February 1988, CPL.

103. NSADC, "Secretary of State Cable to Amembassy New Delhi," 11 February 1988, CPL.

104. NSADC, 6 September 2000.

105. NSADC, "Ambassador Dean Cable to Secretary of State," 3 June 1988, CPL; Deepak Tripathi, "India's Foreign Policy: The Rajiv Factor," *The World Today* 44, no. 7 (1988): 112–14.

106. NSADC, "Cable from Ambassador Raphel, Islamabad, to Secretary of State," 5 June 1988, CPL. See note 58 about Azad Beg.

107. NSADC, "Cable from Ambassador Raphel, Islamabad, to Secretary of State," 5 June 1988, CPL.

108. NSADC, "Ambassador Dean Cable to Secretary of State," 20 June 1988, CPL.

109. Gorbachev, *Otvechaya na vyzov*, 631.

110. NSADC, 7 April 1988.

111. Chernyaev, *V Politburo*, 434–35.

112. Gorbachev, *Otvechaya na vyzov*, 647.

113. Radchenko, *Unwanted Visionaries*, 107, 114–16.

114. NSADC, "Gandhi Letter to Reagan," 3 August 1988, CPL.

115. NSADC, "Cable from Ambassador Oakley," 30 August 1988, CPL.

116. NSADC, "Cable from Ambassador Oakley," 30 August 1988, CPL.

117. NSADC, "Cable from Secretary of State to US Embassy Islamabad," 9 December 1988, USDoS.

118. NSADC, 6 September 2000.

119. "Révélations d'un Ancien Conseiller," 15 January 1998.

120. NSADC, "National Security Directive," 13 February 1989, George H.W. Bush Presidential Library.

121. Tomsen, *Afghanistan*, 458.

122. Coll, *Ghost Wars*, 228.

123. Gromyko, *Pamyatnoe*, 286–87.

124. Coll, *Ghost Wars*, 168.

125. Coll, *Ghost Wars*, 168; Gates, *From the Shadows*, 425. By contrast, Kryuchkov, *Lichnoe delo*, 89 notes that they did not discuss "essential issues" with Gates.

126. NSADC, "Cable from Secretary of State to Amembassy New Delhi," 20 November 1987, CPL.

127. NSADC, "Memorandum of Conversation," 21 February 1988, Reagan Presidential Library (RPL).

128. NSADC, "Memorandum of Conversation," 21 March 1988, RPL.

129. NSADC, 7 April 1988.

130. Chernyaev, *V Politburo*, 70.

131. Akimbekov, *Afghanistan*, 434–38; James Critchlow, *Nationalism in Uzbekistan: A Soviet Republic's Road to Sovereignty* (Boulder, CO: Westview Press, 1991), 42; Riccardo Mario Cucciolla, "Sharaf Rashidov and the International Dimensions of Soviet Uzbeki-

stan," *Central Asian Survey* 39, no. 2 (2020): 185–201; Yaacov Ro'i, "The Islamic Influence on Nationalism in Soviet Central Asia," *Problems of Communism* 39, no. 4 (1990): 49–64.

132. Chernyaev, *Diary, 1984*, 14 July 1984.

133. *AFGHANews* 5, no. 7, 1 April 1989, 3.

134. Martha Brill Olcott, *Kazakhstan, Unfulfilled Promise?* (Washington, DC: Carnegie, 2010), 28–33.

135. Grachev, Interview. Gorbachev could not explain what was happening in Kazakhstan at the politburo. Chernyaev, *V Politburo*, 193.

136. Ro'i, "Islamic Influence," 49–64; Yaacov Ro'i, "The Soviet and Russian Context of the Development of Nationalism in Soviet Central Asia," *Cahiers Du Monde Russe et Soviétique* 32, no. 1 (1991): 123–41; Ro'i, *Bleeding Wound*, 254.

137. Grachev, Interview.

138. Chernyaev, *V Politburo*, 186.

139. Khudonazarov, Interview.

140. RGANI, 11 January 1988, f. 89, o. 51, d. 12, ll. 1–5.

141. RGANI, 14 February 1990, f. 89, o. 51, d. 16, ll. 1–9.

142. Chernyaev, *Diary 1988*, 19 June 1988; Plastun, *Iznanka*, 467–68. Plastun believed the idea to have been so ludicrous that it seemed like the Kremlin hardliners had inspired it to Najibullah as a way of keeping the Soviets engaged in Afghanistan.

143. RGASPI, 11 September 1988, f, 797, o. 1, d. 33, ll. 8–9.

144. RGANI, 16 August 1989.

145. RGANI, 16 August 1989.

146. RGANI, 16 August 1989. According to Pavel Palazhchenko, Gorbachev's interpreter, Central Asian leaders wanted the Soviet-Afghan War to end, seeing it as a source of destabilization. Quoted in Ro'i, *Bleeding Wound*, 259.

147. GFA, 16 December 1989, f. 5, o. 1, d. 0.

148. GFA, 16 December 1989, f. 5, o. 1, d. 0.

149. Coll, *Ghost Wars*, 167; *Mujahideen*, April–May 1990, 16–17.

150. *Mujahideen*, April–May 1990, 25.

151. Khristoforov, *Afganistan*, 276.

152. "Gorbachev meshal vyvodu," Sputnik.kg, 13 February 2019. See also Plastun, *Iznanka*, 495; Plastun and Andrianov, *Nadzhibulla*, 118; Varennikov, *Nepovtorimoe*, ch 6.

153. Gareev, *Voina*, 55.

154. Plastun, *Iznanka*, 480 reproduces the document.

155. Egorychev, *Soldat*, 315.

156. GFA, 16 December 1989.

157. Aleksandr Aksenenok, Interview, Moscow, February 2017.

158. Brutents, *Tridtsat' let*, part 4, ch. 3.

159. GFA, 23 August 1990, 23, 56, 58.

160. GFA, 23 August 1990, 54, 55, 60.

161. GFA, 23 August 1990, 56.

162. GFA, 23 August 1990, 57, 60, 61; Plastun, *Iznanka*, 567. The Soviet embassy in Kabul also conveyed to Afghans that the economic situation in the USSR was now complicated.

163. GFA, 23 August 1990, 56.

164. GFA, 23 August 1990, 60.

165. RGANI, 9 July 1991, f. 89, o. 22, d. 45, ll. 1–4.

166. RGANI, 9 July 1991, f. 89, o. 22, d. 45, ll. 1–4.

167. *AFGHANews* 4, no. 16, 15 August 1988, 1.

168. GARF, December 1991, f. 10026, o. 4, d. 2840, l. 30.

169. Lyakhovsky, *Tragediya*, 624–30; Tomsen, *Afghanistan*, 463–69, 498–503.

170. GARF, 24 February 1992, f. 10026, o. 4, d. 2840.

171. Slinkin, "Afganistan," 94.

172. GARF, 12 July 1989, f. R9654, o. 6, d. 122, ll. 6–16.

173. Kirpichenko, *Razvedka*, 363.

174. Mark R. Beissinger, *Nationalist Mobilization and the Collapse of the Soviet State* (London: Cambridge University Press, 2002); Stephen Kotkin, *Armageddon Averted: The Soviet Collapse, 1970–2000* (London: Oxford University Press, 2008); Leffler, *For the Soul of Mankind*, 338–450; Zubok, *Collapse*, 13–179; Zubok, *Failed Empire*, 303–44. On the Soviet-Afghan War's role in the Soviet collapse: Ro'i, *Bleeding Wound*, 279–307.

175. Chernyaev, *V Politburo*, 303.

176. Zubok, *Failed Empire*, 342.

177. Grachev, Interview.

178. RGANI, 12 May 1991, f. 89, o. 7, d. 40, ll. 137–45.

179. Beissinger, *Nationalist Mobilization*, 27–36.

180. Chernyaev, *Diary*, 5 October 1989.

181. Adamishin, Interview.

182. Beissinger, *Nationalist Mobilization*, 116, 214, 252–70.

183. Ro'i, *Islam in the Soviet Union*, 447, 615; Tasar, *Soviet and Muslim*, 349, 355–61. Authors criticized that argument noting that Soviet propaganda also tended to relegate religion to the cultural realm. A Soviet journal wrote that "religion was the soil that nourishes nationalism and other negative phenomena" in 1977. Quoted in Ro'i, "Task of Creating a New Soviet Man," 35. See also Deweese, "Islam and the Legacy," 326.

184. *AFGHANews* 6, no. 5, 1 March 1990, 4. It was notable the journal still used the derogatory term "Basmachi."

185. *AFGHANews* 6, no. 24, 14 December 1990, 1.

186. *Mujahideen*, April–May 1990.

187. RGANI, 24 August 1990, f. 89, o. 11, d. 5, ll. 1–5.

188. RGANI, 19 April 1991, f. 89, o. 20, d. 66, l. 5.

189. Ro'i, "Islamic Influence," 51.

190. GARF, January–August 1991, f. P9576, o. 20, d. 6485, ll. 6–7.

191. GARF, July 1992, f. 10026, o. 5, d. 422, ll. 1–12.

192. GARF, October 1991, f. 10026, o. 5, d. 1991; Shebarshin, *Ruka Moskvy*, 292.

193. GARF, July 1992.

194. GARF, July 1992.

195. GARF, October 1991.

196. GARF, July–August 1993, f. 10026, o. 5, d. 432, ll. 47–56.

Conclusion

1. Braithwaite, *Afgantsy*, 335; Ali Yawar Adili and Thomas Ruttig, "The Ghost of Najibullah," *Afghanistan Analyst Network*, 21 August 2017.

2. Emran Feroz, "In Afghanistan, the Dead Cast a Long Shadow," *Foreign Policy*, 1 July 2020.

3. "Transcript: Afghanistan's Vision for Peace," *Atlantic Council*, 11 June 2020.

4. M. Zezina, O. Malysheva, F. Malkhozova, and R. Pikhoya, *Chelovek peremen* (Moscow: Novyi Khronograf, 2011), 166–72, 252–62.

5. Yu. Baturin, A. Il'in, V. Kadatsky, V. Kostikov, M. Krasnov, A. Livshits, K. Nikiforov, L. Pikhoya, and G. Satarov, *Epokha Yel'tsina* (Moscow: Prezidentskii Tsentr B. N. Yel'tsina, 2011), 117.

6. Galina M. Yemelianova and Laurence Broers, eds., *Routledge Handbook of the Caucasus* (London: Routledge, 2020).

7. Vassily A. Klimentov, "Bringing the War Home: The Strategic Logic of 'North Caucasian Terrorism' in Russia, *Small Wars & Insurgencies* 32, no. 2 (2021): 374–408; Vassily A. Klimentov and Grazvydas Jasutis, "The Allure of Jihad: The De-Territorialisation of the War in the North Caucasus," *Caucasus Survey* 8, no. 3 (2020): 239–57; Timur Muzaev, *Etnicheskii separatism v Rossii* (Moscow: Tsentr "Panorama," 1999).

8. This section is derived in part from an article published in the *Central Asian Survey* on 10 November 2022, copyright to Taylor & Francis, available at https://doi.org/10.1080/02634937.2022.2134298. See: Vassily Klimentov, "The Tajik Civil War and Russia's Islamist Moment," *Central Asian Survey* 42, no. 2 (2023): 341–58; Vassily Klimentov, "Not a Threat? Russian Elites' Disregard for the 'Islamist Danger' in the North Caucasus in the 1990s," *Kritika: Explorations in Russian and Eurasian History* 24, no. 4 (Fall 2023).

Bibliography

Physical and Online Archives and Notes

Arkhiv Vneshnei Politiki Rossiiskoi Federatsii (AVPRF), Moscow

Gorbachev Foundation (GFA), Moscow

Gosudarstvennyi Arkhiv Rossiiskoi Federatsii (GARF), Moscow

Graduate Institute of International and Development Studies (IHEID), Fonds Micheline Centlivres-Démont (FCFA), Geneva

Khudonazarov, Davlat, Notes from Meetings with Massoud, 1990–1998

National Archives Digital Collection (NARADC), Washington D.C. (aad.archives .gov)

National Security Archives Digital Collection (NSADC), Washington D.C. (nsar-chive.gwu.edu)

Organization of Islamic Cooperation (oic-oci.org)

Rossiiskii Gosudarstvennyi Arkhiv Noveishei Istorii (RGANI), Moscow

Rossiiskii Gosudarstvennyi Arkhiv Sotsial'no-Politicheskoi Istorii (RGASPI), Moscow

United Nations (undocs.org/ digitallibrary.un.org)

Wilson Center, Cold War International History Project Digital Collection (CWI-HPDC), Washington, DC (digitalarchive.wilsoncenter.org)

Published Materials

Abashin, Sergei. *Sovetskii kishlak: Mezhdu kolonializmom i modernizatsiei.* Moscow: Novoe Literaturnoe Obozrenie, 2015.

Adamishin, Anatoly. *V raznye gody: Vneshnepoliticheskie ocherki.* Moscow: Ves' Mir, 2016.

Akhromeyev, Sergey, and Georgy Kornienko. *Glazami marshala i diplomata: Krit-icheskii vzglyad na vneshnyuyu politiku SSSR do i posle 1985 goda.* Moscow: Mezhdunarodnye Otnosheniya, 1992.

Akimbekov, Sultan. *Istoriya Afganistana.* Almaty: IMPE pri FPR, 2015.

Alexandrov-Agentov, Andrei. *Ot Kollontai do Gorbacheva, Vospominaniya diplomata, sovetnika A.A. Gromyko, pomoshchnika L.I. Brezhneva, Yu. V. Andropova, K.U. Chernenko i M.S. Gorbacheva.* Moscow: Mezhdunarodnye Otnosheniya, 1994.

Alexievich, Svetlana. *Zinky Boys: Soviet Voices from the Afghanistan War.* New York: W. W. Norton, 1992.

Andrew, Christopher, and Vasili Mitrokhin. *The World Was Going Our Way: The KGB and the Battle for the Third World: Newly Revealed Secrets from the Mitrokhin Archive.* New York: Basic Books, 2006.

Arapov, D., ed. *Islam i sovetskoe gosudarstvo (1917–1936). Vypusk 2.* Moscow: Mardzhani, 2010.

Arapov, D., and G. Kosach, eds. *Islam i sovetskoe gosudarstvo. Vypusk 1.* Moscow: Mardzhani, 2010.

Arbatov, Georgy. *Svidetel'stvo sovremennika, Zatyanuvsheesya vyzdorovlenie (1953–1985 gg.).* Moscow: Mezhdunarodnye Otnosheniya, 1991.

Arnold, Anthony. *The Fateful Pebble: Afghanistan's Role in the Fall of the Soviet Empire.* New York: Presidio Press, 1993.

Arzumanov, G., and L. Shershnev, eds. *Sovetskomu voinu ob Afganistane.* Tashkent: Politicheskoe Upravlenie Krasnoznamennogo Turkestanskogo Voennogo Okruga, 1981.

Arzumanov, G., V. Gubrii, and V. Sokol. *Sovetskomu voinu ob Afganistane,* 5th ed. Tashkent: Politicheskoe Upravlenie Krasnoznamennogo Turkestanskogo Voennogo Okruga, 1987.

Arzumanov, G. et al. *Byt, nravy i obychai narodov Afganistana, Pravila i normy povedeniya voennosluzhashchikh za rubezhom rodnoi strany.* Tashkent: Politicheskoe Upravlenie Krasnoznamennogo Turkestanskogo Voennogo Okruga, 1984.

Asinovskiy, Dmitry. "'A Priest Does Not Consider the Toppling of the Shah as an Option': The KGB and the Revolution in Iran." *Iranian Studies* (2022): 1–23.

Atkin, Muriel. *The Subtlest Battle: Islam in Soviet Tajikistan.* Lanham, MD: University Press of America, 1989

Aydin, Cemil. *The Idea of the Muslim World.* Cambridge, MA: Harvard University Press, 2017.

Azimi, Nabi. *The Army and Politics: Afghanistan, 1963–1993,* Kindle. Bloomington, IN: AuthorHouse, 2019.

Babadzhanov, B.M., A. K. Muminov, and Martha Brill Olcott. "Mukhammadzhan Khindustani (1892–1989) i religioznaya sreda ego epokhi." *Vostok (Oriens)* 5 (2004): 43–59.

Barfield, Thomas. *Afghanistan, A Cultural and Political History.* Princeton, NJ: Princeton University Press, 2010.

Baturin, Yu., A. Il'in, V. Kadatsky, V. Kostikov, M. Krasnov, A. Livshits, K. Nikiforov, L. Pikhoya, and G. Satarov. *Epokha Yel'tsina.* Moscow: Prezidentskii Tsentr B. N. Yel'tsina, 2011.

Beissinger, Mark R. *Nationalist Mobilization and the Collapse of the Soviet State.* London: Cambridge University Press, 2002.

Bennigsen, Alexandre. "Soviet Islam since the Invasion of Afghanistan." *Central Asian Survey* 1, no. 1 (1982): 65–78.

Bennigsen, Alexandre, and Chantal Lemercier-Quelquejay. *Le Soufi et le commissaire: Les confréries musulmanes en URSS.* Paris: Seuil, 1986.

Bobrovnikov, Vladimir et al., eds. *Musul'mane v novoi imperskoi istorii.* Moscow: Sadra, 2017.

Bondarenko, A. *Aktual'nye problemy formirovaniya u lichnogo sostava ponimaniya tselei i zadach prebyvaniya sovetskikh voisk v DRA, klassovoi nenavisti k vragam Afganskoi revolyutsii (Material k lektsii v sisteme marksistsko-leninskoi podgotovki ofitserov)*. Tashkent: Politicheskoe Upravlenie Krasnoznamennogo Turkestanskogo Voennogo Okruga, 1985.

Borovik, Artyom. *The Hidden War*. New York: Grove Press, 1990.

Braithwaite, Rodric. *Afgantsy: The Russians in Afghanistan 1979–89*. London: Oxford University Press, 2013.

Breslauer, George W., ed. *Soviet Strategy in the Middle East*. Boston: Unwin Hyman, 1990.

Broxup, Marie. "Afghanistan According to Soviet Sources, 1980–1985." *Central Asian Survey* 7, no. 2/3 (1988): 197–204.

———. "Recent Developments in Soviet Islam." *Religion in Communist Lands* 11, no. 1 (1983): 31–35.

Broxup, Marie, and Alexandre Bennigsen. *The Islamic Threat to the Soviet State*. London: Routledge, 2010.

Brutents, Karen. *Tridtsat' let na staroi ploshchadi*. Moscow: Mezhdunarodnye Otnosheniya, 1998

Centlivres, Pierre. "Violence légitime et violence illégitime: À propos des pratiques et des représentations dans la crise afghane." *L'Homme, 37e Année* 144 (1997): 51–67.

Centlivres, Pierre, and Micheline Centlivres-Démont. "Et si on parlait de l'-Afghanistan?" Actes *de la recherche en sciences sociales* 34, no. 1 (1980): 3–16.

Centlivres-Démont, Micheline et al. *Afghanistan. La colonisation impossible*. Paris: Éditions du Cerf, 1984.

Cherneta, Oleg, ed. *Afganistan: Bor'ba i sozidanie*. Moscow: Voenizdat, 1984.

Chernyaev, Anatoly. *The Diary of Anatoly Chernyaev*. Washington, DC: National Security Archive, 2003.

———, ed. *V Politburo TSK KPSS . . .* Moscow: Gorbachev Foundation, 2008.

Citino, Nathan J. *Envisioning the Arab Future: Modernization in the Middle East*. London: Cambridge University Press, 2017.

Coll, Steve. *The Bin Ladens: An Arabian Family in the American Century*. New York: Penguin Press, 2008.

———. *Ghost Wars: The Secret History of the CIA, Afghanistan and Bin Laden*. New York: Penguin, 2005.

Cordovez, Diego, and Selig S. Harrison. *Out of Afghanistan: The Inside Story of the Soviet Withdrawal*. London: Oxford University Press, 1995.

Crews, Robert D. *Afghan Modern: The History of a Global Nation*. Cambridge, MA: Harvard University Press, 2015.

———. *For Prophet and Tsar*. Cambridge, MA: Harvard University Press, 2006.

Critchlow, James. *Nationalism in Uzbekistan: A Soviet Republic's Road to Sovereignty*. Boulder, CO: Westview Press, 1991.

Cronin, Stephane. "Introduction: Edward Said, Russian Orientalism and Soviet Iranology." *Iranian Studies* 48, no. 5 (2015): 647–62.

Cucciolla, Riccardo Mario. "Sharaf Rashidov and the International Dimensions of Soviet Uzbekistan." *Central Asian Survey* 39, no. 2 (2020): 185–201.

Dannreuther, Roland. *The Soviet Union and the PLO*. London: Macmillan, 1998.

Darmanger, Abdul. *L'Afghanistan, terrain du "Grand Jeu."* Neuchâtel: Attinger SA, 2015.

David-Fox, Michael. *Revolution of the Mind: Higher Learning among the Bolsheviks, 1918–1929*. Ithaca, NY: Cornell University Press, 1997.

Daurov, Ramazan, ed. *Dnevnikovye zapisi M.F. Slinkina*. Moscow: IV RAN, 2016.

De Meaux, Lorraine. *La Russie et la tentation de l'Orient*. Paris: Fayard, 2010.

Deweese, Devin. "Islam and the Legacy of Sovietology: A Review Essay on Yaacov Ro'i's Islam in the Soviet Union." *Journal of Islamic Studies* 13, no. 3 (2002): 298–330.

Dorronsoro, Gilles. *Revolution Unending*. London: Hurst, 2005.

Edwards, David B. *Before Taliban: Genealogies of the Afghan Jihad*. Oakland: University of California Press, 2002.

———. *Caravan of Martyrs: Sacrifice and Suicide Bombing in Afghanistan*. Oakland: University of California Press, 2017.

Egorychev, Nikolai. *Soldat, politik, diplomat*. Moscow: Tsentrpoligraf, 2017.

Ehmadi, Hafizullah. *State, Revolution, and Superpowers in Afghanistan*. New York: Praeger, 1990.

Feifer, Gregory. *The Great Gamble, The Soviet War in Afghanistan*. New York: HarperCollins, 2009.

Fraser, Glenda. "Basmachi—I." *Central Asian Survey* 6, no. 1 (1987): 53–65.

———. "Basmachi—II." *Central Asian Survey* 6, no. 2 (1987): 7–42.

Freedman, Robert O. *Moscow and the Middle East, Soviet Policy since the Invasion of Afghanistan*. London: Cambridge University Press, 1991.

Friedman, Jeremy. *Ripe for Revolution: Building Socialism in the Third World*. Cambridge, MA: Harvard University Press, 2022.

———. *Shadow Cold War. The Sino-Soviet Competition for the Third World*. Chapel Hill: University of North Carolina, 2015.

Gai, David, and Vladimir Snegirev. *Vtorzhenie, Neizvestnye stranitsy neob"yavlennoi voiny*. Moscow: SP IKPA, 1991.

Galeotti, Marc. *Afghanistan: The Soviet Union's Last War*. London: Routledge, 1995.

Gareev, Makhmut. *Moya poslednyaya voina*. Moscow: INSAN, 1996.

Garthoff, Raymond. *Detente and Confrontation: American-Soviet Relations from Nixon to Reagan, Revised edition*. Washington, DC: Brookings Institution Press, 1994.

Gates, Robert M. *From the Shadows: The Ultimate Insider's Story of Five Presidents and How They Won the Cold War*. New York: Simon & Schuster, 2011 (1996).

Gibbs, David N. "Reassessing Soviet Motives for Invading Afghanistan: A Declassified History." *Critical Asian Studies* 38, no. 2 (2006): 239–63.

Giustozzi, Antonio. *War, Politics, and Society in Afghanistan, 1978–1992*. London: Hurst, 2000.

Golan, Galia. *Soviet Policies in the Middle East from World War Two to Gorbachev*. London: Cambridge University Press, 1990.

Goodman, Melvin A., and Carolyn McGiffert Ekedahl. "Gorbachev's 'New Directions' in the Middle East." *Middle East Journal* 42, no. 4 (1988): 571–86.

Göransson, Markus Balázs. "At the Service of the State, Soviet-Afghan War Veterans in Tajikistan, 1979–1992." PhD diss., Aberystwyth University, 2015.

Gorbachev, Mikhail, ed. *Otvechaya na vyzov vremeni. Vneshnyaya politika perestroiki: Dokumental'nye svidetel'stva*. Moscow: The Gorbachev Foundation/Ves' Mir, 2010.

Grachev, Andrei. *Gorbatchev, Le pari perdu? De la perestroïka a l'implosion de l'URSS.* Paris: Armand Colin, 2008.

Grau, Lester W., Michael A. Gress, and the Russian General Staff. *The Soviet-Afghan War: How a Superpower Fought and Lost.* Lawrence: University Press of Kansas, 2002.

Green, Nile, ed. *Afghanistan's Islam: From Conversion to the Taliban.* Berkeley: University of California Press, 2016.

Gromov, Boris. *Ogranichennyi kontingent.* Moscow: Progress-Kul'tura, 1994.

Gromyko, Andrei. *Pamyatnoe, Kniga vtoraya.* Moscow: Poltizdat, 1990.

Halliday, Fred. "Gorbachev and the 'Arab Syndrome': Soviet Policy in the Middle East." *World Policy Journal* 4, no. 3 (1987): 415–42.

——. "'Islam' and Soviet Foreign Policy." *Journal of Communist Studies* 3, no. 1 (1987): 217–18.

——. "Soviet Foreign Policymaking and the Afghanistan War: From 'Second Mongolia' to 'Bleeding Wound.'" *Review of International Studies* 25, no. 4 (1999): 675–91.

——. "War and Revolution in Afghanistan." *New Left Review* 119 (1980): 20–41.

Halliday, Fred, and Zahir Tanin. "The Communist Regime in Afghanistan 1978–1992: Institutions and Conflicts." *Europe-Asia Studies* 50, no. 8 (1998): 1357–80.

Hartman, Andrew. "The 'Red Template': US Policy in Soviet-Occupied Afghanistan." *Third World Quarterly* 23, no. 3, (2002): 467–89.

Hegghammer, Thomas. *The Caravan: Abdallah Azzam and the Rise of Global Jihad.* Cambridge: Cambridge University Press, 2020.

Helfont, Samuel. *Compulsion in Religion: Saddam Hussein, Islam, and the Roots of Insurgencies in Iraq.* London: Oxford University Press, 2018.

——. "Islam in Saudi Foreign Policy: The Case of Ma'ruf al-Dawalibi." *International History Review* 42, no. 3 (2020): 449–64.

Hellbeck, Jochen. *Revolution on My Mind, Writing a Diary under Stalin.* Cambridge, MA: Harvard University Press, 2009.

Hunt, Michael M. "Ideology." *Journal of American History* 77, no. 1 (1990): 105–15.

——. *Ideology and U.S. Foreign Policy.* New Haven, CT: Yale University Press, 1987

Hyman, Anthony. *Afghanistan under Soviet Domination, 1964–83.* London: Macmillan, 1984.

Kakar, M. Hassan. *Afghanistan, The Soviet Invasion, and the Afghan Response, 1979–1982.* Berkeley: California University Press, 1995.

Kalinovsky, Artemy M. *The Blind Leading the Blind: Soviet Advisors, Counter-Insurgency and Nation-Building in Afghanistan.* Washington, DC: Cold War International History Project, 2010.

——. *Laboratory of Socialist Development: Cold War Politics and Decolonization in Soviet Tajikistan.* Ithaca, NY: Cornell University Press, 2018.

——. *A Long Goodbye: The Soviet Withdrawal from Afghanistan.* Cambridge, MA: Harvard University Press, 2011.

Kayaoglu, Turan. *The Organization of Islamic Cooperation. Politics, Problems and Potential.* New York: Routledge, 2015.

Kemper, Michael, and Stephan Conermann, eds. *The Heritage of Soviet Oriental Studies.* London: Routledge, 2011.

Kemper, Michael, and Artemy M. Kalinovsky, eds. *Reassessing Orientalism, Interlocking Orientologies during the Cold War*. London: Routledge, 2015.

Kepel, Gilles. *Jihad*. Paris: Gallimard, 2017.

Keshtmand, Sultan Ali. *Political Notes and Historical events: Memories from Moments in the Contemporary History of Afghanistan*. Trans. Hafizullah Nadiri. Kabul, Najib Kabir Publications, 2002.

Khalid, Adeeb. *Central Asia: A New History from the Imperial Conquests to the Present*. Princeton, NJ: Princeton University Press, 2021.

———. *The Politics of Muslim Cultural Reform: Jadidism in Central Asia*. Berkeley: University of California Press, 1999.

Khristoforov, Vasili. *Afganistan: Pravyashchaya partiya i armiya*. Moscow: Granitsa, 2009.

Kirpichenko, Vadim. *Razvedka: Litsa i lichnosti*. Moscow: Mezhdunarodnye Otnosheniya, 2017.

Klimentov, Vassily A. "Bringing the War Home: The Strategic Logic of 'North Caucasian Terrorism' in Russia." *Small Wars & Insurgencies* 32, no. 2 (2021): 374–408.

———. "'Communist Muslims': The USSR and the People's Democratic Party of Afghanistan's Conversion to Islam, 1978–1988." *Journal of Cold War Studies* 24, no. 1 (2022): 4–38.

———. "Not a Threat? Russian Elites' Disregard for the 'Islamist Danger' in the North Caucasus in the 1990s." *Kritika: Explorations in Russian and Eurasian History* 24, no. 4 (Fall 2023).

———. "In Search of Islamic Legitimacy: the USSR, the Afghan Communists and the Muslim World." *Cold War History* 23, no. 2 (2022): 283–305.

———. "The Tajik Civil War and Russia's Islamist Moment." *Central Asian Survey* 42, no. 2 (2023): 341–58.

Klimentov, Vassily A., and Grazvydas Jasutis. "The Allure of Jihad: The De-Territorialisation of the War in the North Caucasus." *Caucasus Survey* 8, no. 3 (2020): 239–57.

Knyazev, Alexander. *Istoriya afganskoi voiny 1990-kh gg. i prevrashchenie Afganistana v istochnik ugroz Tsentral'noi Azii*. Bishkek: KRSU, 2001.

Korgun, Victor. *Istoriya Afganistana, XX Vek*. Moscow: IV RAN/Izdatel'stvo "Kraft," 2004.

Kornienko, Georgy. *Kholodnaya voina, Svidetel'stvo ee uchastnika*. Moscow: Olma-Press, 2001.

Kotkin, Stephen. *Armageddon Averted: The Soviet Collapse, 1970–2000*. London: Oxford University Press, 2008.

———. *Magnetic Mountain, Stalinism as a Civilization*. Berkeley: University of California Press, 1997.

Kozyrev, Nikolai. *Zhenevskie soglasheniya 1988 goda i Afganskoe uregulirovanie*. Moscow: DAMIDRF, 2000.

Kryuchkov, Vladimir. *Lichnoe delo, Chast' pervaya*. Moscow: Olimp, 1996.

Kucherova, Larisa. *KGB v Afganistane*. Moscow: Yauza-Press, 2017.

Laruelle, Marlene. *The Central Asia–Afghanistan Relationship: From Soviet Intervention to the Silk Road Initiatives*. Lanham, MD: Lexington Books, 2017.

Laruelle, Marlene, Botagoz Rakisheva, and Gulden Ashkenova, eds. *Pamyat' iz plameni Afganistana, Kniga 1, Kazakhstan.* Astana: KISI pri Prezidente RK, 2016.

———, eds. *Pamyat' iz plameni Afganistana, Kniga 2, Uzbekistan.* Astana: KISI pri Prezidente RK, 2016.

———, eds. *Pamyat' iz plameni Afganistana, Kniga 3, Tadzhikistan.* Astana: KISI pri Prezidente RK, 2016.

Leake, Elisabeth. *Afghan Crucible: The Soviet Invasion and the Making of Modern Afghanistan.* London: Oxford University Press, 2022.

———. "Afghan Internationalism and the Question of Afghanistan's Political Legitimacy." *Afghanistan* 1, no. 1 (2018): 68–94.

Leffler, Melvyn J. *For the Soul of Mankind, The United States, the Soviet Union and the Cold War.* New York: Hill and Wang, 2007.

Lesch, David W. *The Middle East and the United States, A Historical and Political Reassessment.* Boulder, CO: Westview Press, 2007.

Lobato, Chantal. "Islam in Kabul: The Religious Politics of Babrak Karmal." *Central Asian Survey* 4, no. 4 (1985): 111–20.

Lüthi, Lorenz M. *The Sino-Soviet Split, Cold War in the Communist World.* Princeton, NJ: Princeton University Press, 2008.

Lyakhovsky, Alexander. *Inside the Soviet Invasion of Afghanistan and the Seizure of Kabul, December 1979.* Washington, DC: Cold War International History Project, 2007.

———. *Tragediya i doblest' Afgana.* Moscow: GPI Iskona, 1995.

Lyakhovsky, Alexander, and Vyacheslav Nekrasov. *Grazhdanin, politik, voin.* Moscow: Grif i K, 2007.

Maher, Shiraz. *Salafi-Jihadism: The History of an Idea.* London: Oxford University Press, 2016.

Maiorov, Aleksandr. *Pravda ob Afganskoi voine.* Moscow: Prava cheloveka, 1996.

Mamdani, Mahmood. *Good Muslim, Bad Muslim: America, the Cold War, and the Roots of Terror.* New York: Pantheon Books, 2004.

Martinez-Gros, Gabriel, and Lucette Valensi. *L'Islam, l'Islamisme et l'Occident.* Paris: Seuil, 2004.

Merimsky, Viktor. *Zagadki Afganskoi voiny.* Moscow: Veche, 2015.

Minkov, Anton, and Gregory Smolynec. "4-D Soviet Style: Defense, Development, Diplomacy and Disengagement in Afghanistan during the Soviet Period. Part I: State Building," *Journal of Slavic Military Studies* 23, no. 2 (2010): 306–27.

———. "4-D Soviet Style: Defense, Development, Diplomacy, and Disengagement during the Soviet Period. Part II: Social Development." *Journal of Slavic Military Studies* 23, no. 3 (2010): 391–411.

———. "4-D Soviet Style: Defense, Development, Diplomacy, and Disengagement during the Soviet Period, Part III: Economic Development." *Journal of Slavic Military Studies* 23, no. 4 (2010): 597–611.

Mitrokhin, Vasiliy. *The KGB in Afghanistan.* Washington, DC: Cold War International History Project, 2002.

Morgan, Gerald. "Myth and Reality in the Great Game." *Asian Affairs* 4, no. 1 (1973): 55–65.

Musalov, Andrei. *Zelenye pogony Afganistana.* Moscow: Yauza-Katalog, 2019.

Muzaev, Timur. *Etnicheskii separatism v Rossii*. Moscow: Tsentr Panorama, 1999.

Nabat, Maria. "The USSR's Economic Assistance Strategy to Afghanistan on the Threshold of the Soviet Troops' Withdrawal." *Vestnik of Saint Petersburg University* 10, no. 1 (2018): 118–32.

Naumkin, Vitaly. *Radical Islam in Central Asia: Between Pen and Rifle*. Lanham, MD: Rowman & Littlefield, 2005.

Nunan, Timothy. "'Doomed to Good Relations': The USSR, the Islamic Republic of Iran, and Anti-Imperialism in the 1980s." *Journal of Cold War Studies* 24, no 1 (2022): 39–77.

——. *Humanitarian Invasion, Global Development in Cold War Afghanistan*. London: Cambridge University Press, 2016.

Olcott, Martha. "The Basmachi or Freemen's Revolt in Turkestan 1918–24." *Soviet Studies* 33, no. 3 (1981): 352–69.

——. *Kazakhstan, Unfulfilled Promise?* Washington, DC: Carnegie, 2010.

——. *Roots of Radical Islam in Central Asia*. Washington, DC: Carnegie, 2007.

Penati, Beatrice. "The Reconquest of East Bukhara: The Struggle against the Basmachi as a Prelude to Sovietization." *Central Asian Survey* 26, no. 4 (2007): 521–38.

Pikov, Nikolai. *Spetspropagandist o Dubynine V.P.* Moscow: Soyuz veteranov Voennogo instituta inostrannykh yazykov, 2018.

Pirzada, Syed Sharifuddin. "Pakistan and the OIC." *Pakistan Horizon* 40, no. 2 (1987): 1–36.

Plastun, Vladimir. *Iznanka Afganskoi voiny*. Moscow: IV RAN, 2016.

Plastun, Vladimir, and Vladimir Andrianov. *Nadzhibulla, Afganistan v tiskakh geopolitiki*. Moscow: Russkii biograficheskii institut / "Sokrat," 1998.

Power, Jonathan. "From Stalin to Putin, An Insider's View: Talking with Georgi Arbatov." *World Policy Journal* 24, no. 3 (2007): 83–88.

Prados, John. "Notes on the CIA's Secret War in Afghanistan." *Journal of American History* 89, no. 2 (2002): 466–71.

Primakov, Yevgeny. *Konfidentsial'no, Blizhny Vostok na stsene i za kulisami*. Moscow: Tsentrpoligraf, 2016.

Pulyarkin, Valerii. *Afganistan*. Moscow: Mysl', 1964.

Radchenko, Sergey. *Unwanted Visionaries. The Soviet Failure in Asia at the End of the Cold War*. London: Oxford University Press, 2014.

Redissi, Hamadi. *Une histoire du wahhabisme. Comment l'Islam sectaire est devenu l'Islam*. Paris: Seuil, 2007.

Robinson, Paul, and Jay Dixon. *Aiding Afghanistan, A History of Soviet Assistance to a Developing Country*. London: Hurst, 2013.

Ro'i, Yaacov. *Islam in the Soviet Union, From the Second World War to Gorbachev*. London: Hurst, 2000.

——. *The Bleeding Wound, The Soviet War in Afghanistan and the Collapse of the Soviet System*. Redwood City, CA: Stanford University Press, 2022.

——. "The Islamic Influence on Nationalism in Soviet Central Asia." *Problems of Communism* 39, no. 4 (1990): 49–64.

——. "The Soviet and Russian Context of the Development of Nationalism in Soviet Central Asia." *Cahiers Du Monde Russe et Soviétique* 32, no. 1 (1991): 123–41.

——. "The Task of Creating the New Soviet Man: "Atheistic Propaganda" in the Soviet Muslim Areas." *Soviet Studies* 36, no. 1 (1984): 26–44.

——. *The USSR and the Muslim World. Issues in Domestic and Foreign Policy.* London: Routledge, 2016.

Roy, Olivier. *The Failure of Political Islam.* Cambridge, MA: Harvard University Press, 1994.

——. *Globalized Islam.* London: Hurst, 2004.

——. *Islam and Resistance in Afghanistan.* Cambridge: Cambridge University Press, 1990.

——. *La Nouvelle Asie centrale ou la fabrication des nations.* Paris: Seuil, 1997.

Rubin, Barnett R. *The Fragmentation of Afghanistan, State Formation and Collapse in the International System.* New Haven, CT: Yale University Press, 2002.

Rubin, Dominic. *Russia's Muslim Heartlands, Islam in the Putin Era.* London: Hurst, 2018.

Runov, Valentin. *Afganskaya voina.* Moscow: Yauza, 2016.

Said Aly, Abdel Monem, Shai Feldman, and Khalil Shikaki. *Arabs and Israelis: Conflict and Peacemaking in the Middle East.* London: Red Globe Press, 2013.

Saikal, Amin, with Ravan Farhadi and Kirill Nourzhanov. *Modern Afghanistan. A History of Struggle and Survival.* London: I.B. Tauris, 2004.

Saivetz, Carol R. "Islam and Gorbachev's Foreign Policy in the Middle East." *Journal of International Affairs* 42, no. 2 (1989): 435–44.

Sen Gupta, Bhabani. *The Afghan Syndrome, How to Live with Soviet Power.* London: Croom Helm, 1982.

Shebarshin, Leonid. *Ruka Moskvy, Zapiski nachal'nika vneshnei razvedki.* Moscow: Algoritm, 2017.

Shershnev, L., and V. Granitov, eds. *Islam v sovremennom Afganistane. Politika NDPA v otnoshenii religii.* Tashkent: Politicheskoe Upravlenie Krasnoznamennogo Turkestanskogo Voennogo Okruga, 1982.

Shevardnadze, Eduard. *Kogda rukhnul zheleznyi zanaves.* Moscow: Evropa, 2009.

Shur, V. *Real'naya sushchnost' islamskoi "svyashchennoi bor'by za veru."* Tashkent: Politicheskoe Upravlenie Krasnoznamennogo Turkestanskogo Voennogo Okruga, 1987.

Siasang, Saburulla. *Aprel' 1978: Nachalo tragedii Afganistana.* Moscow: "U nikitskikh vorot," 2009.

Sierakowska-Dyndo, Jolanta. "Peculiarity of the Afghan Clergy." *Afghanica* 4, no. 6–7 (March–September 1990): 14–17.

Silantyev, Roman. "Mezhdunarodnaya deyatel'nost' dukhovnykh upravlenii musul'man SSSR v gody perestroiki (1985–1991 gg.)." *Vlast'* 22, no. 3 (2014): 154–56.

Slinkin, Mikhail. "Afganistan: Uroki informatsionnoi voiny." *Kul'tura narodov Prichernomor'ya* 15 (2000): 82–96.

——. *Afganskie stranitsy istorii.* Simferopol: TGU, 2003.

——. "Afganskie vstrechi i besedy." *Kul'tura narodov Prichernomor'ya* 113 (2007): 7–60.

——. "Khal'k i Parcham." *Kul'tura narodov Prichernomor'ya* 9 (1999): 98–107.

——. "Myatezh Generala Sh. N. Tanaya." *Kul'tura narodov Prichernomor'ya* 8 (1999): 94–100.

Snegirev, Vladimir, and Valerii Samunin. *Virus "A," Kak my zaboleli vtorzheniem v Afganistan.* Moscow: Rossiiskaya Gazeta, 2011.

Snyder, Timothy. *Bloodlands: Europe between Hitler and Stalin.* New York: Basic Books, 2012.

Spolnikov, Victor. *Afganistan, Islamskaya oppositsiya.* Moscow: Nauka, 1990.

Tanwir, M. Halim. *Afghanistan: History, Diplomacy and Journalism.* Bloomington, IN: Xlibris Corporation, 2013.

Tarzi, Shah M. "Politics of the Afghan Resistance Movement: Cleavages, Disunity, and Fragmentation." *Asian Survey* 31, no. 6 (1990): 479–95.

Tasar, Eren. "The Central Asian Muftiate in Occupied Afghanistan, 1979–87." *Central Asian Survey* 30, no. 2 (2011): 213–26.

——. "The Official Madrasas of Soviet Uzbekistan." *Journal of Economic and Social History of the Orient* 59, no. 1–2 (2016): 265–302.

——. *Soviet and Muslim, The Institutionalization of Islam in Central Asia.* London: Oxford University Press, 2017.

Taubman, William. *Khrushchev: The Man and His Era.* New York: W. W. Norton, 2003.

Tema: "'Znat' i uvazhat' traditsii, nravy i obychai afganskogo naroda, Za rubezhom strany vysoko derzhat' chest' i dostoinstvo sovetskogo voina" (V pomoshch' rukovoditelyam grupp politicheskoi ucheby praporshchikov i politicheskikh zanyatii s soldatami i serzhantami).* Tashkent: Politicheskoe Upravlenie Krasnoznamennogo Turkestanskogo Voennogo Okruga, 1985.

Tikhonov, Yu. ed. *Sovetskaya Rossiya v bor'be za "afganskii koridor" (1919–1925).* Moscow: Kvadriga, 2017.

Tomsen, Peter, *The Wars of Afghanistan: Messianic Terrorism, Tribal Conflicts, and the Failures of Great Powers.* New York: PublicAffairs, 2011.

Toporkov, Vladimir. *Afganistan: Sovetskii faktor v istokakh krizisa.* Cheboksary: TSNS Interaktiv Plyus, 2014.

Tribe, Keith, ed. *Max Weber, Economy and Society, A New Translation.* Cambridge, MA: Harvard University Press, 2019.

Tripathi, Deepak. "India's Foreign Policy: The Rajiv Factor." *The World Today* 44, no. 7 (1988): 112–14.

Varennikov, Valentin. *Nepovtorimoe, Kniga 5.* Moscow: Sovetskii pisatel', 2001.

Volkov, Y., K. Gevorkyan, I. Mikhailenko, A. Polonsky, and V. Svetozarov. *The Truth about Afghanistan.* Moscow: Novosti Press Agency Publishing House, 1980

Vorotnikov, Vitaly. *A bylo eto tak . . .* Moscow: Sovet Veteranov Knigoizdaniya SI-MAR, 1995.

Voslensky, Mikhail. *Nomenklatura.* Moscow: Zakharov, 2016 (1990).

Wakil, Abdul. "Iran's Relations with Afghanistan after the Islamic Revolution." *Orient* 32, no. 1 (1991): 97–115.

Welch, David A., and Odd Arne Westad, eds. *The Intervention in Afghanistan and the Fall of Détente.* Nobel Symposium 95, Lysebu, 17–20 September 1995. Oslo: Norwegian Nobel Institute, 1996.

Westad, Odd Arne. *The Cold War: A World History.* New York: Basic Books, 2017.

——. *The Global Cold War: Third World Interventions and the Making of Our Times.* London: Cambridge University Press, 2011 (2005).

——. "Prelude to Invasion: The Soviet Union and the Afghan Communists, 1978–1979." *International History Review* 16, no. 1 (1994): 49–69.

Whitlock, Craig. *The Afghanistan Papers: A Secret History of the War.* New York: Simon & Schuster, 2021.

Yemelianova, Galina M., and Laurence Broers, eds. *Routledge Handbook of the Caucasus.* London: Routledge, 2020.

Yousaf, Mohammad, and Mark Adkin. *Afghanistan—The Bear Trap, The Defeat of a Superpower.* Barnsley, UK: Leo Cooper, 2001.

Yurchak, Alexei. *Everything Was Forever, Until It Was No More: The Last Soviet Generation.* Princeton, NJ: Princeton University Press, 2006.

Zakharov, V. et al. *I. Znat' i uvazhat' traditsii, nravy i obychai Afganskogo naroda, II. Masterski vladet' oruzhiem i boevoi tekhnikoi. III, Sovetskii voin—patriot i internatsionalist (Materialy v pomoshch' rukovoditelyam grupp politicheskikh zanyatii).* Tashkent: Politicheskoe Upravlenie Krasnoznamennogo Turkestanskogo Voennogo Okruga, 1987.

Zezina, M., O. Malysheva, F. Malkhozova, and R. Pikhoya. *Chelovek peremen.* Moscow: Novyi Khronograf, 2011.

Zhuravlev, I., S. Mel'kov, and L. Shershnev. *Put' voinov Allakha.* Moscow: Veche, 2004.

Zierler, David, and Adam M. Howard, eds. *Foreign Relations of the United States (FRUS), 1977–1980, Volume XII, Afghanistan.* Washington, DC: Government Printing Office, 2018.

Zubok, Vladislav M. *Collapse: The Fall of the Soviet Union.* New Haven, CT: Yale University Press, 2021.

——. *A Failed Empire, The Soviet Union in the Cold War from Stalin to Gorbachev.* Chapel Hill: University of North Carolina Press, 2007.

Index

Note: Figures are indicated by *f* after page numbers.

AAPSO. *See* Afro-Asian People's Solidarity Organisation
Adamishin, Anatoly, 39, 119, 141, 221, 242–43
"Address of the Presidium of the DRA to the Muslims of Afghanistan and the World" (Bakhtar), 74, 146
advisers, 57, 257–58; activism by, 56; ethnicities of, 70, 248; Khalq and, 36; worldviews of, 55–56
Afghan Constitution, 124–25, 129
AFGHANews (journal), 133, 135–39, 148, 167–68, 170; Cotton Affair and, 206; OIC and, 175–76; on operations in USSR, 194; POWs and, 218; on Soviet Muslims, 222
Afghani, Sayyed, 77, 80
Afghan Interim Government, 167, 188
Afghanistan: areas controlled by insurgent groups, 132*f*; availability of information about, 55; ethnic map of, 21 (map); Iran diplomatic relations with, 159; Islam and national reconciliation program in, 107–13; Islam and rural, 32–33; Marxism-Leninism and, 14–16, 101; OIC understanding with, 170–78; refugees from, 2, 110, 128–30, 147, 159, 162, 185, 199; Soviet advisers in, 55–57; Soviets and national reconciliation program in, 113–23, 257; Soviet Treaty of Friendship with, 21; study of Soviet-Afghan War and, 7; US war in, Soviet-Afghan War parallels to, 4–5, 10, 98
Afghanistan Information Centre (AIC), 65, 76, 81, 126, 130, 183, 186, 188
The Afghan Mujahid (journal), 169*f*
Afghan Red Crescent Society, 165
Afghan Syndrome, 2
Afro-Asian People's Solidarity Organisation (AAPSO), 153, 155–56

agitprop units, 72–73, 84, 122, 149
AIC. *See* Afghanistan Information Centre
Akayev, Askar, 232
Akhromeyev, Sergey, 67, 107
Aksenenok, Aleksandr, 214
Alexandrov-Agentov, Andrei, 244
Algeria, 153, 228
Aliyev, Heydar, 231
Allende, Salvador, 13
"All the Toiling Muslims of Russia and the East" (Lenin), 19
Amanullah Khan, 21, 133
Amin, Hafizullah, 29, 43, 153; Blood meeting with, 41; infighting and, 40; International Department criticisms of policies, 78; Iran and, 159; Islam and, 48–50, 97, 244; Karmal removing, 85, 88; killing of, 46; Pakistan and, 45; Soviets meeting with, 38
Andropov, Yuri, 13, 36, 41, 45, 63–65, 67, 205–6
anticlericalism, 47, 83
anticolonialism, 3
anti-Islamic propaganda, 83
April Revolution, 28–29, 74, 126; Afghan Constitution and, 124–25; information campaign and, 144, 146; Islam and, 110; Soviet handbooks on, 85, 88–89; Soviet thinking on, 36
Al-Aqsa Mosque, 165
Arab Afghans, 4, 186, 269
Arab League, 143, 261
Arafat, Yasser, 160, 165–68
Armacost, Michael, 203
al-Assad, Hafez, 13, 154, 166
atheism, 228–29; Central Asian soldiers and, 93–95; information campaign and, 144–46, 148; PDPA and, 47, 63, 142, 152; of USSR, 25, 70, 223

Azerbaijan, 26, 222, 224, 231
al-Azhar University, 80, 132–33, 143
Azimi, Nabi, 117, 246
Azzam, Abdullah Yusuf, 4, 130

Babakhan, Ziyauddinkhan ibn Eshon, 69–70
Bakhtar news agency, 74, 145, 175
Baku conference, 149–52, 175, 213
Bangladesh Liberation War, 195
Banisadr, Abolhassan, 157–58, 160
Baryalai, Mahmoud, 155
Basmachi, 20–23, 33, 37, 44, 64, 115, 230,
    239; Islam and cohesion of, 21; jihad
    and, 21
Basov, Vladimir, 58
The Beast of War (film), 7
Beg, Azad, 191, 193, 208, 270
Beg, Mirza Aslam, 199, 201, 270
Bek, Ibrahim, 21
Beloe solntse pustyni (White Sun of the Desert)
    (film), 21, 73
Bendjedid, Chadli, 27
Bennigsen, Alexander, 19, 192
bin Laden, Osama, 4, 130, 186
Blood, Archer, 41
Bolsheviks, 19; Amanullah Khan and, 21
Bratstvo (Leaving Afghanistan) (film), 9
Brezhnev, Leonid, 12–13, 24, 36, 37f, 38, 45,
    161, 243
bride price, 31
Broxup, Marie, 19
Brutents, Karen, 37, 42, 51, 155, 214
Brzezinski, Zbigniew, 202
Bukharan People's Soviet Republic, 20–21
Bush, George H. W., 202

Camp David Accords, 143, 165–67
caravans of peace, 72
CARC. See Council for the Affairs of
    Religious Cults
Carter, Jimmy, 202
Castro, Fidel, 13
Central Asians: atheism and, 93–95; Islam
    and, 94, 96, 204–5, 274; Jamiat-e-Islami
    and, 136; in LCST, 91–96, 248, 253; oral
    history accounts of, 95–96; Soviet-Afghan
    War views among, 190
Central Committee CPSU (CC CPSU), 29;
    Agitation and Propaganda (Ideology)
    Department, 70, 223; Department of
    Information, 73; International Depart-
    ment, 15, 28, 41, 70, 77–79, 98, 214, 218;
    Plenum of, 54–55, 107; Pravda report to, 60

Central Intelligence Agency (CIA), 130;
    Hekmatyar and, 210; information cam-
    paign and, 144–48; insurgent group areas
    map by, 132f; Islamic propaganda and,
    192; operations in USSR and, 192–93;
    Program-M, 191, 193; on support for
    Soviet-Afghan war, 190
CFM. See Council of Foreign Ministers
Chatty, Habib, 173
Chebrikov, Victor, 97–98, 189, 193, 207
Chechnya, 232–33
Chernenko, Konstantin, 13, 55, 59
Chernyaev, Anatoly, 25, 106, 106f, 115, 221;
    on Cotton Affair, 205
China, 38
CIA. See Central Intelligence Agency
clergy, 50, 68, 238, 241; army and, 85; assem-
    blies of, 76; KhAD and, 81; national recon-
    ciliation and, 111–12; proregime scholars,
    76–77; repressions of, 81
Cold War, 2–3, 5; debate between ideology
    and realpolitik in, 10; geostrategic
    frameworks of, 41, 63; OIC and, 174;
    Soviet foreign policy and, 13
Commissariat for Internal Affairs, 21
Committee for State Security (KGB), 13,
    15; anti-Amin plot and, 40; information
    campaign and, 145, 147; Iran and, 158;
    on "Islamic factor," 191, 241; Islamism
    concerns in, 26, 44–45, 207, 212–13, 244;
    Ittehadiya and, 192; Karmal and, 98;
    official clergy and, 39; religion and, 39;
    training for Afghanistan deployments,
    59, 65; unregistered clergy and, 25
Communist International, 19
communist internationalism, 2
Communist Party of the Soviet Union
    (CPSU), 1, 9, 13–14; advisers from,
    55–57; Afghan policy factionalism and,
    61; centralization under, 11; ethnicities
    of advisers from, 70, 248; Kazakh, 24;
    propaganda advisers from, 36; Turkmen,
    25–26
Cotton Affair, 205–6
Council for Mutual Economic Assistance, 62
Council for Religious Affairs (CRA), 19, 24,
    69, 158, 171, 187
Council for the Affairs of Religious Cults
    (CARC), 19, 24
Council of Foreign Ministers (CFM), 153,
    171–74, 177
Council of Ulemas, 49–50, 69, 125
counterpropaganda, 146

CPSU. *See* Communist Party of the Soviet
    Union
CRA. *See* Council for Religious Affairs
Cuba, 13
Cultural Revolution, 20

Daoud Khan, Mohammad, 28–29, 51, 133
Darmanger, Abdul, 31, 48, 103–4, 240
Dean, John Gunther, 196, 198–201, 259–60
decolonization, 10
defections, 93, 96
Democratic Front for the Liberation of
    Palestine (DFLP), 165
Democratic Republic of Afghanistan
    (DRA), 4, 15, 124–25, 230; creation of,
    28; diplomacy by, 152–56; outreach by
    religious institutions of, 150–51; propa-
    ganda in, 59; Soviet-style symbols and,
    32–33
Democratic Youth Organisation of
    Afghanistan (DOMA), 67–68, 112
Department for Safeguarding the Interests
    of Afghanistan, 39
détente, 42
development assistance, 62
DFLP. *See* Democratic Front for the
    Liberation of Palestine
diplomacy: by India, 195–202; mujahideen
    reactions to, 168, 170; in Muslim world,
    152–56; Palestinians and, 164–68; Soviet,
    with Islamic world, 148–52
Directorate for Islamic Affairs, 71
Dobrynin, Anatoly, 42
DOMA. *See* Democratic Youth Organisation
    of Afghanistan
Dost, Shah Mohammad, 142, 145, 153, 161,
    165–66
DRA. *See* Democratic Republic of
    Afghanistan
Dudayev, Dzhokhar, 232–33

education, 31, 65, 80; Islamic, 112;
    mujahideen targeting, 76; Najibullah
    and, 112
Egorychev, Nikolay, 9, 70, 105, 114, 119, 121,
    213
Egypt, 142–43, 156, 214, 228; information
    campaign and, 144
Eid al-Fitr, 48, 75, 138
Elmi, Mohammad Salem, 77
Enver, İsmail, 20
Ermakov, Viktor, 2, 45
Eskandari, Iraj, 158

Faisal (King), 171
Fatah, 166–68
Fergana Valley, 21
First Anglo-Afghan War, 63
First Chechen War, 226, 233
First Congress of the Peoples of the East, 19
fundamentalist Islam, 4, 45, 195
Fundamental Principles (DRA), 124

Gadhafi, Muammar, 154
Gaidar, Egor, 232
Gailani, Sayyid Ahmed, 34, 39, 132–34, 182,
    189
Gandhi, Indira, 195
Gandhi, Rajiv, 195–201
Gankovsky, Yuri, 58, 116
Gapurow, Muhammetnazar, 26
Gareev, Makhmut, 45, 212
Gates, Robert, 203
General Department of Islamic Affairs, 76–77
Geneva Accords, 128, 177–78, 182, 200–201,
    203–4, 212
Ghafar Khan, Khan Abdul, 156
Ghani, Ashraf, 228
Ghotbzadeh, Sadegh, 160–61
glasnost, 222
Gorbachev, Mikhail, 1, 102, 114, 141, 181,
    227, 232, 234; Arafat and, 166; "bleeding
    wound" speech, 115; collapse of USSR
    and, 219–21; Cotton Affair and, 206; coup
    attempt against, 188; Gandhi, R., and,
    195–96, 200; handbook revision and, 86;
    India and, 195–96; Iran and, 163–64;
    Islamism and, 205; Karmal and, 99–100,
    100f; Najibullah and, 106f, 118–20, 120f,
    139, 195–97, 200, 205, 208, 215–17, 230;
    New Political Thinking, 109, 155, 164,
    214; OIC and, 175; reforms, 17, 219–20;
    on US and Islamism, 216–17; US visit,
    203, 204f; withdrawal ordered by, 105–7,
    124, 127, 155, 179
Gorbacheva, Raisa, 120f
Grachev, Andrey, 28, 36, 42, 107, 142, 148,
    157, 220, 240, 264–66; on Islamism and
    Central Asia, 206
Grachev, Pavel, 232
Great Game mindsets, 197, 199, 226
Great Terror, 20
Gromov, Boris, 2, 45, 180, 232
Gromyko, Andrei, 13, 36, 37f, 41–42, 100f,
    127, 145, 153; Assad and, 166; interven-
    tion encouraged by, 46; Plenum speech,
    54–55; on Saudi Arabia diplomacy, 127

GRU. *See* Main Intelligence Directorate
Gulabzoi, Sayed Muhammad, 104, 118, 120
GULAG, 11

handbooks: ideology and, 101; for LCST,
   83–91
Harakat-i-Inqilab-i-Islami (Islamic Revolution
   Movement), 133
hearts-and-minds strategy, 72
Hekmatyar, Gulbuddin, 3, 129–31, 133–34,
   209, 211*f*, 231; infighting by, 187–88;
   Soviets meeting with, 182; US and, 203–4
Herat revolt, 35, 39, 48
Hezb-e-Islami, 4, 35, 131, 211*f*, 218, 225;
   Azerbaijan and, 222; India concerns
   about, 199; Najibullah and, 183, 200;
   Soviets working with, 134–35; Soviet
   thinking about, 209–10; Tanai coup
   attempt against, 187; US and, 213; USSR
   operations and, 191, 193
Hezb-e Watan, 185, 188, 215
High Council of Ulemas and the Clergy, 76,
   124, 150, 156, 160, 162
High Sunni Council, 142
Hindustani, Muhammadjan, 190, 207
Hojjat, Abdul Wali, 71, 76, 80
humanitarian assistance, 62; *agitprop* and, 73
Hussein (King), 177
Hussein, Saddam, 152, 154

ideology, 9–11; intervention decision
   and, 42; modernization, 14; politburo
   decisions and, 42–43; as trap, 54–60;
   USSR foreign policy and, 36. *See also*
   Islamism; Marxism-Leninism
IEWSS. *See* Institute of the Economy of the
   World Socialist System
Imam al-Bukhari Islamic Institute, 69, 187
India, 38, 153, 156; Pakistan and, 197; Sri
   Lanka intervention, 201; triangular
   diplomacy by, 195–202
industrialization, 11, 54
infrastructure projects, 62–63
Institute of the Economy of the World
   Socialist System (IEWSS), 143
International Committee for Solidarity
   with the Arab People and their Central
   Cause–Palestine, 153
Inter-Services Intelligence (ISI), 76, 212;
   Hekmatyar and, 187; Islamic propaganda
   and, 192; operations in USSR and, 192–93;
   Program-M, 191, 193; support channeled
   through, 130–31
intra-Soviet rivalries, 66–67

Iran, 1, 38, 41, 142, 148, 228, 231; Afghani-
   stan diplomatic relations with, 159;
   Afghanistan fighters from, 131; Central
   Asian Islamism and, 207; mujahideen
   and, 158, 161; OIC and, 173, 176; refugees
   in, 159, 162; Saudi Arabia and, 173; US
   and, 160, 163; USSR and, 145, 153, 156–64
Iran-Contra Affair, 163
Iranian Revolution, 3, 18, 26
Iran-Iraq War, 160–63, 173
Iraq, 4, 6, 142, 153–54, 167, 228
IRPT. *See* Islamic Renaissance Party of
   Tajikistan
ISCHS. *See* Islamic Summit Conference of
   Heads of States
ISI. *See* Inter-Services Intelligence
Islam, 1; April Revolution and, 110; Basma-
   chi cohesion and, 21; Central Asians and,
   94, 96, 204–5, 274; fundamentalist, 4, 45,
   195; historiography of, in USSR, 18–19;
   Karmal and, 97; Khalq and, 31–32, 46–52,
   245; Marxism-Leninism and, 9–10, 14–16,
   48–49; national reconciliation in, 107–13;
   PDPA conversion to, 124–30; PDPA
   Marxist playbook and, 28–35; as political
   force, 10; in rural Afghanistan, 32–33;
   Shevardnadze and Kryuchkov report on,
   208–9; Soviet priorities and, 67–73; Soviet
   repression and, 19–20; study of Soviet-
   Afghan War and, 6; USSR and, 9–10,
   16, 18
Islamic Committees, 110, 133
Islamic education, 112
Islamic Guidance (Ershad Islami) (journal),
   124
Islamic Renaissance Party of Tajikistan
   (IRPT), 207, 224
Islamic Revolution, 18, 44, 146, 149, 156–64,
   172
Islamic socialism, 73–83
Islamic State, 231
Islamic Study Centre, 116, 125
Islamic Summit Conference of Heads of
   States (ISCHS), 172
Islamism, 3, 26, 225, 233; Central Asia
   protests and, 204–5; Gorbachev and, 205;
   KGB concerns about, 26, 44–45, 212–13,
   244; KGB monitoring of, 207; as Pakistani
   influence tool, 201; radical, 4, 15, 183,
   186, 228, 231; Soviet policies and, 208–14;
   in Tajikistan, 190–91; US and, 216–17;
   Yeltsin and, 188
Islamization, 113–23, 126, 136, 143, 187, 205
Israel, 143, 165

Ittehad-e-Islami bara-ye Azadi-ye Afghanistan (Islamic Union for the Liberation of Afghanistan), 131–32, 193, 208

Ittehadiya Islami-ye Wilayat-i Shamal (Islamic Union of the Northern Provinces, Ittehadiya), 191–93, 208, 212

Jamiat-e-Islami, 35, 210, 218, 225; infighting by, 134; national reconciliation and, 135–39; OIC and, 176; on Tanai coup, 176; USSR operations and, 191, 194. *See also AFGHANews*

Jebh-i-Nejat-i Melli (National Liberation Front), 132, 138

jihad, 35, 187, 245; Arab fighters and, 186, 269; attempt to discredit idea of, 91; Basmachi and, 21; Iranian parties in, 131; Pakistani parties in, 131

jirga, 49

Jordan, 143, 154, 177

Kabul New Times (newspaper), 50, 74, 112

al-Kaddoumi, Farouk, 166

Kadir Dagarwal, Abdul, 58

Kalakani, Habibullah, 21

Kandahar (film), 9

Karimov, Islam, 209, 231

Karmal, Babrak, 6, 16, 29, 46–49, 53, 61–63, 82f, 243; diplomacy and, 154; Gorbachev and, 99–100, 100f; information campaign and, 144–47; Iran and, 159–62; Islam and, 85, 97; Islamic socialism of, 73–83, 89; KGB and, 98; Khalq reforms and, 78; land reform and, 78–80; LCST expectations of, 100; Marxism-Leninism and, 97; OIC and, 172; ousting of, 103–7, 139, 255; PLO and, 165–67, 178; problems with leadership of, 96–102; religious leaders and, 77, 81; return of, 189; as scapegoat, 98–99, 122; Soviet scrutiny of, 97–98; tactics for dealing with Soviets, 65–66

Karmalism, 127

Kashmir, 197

Kazakhstan, 206, 231

Keshtmand, Ali, 61, 76, 107, 118, 152

KGB. *See* Committee for State Security

KhAD. *See* State Information Services

Khakikat-e Inquilab-e Saur (*Truth of the April Revolution*) (newspaper), 74, 161–62, 247

Khalis, Younas, 131, 133

Khalq, 28–30, 37–38, 43, 65, 67, 122–23, 227, 229; CPSU advisers to, 36; diplomacy and, 152–53; infighting in, 40; Iran and, 159; Islam and, 31–32, 46–52, 245; land reform

and, 78; leftist radicalism of, 33; reforms by, 48–49, 78; socialism interpretations of, 40

Khanate of Kazan, 18

Khasbulatov, Ruslan, 223–24

Khivad (*Motherland*) (newspaper), 74

Khomeini, Ruhollah (Ayatollah), 3, 48, 153, 159, 161, 163–64

Khristoforov, Vasili, 7

Khrushchev, Nikita: antireligious campaigns, 24; international commitments, 12–13; on Muslims, 25; reforms by, 12

Khudonazarov, Davlat, 207, 239–40, 246, 271

Khyber, Mir Akbar, 126

Kirilenko, Andrei, 36

Kirpichenko, Vadim, 98, 220

Kolbin, Gennady, 206

Komsomol, 14, 26, 67, 112

Kornienko, Georgy, 32, 127

Kosygin, Alexei, 35, 45

Kozyrev, Andrei, 188

Kryuchkov, Vladimir, 34, 134, 182, 188, 230; on Islamism and Central Asia, 206–7; on Islamism in Afghanistan, 44–45; Islamism report, 208–9; on KGB training programs, 64–65; Najibullah and, 208; on Najibullah Islamization initiatives, 115

Kunaev, Dinmukhamed, 206

Kuwait, 143, 154–55, 176–77, 214

Kyrgyzstan, 20, 232

land reform, 21, 57, 62; under Khalq, 29–35; under Parcham, 78–80; Soviet criticisms of, 32–34

Layeq, Suleiman, 47, 56, 117

LCST. *See* Limited Contingent of Soviet Troops

League of Arab States, 224

Lebanese Independent Nasserite Movement, 155

Lebanon, 155, 165

leftist movements: USSR support of, 12

Lenin, Vladimir, 12–13, 19, 21

Libya, 142–43, 154, 167, 174, 228

Life of the Party (journal), 68

Limited Contingent of Soviet Troops (LCST), 2, 15, 29, 38, 41, 53–54, 257–58; Afghan policy factionalism and, 61; army reserve units and, 92–93; Central Asians and, 91–96, 253; criticisms of, 122; handbook for, 83–91; ideological support units, 72–73; Islam and training for, 68; Karmal expectations of, 100; withdrawal of, 105–7, 180, 182–83

literacy programs, 31
Literaturnaya Gazeta (newspaper), 194

Madrasas, 21, 33, 50; national reconciliation
and building of, 111–12; state education
replacing, 65
Mahaz-i-Milli-ye Islami-ye Afghanistan
(National Islamic Front for Afghanistan),
132
Mahkamov, Qahhor, 222
Main Intelligence Directorate (GRU), 39
Maiorov, Aleksandr, 43, 55, 61, 67, 70–71, 75,
117, 189
Maoism, 3
Mariam, Mengistu Haile, 13
Marxism-Leninism, 1, 227; Afghanistan and,
14–16, 101; argument against jihad from,
91; as ideology, 9–11, 13; intervention
decision and, 42; Islam and, 9–10, 14–16,
48–49; Karmal and, 97; Najibullah and,
17, 185; PDPA playbook and, 28–35;
Soviet advisers and, 55–57; Soviet-Afghan
War and, 14–16; Soviet approach to
Afghanistan and, 101; Third World leftist
movements and, 12
Massoud, Ahmad Shah, 3, 132, 134, 136f,
138, 188, 209–10, 228, 231
Maudoodi, Abul A'la, 3
media: Karmal use of, 74
MID. *See* Ministry of Foreign Affairs
military-industrial complex, 42–43
Ministry of Foreign Affairs (MID), 40, 98,
127; Ittehadiya and, 191–92
Ministry of Islamic Affairs, 76
Ministry of Islamic Affairs and Waqfs,
109–11, 150
modernization, 1, 54, 190, 222; ideology
and, 14
Mohammadi, Mohammad Nabi, 133
Mohib, Hamdullah, 228
Moiseev, Mikhail, 2
Morocco, 143, 174
mosques, 50; Karmal and, 75; national
reconciliation and building of, 111–12;
near garrisons, 85
Mozhaev, Pavel, 118
Mujaddidi, Sibghatullah, 35, 48, 132–34, 167,
182, 189, 245
Mujaddidi family, 34–35
mujahideen, 1–2, 9, 15, 44f, 61, 228; Central
Asians and, 93; educational institutions
targeted by, 76; handbooks and, 85, 89;
infighting among, 134, 187–88; information campaign and, 145, 147f, 148; Iran

and, 158, 161; national reconciliation
program and, 109–10, 120–21, 128–29;
OIC and, 172, 175–76; Pakistan and, 41,
187, 212; PDPA criticisms by, 135–38;
PDPA negotiating with, 133–35; post-
withdrawal gains by, 180–81; pro-Kabul
Islamic institutions targeted by, 76; propaganda by, 83, 89, 135; reactions to diplomacy, 168, 170; response to Soviet
training programs, 64–65; Saudi Arabia
and, 155; Soviet Muslims and, 222–23;
US and, 41, 131f, 142; USSR negotiating
with, 134–35, 182–83; USSR operations
of, 189–94
A Muslim (film), 96
Muslim Brotherhood, 32, 35, 47–49, 131,
207; Tajikistan and, 190
Muslim internationalism, 3
Muslims in the USSR (journal), 158
Muslim World League (MWL), 151, 171,
224
Muslim Youth, 47
MWL. *See* Muslim World League

Naghlu Dam, 62
Nagorno-Karabakh, 231
Najibullah, Mohammad, 4, 17, 73, 106f, 120f,
139–40, 226–27; becoming PDPA general
secretary, 103–7, 255; concessions by, 188;
death of, 180; diplomacy and, 154; end
of Soviet support to, 215–19; Gandhi, R.,
and, 198–99; Gorbachev and, 195–97, 200,
205, 208, 215–17, 230; handbook revision
and, 86; India support for, 200; Iran and,
163–64; Islamization and, 184–85, 187,
205; Karmal and, 99; Kryuchkov and, 208;
Marxism-Leninism and, 185; national
reconciliation program, 109–13, 115,
118–19, 122–23, 149, 175, 179, 257; OIC
and, 173, 175, 177; PDPA conversion to
Islam and, 124–27, 129–30, 228; peace
negotiations and, 133–34, 148; PLO and,
178; Shevardnadze and, 208; Soviet POWs
and, 219; Soviet withdrawal and, 188–89;
Wahhabism and, 183; withdrawal
negotiations and, 182–83
NAM. *See* Non-Aligned Movement
Naqshbandiyah Sufis, 34, 132
Nasser, Gamal Abdel, 47
National Council, 125
National Fatherland Front (NFF), 77,
109–10
nationalism, 222
National Security Council (NSC), 144

NATO, 3, 145
Nazarbayev, Nursultan, 231
Neto, Agostinho, 13
New Economic Policy, 21
New Political Thinking, 109, 155, 164, 214
News of Jihad (journal), 138
NFF. *See* National Fatherland Front
9/11. *See* September 11, 2001 terrorist attacks
9 rota (*The 9th Company*) (film), 7, 9
Nishanov, Rafiq, 120f
Niyazov, Saparmurat, 231
Noga (*The Leg*) (film), 7
Non-Aligned Movement (NAM), 141, 145, 152, 161
Novosti Press Agency, 59, 69, 146, 158
NSC. *See* National Security Council
Nuri, Sayid Abdulloh, 207

Oakley, Robert, 201
official clergy, 39
Ogarkov, Nikolai, 67
OIC. *See* Organisation of Islamic Conference
Oman, 176
Operation Magistal', 77
Operations Group on Afghanistan, 61
opiates, 2
Organisation of Islamic Conference (OIC), 17, 153, 161, 168, 224, 231; understanding with, 170–78
Oriental Studies Institute, 27, 58–59, 62, 114–15, 156–58, 195; on Iran, 157; on Pakistan, 143–44
Orthodox Christianity, 20
Ottoman Empire, 18

Pakistan, 1, 38, 45, 143–45, 148, 151–52, 158, 195, 228; Federally Administered Tribal Areas, 156; fundamentalism and, 208; India and, 197; Inter-Services Intelligence, 76; Islamism as influence tool of, 201; mujahideen and, 41, 187, 212; Muslim conferences in, 170; negotiations hosted by, 182; North-West Frontier Province, 156; OIC and, 176; operations in USSR and, 192–93; refugee camps in, 128–30, 147; support channeled through, 130–31; US and, 142
Palestine Liberation Organization (PLO), 143, 164–68, 178, 228–29; Soviet-mujahideen negotiations and, 182
Palestinians, 164–68, 174

Parcham, 28–29, 30f, 38, 45, 47, 65, 67, 122, 227; Iran and, 159; land reform under, 78–80; purges of, 40
Pashazadeh, Sheikh ul-Islam Allahshukur, 70
Pashtunwali, 49
PDPA. *See* People's Democratic Party of Afghanistan
PDRY. *See* People's Democratic Party of Yemen
People's Democratic Party of Afghanistan (PDPA), 1–4, 9, 14, 18, 51, 154, 235; anticlericalism in, 83; atheism and, 47, 63, 142, 152; attempts to moderate, 33–34; cadres, 32; clergy and, 50; collapse of, 180, 182; factionalism in, 40, 65, 120; information campaign and, 144–48; International Department, 150; Islam conversion of, 124–30, 228; Islamic policies, 85; Islamization of, 113, 126; land reform and, 79–80; Marxist playbook, and Islam, 28–35; mujahideen criticisms of, 135–38; mujahideen negotiating with, 133–35; mullahs condemning, 35; national reconciliation program and, 107–23; PLO and, 164–68; Propaganda Department, 109; reform programs, 31–32, 48–49; revolt against, 35–36; shift in discourse on religion in, 74–75; Soviet criticisms of, 15; Soviet encouraging tolerance of Muslims by, 38; Soviet support of, 16; tactics for dealing with Soviets, 65–67
People's Democratic Party of Yemen (PDRY/South Yemen), 6, 172
People's Party of Iran (Hezb-e Tude-ye Iran/Tudeh), 158, 163
perestroika, 54, 57, 121, 232
Pershing missiles, 42
Peshawar-7, 131, 188, 191, 218
PFLP. *See* Popular Front for the Liberation of Palestine
Pikov, Nikolai, 72–73, 94
Pirzada, Sharifuddin, 171, 174–76
Plastun, Vladimir, 7, 58–59, 66, 113, 116–17, 249
Plenum, 54–55, 107
PLO. *See* Palestine Liberation Organization
politburo, 7, 13; Afghanistan debates in, 16, 36–37; ideology and decision by, 42–43; information sources for, 39–40
political propaganda, 72
political reforms, 124
Polyanichko, Victor, 56, 68, 80, 101, 109, 114–16, 118–20, 125

Ponomarev, Boris, 36, 40–41, 58
popular culture, 7, 9
Popular Front for the Liberation of
    Palestine (PFLP), 165
Popular Islamic Party of Afghanistan, 124
Pravda, 60–62, 79, 161
Primakov, Yevgeny, 27, 58, 114, 233–34
Proclamation 5621, 147*f*
Program-M, 191, 193
propaganda, 59, 88; anti-Islamic, 83; CIA
    and, 192; countering, 90; information
    campaign, 144–48; Iran and, 158; by
    mujahideen, 83, 89, 135; units for, 72–73;
    US and, 144; in USSR, 192
Pul-e-Charkhi Prison, 219
Putin, Vladimir, 234
Puzanov, Alexander, 31, 33, 38, 152

Qadiriyyah Sufis, 34, 132
al-Qaeda, 4, 6, 231
Qubba'ah, Tayseer, 166
Qutb, Sayyid, 3, 47

Rabbani, Burhanuddin, 132–36, 182, 189,
    203, 209, 269
radical Islamism, 4, 15, 183, 186, 228, 231
radical reformism, 47
Radio Kabul, 88
Radio Liberty, 144
Rafsanjani, Akbar Hashemi, 163–64
Rahman, Akhtar Abdur, 199
Rajai, Mohammad-Ali, 160
Rakhmon, Emomali, 232
Ramadan, 31, 48–49, 75, 112, 138
Rambo III (film), 7
Raphel, Arnold, 199
Rashidov, Sharof, 205
Ratebzad, Anahita, 71
Reagan, Ronald, 131*f*, 147*f*, 195, 198, 204*f*
realism, 72
realpolitik, 10
refugees, 2, 110, 185, 199; in Iran, 159, 162;
    in Pakistan, 128–30, 147; Palestinian, 165
Republic of Afghanistan, 125
Resalat (newspaper), 164
The Role of Ulemas in the Invitation to Peace
    (brochure), 110
Russia, 232; post-Soviet views of Soviet-
    Afghan War, 2–3; reengagement with
    Afghanistan, 3; study of Soviet-Afghan
    War and, 7
Rutskoy, Alexander, 232
Ryzhkov, Nikolai, 197

Sabra and Shatila massacres, 165, 174
SADUM. *See* Spiritual Administration of the
    Muslims of Central Asia and Kazakhstan
SAFS. *See* Soviet-Afghan Friendship Society
Salafi-Jihadism, 4
SALT II. *See* Strategic Arms Limitation Talks
    II Treaty
Saudi Arabia, 1, 3–4, 214, 223–24, 228, 231;
    Afghanistan diplomatic mission to, 155;
    information campaign and, 144, 148; Iran
    and, 173; Islamists and, 130; MWL and,
    151; OIC and, 171, 176; Pakistan and, 143;
    PDPA atheism and, 142
Saur Revolution. *See* April Revolution
Sayyaf, Abdul Rasul, 132, 203
Second Chechen War, 234
Sen, Rohen, 197–98
September 11, 2001 terrorist attacks (9/11),
    4, 231
Sevruk, Vladimir, 70
Shahi, Agha, 172
Shakhnazarov, Georgy, 209–10, 213, 220
sharia courts, 18, 21, 112
Shark, Mohammed Hassan, 127
Shebarshin, Leonid, 55, 98, 125, 158,
    160–61
Shershnev, Leonid, 72, 84
Shevardnadze, Eduard, 106*f*, 117–18, 120*f*,
    182, 206, 231–32; Afghanistan interven-
    tion promoted by, 54; Iran and, 163;
    Islamism report, 208–9; Massoud and,
    134; Najibullah and, 208; Pakistan and,
    201; Shultz talks with, 203–4
Shinwari, Wakil Azam, 125–26
Shultz, George, 199, 203–4
Shura-e Nazar (Supervisory Council of the
    North), 132
Sino-Soviet split, 10, 12
Slinkin, Mikhail, 56, 103, 118–19, 155
smallpox vaccination, 33
Snegirev, Vladimir, 7, 246
socialism, 1, 230; belief in, 54; Islamic, 73–83
Sokolov, Sergei, 61, 67
South Yemen. *See* People's Democratic
    Party of Yemen
Soviet-Afghan Friendship and Cooperation
    Treaty, 46
Soviet-Afghan Friendship Society (SAFS),
    71, 76
Soviet-Afghan War, 1–3; Central Asia as
    basing for, 92; Central Asians views on,
    190; costs of, 62, 247–48; framings of,
    138; information campaign, 144–48;

international framing of, 142; Islamism and, 4; Marxism-Leninism and, 14–16; motivations for intervention, 40–46; Muslim country condemnations of, 141–44; OIC and, 171–75; oral history accounts of, 95–96; phases of, 53–54; popular culture and, 7, 9; Soviet withdrawal, 105–7, 180, 182–83; study of, 5–9; US war parallels to, 4–5, 10, 98

Soviet Council of Ministers, 35

sovietization, 33, 54, 65, 94, 108

Soviet Union (USSR), 1–2; advisers from, 55–57; Afghanistan Treaty of Friendship with, 21; Afghan tactics for dealing with, 65–67; anti-Islamic policies in, 24; atheism of, 25, 70, 223; CIA and Islamic propaganda in, 192; collapse of, 4; development and humanitarian assistance from, 62; end of, 219–25; end of Najibullah support from, 215–19; Fatah and, 167; foreign policy of, 12–13, 36, 155; Gulf countries and, 214; hearts-and-minds strategy of, 72; Hekmatyar and, 210; historiography of Islam in, 18–19; ideology and foreign policy of, 36, 246; ideology and playbook, 9–11; India diplomacy with, 195–202; information campaign and, 144–48; Iran and, 156–64; Islam and, 9–10, 16, 18, 274; Islam and priorities of, 67–73; Islamic diplomacy, 148–52; Islamism and policies of, 208–14; Islamism and protests in, 204–5; Islamization and, 113–23; Karmal scrutinized by, 97–98; land reform and, 78; leftist movements supported by, 12; loyalty of Muslims in, 26; Marxism-Leninism and approach to Afghanistan of, 101; military-industrial complex of, 42–43; mobilization strategies in, 122; modernization in, 11; mujahideen negotiating with, 134–35, 182–83; mujahideen operations in, 189–94; Muslim world diplomacy and, 153–54; national reconciliation program and, 113–23, 257; PDPA criticized by, 15; PDPA support by, 16; PLO and, 165–66; POW and MIA retrieval, 218–19; reforms in, 12; religious repression in, 19–20, 24–25; rivalries in, 66–67; tolerance of Muslims encouraged by, 38; training programs, 64–65. *See also* Russia

Special Commission for National Reconciliation, 112–13

spetspropagandists, 72–73, 94, 122

Spiritual Administration of the Muslims of Central Asia and Kazakhstan (SADUM), 19, 24–25, 37, 69–70, 171, 187, 224

Spiritual Administration of the Muslims of Transcaucasia, 70

Spolnikov, Victor, 134

Sri Lanka, 201

Stalin, Joseph, 11–12, 21; antireligious campaign, 19–20

state education, 65

State Information Services (KhAD), 39, 50, 57, 65, 76, 81, 114, 145, 188; Iran and, 164; Ittehadiya and, 191; Karmalism in, 127; Najibullah and, 110

Steadfastness and Confrontation Front, 172

St. Petersburg International Economic Forum, 3

Strategic Arms Limitation Talks II Treaty (SALT II), 42

Sufis, 27, 34

Sunni Islamism, 3, 224

Suslov, Mikhail, 243

symbols, 33

Syria, 2, 6, 13, 143, 154, 166, 214

Tabeev, Fikryat, 41, 43, 61, 71, 116; Amin and, 78; dogmatism of, 56–57, 66–67; India and, 195; recall of, 67, 118

Tadzhuddin, Talgat, 223

Tajik Civil War, 224, 226, 233

Tajikistan, 13, 20, 45, 69, 95, 192–94, 207, 222, 232–33; Islamism in, 190–91; soldiers from, 91

Taliban, 2–3, 111, 180, 228, 231

Tanai, Shahnawaz, 120, 187–88, 200, 211*f*

Taraki, Nur Muhammad, 29, 30*f*, 31, 34–36, 38, 47–51, 58, 97, 152, 243; assassination of, 40; Pakistan and, 45; PLO and, 165

Tashkent conference, 90, 149, 151

TASS. *See* Telegrafnoe Agentstvo Sovetskogo Soyuza

Tatarstan, 232

Telegrafnoe Agentstvo Sovetskogo Soyuza (TASS), 114–15, 124, 145, 167, 210

Third World: internationalism and, 171; USSR support of leftist movements in, 12

Tomsen, Peter, 202

The Truth about Afghanistan (brochure), 146; Iran and, 158

Tsagolov, Kim, 116, 127–28

Tudeh. *See* People's Party of Iran

Tunisia, 167

Turkestan, 20, 194

Turkestan Military District: Political
Directorate of, 84, 87
Turkey, 155, 223–24, 231
Turkmenistan, 21, 25–26, 192, 231; soldiers
from, 91

ulemas, 110–11, 156
Ulyanovsky, Rostislav, 58
United Arab Emirates, 176, 214
United Nations: Afghanistan resolution, 141;
negotiations brokered by, 182
United Nations Special Rapporteur on
Human Rights, 129
United States (US), 1–2, 4–5, 38; India
diplomacy with, 195–202; information
campaign and, 144–48, 147f; Iran and,
160, 163; Islamism and, 216–17; mujahideen and, 41, 131f, 142; Pakistan and,
142; post-Soviet Afghanistan policies
of, 202; propaganda and, 144; Soviet-
Afghan War parallels to Afghan war
of, 4–5, 10, 98; study of Soviet-Afghan
and, 6–7
University of Kabul, 80, 112, 187
unregistered clergy, 25–26
urbanization, 222
US. *See* United States
USSR. *See* Soviet Union
Ustinov, Dmitry, 13, 36, 39, 41, 43, 45, 97
usury, 49
Uzbekistan, 20, 45, 95, 192, 209, 219, 231,
233; Cotton Affair in, 205–6; soldiers
from, 91

Varennikov, Valentin, 43, 98, 116, 118, 121,
127, 134, 192–93, 212
Vinogradov, Vladimir, 153, 157–58
The Voice of the Islamic Revolution (radio
broadcast), 159
Vorontsov, Yuli, 114, 118, 203

Wahhabism, 15, 183, 186
Wakil, Abdul, 118, 154, 177, 182
Wali Khan, Khan Abdul, 156
waqf lands, 21, 50
White Sun of the Desert. See Beloe solntse pustyni
WMC. *See* World Muslim Congress
World Health Organization, 33
World Muslim Congress (WMC), 151,
170–71
World Peace Council, 153

Yacoub, Talaat, 167
Yakovlev, Alexander, 68
Yazov, Dmitry, 128, 182
Yeltsin, Boris, 188, 216, 221, 232–33
Yemen Socialist Party, 51
Yousaf, Mohammad, 76
Yusufi, Jalil, 80

Zagladin, Vladimir, 57
Zahir Shah (King), 28, 130, 197
zampolits, 87, 93–94, 101, 186
Zaplatin, Vasili, 34
Ziarmal, Zabihullah, 66, 122
Zia-ul-Haq, Muhammad, 195, 271
Zinoviev, Grigory, 19

Printed in the USA
CPSIA information can be obtained
at www.ICGtesting.com
CBHW022313280624
10860CB00002B/8